HALF AND

D1434241

'A remarkable story' was the reactio<del></del> <del></del> managing-editor of Auckland Univers<del></del> Nalden's *Half-and-Half*. It was accorded a<del>n honourable mention in Oxford</del> University Press's quincentennial biography competition.

Abandoned by his mother at three weeks old, the author was received into the London Foundling Hospital, established in 1739 for illegitimate children.

Half-and-Half discusses in absorbing fashion the four distinct phases into which his life naturally fell, with his first six years in the care of foster-parents and the ensuing eight years as an inmate of the Foundling Hospital.

The opening chapter gives a brief but vivid account of the hospital's early, and at times turbulent, history such as the infamous 'basket-baby' years of 1756-9, when thousands of infants, many already at the point of death, were dumped, quite shamelessly, into a basket provided by the hospital for that express purpose. As the author observes, the infant mortality rate during those years reads more like a casualty list of a bloody Passchendaele; for of the 15,000 'admissions' some 10,000 died, with half that number failing to reach the age of six months.

On the happier side the author gives a brief account of the institution's greatest single benefactor, George Frederick Handel, whose personally directed performances of *Messiah* in the chapel of the Foundling Hospital set 'this most regularly and frequently performed work of all time' on its unparalleled career.

Nalden recalls certain of the hospital's unnatural practices, legacies of the 18th century and extant in his own time, in the upbringing of its young charges. One such practice was the rigid, almost pathological, obsession on the part of the authorities in perpetuating the archaic regulation which sternly decreed the total segregation of the sexes — a well-intentioned nonsense pushed to its absurd limits when twin brother and sister might seldom, if ever, communicate in any form with each other — less bastard begat bastard no doubt.

His third and fourth phases spanned some 26 years apiece, hence the book's title, *Half-and-Half*.

Phase three tells of the abrupt transition from the sequestered monastic-like lifestyle of the Foundling Hospital to the sordid, and at times brutal, realities of an army barrack room into which the author was rudely pitchforked at the not-altogether mature age of 14. Monica Baldwin's *Leap Over the Wall* could hardly have resulted in a greater emotional shock than that sustained by the author as a consequence of his Leap Over the Wall.

Even so, these hardships whether real or imagined, failed to deter the author from embarking upon a self-imposed course of correspondence study, unaided by any form of monetary assistance, which led ultimately to his graduating Doctor in Music at the University of London. Concurrently with his academic studies and again at his own expense, he attended for six years the London Guildhall School of Music as a harp student. For a time, in order to support these studies, he supplemented his army pay of seven shillings per week by undertaking menial tasks such as polishing other soldiers' equipment.

In 1942 he was appointed lecturer in harmony at the Royal Military School of Music (more widely known as Kneller Hall). It was to prove itself a disastrous move, for within a short time of his appointment he found himself caught up, unwittingly, in a major scandal which led to the director of music himself being court-martialled.

But as the author now admits, these early years' 'vile blows and buffets of the world' turned themselves to advantage, in that forever after, life, by comparison, became one unending soft option; so that his literal overnight exchange of army battledress for hood and gown, barrack room for Milton's 'olive grove of Academe' was effected with relative ease.

Phase four relates to the author's years in New Zealand. He left England in 1948 to take up a lectureship in Auckland University College (now the University of Auckland).

He was appointed to the chair in music in 1956 and in this capacity played the central role in the establishment of New Zealand's first conservatorium of music.

He has conducted the New Zealand Symphony Orchestra on a number of occasions as well as appearing as a casual player on his principal instrument, the harp. He has also given frequent broadcast talks on music.

His book *Fugal Answer* was acclaimed by Watkins Shaw *(Music and Musicians*, October 1972) as 'the most penetrating and precise treatment of the subject available'. Another publication *A History of the Conservatorium of Music* — University of Auckland 1888-1981 was the author's personal contribution to his university's centenary celebrations.

His work with amateur orchestras spans the whole of his years in New Zealand.

On his retirement in 1974 the University of Auckland elected him Emeritus Professor of Music and in 1976 he was awarded the CBE for Services to Music.

Half and Half

The Memoirs of a Charity Brat

Charles Nalden

1908 — 1989

© Charles Nalden, 1989

ISBN 0-908705-48-4
Published by Moana Press
19 Roderick Street
Tauranga, NEW ZEALAND
Phone (075) 63-011
and 112 Pope Street
Plimmerton, Wellington
NEW ZEALAND
Phone (04) 331-842

Printed and Typeset by
Printcorp Services Ltd, Tauranga

Dedicated in Love and Gratitude
to the Memory of
Peggy

CONTENTS

Contents (continued)

ILLUSTRATIONS

Preface
In which the Skeleton in the Cupboard is Revealed.

It could prove somewhat disconcerting to discover when well past your allotted span of three-score-years-and-ten that you are automatically debarred from inheriting titles or entailed property, from joining the Metropolitan Police, and (until 1964) from becoming ordained a priest without special dispensation; and further to discover that you may be refused admission to 'one of the biggest clubs in Britain, Freemasonry'.

Yet this happens to be my position — because I am illegitimate, one of 'us'.

Insofar as the Metropolitan Police is concerned, I can pass that one off as 'sour grapes' quite easily, as the fact of my falling short by several inches of the required minimum height in itself would have debarred me from joining. As to the Church (had I been afforded opportunity of entering it), short of becoming Primate of Canterbury or at the very least Primate of York, I would have ended up a frustrated, disappointed cleric, and certainly not a useful servant of God. Which brings me to Freemasonry, whose ancient brotherhood I never have contemplated joining — never, that is, since the evening, some 60 years since, when I was rudely ejected by a brother of the Farnham (Surrey) Lodge, when surprised in the process of devouring in wolfish fashion the remains of that lodge's sumptuous annual banquet.

And as I happen now (but only just now) to know that my father was not titled, all in all, I find that I am no more an embittered person since my being enlightened on these matters than I was when living in blissful ignorance of them.

Even so, I do not deny that on occasions I have harboured some resentment, as for example when required in the past to produce my original Foundling Hospital birth certificate which stated my parentage as 'unknown'.

When in 1953 the shortened form of birth certificate (which excludes reference to parentage) was introduced, the Foundling Hospital (now The Thomas Coram Foundation for Children)* authorities believed in all good faith that they had found in it the solution to the embarrassing predicaments in which their ex-scholars were liable to find themselves. An arrangement was agreed upon (between the hospital and the London General Register Office presumably) whereby ex-foundlings could obtain the shortened form of birth certificate in the names bestowed upon them by the hospital at baptism.

But as I myself have come to discover , although constituting a decided improvement over the old Foundling Hospital form of birth certificate which proclaimed to the whole universe its holder's illegitimacy, the shortened form is still inadequate a safeguard; for when recently I had a mind to apply for New Zealand citizenship, I blenched from seeing it through when I found myself obliged to give answers to questions as —

My father's name is . . . .

My mother's name is . . . .

The Hydra was not going to be despatched as easily as that.

I was born in London in the year 1908. Charles Nalden are the names by which I have been known since I was 29 days old, these being the names which were bestowed fortuitously upon me when I was baptised in the chapel of the old London Foundling Hospital in the Anglican faith. For those first 29 days of my life my names were John Leslie Simpson. These are the names in which my mother registered me.

This change of names was not effected by deed poll, and neither do I recollect having had any say in the matter either of having them changed or in the acceptability or otherwise of the substitutes. Nor was mine an isolated case of its kind, for there had been 23,061 similar cases before my own. The very first case of its kind occurred on 25 March, 1740/1, when the London Foundling Hosital came into being; and there will continue to be cases similar to mine to the end of time.

The title of my book, *Half-and-Half,* is a shameless borrowing of a term which is readily understood on both sides of the bar counter by publican and patron alike, and which conveys in a minimum number of words the

---

* As far back approximately as the middle of the last century the anonymous author of *Observations on the Foundling Hospital* advocated changing the name Foundling Hospital to something different to 'remove from them [the inmates] the odium attached to their birth'.

required proportions of the two different kinds of beer that go in the making up of the Englishman's 'pint'. In short, 'arf an' 'arf; in full, 'arf o' Mild an' 'arf o' Bitter, thanks, an' Gawd bless yer; or, as etherealised in Albert Ketelby's immortal masterpiece *A Cockney Suite* for Military Band —

　　　Largo molto affetuoso (Whistled by Bandsmen)

Half-and-Half appeared to me as being the most appropriate title that would summarise accurately, yet succinctly, the proportions that went into the making up of my own life's brew; for it so turned out that the first 25 years of my working life were spent in the British Army (into which I was rudely pitch-forked at the mature age of 14 — hence Bitter) and the ensuing 25 years as a university teacher (hence Mild, or relatively so).

I am grateful to Mrs Dora Hessell, of Papakura, New Zealand, for her generosity in making available to me a letter written on 3 May 1842, by her great-aunt Lizzie Longmore, who at that time was living at No. 2, Landsdown Place*, Brunswick Square, whose eastern side shared a common boundary line with the old London Foundling Hospital's western side. Lizzie Longmore writes, 'I am getting on pretty well with the organ. I like Miss Wesley** [her organ teacher]. I am going to tea with her tomorrow at Kings Row, Pentonville. George [a younger member of the family] only blew the bellows once and he got tired, so now I have a charity brat, and pay him threepence a week, which he opens his eyes at.'

This explains the choice of phrase for the sub-title of my work, *The Memoirs of a Charity Brat;* for although not mentioned in the letter, I agree with Mrs Hessell that the organ-blower must have been a Foundling boy.

---

* Since re-named Lansdowne Terrace. A site plan of the Foundling Hospital, drawn in 1912, shows it as Lansdown Place.

** This almost certainly is Eliza Wesley, one of the several children of the liaison formed by her father, Samuel Wesley, with Sarah Suter; and this even though his wife, Charlotte Louisa, was still living. Eliza Wesley was organist of St. Margaret Pattens. She died unmarried in 1895.

The title for Part I, A Blank Childhood, is borrowed from an article by Charles Dickens, *Received, a Blank Child,* which he wrote following a visit to the Foundling Hospital in 1853. As one of Dickens's blank children, I was cared for by foster-parents for the first six years of my life, spending the next eight as an inmate of the London Foundling Hospital. I considered it imperative therefore that I prefaced this work with an account, however brief, of this long-since vanished, but once-famous, home for illegitimate children; for without such an account the work must stand as being incomplete.

My thanks go to Cathie Hutchinson of the University of Auckland Library's Reference Department, who far exceeded her official call of duty in helping me trace the sources of many an obscure document; and to Alison Grant, who by checking several references in the university library saved me many a time-consuming journey.

I should like to acknowledge Garth Tapper's consummate skill in translating unerringly the things in my imagination into the reality of animated cartoons.

I am particularly grateful to Pamela Constance and June Rose, who transformed some thoroughly untidy drafts into impeccable typescripts.

I am grateful to my old Royal Artillery (Mounted) Band friends, Frederick Goddard and William Walden-Mills; to Charles King, for making available to me certain old photographs and to Lt-Colonel Rodney Bashford (one-time Director of Music of the Grenadier Guards and of the Royal Military School of Music, Kneller Hall) for advising me on a number of matters relating to British Army Bands.

Finally, I wish to acknowledge with gratitude the expert advice relating to matters of style and presentation given me by the late Dr James Newman, and Denis McEldowney, Managing Editor, Auckland University Press.

A note on Part III — Mild - or Relatively So.

After writing these memoirs I was invited by the University of Auckland to write a History of the Conservatorium of Music in connection with the university's centennial year, 1983. This will explain why some of the material of Part III of the memoirs and Chapter IV of the history is virtually the same.

Charles Nalden,
Auckland 1989.

PROLOGUE

The Foundling Hospital c.1920.

1: The Foundling Hospital

The children's playground known as Coram's Fields, which lies in the heart of Bloomsbury, was originally the site of the long-since demolished Foundling Hospital.

Founded in 1739 by Captain Thomas Coram, a retired Merchant Service seaman, the Foundling Hospital was England's first incorporated charity for illegitimate children.

Coram's inspiration for his project emanated from his frequent business journeys to and from the Royal Exchange in the City of London. During these journeys he was moved by the sight of dead infants who either had been outright murdered, their bodies literally flung on the dunghills, or else left deserted to die.

Coram's efforts to establish a Hospital for the Maintenance and Education of Exposed and Deserted Young Children (as it was originally styled) occupied him a full 17 years. His efforts finally met with success when in 1739 he himself petitioned the King.

The annals of bastardy as recorded in the early years of the Foundling Hospital are frightful. The scenes at the opening of the hospital are vividly described in the Daily Committee's Minutes of Lady Day, 25 March 1741:

> Having according to the Resolution of the General Committee with all possible diligence put this Hospital into a Condition proper for the Reception of Children This Committee met at seven o'Clock in the Evening. They found a great number of People crowding about the door, many with Children and other's for Curiosity, the Committee were informed that Several Persons had offerd Children but had been refused admittance The Order of the Gen[l] Committee

being that the House sho^d not be open'd till Eight o'Clock at Night. And this Committee were resolved to give no Preference to any person whatsoever — The Committee were immediately attended by the Peace Officers of the Parish and Two Watchmen of theirs were ordered to assist the Watchman of the Hospital. He had orders to prevent any Child being laid down at our Door and to give a Signal to the Parish Watchman in Case any Child was refused to be admitted into the Hospital, who thereupon was to take Care that it was not Dropt in the Parish.

At Eight o'Clock the Lights in the Entry were Extinguished, the outward Door was opened by the Porter, who was forced to attend at that Door all night to keep out the Crowd imediately the Bell rung and a Woman brought in a Child the Messenger let her into the Room on the Right hand, and carried the Child into the Stewards Room where the proper Officers together with Dr Nesbitt and some other Gov^rs were constantly attending to inspect the Child according to the Directions of the Plan. The Child being inspected was received Number'd, and the Billet of its Discripton enter'd by three different Persons for greater Certainty. The Woman who brought the Child was then dismised without being seen by any of the Gov^rs or asked any Questions w^tsover. Imediately another Child was brought and so continually till 30 Children were admitted 18 of whom were Boys and 12 Girls being the Number the House is capable of containing. Two Children were refused. One being too old and the other appearing to have the Itch.

About Twelve o'Clock, the House being full the Porter was Order'd to give Notice of it to the Crowd who where without, who thereupon being a little troublesom One of the Gov^rs went out and told them that as many Children were already taken in as Coud be made room for in the House and that Notice shoud be given by a publick Advertisement as soon as any more Could possibly be admitted, And the Gov^rs observing Seven or Eight Women with Children at the Door and more amongst the Crowd desired them that they woud not Drop any of their Children in the Streets where they most probably must Perish but to take care of them till they could have an opportunity of putting them into the Hospital which was hoped would be very soon and that every Body would immediately leave the Hospital without making any Disturbance which was imediately complyed with great Decency, so that in two minutes there was not any Person to be seen in the Street Except the Watch.

On this Occasion the Expressions of Grief of the Women whose

Children could not be admitted were Scarcely more observable than those of some of the Women who parted with their Children so that a more moving Scene can't well be imagined.

All the Children who were received (Except Three) were dressed very clean from whence and other Circumstances they appeared not have been under the care of the Parish officers, nevertheless many of them appeared as if stupifyed with some Opiate, and some of them almost Starved, One as in the Agonies of Death thro' want of Food, too weak to Suck, or to receive Nourishment, and notwithstanding the greatest care appeared as dying when the Gov^{rs} left the Hospital which was not till they had given proper Order's and seen all necessary Care taken of the Children.

Within a little over a year following the opening of the hospital, the number of women seeking admission for their babies far outstripped the number of vacancies. John Brownlow (himself a foundling who was to become the hospital's senior administrator) relates: 'As the hospital became more generally known, the applications for admissions greatly increased, so that there were frequently 100 women at the door when 20 children only could be received. This gave rise to the disgraceful scene of women scrambling and fighting to get to the door, that they might be of the fortunate few to reap the benefit of the Asylum.'[1]

It was situations such as these the governors feared most, for they strengthened the hand of those who were vociferous in their denunciations of the basic principle of such an institution on moral grounds. In an endeavour to overcome the accommodation problem, a system of balloting was introduced. The method proposed:

That all the Women who bring any Children be let into the Court Room as they come, and there set on Benches to be placed round the Room, with strict Orders not to stir from their Seats on pain of being turned out with their Children. And that two of the House-Maids stay in the Room with them to prevent any Children being dropped or other Tricks being put upon the Hospital.

That as many White Balls as there shall be Children to be taken in, with five red Balls for every Twenty Children who are to be taken in and so in Proportion for any greater or lesser number, and as many black Balls as with the white and red shall be Equal to the number of Women present, shall be put into a Bag or Box and drawn out by the Women who bring the Children.

That each Woman who draws a black Ball shall be immediately turned out of the Hospital with her Child.

If any Woman desire to be concealed the Bag or Box may be carried to them, or the Matron or some other person may draw for them. The Lotts to be drawn in the Court Room in the presence of all the Women to prevent all Suspicion of Fraud or Partiality.

And finally the sensible precaution, 'That the Room be strewn with Sand'.[2]

Among the foundation's collection of pictures you may see an engraving by N. Parr after a drawing by the 18th century artist Samuel Wale, whose legend reads, 'An exact Presentation of the Form and Manner in which Exposed and Deserted Young Children are admitted into the Foundling Hospital.' Parr's engraving, published in 1749, depicts such a scene, from the dejected expression on the face of the 'unlucky' mother who has drawn a black ball, to the look of relief on that of the 'lucky' mother who has drawn a white ball.

The Admission of Children by Ballot, engraved by Nathaniel Parr after a drawing by Samuel Wale, 1749

The darkest period of the hospital's early history was between the years 1756-60. This was the era of the 'basket babies', or 'indiscriminate admissions'.

By then the hospital had fallen upon hard times. The cold truth was that the admission rate of children was governed by the amount of finance available, so that the upper limit was determined by the extent to which private effort was willing to stretch itself. Private benefactions had rendered possible the erection of the hospital buildings, and the admission of approximately 100 children each year.

As the finances of the hospital continued to be depressed, a special committee was formed which recommended that a petition be presented to the House of Commons. The petition was successful, the Commons voting the hospital the sum of £10,000, with the mandatory condition that it receive all children offered under a certain age, which the hospital first set at two months.

Elaborate preparations were devised by the hospital to meet Parliament's condition. These included that the children should be taken in 'at all Hours, both Day and Night'. That the hospital's inspectors provide '60 wet Nurses and 20 dry'; and finally that a basket be hung at the gate of the main entrance in Guilford Street 'into which the mother, after giving the Porter notice by ringing the bell, could deposit her child'.[3]

Never in the history of the hospital had such precautions as these been rendered so necessary. The new system of general admissions became fair game for everybody, so that 'infants from villages, 50, 100 or even 200 miles distant, were sent to town, oftentimes in a manner too shameful to relate, to take their fortune with the parish children of the metropolis'.[4]

It was almost three years before Parliament decided to intervene. In the April of 1759 the hospital was asked by the House of Commons to provide a return of the number of children received into the hospital, and the number of children who had died.

The return was duly laid before the House, whereupon it resolved 'That the general admission of all children, indiscriminately, had been attended with many evil consequences, and that it be discontinued.'[5]

The death rate had been appalling, the statistics reading more like casualty lists of a bloody Passchendaele.

During the period of general admission (which went on for a little over three years) 14,934 children were received of whom 10,204 died. Of those who died, 4735 were under the age of six months; 971 under the age of one year, and 967 under two years. In the words of Thomas Bernard: 'The seite of the Hospital was in many instances converted into a burying ground.'[6]

Some children were actually stripped of their clothing before being deposited in the basket. Brownlow relates the case of an aged banker received into the hospital during this period who was desirous of becoming acquainted with his origin. 'All the information afforded by the hospital was that he was put into the basket at the gate — naked.'[7]

The period of indiscriminate admission was brought to a close at the hospital's baptismal font, when the foundling chaplain christened the last child to be received under the system with the names, Kitty Finis.

One of the many prominent benefactors who came forward during the earliest years of the hospital was William Hogarth. He conceived the plan of decorating the bare walls of the newly-built hospital with various works of art. To carry out his plan, Hogarth obtained the co-operation of some of the most prominent artists of his day including Thomas Gainsborough, Francis Hayman, Joseph Highmore, Thomas Hudson, Allan Ramsay, Sir Joshua Reynolds, James Wills, Richard Wilson and Michael Rysbrack, 'the leading sculptor and one of the most fashionable artists in Britain'.[8]

Before the turn of the half-century, the foundation had been laid for the Foundling Hospital's considerable collection of pictures and other art works, which is described by Benedict Nicolson as 'an admirable cross-section of a particular phase in British art, unparalleled elsewhere',[9] and by Ronald Paulson as 'an illuminating cross-section of all the developing styles of the 1740s and 50s'. [10]

Four of the paintings, Highmore's *Hagar and Ishmael*, Wills's *Little Children Brought to Christ*, Hayman's *The Finding of the Infant Moses in the Bullrushes* and Hogarth's *Moses Brought to Pharoah's Daughter* occupy the same four places in the Coram Foundation's exquisite Court Room as they first occupied those two centuries ago.

From the historical viewpoint, the most fascinating piece of the Coram Foundation's entire collection, possibly, is Hogarth's *March of the Guards to Finchley*.

An announcement in the *General Advertiser* of 14 April 1750 read:

Mr Hogarth is publishing by subscription, a print representing *The March to Finchley*, in the year 1746, engraved on a copperplate 22 inches by 17, the price 7s.6d.

In the subscription book are the particulars of a proposal whereby each subscriber of three shillings, over and above the said seven shillings and sixpence for the print, will in consideration thereof be entitled to a chance of having the original picture, which shall be delivered to the winning subscriber as soon as the engraving is finished.

Some few days later, Hogarth announced the day and time appointed for the draw: Monday 30 April at 2 pm.

The result of the draw was made known on the following day, through the media of the *London Evening Post*, and the *General Advertiser*:

General Advertiser, May 1, 1750:

Yesterday Mr Hogarth's subscription was closed; 1843 chances being subscribed for, Mr Hogarth gave the remaining 167 chances to the Foundling Hospital, and the same night delivered the picture to the governors.

The contemporary diarist George Vertue (who clearly was no admirer of Hogarth the man as against Hogarth the artist) gives a somewhat more colourful account of the transaction:

Mr Hogarth having proposed to publish a print the march to finchly the army raisd. in 1745. a drolle humorous ridiculous print. from a painting he had done — the print to be subscribed at 7s6. each, those that woud pay half a guinea. should be intituled to a chance of Lottery for the painting also, so that every person rather subscribed half a guinea than 3 half Crowns; by which means he gatherd about 1800 for Ticketts subscription before hand — thus cunning & skill joynd together. changes the proverb. (say well is good, do well is better.) — for here in this case he valud the painting at 200 pounds its said — a great unbounded price, however, by this means. he has raised 900 pounds and still has the Engraved plate to dispose of prints at half guineas more — therefore, it may well be said. do well is good, but say well is better) such fortunate successes are the effect of cunning artfull contrivances. which men of much greater merrit coud never Get or expect — of this picture its said he having 200 Tickets unsubscribed, on the day (30 April 1750) the Lot was to be drawn — he gave them to the Governors, & for the Hospitals of the Foundlings. for their benefit — whereby they became (by the Lot being drawn in one of their numbers) the possessors of the painted picture — and all the rest went without it — (but there it remains —), [11]

By no means was this the end of this already colourful romance, for according to an anonymous writer in the *Gentleman's Magazine*, 'A Lady was the possessor of the fortunate number, and intended to present it to the Foundling Hospital. But that same person having suggested what a door would be open to scandal, were any of her sex to make such a present, it was given to Hogarth, on the express condition that it should be presented in his own name.' [12]

The Foundling Hospital collection of paintings was subsequently made available all the year round for public viewing, drawing 'a daily crowd of spectators in their splendid equipages; and a visit to the Foundling Hospital became the most fashionable morning lounge of the reign of George II'. [13]

The Foundling Hospital was to remain the most important centre of public art and a common meeting ground for London's most prominent artists until the founding, some 16 years later, of the Royal Academy.

Meanwhile, the artists decided to meet annually at the Foundling Hospital, and it was out of these meetings that the Royal Academy ultimately took birth:

> The donations in painting, which several artists presented to the foundling hospital, were among the first objects of this nature, which had engaged the attention of the public. The artists, observing the effects that these paintings produced, came, in the year 1760, to a resolution to try the fate of an exhibition of their works. This effort had its desired effect: the public were entertained, and the artists were excited to emulation.
>
> These exhibitions, so flattering to every artist of true genius, were annually renewed: they were the means of bringing to light the works of many ingenious young men, who might otherwise have remained in obscurity. [14]

A little less than five years later, on 26 January, 1765, the Incorporated Society of Artists of Great Britain, as it was then named, received the Royal Charter.

Thus the chain, in which Hogarth unintentionally forged the first link, was now virtually complete. John Ireland could claim, with justification, that 'This gives Hogarth a right to be classed, if not among those who were founders of the Royal Academy, as one of the first causes of its establishment.' [15]

And nearer our own day, Sydney Hutchison could claim, with equal justification, 'the father and ultimate breadwinner [of the Royal Academy] was the Foundling Hospital'. [16]

The hospital's greatest benefactor during the fifth and sixth decades of the 18th century was George Frederick Handel.

An item from the minutes of a meeting of the hospital's general committee of 14 May 1749 records:

> 'Mr Handel being present and having Generously and Charitably Offered a Performance of Vocal and Instrumental Musick to be at this Hospital, and that the money arising therefrom should be applied to the finishing the Chapel of this Hospital.'

Handel himself directed the performance which took place on 24 May 1749. It included his *'Musick for the Royal Fireworks, Select Pieces from the Oratorio of Solomon relating to the Dedication of the Temple and*

Several Pieces composed for the Occasion, the words taken from the Scripture and applicable to this Charity, and its Benefactors'. *

Certain musical ears apparently were not as yet attuned to the Handel idiom, for the contributor to the *London Evening Post* commented, 'Last Saturday several Curious pieces of Musick, composed by Mr Handel, were performed in the new Chapel at the Foundling Hospital.'

In the following year an advertisement put out by the hospital announced:

> George Frederick Handel Esq. having presented this Hospital with a very fine Organ for the Chapel thereof, and repeated his Offer of Assistance to promote this Charity; on Tuesday the First Day of May of 1750, Mr Handel will open the said Organ; and the Sacred Oratorio called *Messiah* will be performed under his direction![7]

So vast was the audience for the 1749 performance (the *Gentleman's Magazine* reporting it as being 'above a thousand')[18] that invitations for the 1750 performance of *Messiah* desired 'The Gentlemen to come without Swords and the Ladies without Hoops'. ** And in the following year the *General Advertiser* of 18 April gossiped, 'We hear that the Ladies who have Tickets for the Oratorio of *Messiah* at the Foundling Hospital intend to go in Small Hoops, and the Gentlemen without Swords, to make their Seats more convenient to themselves.'

In the spring of each successive year until his death in 1759, Handel arranged for performances of *Messiah* in the hospital chapel — a total in all of 12 performances, which enriched the charity by a net total of £6725 10s. 6d. Moreoever, Handel personally directed these performances until compelled by failing health to hand over their physical direction to John Christopher Smith.

Previous to the series of Foundling Hospital performances of *Messiah*, the work had hardly prophesied its ultimate triumph. His contemporary biographer, John Mainwaring, wrote, 'He hoped to find that favour in a distant capital [meaning Dublin] which London seemed to refuse him. For even his *Messiah* had met with a cold reception.' [19]

Posterity was thus to prove the Foundling Hospital performances as epoch-making in that it was these which set this most regularly and frequently performed work of all time on its unparalleled career.

---

* *The Several Pieces composed for the Occasion* are now known as *The Foundling Hospital Anthem*. The original manuscript which is partly in Handel's own hand and partly in that of his amanuensis, John Christopher Smith, is part of the Thomas Coram Foundation's Handel collection. (In 1954 the name was changed from the Foundling Hospital to The Thomas Coram Foundation for Children.)

** A copy of this Invitation Card together with the keyboard of Handel's presentation organ is displayed in the Thomas Coram Foundation's museum.

In the third codicil to his will, Handel bequeathed to the hospital 'a Fair Copy of the Score, and all the Parts of my Oratorio called The Messiah to the Foundling Hospital'.[20]

The copying was done by John Christopher Smith, and both score and parts are in the possession of the Thomas Coram Foundation.

During Handel's own lifetime, we see the reigning Professor of Music of Oxford University, Dr William Hayes, paying this eloquent tribute to Handel:

> As a moral, good, and charitable Man, let Infants, not only those who feel the Effects of his Bounty, but even such who are yet unborn, chaunt forth his Praise, whose annual Benefaction to an Hospital for the Maintenance of the Forsaken, the Fatherless, and those who have none to help them, will render HIM and his MESSIAH, truly Immortal and crowned with Glory, by the King of Kings and Lord of Lords.[21]

We thus lower the curtain on one of the world's most happy, romantic and enduring of love affairs. It was happy, because the prime giver neither asked for, nor expected, any return; it was romantic, because it brought together two extremes of social degree; and it was enduring because neither party was wholly on the receiving end.

My own mother attended the Foundling Hospital with her petition on Friday, 10 April 1908. An item in the Minutes of the General Committee's meeting of the following week records:

> Read the report of Hannah . . . for the admission of her child and it appearing to be a proper object of this Charity
> RESOLVED
> That the child of the said Petitioner be admitted subject to the fifth regulation relating to the admission of children.

Thus (vide the said fifth regulation) was my mother able to 'hide her shame' and be replaced 'in the course of virtue, and the way of an honest livelihood'.

It was to be the last time we were to see each other.

Part of the third codicil to Handel's will, and his signature. He bequeathed 'a fair copy of the Score and all the Parts, of my Oratorio called The Messiah to the Foundling Hospital'.

As far as I am aware, my mother made no enquiries of the hospital during my eight years there as to my well-being. This was as well perhaps (more for her sake than for my own), for she was thus spared the coldly formal reply which went out in stereotyped fashion to all such enquiries:

'Dear Madam,

I am in receipt of your letter this morning and am pleased to inform you that the [sic] child is quite well.'

In the words of Robert Southey: 'Cold is thy heart and as frozen as Charity!'

FOOTNOTES TO CHAPTER 1

[1] John Brownlow, *Memoranda; or Chronicles of the Foundling Hospital* (London, 1847), pp.166-7. Also, Brownlow, *The History and Design of the Foundling Hospital* (London, 1858), p.7.

[2] Gen.Com.* 27 October 1742.

* General Committee Minutes of the Foundling Hospital.

[3] Ibid., 18 and 24 May 1756.

[4] Sir Frederick Morton Eden, *The State of the Poor, or An History of the Labouring Classes in England* (London, 1797), Vol.1, pp.338-9.

[5] Quoted from Nichols and Wray, *The History of the Foundling Hospital* (London, 1935), p.69.

[6] Thomas Bernard, *An Account of the Foundling Hospital* (London, 1799), p.29.

[7] *Memoranda*, p.173 and *History and Design*, pp.13-14.

[8] M.I. Webb, *Michael Rysbrack, Sculptor* (London, 1954), p.48, quoted in Ronald Paulson, *Hogarth his Life, Art, and Times* (London, 1971), pp.42 and 429 n20.

[9] Benedict Nicolson, *The Treasures of the Foundling Hospital* (Oxford, 1972), p.53.

[10] Ronald Paulson, *Hogarth; His Life, Art, and Times* (London, 1971), Vol.II, p.50.

[11] The Walpole Society, *Vertue Note Books* (Oxford, 1933-4), p.153. George Vertue (1684-1756) Engraver, Antiquarian and a devoted musician. He was only 29 when he commenced his researches into the lives of artists. His *Note Books*, relating to artists and collections in England were purchased after his death by Horace Walpole, and formed the basis for his *Anecdotes of Painting in England*.

[12] Quoted from *Memoranda*, pp.14-15. I have searched in vain through numerous volumes of *Gentleman's Magazine* for the source of this story.

[13] Ibid., p.12. Brownlow in turn quotes from *Catalogue Raisonne* of West's pictures.

[14] Sir Robert Strange, *An Inquiry into the Rise and Establishment of the Royal Academy of Arts* (London, 1775), p.63.

[15] John Ireland, *Hogarth Illustrated* (London, 1791), Vol.II, p.348.

[16] Sydney C. Hutchison, *The History of the Royal Academy* 1768-1968 (London, 1968), p.34.

[17] Gen.Com. 18 April 1750.

[18] *Gentleman's Magazine*, May 1749, p.235.

[19] John Mainwaring, *Memoirs of the Life of the late George Frederick Handel* (London, 1760), p.131.

[20] A copy of the Third Codicil to Handel's Will was kindly made available to me by Mr Gerald Coke.

[21] William Hayes, *Remarks on Mr Avison's Essay on Musical Expression* (London, 1753), p.130.

PART I

A BLANK CHILDHOOD

When my Father
and my Mother
forsake me
the Lord taketh
me up. Psalm 27.12

2: *Received, a blank child*

"Familiar in their Mouths as HOUSEHOLD WORDS." — Shakespeare.

A Weekly Journal
conducted by Charles Dickens

No.156   Saturday, March 19, 1853.   Price 2d.

Received, A Blank Child

The blank day of blank, Received a blank child.

Within a few weeks, this office form, printed on a piece of parchment, happened to come in our way. Finding it to be associated with the histories of more than 20,000 blank children, we were led into an enquiry concerning those little gaps in the decorous world. Their home and head quarters whence the document issues, is the Foundling Hospital, London.

This home of the blank children is by no means a blank place. It is a commodious roomy comfortable building, airily situated, though within advertisement distance of Temple Bar, which, as everybody knows, is precisely ten minutes' walk. It stands in its own grounds, cosily surveying its own shady arcades, its own turf, and its own high trees. It has an incredible fishpond behind it, no curious windows before it, and the wind (tempered to the shorn lambs within) is free to blow on either side of it. It preserves a warm, old fashioned, rich-relation kind of gravity, strongly indicative of Bank stock.

What these are [the existing rules of admission], may be best described through our own observation of the admission of two children who happened to be brought there by two mothers while we were inspecting the place.

Each of the mothers had previously rung the porter's bell to obtain a printed form of petition to the Governors for the admission of her child. No petition is allowed to be issued, except from the porter's lodge: no previous communication with any officer of the Hospital must have been held by the mother: the child must have been the first-born, and preference is given to cases in which some promise of marriage has been made to the mother, or some other deception practised upon her. She must never have lived with the father. The object of these restrictions (careful personal inquiry being made into all such points) is as much to effect the restoration of the mother to society, as to provide for her child.

My mother was employed as a children's nurse in West Kensington; and my father, in George Crabbe's words, 'The cause of all, the faithless lover cold', a courier and interpreter. When my mother knew him, he lodged with his brother and sister-in-law in Brompton, London.

They became engaged, but before arrangements for the wedding were made, upon hearing that my mother had become pregnant, my father deemed it prudent to disappear (as his sister-in-law told my mother) to Germany.

My mother was then 27 years old. With both her parents dead, she found herself faced with the most unenviable and tragic of all human problems; for the unmarried mother's prospects, particularly for the less than well-to-do classes of those times, were singularly unpromising. The tragedy of the unmarried mother was described by Goldsmith:

Woman

When lovely woman stoops to folly,
And finds too late that men betray,
What charm can soothe her melancholy?
What art can wash her tears away?

The only art her guilt to cover,
To hide her shame from ev'ry eye,
To give repentance to her lover,
And wring his bosom is — to die.

My mother decided upon the only sensible course open to a single woman who must provide wholly her own means of support — that of submitting a petition to the Governors of the Foundling Hospital, asking that they receive her child.

My mother's petition (which she presented when I would have been 26 days old) proved successful. She at least was spared the agonising suspense of the old balloting system, which long since had been swept into limbo.

I was received officially into the Foundling Hospital on the following Tuesday, when a ribbon-threaded off-white bone locket stamped with my hospital number, 23062, was hung around my neck. I was then handed over to my foster-mother, who at the same time received the customary caution, 'and it is especially required of you that you keep the number of the child always affixed to its person', which caution, once clear of the hospital gates, she proceeded conveniently to ignore. I was then taken into the chapel (the very same chapel that under Handel's personal direction had started *Messiah* 'on its unexampled career'), when I was deprived of the names given me by my mother, and baptised in the names of Charles Nalden.

My natural mother was now free to walk out of the hospital gates to a fresh and unencumbered start in life.

May God have blessed and protected her.

Chertsey Town Church, **by James S. Ogilvy, 1912.**

3: Foster child

A foster parent is just an ordinary kind of common or garden saint — (Mr Tony Liddell, regional officer for the National Children's Homes, in Britain.)

From being an unwanted baby, I now became a very much wanted foster-child. My foster parents were Mr and Mrs Mills of Holly Cottage, 100 Station Road, Chertsey, Surrey.

There was nothing fortuitous in the choice of Chertsey, for the good townspeople of that area had been providing foster homes for literally thousands of baby foundlings for the better part of two centuries. Chertsey shared the distinction with half-a-dozen other towns near London of being first in the field with this humanitarian service. Foster-mothers were engaged by a visiting committee of the Foundling Hospital as far back as 1740 — a few months before the official opening of the institution on (appropriately) Lady Day, 1741.

The last time I visited Chertsey (in 1970) I found it the same charming, relatively unspoilt, place I knew earlier in the century. The town council in its wisdom must have decided against admitting those abominations, the chain-store and the supermarket, and I was overjoyed to see many of the landmarks such as the picturesque old houses in Guildford, Windsor and London Streets, together with the 17th and early 18th century 'George', 'Queen's Head', 'King's Head' and 'Swan' inns. Although altered a good deal over the course of years, they still retained some of their original brickwork and evidence of their respective period's construction. *Cowley*

House (once the residence of Abraham Cowley) and *Pyrcroft* (the scene of the burglary in *Oliver Twist* and now used by the Surrey County Council as a nursery school) have been spared the attentions of the 'developers'.

It was this Chertsey that was to be my home for the next six years.

My foster-mother's first name was Fanny, and my father's William. Undoubtedly my mother's greatest claim to fame was her feat of bringing up 24 foster children in addition to the one surviving son of her own seven children. And my father's? Undoubtedly his feat of catching two fish simultaneously on the same hook in the River Thames, which, to his eternal delight, was reported in the local paper.

I must have been about three years old when my parents moved from Holly Cottage (a bungalow) to 98 Station Road — next door. Why they moved I never really knew; maybe it meant a lower rent, or that they preferred a house with an 'upstairs', or whether my mother simply wanted a change. The most plausible reason for the change (which came from my mother) was that the previous tenant, a drink-besotted old woman, kicked the amply-filled chamber pot from the top of the stairs to the bottom, and that my parents were the only couple in Chertsey sufficiently game to take on this otherwise desirable mod-cons residence.

My most vivid memories of Holly Cottage are connected with the amputation of my father's big toe by the town's GP, Dr Milsome. I still retain, albeit deep down in my subconscious, memories of the sickly smell of chloroform, of my father's agonised yells once its effect had worn off, and of the ministering attentions of my mother, who plied ceaselessly it seemed between kitchen and bedroom with a constant supply of hot water bottles. In those days they were made of the same fawn-coloured stone used in the manufacture of ginger-beer bottles, 7 lb jam jars, and half-gallon vinegar bottles — all collectors' pieces today. But my most treasured memory of that operation is my father's hymn singing which alternated with his bouts of groaning. I do not recollect either of my parents going to church and can only assume that the hymns were a legacy of the compulsory church parade system of his army days.

Other memories of Holly Cottage include the greengage and apple trees, my staring up at the exposed wooden laths following a collapse of the plastered bedroom ceiling, and of my father whitewashing the ceilings (another characteristic smell which I still recall) and papering the walls. The bedroom ceiling episode was kept alive by fear — fear of what lay hidden beyond that frightening alternation of white laths and pitch blackness.

The move into No.98 was done without any fuss, as in those days a small wicket gate connected the two houses. No.98 was the normal type of 'rent-catcher'. As you went in at the 'front door' (which was situated at the side of the house), immediately facing you was a steep staircase. It had to be steep, on account of the house's narrow width in relation to its height. Bottom right was the 'front room', and bottom left the kitchen and scullery. Top right was bedroom No.1, and top left, bedroom No.2. There was of course no bathroom, hot water system (short of a relay of hob- and gas-heated kettles), or electricity, but there was an outside lavatory.

A wooden out-shed housed the mangle, an Amazonian affair, whose heavy handle my mother would begin to turn at some unearthly hour every Monday morning to the accompaniment of a chorus of demoniacal shrieks.

Even so, my mother's lot was no different from that of countless thousands of other working-class British housewives of the pre-electric, pre-domestic-gadget era, who, within all too few years of marriage found themselves reduced (by a taken-for-granted unbroken run of pregnancies and exhausting domestic chores of the 'Monday morning wash' type) from fresh-complexioned country wenches to prematurely old women.

A shallow sink was positioned in the corner of the scullery, which was used for ablutions and washing up alike, for the good reason that it boasted the only running water tap in the house. In the corner opposite stood the copper — another dual-purpose appliance used for the Monday morning wash and boiling the Christmas puddings. But ah! what puddings!

At the far end of the same wall stood the gas stove, and opposite that (on the same side as the sink) the back door. The 'front room', in common with thousands of other front rooms of this strata of society, was virtually a Victoriana showcase. The mantel-shelf, and indeed every available flat surface (other than floor and ceiling) was literally crowded with choice pieces of Goss china — 'A Present from Margate' sort of thing. The place-names on the several pieces of china meant nothing to my mother, for never once during her 73 years on this earth did she catch even a glimpse of the sea, let alone enjoy a seaside holiday; or for that matter, any other sort of holiday, for she was born in Chertsey, lived all her life in Chertsey, and was buried in Chertsey.

Hanging on the wall in pride of place was a framed portrait of Queen Victoria. Then there was a picture of a contemporary music-hall dancer with a bejewelled dagger in hand (Polly somebody or other), a suite of leather covered horse-hair stuffed chairs and sofa, a table made from genuine 'meoggomamy' (the show-piece par excellence), some magnificent potted aster-me-desters,* whose leaves were washed with loving care in pure milk. The whole was rounded off by a permanent musty smell due to the

* Aspidistras

fact that both window and door remained firmly shut, wooden-slatted venetian blinds drawn to half-mast, and the room staying unused between Christmas festive seasons.

In bedroom No.1 there hung a picture of Windsor Castle, viewed from the Thames and surrounding fields, and a print of Holman Hunt's *The Light of the World*. Both these pictures remained undisturbed in their respective positions right up to the time of my mother's death in 1937. Positioned underneath the staircase was the larder, dark and ill-ventilated.

Gas was used for cooking and lighting on the penny-in-the-slot system. Periodically, and without warning, the house would be plunged into darkness, when minor chaos would ensue until one or the other of my parents located the re-vitalising penny. So far as the kitchen and front room were concerned, the gas lighting was reasonably adequate, for affixed to their respective jets was a gas mantle, which in turn (because of its fragile, gossamer-like texture) was protected by a white glass globe. Apparently my parents could not run to the expense of installing mantles in either of the bedrooms, so that we had literally to grope our way around these with the dubious aid of a pale flicker of gas light, which cast Edgar Allan Poe-like silhouettes on to the surrounding walls, when

Mole hills seems mountains, and the ant
Appears a monstrous elephant.

A low gas was allowed to burn all night, so that I never knew what it was to sleep in complete darkness — a habit which I did not encourage within my own family. There was no provision for light of any kind in either the larder, scullery or outside lavatory.

Saturday night was the traditional bath night. An oval galvanised iron bath was used for this purpose, and as the method of filling it (kettle by kettle of boiling water) was laboriously slow, my mother would bath all her children in the same water. And my guess is that both my mother and father bathed in the same water once we were safely in bed. In the summer, we were bathed in the scullery, but in the winter in front of the kitchen fire.

The fireplace hearths, and the little oblong stone slab which stood outside the front door, were kept in spotless off-white condition by my mother's regular and expert use of what she termed 'arse-stone'. The method was first to wash the stone surface, apply the hearth-stone, using brisk, circular motions, and finally finish off with a barely moistened cloth in a series of left-to-right lines.

At the front of the house was a tiny plot in which my father grew Sweet Williams, wallflowers and flags (a species of Iris). That part of the back garden which was not encroached upon by the shed, the outside lavatory, the clothes line and the chicken run, was planted out with gooseberry bushes, red and black currants, 'roobub', but little else; for my father ran an allotment situated hard by the town cemetery.

My father's was classified as an 'official' allotment, whose history goes back to the beginning of the last century, when areas of land were set aside in such villages as Chertsey for the 'labouring poor'. Running an allotment meant rather more than a weekend hobby to my father and others like him, for its produce became a necessary supplement to their meagre weekly pay packets. A gravel walk (which led through hedgerowed fields to Addlestone) divided the 'new' from the 'old' cemetery, the little lodge at the entrance providing accommodation for the sexton. At the tolling of the cemetery bell, my mother audibly would murmur "another poor soul gone to rest".

A dead person's body was placed in its coffin, and kept in the bereaved family's front room until the day of the funeral. During this period, the blinds in the bereaved household would be lowered to their fullest extent, the near neighbours lowering theirs as a mark of respect. Some half-hour or so before the funeral procession was due to leave the house, relatives and friends filed past the coffin for one final look at the deceased's face. On these occasions, my mother would encourage me to touch the dead person's forehead as a precaution against dreaming about him. It did not occur to her that to set her face (and mine) against the practice of 'one final look' might have provided an even surer precaution. Next to market day, a local funeral was the guarantee of a record turn-out of the town's women-folk.

Our 'backyard' backed on to Laburnum Road, whose frontages faced the London and South Western Railway, as it was then called. This was convenient for householders along the entire lengths of Station and Laburnum Roads, as the 7.19 am 'Workmans Train' (as it was designated) to Waterloo provided an unfailing time-check, for running on a branch line, it could be relied upon to run on time.

These, then, were to be my home and surroundings until I arrived at the age for admission to the Foundling Hospital. My mother displayed a great deal of common sense on this score, for as soon as I was old enough to appreciate the significance of it all, periodically she would gently remind me that one day I must leave home to go back to the 'Fondling 'orsepiddle'; so that the shock when ultimately it did come was at least partially numbed.

It was in situations such as this that my foster parents demonstrated in their simple way their deep love and compassion for their foster children; and I do believe that they lavished at least as much, if not more, love upon us than upon their own son. Moreover, their love for us never diminished, for until my father's untimely death on July 18, 1918, either one or the other parent (or both) visited us in the March, June, September and

December of each year during the whole of our stay in the London institution.

Before their marriage, my mother worked in a 'larndry' for upwards of 10 hours each day, her wages amounting to 19/3d per week. Dutifully, she would hand over her wages in full to her mother (from her photograph a stern, humourless Victorian), who, just as dutifully (according to my mother), would hand her back the odd 3d. In later years my mother would recall, not without a touch of venom, that she was made to suffer this humiliation right up to, and including, her last pay packet before her wedding day. The sole memories I retain of my grandfather are of his 19th century styled 'face-do' which took the form of a shaved upper-lip, and a fringe of whisker extending from ear to ear; of his riding to visit us on his solid iron, solid-tyred tricycle, and of his gentleness of manner.

Following her marriage, my mother became consumed with two overriding passions which she regarded (not without a show of pride when discussing them) as her 'pussonal' contribution to the welfare of the town's community, which included both the quick and the dead. Her first passion was assisting the local midwife in 'delivering', and the second, in assisting the local undertaker in 'laying-out'. A generous person herself, her experience in the second of her two community services gave rise no doubt to her oft-repeated castigation 'so mean that he would nick the 'ape-nies from a dead kid's eyes'.

My father joined the Army as a regular soldier in the Leicestershire Regiment, serving for the greater part of his time in Burma. He was born in 1867, so that his soldiering would have been done during the last decade or so of the 19th century, which saw the publication of several editions of Kipling's *Barrack Room Ballads*. Soldiers below officers' rank (termed 'other ranks') were still regarded as little better than scum; the degrading conditions of service life, his lack of education, and his unpolished manners notwithstanding, my father emerged from it all as the most kindly and gentle of men. Vocational training courses which were introduced to help the time-expired serviceman's transition from army life to 'Civvy Street' had yet to be established, so that in common with the majority of ex-servicemen, my father left the army fitted only for unskilled labour. This he found in Herring's Iron Foundry in Chertsey, where he was employed as furnace-stoker. There he remained until his death in 1918 at the relatively early age of 51. How my mother managed to pay for things I shall never know, but she arranged for a suitably inscribed kerbstone to be put around his grave (in the 'new' section of Chertsey Cemetery), had an in memoriam card printed, and for some considerable time after his death used the then fashionable black-edged notepaper, which was not cheap. Her choice of

words for the in memoriam card epitomises within the space of a couple
of verses her own simple beliefs, and affords an insight into the type of
sentiments which appealed to the average mind of the English 'lower'
classes:

> Day by day we all do miss him
> Words would fail our loss to tell.
> But in Heaven we hope to meet him,
> Evermore with him to dwell.
>
> We loved what God has taken
> We loved but could not keep.
> We strove but death was stronger
> So we must cease to weep.

   In the early days of their married life my mother went on working in
the 'larndry' as a means of helping establish a home; but an unbroken
sequence of pregnancies soon put paid to that. They had seven children,
all of whom save one (a boy they named William), died in early infancy.
And even the young William's life was precariously in the balance, my
mother recalling how she moistened his parched lips with brandy, which
she applied with a feather. Whether 'Bill' survived because of, or in spite
of, this drastic treatment (which in this case the doctor didn't order), I
cannot say; all I can vouch for is that this taste, cultivated so early in life,
never quite left him.
   And while we are on the subject of what my mother termed 'intopsicating
liquor', my parents' favourite drink appears to have been stout — not
straightout stout, but stout with a difference. A curious practice existing
among country people of those times was to place a red-hot poker in their
stout* and hold it there until the hissing ceased. Whether the red-hot poker
gave it some distinctly characteristic flavour, or whether they believed it
to endow the stout with some additional property (such as 'iron'), I can
but conjecture. What is not conjecture is my being encouraged to 'take
a sip out of dad's glass', but not until promising that I would not 'let on'
to the people at the 'orsepiddle'. Occasionally my parents would repair to
the 'Swan' at the top of the town, bribing me with a huge biscuit to remain
on the footpath outside. Never do I recall either of my foster-parents coming
home the worse for drink — which is saying something for those days of
cheap booze.

---

* Mulled stout.

Although my father was not an addict in this direction, he was in another — snuff-taking. As became the fashion, he kept his supply of snuff in a tiny metal box, which was lodged in one of his 'weskit' pockets. He must have considered it harmless stuff, for in introducing me to the filthy habit (as mum called it) he did not, as in the case of stout sampling, swear me to secrecy.

The local GP whose auxiliary functions were those of surgeon and dentist (a not unusual combination for those times) was a Dr Milsome, whose thick, shaggy eyebrows and gold-rimmed spectacles endowed him with a stern, forbidding presence. He lived in a charming old Georgian house in Guilford Street, long since demolished to make way for the town's public library and car park — commendable additions as social amenities, but a poor exchange of architectural styles.

My mother never forgave him for the suffering he caused my father in his big toe amputation, and the alleged mess he made of my initial vaccination. So that although the very model of propriety, respect and deference to his face (characterised by an ever-so-slight sideways tilt of the head), behind his back she always referred to him as 'that bleedin' butcher'.

Dr Milsome was appointed by the governors of the Foundling Hospital as medical superintendent for the Chertsey district. I recall his visiting me when I was confined to bed with chicken pox, and my visiting his surgery for a tooth extraction; but apart from these and other minor ailments (such as measles), I had a clean bill of health.

The one complaint which caused me constant distress was headache. When I returned to the hospital, this took a more agonising form; the ache would commence in my forehead, and then move to the back of my head, to persist, on and off, for a minimum of three days. My mother also suffered from headaches, which she attempted to ease by applying a vinegar-soaked bandage to her forehead — a time-honoured remedy among people of her class. Other, and equally ineffectual, remedies included menthol (marketed in acorn-shaped containers), smelling salts, and mustard plaster. The remedy she used on me for headache and constipation alike was a somewhat more drastic affair; she would dose me with a loathsome concoction called liquorice powder — a drab, greyish substance, which made me feel physically sick every time I took it, the mollifying effect of the post-medicine 'boo-boo' bribe nothwithstanding. The 'boo-boo' was generally a pink cone-shaped sweet, topped with a hazel nut.

The nickname given me by my parents was Barley (abbreviated to Bar) on account of my alleged over-fondness for barley-sugar. But it is the pink hazel-nut-topped sweet, the 'marshmaller', and the 'joo-joo', and not the barley-sugar, that I recall as being my favourite confection.

For straightout constipation her remedy, although tasteless, was no less drastic and effective than the liquorice powder. I might add, that but for my tender years, it would also have been embarrassing. Her remedy was to insert up my rectum a cone-shaped piece of soap (expressly fashioned for the purpose) which she would work up and down until my 'bells' decided to co-operate.

Unlike her Maker, my mother was quick to anger, and equipped with a vituperative lashing tongue. 'Take that, you perishin' bleeder' was the set phrase which accompanied the stinging 'wipe' across her teenage son's 'moey'*, or maybe a well-placed kick at our fox-terrier bitch, Nell. Yet never once do I recall being chastised by either of my foster-parents.

I can remember but one occasion only when my mother was really angry with me. My 'Sunday best' (which literally it was) ran in the fashion of the day as befitted a child of humble origin — Norfolk-style jacket with knickerbockers to match, long stockings (which reached well above the knees), celluloid collar with ready-made bow-tie, and button-up, patent-leather-toecapped black boots. (I still recall the tedious process of button-hooking up this particular pair of boots.) It was my kicking a chunk of leather out of the patent-leather toecap of one of my Sunday-best boots that moved my mother to real anger. This incident took place outside Jago the Chemist, whose shop stood on the corner of Guildford Street and Station Road. Although no longer a chemist's shop, a close, sideways look will reveal the word CHEMIST underneath its countless coats of paint.

In those days, the milkman did his rounds with a handcart (called a milk-pram) into which was fitted a couple of large capacity milk churns. The milk was drawn off by means of a brass tap. This brings me to the one and only time I recall arousing my father's wrath. It was when I turned on the tap of a temporarily unattended milk cart, and like the Sorcerer's Apprentice in Eucrate's story, was unable to reverse the mischief I had set in motion. My guess is that my father's outburst of anger was sparked off by his having to make good the milkman's loss, which in terms of milk must have been not inconsiderable.

I cannot pretend to write authoritatively on women's fashions of those days, as I had but my mother and her sister (Aunt Lil) as my sole yardsticks. What I do remember is their appearing in what were known as hobble skirts.

---

* A colloquialism, and probably a corruption of 'mow', a wry face:

       Ariel   'Before you can say 'Come' and 'Go'
                And breathe twice; and cry 'So, so,
                Each one, tripping on his toe,
                Will be here with mop and mow'.
                (Tempest, iv, I, 44-7)

Both their dresses were knitted in different shades of blue. The hobble skirt was an ankle-length affair, which tapered off to a narrow circumference at the bottom. The fashion took its name from the short, shuffling steps (somewhat in the manner of the popular conception of a Japanese 'Lady') which the skirt's absurdly narrow width at the ankle compelled the wearer to take.

This fashion must have been 'the rage' about 1913, that is, when I was between five and six years old. If the heavily-bustled, full bosomed woman of the 1870s set out to ape a centaur (which she managed to do with a remarkable degree of success) then the hobble-skirted, amply bottomed woman of the second decade of the present century set out in no less a determined manner, and with no less remarkable a degree of success, to resemble one of the fashionable toys of the period, the peg-top.

From Monday to Saturday my father wore his working clothes, but on Sunday he would wear a suit, set off by a spotlessly white starched dicky, and a bowler hat. On Saturday afternoons he worked on his allotment, where he raised 'taters', 'marrers', 'roobub', 'parznips', 'parzley', and so on; but on Sunday mornings during the summer months, he would delay changing into his Sunday best and take me and Nell to the Thames for a morning's fishing.

Another treat was to be taken on a Sunday evening to hear the Chertsey Town Brass Band. Some few years later the band was to steal a march on its local rival, the Addlestone Brass Band, by investing in a set of silver-plated instruments, and so emerging with the more elevated title of Chertsey Town Silver Prize Band. The band's performances took place on the small patch of green on the Middlesex bank of the Thames, just alongside the old Bridge Hotel. This goes back of course to the pre-motorised era, when pleasures were more simple, and simple pleasures more appreciated. As to the quality of the band, I do not think it would give offence were I to suggest that neither the Chertsey nor the Addlestone Brass Band was exactly a Grimethorpe, a Black Dyke or a Fodens.

The quality of the Chertsey Town Silver Prize Band notwithstanding, a performance was guaranteed to attract a large crowd. This would break itself up into small social knots, who would either recline on the grass, or promenade up and down the riverbank; for a concert by the local band provided good justification for a social gathering of the town's men and womenfolk, when the latter would vie with each other in such matters of dress, deportment and offspring. Quite clearly do I recall the men's 'boaters' (hard, oval-shaped straw hats) which were securely moored against the occasional gust of wind by a cord fastening at one end to the hat itself and the other to the lapel of the jacket.

The vantage point for taking in these brilliant social gatherings was Chertsey Bridge. On one side of the bridge were the locks and weir, and on the other a flat expanse of green meadows (through which the Thames idled along its tortuous route) known to locals as the Meads. It must have been in the summer of either 1912 or 1913 that I saw the take-off of an aeroplane, which used the Meads for a runway. Much of the charm of this one-time idyllic spot has been marred by a span of the M3 motorway, which spews itself across the river; and by the removal of the lion which once stood on the roof of the public house of that name, as proud and defiant guardian of the Surrey bank of the Thames.

Apart from their going to hear the local brass band, my parents' only other cultural outlets were by way of *Reynolds News* and (if and when they might be passed on by a rather more affluent and widely-read neighbour) *John Bull* and the *Daily 'Marrer'.*

At other times my parents would take me for a walk to the still beautiful and unspoiled St. Anne's Hill, whose romantically-concealed wishing well has shared the innermost secrets of countless generations of Chertsey's lasses and lads. Another walk took us over the railway level-crossing, leaving the Recreation Ground (the 'Rec') on our right, and along the Ottershaw Road. My mother was always at pains to point out the then solitary landmark on this still beautiful country road — the local 'orsepiddle'.

Once a year, my father's firm gave its employees an outing, which generally took the form of a pleasure-steamer excursion from Chertsey to Maidenhead. This was not a trip for male employees only, but for the entire family. I still retain vivid memories of two incidents which took place during one of these excursions; the landing at Maidenhead and the scrumptious meal provided by my parents, and the spontaneous burst of laughter from the trippers when an unexpected blast from the boat's siren caused a thoroughly startled riverside housewife to drop her basket of freshly-laundered clothes. Such was these simple people's Laurel and Hardyish sense of humour.

Then there were the seasonal visits of fairs and circuses, which would pitch their camps 'over the Station', or on a piece of waste ground in Free Prae Road, hard by Stepgates, the local council school. Those were the days when the roundabouts were propelled by steam engine. The combined smell of steam, oil and carbide (which provided flare lighting) created a heady, nostalgic odour, which never quite left the senses. It was an integral part of the fair's atmosphere.

I remember on one occasion, one of the roundabouts stubbornly refusing to budge, and in like manner my mother's equally stubborn refusal to budge from her seat until the unhappy proprietor had refunded her her fare. We were thus the roundabout's sole remaining passengers, and young though I was, I still recall the sense of acute embarrassment this incident caused me; for the more protracted the argument (and my mother had a shrill voice when roused) the larger became the crowd of onlookers.

Other fair attractions included the Hoop-la, in which the prize aimed at must be encircled, but untouched by the hoop. In view of the sloping, highly varnished stall which contained the prizes, the chances of winning one were remote. But however long the odds against winning a prize from the Hoop-la stall, the odds against negotiating successfully the 'Greasy Pole' were well-nigh impossible. The 'Greasy Pole' was about 12 feet long and 12 to 15 inches in circumference. It was suspended in a horizontal position, sufficiently high to ensure that competitors' feet could not touch the ground. To win a prize, the challenger had to sit astride the pole and edge himself from one end to the other. Failure to go the full distance meant a ducking in the water trough below. Naturally enough, youths would come suitably clothed for this event, as fair proprietors adhered to the sound economic principle that the more liberal the grease, the less liberal their prize handouts.

A sterner test of manhood was provided by the 'Test your Strength' machine. The competitor, armed with a great wooden mallet, would aim a sledgehammer blow at a heavily-sprung valve, which would send a strength-measuring indicator whizzing up a contraption having the appearance of a giant thermometer. The admiration of the crowd in general and the girls in particular was reserved wholly for the man who could deliver such a Thor-like hammer blow as to send the indicator racing to the top of the pole to ring the bell and so win a prize.

The area of waste land in Free Prae Road was regularly used as a site for a gypsy encampment; and as the scare-weapon for the erring 19th century child was Napoleon, and for the Irish child Cromwell, so for many a country-bred child was it the gypsy. This was understandable, as this enigmatic, and at times fierce-looking people, whose style of living (particularly in their sanitary arrangements) put them beyond the pale of polite society, and their nomadic existence beyond the reach of the township's rates and taxes collector, struck unholy terror into the imagination of many a country-bred child. We were taught not to go near them in such sing-song rhymes as:

> My mother said
> I never should
> Play with the Gypsies in the wood.

> If I did
> She would say
> Naughty boy to disobey!

The distinguishing characteristics of the English gypsy around our parts were the men's swarthy complexions, black, lank, greasy looking hair, fierce drooping moustaches, and great golden earrings. And the women? The average person's conception of the fairground fortune-teller; weather-beaten, grime-furrowed face, with hair concealed under a tightly-fitting red kerchief, low-cut blouse revealing low-cut bodice revealing ...., bedraggled skirt (rendering unnecessary, so they must have decided, a certain undergarment), heavily ringed fingers, and little or no pretence to cultivate the body beautiful. These then were the type of gypsies who would present themselves at our back door in the hope of hawking clothespegs, basket-ware, or tinkering services such as mending kettles and sharpening knives. Little wonder that the gypsies were one of my mother's most formidable scare weapons.

A further successful scare weapon was the nun. Very near to where we lived was a convent, and my mother planted firmly into my then innocent little head that the ground-length dresses worn by the nuns were designed for spiriting away disobedient children. (The recently-introduced, Pope-approved, mid-calf length habit has, of course, rendered this scare weapon ineffectual.) This particular scare weapon had an added twist to it, for my mother never identified these holy women as nuns.

It was during the years 1912-14 that suffragette militancy reached its climax, so that the term 'suffragette' was on everybody's lips, whatever their social class. Now the suffragette, unlike the nun or the gypsy, could not be identified as such; and as the child is more likely to be scared by the devil he can see than by the one he cannot see, clearly something had to be done to make the suffragette scare weapon effective. Wily old bird that my mother could be, she implanted in my mind the belief that those women who wore the long black hooded dresses with the jet crucifixes were, in fact, suffragettes. Thus conditioned, together with the fact that I was sent to the nearby Wesleyan Chapel for my Sunday schooling (my being 'babtised' in the Anglican faith notwithstanding), the signpost to my future spiritual salvation hardly pointed in the direction of Rome.

The annual Wesleyan Sunday School outing took the form of a ride in a brake (in our case a double-decker horse-drawn carriage) to some leafy glade, where we participated in competitive sports (of the egg-and-spoon race type) followed by a picnic meal. The Wesleyan Chapel also presented each member of its Sunday School class with a china mug to mark the coronation of King George V, a memento I retained until well into adulthood, when unaccountably it disappeared.

Saturday was my father's pay day, and also his half-day off work. Without fail, he would give me my 'Saturday 'ape-ny' which was the required sum to get me into the Chertsey Constitutional Hall for the afternoon film session. These years were the heydey of the cowboys (the goodies) and the Indians (the baddies); in short, the years which set in motion a base and fraudulent distortion of the true historical facts. It was all too good box-office stuff for the film companies' directors to let a handful of dispossessed Indians stand in the way of their script-writers. And so we learnt to regard every cowboy a hero, and every Indian a villain.

The only film which made a lasting impression on me was *The Indian Mutiny*, which I avow was in colour! Periodically the cinema proprietor would give his young patrons a special bonus in the form of a 'lucky dip'. A tub was filled with bran, into which you plunged your arm to draw out your prize. One of my prizes was a china doll, which in my rage I smashed to the ground, only to weep for the injury that I had done it. These were, of course, the days of the silent films (the 'flicks'), appropriate music being provided throughout each session by pit musicians, whose number varied according to local conditions; so that whereas the old Tivoli Cinema in London's Strand, or the Stoll Theatre in Kingsway, would support a film with a large pit-orchestra, country-town cinemas such as those in Chertsey and nearby Addlestone and Weybridge had to content themselves with a solo pianist.

An aroma no less characteristic than that of the fairground (though more seductive perhaps) was that which hung around the pre-1914 cinema. In its crude way, the scent-spray served the same purpose then as the air-conditioning system does today. At the time, it was as good an antidote as could be devised to help counteract the foul and smoke-laden atmosphere that pervaded some of the more primitive structures which were passed off as cinemas.

Which leads me to the thankless, soul-destroying job of cinema pianist. In those days, the pianist would be required to play right through the two evening sessions and the Saturday afternoon matinee, breathing in the foul air, and reading his or her music in the glare of a high-powered electric-light bulb. Here I write with first-hand knowledge, as I was to sample this sort of life myself. The pianist was responsible for fitting appropriate music to the unfolding drama, and to avoid such absurd situations as, say, the *Chocolate Soldier* song, *'I love you only'* being played as background music to a prison breakout scene, he was compelled to move his head from music to screen, and vice-versa throughout the film's showing. It was as though he had been smitten early in life with senile tremor. It was from the cinema that I picked up what pathetically small store of tunes I came to know during my Chertsey years. These included *Come, come, my hero* from *The Chocolate Soldier, Come to the Ball* from *The Quaker Girl*, and *Love's Kisses*, a popular waltz tune of the day, which I traced subsequently to the then-popular *Star Folio Album*. The only other tunes I recall knowing are *Itchy-Koo, Yip-i-addy-i-ay, We all go the same way home*, and *God bless the Prince of Wales*. As I came to know both words and music of *Yip-i-addy-i-ay* and *Itchy-Koo*, I can only presume that I picked them up from hearing other people singing them, or maybe from my parents' gramophone, which was the type that played wax-cylinder records. My musical education was rounded off with an occasional visit of the German band,* and listening to Aunt Lil's distinguished guest 'making her violeen talk'. **

The country child's toys were just as simple as other aspects of country life. Perhaps the most popular toy was the hoop, a circle made either of wood or iron and propelled by means of a beater. The hoop provided a stimulating (even though unconscious) form of exercise, as the faster one propelled it, the faster one ran to keep abreast of it. It mattered not a great deal whether one rolled it on the footpath or on the road, as the motor car was still something of a rarity. Due in part no doubt to changing fashions, but in greater part to the rapid growth of motorised traffic, it is a sad thought that for today's child it is no longer safe to 'chase the rolling circle's speed'. ***

Other popular toys were the top and whip (the peg-top requiring a greater degree of skill, was for older boys), the pop-gun and the 'repeater' revolver. This was a cowboy-style revolver, which was loaded with a roll of 'caps' for successive firings.

Then there was the rag-and-bone man, who walked slowly up and down the street pushing his costermonger-style barrow and crying his trade 'Any old iron, **** rags, bottles and bones!' In exchange for discarded household rubbish such as iron bedstead frames, pots and pans, rags, bottles and rabbit skins (it was cheaper to skin your own rabbit than to buy one ready dressed), the child of the household would be given a toy windmill, which was simply

---

* Itinerant German bands were quite common in all parts of Britain up to the outbreak of the 1914-18 War, when they disappeared from the scene for good. Although known to the British public as 'German' bands, their members (who might number anything from six to 15), were actually Bavarians, who worked at their respective trades during winter and toured outside their homeland each summer. (Ox.Comp. 'Street Music').

** These good country people frequently pronounced the syllable 'in' as 'een'; thus, 'Good Save the Keene', 'Mandoleen'. Like-wise 'telephone' became 'tallyphone', marshmallow 'marshmaller', and monkey antics 'monkey antiques'.

*** Gray, of Eton College.

**** Probably the inspiration for the music hall song of that name.

a few shaped pieces of gaily-coloured cardboard tacked on to a stick. There is scarcely need for me to say who got the better of the bargain; I can speak with a certain degree of first-hand knowledge on this topic, for my 'Uncle' Harry, a rag-and-bone man (who lived next door but one) became one of the town's more affluent tradesmen.

He could afford not only to employ a number of sorters (a skilled trade in itself) but also to run a motorcycle and sidecar, an acquisition which in those days struck envy deep into the hearts of the common wage-earners' wives; for the sidecar in itself was sufficient to elevate my Aunt Lil above the town's less affluent womenfolk to the extent of at least six rungs on the local social ladder. Aunt Lil was to mount the top rung of Chertsey's social ladder when Uncle Harry exchanged his motorbike for a two-seater Rover car, fitted with the 'latest Sinker-Mash gears'.

The natural corollary was the drive to 'Margit' for the annual summer's holiday, their becoming lost en route no doubt in the intricate maze of Chertsey's unfamiliar streets. Never would it have occurred to Aunt Lil that she might have taken her widowed sister Fanny Mills with her, who, after all, had had more than her fair share of this world's ill-luck and drudgery, and yet had managed to contribute more than her fair share of time and energy to humanitarian causes. But then the Rover's dickey-seat was reserved exclusively for the young Harry.

The vital clue to the basic differences in character between the two sisters, my mother and Aunt Lil, lay in their respective tea-drinking procedures. Whereas Aunt Lil would crook her little finger genteelly as she sipped her (hob-brewed) tea from the cup, my mother would pour her tea into the saucer and, after blowing on it, drink from that. So that, although they both came from the same womb, from their earliest childhood recollections, there grew between them an ever-widening and unbridgable social gulf.

My uncle and aunt's affluence also meant a grand pedal motorcar for my 'cousin' Harry, who was within a mere three weeks of my own age. Yet never once do I recall being allowed to ride in it — a typically selfish attitude, I suppose, of an only child. Most likely it was his selfishness that prompted my over-generous parents to buy me a tricycle (albeit a second-hand one). My one and only memory of this same tricycle is a hurtful one. In attempting to cultivate the demon speed, I once came a fearful cropper by executing what my mother would describe as a perfect 'arse-over-'ead somersort', landing on my nose, which bled profusely.

On occasions, the reigning peace and quiet of the neighbourhood would be shattered by a series of thin piping yelps of anguish. When this happened my mother would soothe me by explaining 'It's only your Uncle Harry biting the tails orf another batch of puppy-dogs'.

Uncle Harry was proud of his reputation as the town's leading dog-tail fashion designer, and was willing, apparently, to oblige with any breed of dog whose tail, according to the prevailing dictates of canine fashions, was in need of shortening — the Creator's ideas on what its length should be notwithstanding. I discovered in later years that dog owners favoured the biting over the cutting method on grounds of hygiene — from the dog's viewpoint, that is. But recalling Uncle Harry's fondness for his pint, his pickled onions, his snuff-pinching and tobacco-chewing habits, always have I harboured strong reservations as to the efficacy of this method.

Uncle Harry was of the type, who, having volunteered (in all innocence) a piece of wrong information, stretches his upper lip tightly across his teeth, and proclaims in self-deprecatory fashion, 'No! I'm a liar!'. He could also be categorised as the plural-singular type — 'They're a lovely plum, they are'.

Birthdays, Christmas and Guy 'Fox' night meant a great deal to these simple country people. Poor though they were, nothing was spared by way of decorations, toys etc. to make these festive occasions never-to-be-forgotten events in their 'Children's Calendar'. When Christmas came round, my father himself would make the paper-chains, patiently intertwining and pasting together the coloured strips of paper, which were sold by the bundle. As we lived first in, and subsequently next door to, appropriately named Holly Cottage, the acquisition of that particular decoration caused us neither difficulty nor expense.

A few days before Christmas, my mother would take me to Stotts, on the corner of Eastworth Road and Guildford Street, or to Foster's Bazaar in Guildford Street. She would invite me, not to choose a Christmas present, but to choose a present I would like Father Christmas to bring me, which in the mind of a child means a world of difference. I do not remember Father Christmas ever failing me.

The outward and visible sign which heralded Christmas Day in our family was not the decorations; neither was it the liberal Christmas fare, nor indeed, the array of presents, but the fire which greeted us early on Christmas morning in the front room. As I mentioned earlier, for 363 days in the year (364 in the case of leap years), the front room was inviolable. Indeed, had its portal powers of speech, it would, I am sure, have boomed out to the would-be trespasser 'Put off thy shoes from off thy feet, for the place whereon thou standest is holy ground'. It is a pity that it was not articulate, for rather a thousand such booms than a solitary lashing from my mother's virulent tongue. Thus it was that for these two days in the year, this otherwise hallowed atmosphere (which by comparison would have made the atmosphere of a Trappist monastery appear little different from that of an FA cup final), would be irreverently shattered by the delighted shrieks of childish laughter from the grown-ups.

Uncle Harry owned a piano, but as neither family boasted a pianist, our sing-songs were unaccompanied. This same uncle usually saw to it that he opened the batting. Adopting his characteristic 'give us a "chune" ' pose of back to the fireplace, legs astride with the authority of one in his own house (even though he may have been in ours), slightly sagging knees, hands stuck deep down in trousers pockets, and eyes turned heavenwards (with agonised expression in mute appeal to the Almighty so it seemed), he would reduce the gin-laced womenfolk to tears with his soulful renderings of *Don't go down the mine, Daddy,* and *Ring down the curtain, I cannot sing tonight, my little one is dying, I cannot sing tonight.* ('Nor any other night' was to be my silent verdict in later years.) Tears would give way to laughter, however, when Uncle Harry gave a rendering of that singularly appropriate song, *Any old Iron.* He would also make it his business to lead the assembled company in singing —

> I'm 'Enery the Eighth I am!
> 'Enery the Eighth I am, I am!
> I got married to the widow next door,
> She's been married seven times before.
> Ev'ry one was an 'Enery,
> She wouldn't 'ave a Willie or a Sam.
> I'm 'er eighth old man named 'Enery,
> 'Enery the Eighth I am!

Then my mother's 'lodger' Fred would entertain us with his 'mandoleen' (which he practised in his railway signal box at Chertsey station between train arrivals and departures) and I was encouraged to sing *God Bless the Prince of Wales.*

I cannot recall us singing even one carol, due to the fact I suppose that the adult members of the two families were non-churchgoers. Unlike my uncle, my dear old dad must have realised his limitations musically and so confined his contribution to a recitation. The one and only poem I recall was a bawdy parody (a relic of his barrack-room days no doubt) of George R. Sims' sensitive, if somewhat sentimental, *Christmas Day in the Workhouse.*

The sumptuous Christmas fare was due, mainly, to my parents' prudence in joining a Christmas club. Poultry was plentiful at Christmas, as my father kept a few 'ens. I still retain a picture of him plucking his 'birds' and showing me the undigested corn which was still lodged in the unfortunate bird's crop. On another occasion I recall him removing an egg from whatever part of an 'en's anatomy eggs are harboured. Then there were my mother's delicious Christmas puddings.

Like most country house-wives of her class, she was an excellent cook, especially in view of her meagre budget. Her specialties included 'biled' bacon and 'parzley' roll (identical in shape, but with different filling naturally, from the illustration on p.58 of Beatrix Potter's *Tale of Samuel Whiskers or The Roly-Poly Pudding*), faggots, 'chidlings' (chitterlings), steak and 'kitney' pie, 'peeze' pudding, sausages and tinned 'marters', 'tabiocco' pudding, and treacle tart. Her meagre budget meant that our bread was spread with lard rather than butter.

Another of my mother's specialties went by the odd name of liver and crow, but for the life of me, I cannot now imagine what the crow part of it could have been. The basis for her soups was a packet of Edward's Desiccated Soup, whose wrapping bore the then familiar trademark of a well-proportioned, happy-looking, middle-aged uniformed cook, carrying an equally well-proportioned, happy-looking tureen of steaming soup. Allowing that these foods (mainly offals) were inexpensive, it was the innate genius of these country women for cooking that they (the foods) were transformed into appetising, if not exactly nourishing, dishes.

Socially speaking, the supreme moment of the week came with Sunday afternoon tea, for it was then that my mother's fine friends and relations would 'drop in', for formal invitations were hardly in keeping with this severely egalitarian society. On these occasions the oilcloth which covered the table from Monday breakfast to Sunday dinner would be discreetly concealed from view by a spotlessly white table cloth, expertly 'larndered', naturally enough, by my mother.

The basis of afternoon tea would be bread and butter (always a cottage loaf which was shaped like the figure 8), jam, and home-made cake and treacle tart. Even though dinner would have been eaten only some two hours previously, the Sunday afternoon tea, like week-day afternoon tea, had to be 'high' tea. The 'high' part of it varied according to the season.

During the winter months, all ears would be alerted for the sound of the muffin man's bell, who would ply his trade up and down the street, his tray balanced expertly on his head as he walked slowly along. Then in the appropriate season we would listen for the familiar cry of the shellfish hawker — 'I sell shrimps' (pause) 'and winkles!' I seem to recollect that the 'I sell shrimps' section of the cry came very close to the 'Muss es sein' motto which prefaces the last movement of Beethoven's Op.135 Quartet. In fairness to the hawker, let me hasten to add that any resemblance to Beethoven's theme was, I am sure, purely fortuitous and not an impertinent plagiarism on the winkle-seller's part.

It was the custom in those days to sell shrimps and winkles not by the pound, but by the pint or half-pint. When it was time to dispose of these delicacies, pins were handed round to the assembled company and the central repository (a white plate) for the inedible blackcaps from the winkles gradually took on the appearance of a decapitated Dalmatian dog.

And as for Christmas, so also for the few birthdays I can still remember. Nothing was spared either by my parents or near-neighbours to ensure that a child's dream of happiness became reality. To an enquiry as to the age of a child, the reply would be, 'Five come Sunday'; or should the birthday be not so near, 'Five come May next'. This quaint turn of phrase was not peculiar to Surrey but to many other English counties.

Next to birthdays and Christmas, Guy 'Fox' night was the most eagerly anticipated day of the year; for here was real excitement which did not commence until well beyond the normal bedtime hour. Guy 'Fox' Night was a celebration with a difference, the difference being that whereas parents did all the 'forking out' for Christmas and birthdays, a goodly proportion of the money needed for the purchase of Guy Fawkes masks, rockets, catherine wheels, jumpers, squibs and the rest came in part from the initiative and enterprise of the children themselves; for it was a recognised and time-honoured custom for children to go from door to door chanting verses such as:-

Guy, Guy, Guy,
Stick him up on high,
Hang him on a lamp post
And there let him die.

Guy, Guy, Guy,
Poke him in the eye,
Put him on the bonfire
And there let him die.

Remember, remember the Fifth of November,
　　　The poor old Guy
With a hole in his stocking
A hole in his shoe,
A hole in his hat where his hair comes through.
If you haven't got a penny a halfpenny will do,
If you haven't got a halfpenny
　　　God bless you.

Whichever verse one recited, the follow-up would take the same form — a knock on the door, a proffered money-box (which by custom was nailed to the end of a foot or so long stick), and 'Penny for the Guy please'. To the generous giver, Guy Fawkes night could be quite an expensive occasion, for although nothing in excess of a penny was asked for, house-to-house appeals would start well in advance of November 5th*, and come from all the children in the near and not-so-near neighbourhoods.

Then again, a Guy Fawkes custom (long since discontinued) was for children to wear Guy Fawkes masks, whose colour I can describe only as 'Toper's Pink', so garish was it. Masks were secured to the wearer's face either by a piece of string or elastic, or held in position by a stick, to which the mask was fixed. The point I am about to make is this; believing that masks gave them complete anonymity, it was by no means uncommon for some of the more enterprising children to knock up the same household on successive days. Was I one of the more enterprising of Chertsey's children? At this point my memory becomes a complete and utter blank.

In those now remote, far-off days, there was one event in the year which to a child was markedly different from Guy Fawkes Night, Christmas, birthdays, and indeed every other day, in that it involved partisanship and blind loyalties. I refer to the Oxford and Cambridge annual boat race. With the tremendous upsurge of interest since the Second World War in commercialised sports, coupled with a more ready access to higher education (resulting in a higher degree of sophistication), the excitement which the annual boat race once aroused appears largely to have disappeared.

I would imagine, for example, that the kind of pre-1914 Boat Race Night, when varsity undergraduates and young society bucks vied with each other in seeing who could paint Piccadilly Circus the most vivid shade of red (and Eros the most vivid shade of some other colour) is lost to us for ever; for the spontaneity and spirit of fun which characterised Boat Race Night during the opening years of the century appears alien to present-day youth. Rags and good-natured tussles with the police may still take place, but the fun appears no longer spontaneous, but forced. As Ben Travers once put it: present generations have lost their sense of fun.

The curious paradox relating to the boat race fever of those days was that the great majority of the rival crews' supporters never saw a race at all, and were less enlightened than was Hardy's Jude even as to what went on in the two universities. Yet for days, if not weeks, in advance

* 'I have just been asked "Any money for the guy?" Is this a record?' — Letter to *The Times*, written from the Reform Club, 18 September, 1951.

of the actual race, children would sport their respective favourite's colour, light or dark blue, with an air of proud and even aggressive defiance. For some reason or other, I came to 'stick up' for Oxford, and my mother would make me a dark blue rosette, which she would pin to my guernsey, as our shoulder-buttoned woollies were styled.

Rivalries would find their verbal expression in harmless taunts such as:

Oxford the winner,
Cambridge the sinner
Put them in a match-box
And throw them in the river.

Cambridge upstairs
Putting on their braces
Oxford downstairs
Winning all the races.

Oxford upstairs
Eating bread and butter
Cambridge downstairs
Playing in the gutter.

Naturally enough, Light-Blue supporters would reverse these scurrilous libels.

Naive sort of stuff? Perhaps it was; yet I cannot bring myself to believe that today's child who regards his car ride to and from school as much a right as we regarded our ride on shanks's mare as part of our lot in life, whose remote-controlled model aircraft would make our string-drawn wooden horse-and-cart by comparison appear faintly infantile, and whose TV children's hour would put our *Comic Cuts Weekly* type of entertainment beyond the pale — I cannot bring myself to believe that today's child is any the happier, or the more contented, for it.

Periodically my mother would take her children and her bitch Neil to Mr Foster's studio in Chilsea Green (about a mile from Chertsey township) to 'have their photos took'. Well-meaning as these photographers no doubt were, I would say that they did more than any other professional man of the day to implant into the mind of the late 19th and early 20th century child the twin seeds of mistrust and disbelief. I mean, having managed to scare his young sitter by taking on the sinister appearance of William Blake's picture *Vultures of the Mind* (this being accomplished by his disappearing under a toe-length black drape) he then proceeded to practise his cruelly Machiavellian deception by inviting his now thoroughly frightened young victim to 'watch for the dicky-bird', which, of course,

The author (left) at about five years old.

never obliged. Little wonder that in later life the oft-photographed child found himself lying prone on some chuckling, hand-rubbing psychiatrist's couch — for by then the early seeds of mistrust had germinated into a bumper crop of psychic ills.

The route to Mr Foster's studio lay via the 'Bell' public house in Guildford Street, and through the Italian quarter of Chertsey. In those days there was a well in the road hard by the Chertsey Fire Station, and I recall seeing the 'Eye-tyes' (as my mother called them) doing their washing at the town's well-head. In common with many another of their fellow-countrymen, the Chertsey Italians became ice-cream vendors in the summer, exchanging their ice-cream barrows for chestnut-roasting braziers 'come the winter'.

I have grave doubts as to whether their methods, or the ingredients they used in the manufacture of ice-cream, would have measured up to today's required standard of hygiene; for local gossip had it that the mixture, when in its unfrozen state, was stored (for want of a better place) beneath their beds. Happily, one could hardly have levelled a similar complaint against their methods of roasting chestnuts, for these were done in coke-braziers positioned at tactically well-chosen kerbsides. Upon returning to Chertsey some few years later, I was to discover how few people on a cold winter's evening were able to resist the welcoming glow and warmth of the chestnut vendor's brazier.

Chilsea Green as I knew it, a sleepy hamlet up a dusty back lane, has long since ceased to be. It is now a smart up-to-date tarmac-sealed road affair, with rows of council houses whose very design, in some curiously mute fashion, informs the would-be purchaser 'We are not for sale — renting only'.

'Come four year old' (or maybe 'come five') I was sent to the local council school in Free Prae Road. For obvious reasons I never advanced beyond the infant school. Two of our infant school mistresses were sisters, who to the children were 'Big' Miss Mallom and 'Little' Miss Mallom. They lived together in a 'superior' house at the Guildford Street end of Eastworth Road. Another of the infant school mistresses revelled in the delicious and (for a pre-1914 school ma'am) quaintly appropriate name of Bungard; for the very name Bungard conjures up the enormous and then-fashionable clump of hair, ankle-length skirts barely concealing a pair of button-up boots, a neck-high leg-of-mutton sleeved blouse and a pair of steel-rimmed spectacles perched perilously near the end of a long thin nose. But perhaps I do Miss Bungard an injustice, for I remember both her and the Misses Mallom as being three very kind persons.

Our main occupation, as I recall it, was modelling with sand. Each of us would be given a tray into which was poured some moist sand. One of the mistresses would spend some time with each of us in turn, bestowing either praise or blame according to the quality of our individual efforts.

The traditional custom of dancing round the maypole was still being observed in many country towns and villages throughout Britain (including Chertsey), and was celebrated on May Day. In our own school the maypole was erected in the playground near Free Prae Road, presumably for the benefit of adoring parents. I was soon to discover that the Maypole dance (which required the dancers to weave in and out of each other in clockwise and anti-clockwise directions) was seized upon by the children as a heaven-sent opportunity for settling old scores amongst themselves — when the bigger boys would deliberately bump into the smaller boys, and the smaller boys into the girls. To the young dancers' credit be it said that this sort of behaviour was reserved for rehearsals only, best behaviour being put on for the display itself.

I recall also what must have been our school's end-of-year breaking-up party. Its main attraction was an all-round entertainer-conjuror, ventriloquist and chapeaugraphist. The art of the now-forgotten music hall science of chapeaugraphy consisted in the chapeaugrapher taking a black felt ring which he would manipulate into several different varieties of characteristically-shaped hats; so that now, say, he would impersonate a bishop wearing a shovel hat; now Napoleon (adopting at the same time no doubt that hero's best 'On board the Bellerophone' pose) and now a London street cleaner in regulation slouch hat.

From time to time I was to receive uneasy reminders of the fact that the happiness I had found with my foster-parents was but transient. For example, periodically, foster homes would be visited by one or two Foundling Hospital representatives accompanied by the local doctor.

In my own day, notice of an intended visit having been received, I would be excused school, have my 'moey' washed, change into my Sunday clothes, with my mother herself changing into a clean pinafore, which was the customary Monday-to-Saturday house garment. The ultimate precaution was for my mother to go through my hair in depth with a nit-comb. Fully experienced as she was in the art of foster-mothering, mum knew better than to run the risk of presenting a 'lousy' bastard to so distinguished a party of Foundling Hospital visitors.

It was customary for hospital visitors to give each child a threepenny piece. The moment the visitors had gone, my mother would gull me into parting with my 'threppney Joey' (as she termed it) in exchange for a bigger one — a penny. Premissing that these acts of charitable benevolence on the part of the hospital were bestowed upon me quarterly, commencing, say, when I was three years old, over the years my mother would have netted a gross profit of two shillings. Downright 'besting' though it may have been, let me hasten to stifle my readers' indignant cries of 'Shame!' which my touching tale might otherwise provoke; for it would be unjust on my part to foster the notion that my parents (and foster-parents in general) took us for what they themselves could get out of it.

Here are the material facts. In the earliest days of the Foundling Hospital, foster-mothers (or nurses, as they were then called) were paid 1/6 weekly for each child. This rate was increased in 1753 to 2/- weekly, the nurse now having to provide the child's clothing!

A century and a half later foster-mothers were paid 10/- per month, plus an annual grant of four guineas for clothing. I would estimate therefore that my parents were paid somewhere in the region of 4/- per week, plus a small clothing allowance. I trust that this exposition of facts places in fairer perspective my mother's truly feminine wile. In the years to come, my good parents were to redeem a thousand-fold this piece of honest dishonesty.

As I have already said, my mother had the good sense to give me periodic reminders that one day I must leave home, to live in the big 'orspiddle' in London. Thanks to her unfailing love and plain common sense, the wrench, when ultimately it did come, proved not nearly so great a shock as it would otherwise have done. Once my sixth birthday had passed, I knew that time was rapidly running out. The dreaded day came in the April of 1914. It started with my mother hanging around my neck the bone locket on which was stamped my Foundling Hospital number — 23062.

My mother then took me round to say my goodbyes to the neighbours. First to the lovable Miss Bixley who owned a little general store on the corner of Station Road and Queen Street. She was short, swarthy complexioned, with raven black hair, and deeply-set eyes. I was going to miss running those errands to her shop, when she would encourage me to climb up the small pair of steps and perch myself on the spotlessly clean wooden counter. Poor Miss Bixley: local gossip had it that she was swindled out of her pathetically small business, to end her days in the workhouse.

Thence to the gentle, moustachioed Miss Williams, who, because of her acute deafness, would either descend to my ear level, or lift me up to her own. And so to Lizzie Miller, the girl who lived opposite, and who kept me company during my confinement in No.1 bedroom with the chicken-pox. These, and other neighbours (who over the years had developed a very real affection for their local 'fondlings') were kindness itself, showering me with presents and money. Among my presents was one from the Misses

Mallom and Bungard, who had announced my impending departure in assembly on my last day at school.

My father must have taken time off work, for he came to the station to see me off. I bought him a penny bar of chocolate from the station's automatic vending machine. Years later, my mother told me he had carried the wrapping paper in his waistcoat pocket right up to the day of his death. On the few occasions he was able to visit me in the Foundling Hospital, he would produce the wrapping paper and ask, 'Remember that, Bar?' Such was this untutored, but kindly man's affection for me.

It so happened that the contingent of children from the Chertsey — Addlestone — Ottershaw districts was quite a large one.

We were met at Waterloo Station by a horse-drawn bus, christened by foster-mothers 'The Black Maria' on account of its darkened opaque windows. The Black Maria provided an unintended touch of grim irony, for it was strangely symbolic of our approaching severance from virtually all contact with the outside world. We were driven to No.40 Brunswick Square, known to all who had connections with the hospital as 'House Forty'.

A group of Foundlings in their 'touching' hospital uniforms.

4: *House Forty*

London's 40 Brunswick Square is the headquarters of The Thomas Coram Foundation for Children. The original 'House Forty' (as it was known to many generations of foundling children) was demolished in 1937 to make way for the present building. 'House Forty' was used to accommodate new admissions to the hospital — children who for the first five or six years of their lives had been reared in the country (in either Kent or Surrey) by their foster-parents.

It was as well, perhaps, that the old House Forty, a sad witness for over a century to so unfeeling a practice, should have been demolished. And I have it on unimpeachable authority that when the demolition squad moved in, its foundations and floors were still damp from the tears of countless hundreds of weeping foster-mothers and their bewildered foster-children. Still damp, although 11 years had elapsed between the final exodus of the foundling children and the arrival of the demolition squad. Children remained in House Forty for some months before being transferred to the infant school proper.

On arrival we were herded together in the playroom and told to take off our clothes — the first stage of our initiation ceremony. In exchange for the clothes provided by our foster-parents — the knickerbocker suits, the sailor suits (most fashionable at the time) and the rest — we were issued with the Hospital Infant School uniform — a coarse woollen chocolate-brown jacket and knickers, blue check shirt, white starched collar and red ribbon bow-tie, stockings, lace-up boots, sailor-style flannel vest and calico underpants (which we termed linings), and red and white spotted handkerchief which in those days was one of the hallmarks of the British navvy. The girls were issued with frocks of the same material, together with what was worn underneath those frocks. I do know that the girls' undergarments included a pair of unbleached calico drawers, which at one time (according to a 19th century old girl's account of life at the hospital) was not considered an essential piece of lingerie. Little was I to know that from that day on, I was to be in and out of one uniform or another (and I can account for at least eight different changes) for the next 34 years.

Our respective foster-mothers were permitted to farewell us, which I recall was done with no small show of emotion on both sides: on the mother's side, who even at this late hour still refused to recognise the fact that her foster-child had been simply on loan to her; and on the child's side, who to the last continued to cling to the skirts of the woman he had come to regard as his mother. Mothers wept just as openly and as heartily as the children.

But the most poignant moment insofar as the mothers were concerned came, not with their leave-taking, but with the return to them of our discarded clothing, still warm from the heat of our young bodies. From then on, further contact between our respective foster-mothers and ourselves 'depended', as D.M. Dyson aptly puts it, 'on the persistence of the foster-mothers'. [1]

Nichols and Wray in their *History of the Foundling Hospital* comment:
> 'In numerous cases a great bond of affection sprang up between the child and foster mother, and it was frequently a wrench for both when the child was returned to the Hospital'.

This is all very true; but I must confess to raising my eyebrows when first I read the next paragraph:
> 'So much was this the case that the child on arrival at the Hospital was allowed to spend its time in play for the first few days.' [2]

And then what? For however well-intentioned, one would hardly attribute this settling-in programme to a child psychologist. Although it may have been quite impracticable, I am of the opinion that it would have been a more humanitarian course had we been institutionalised from the day of our reception into the hospital, which in my own case would have been at about three weeks old. The only commonsense alternative is the Coram Foundation's present-day policy of placing the children in permanent foster homes.

With our foster-mothers safely out of the way, the next stage of our initiation began. The nurse in charge of House Forty was a downright sadist, and the very last person to have been entrusted with the task of helping children adjust from a normal home atmosphere to life in a Dickensian-style board school. Her method of helping us effect the adjustment was absurdly simple; after ordering the children who were crying to be silent, she flew round the room in whirlwind fashion, boxing the ears of those who were slow in complying.

I was one of the lucky ones who got away with it simply because my weeping was not audible. But my turn was not long in coming. The most forceful recollection of life in House Forty is Nurse Cullen's bestiality. I learned some years later of her dismissal from the hospital on grounds of cruelty to the children.

Next to Nurse Cullen, the most terrifying experience of my House Forty days was my first bath. Coming from homes whose baths invariably were of the portable, galvanized-iron type, it is doubtful whether any of us had ever seen the like of the gargantuan monster which confronted us on our first bath night. There it stood, a great, cavernous affair, surrounded by a wide wooden bench (upon which we were perched for part of our ablutions), its two enormous brass H & C taps noisily belching water at a high velocity.

Its capacity can be gauged from the fact that we fitted into it, four or five at a time, without any sense of overcrowding, whether in sitting or standing position.

As far as I am aware, the only other foundling to have written an account of the institution is Hannah Brown* (nee Sherman) who was born in 1866. The self-declared object of her book, *The Child She Bare* (which is a graphic account of life in the hospital during the 1870s and her subsequent experiences as a domestic servant), is that of 'drawing attention to the iniquitous practice of mothers giving up their children to any stranger or governing Body where the child's happiness and future interests are at stake'.

For the majority of readers, probably, her book would appeal as a document of social history. But for myself, its main interest is contained in the fact that although a gap of about 50 years separated Hannah Brown's admission to the hospital from my own, life there during my own day was virtually the same in every one of its fundamentals as it was in hers.

---

* Hannah Brown was a woman of many parts. According to her entry in *Who's Who* (1940) she worked as a domestic servant 'in seventeen different situations until the age of twenty-eight, threw it up as unbearable and was an artist's model for the next eight years; through the kindness and generosity of a stranger lived for five years in retirement, prior to its termination entering the City of London Maternity Hospital for training in midwifery; gained Diploma. In 1929 lived for nearly six months in Italy; came back and worked at painting in her own home; exhibited and sold first picture entitled, *A road in Tuscany* at the Royal Academy Exhibition, 1930. Illustrations in London Paintings and London Sculpture by Frank Brown [her husband]. The one aspect of life in the Foundling Hospital which appears to have rankled most (for she mentions it in her book on three separate occasions) is that in her day the girls were not equipped with 'a certain undergarment'. Although throughout her story she complains repeatedly of being 'shamefully put upon by mean natures', of 'arduous domestic duties' and of her employers working 'an orphan girl of fourteen like a cart-horse', she managed to reach the ripe old age of 106½ years!

Hannah recalls the 'humiliating initiation ceremony':
>'Meanwhile, the hairdresser would make his appearance and cut off their hair close to the ears. Sometimes, beautifully long curls were cut. On one occasion a little girl smacked the hairdresser's face, as she stood on a chair in front of him, stamping and screaming out: "I'll tell my Mother"; not having realised that she had again lost a 'Mother'.'

We were marched 100 or so yards to the Infirmary (as the school sick bay was called) for stage three. One by one, boys and girls alike, our hair was literally shorn off fore to aft with what must have been the barber's closest-set clippers. For this, and all future hair-cutting parades, we were lined up so that the 'next for a shave' (for that is what it was) saw mirrored in front of him his own approaching fate. Whether it was sheer vanity or (a more likely reason) the frightening convict-like transformation of my newly-made friends, all I can say is that this was the first time since my admission when, like little Tom Dacre,
>'who cried when his head
>That curled like a lamb's back was shaved',

I really broke down and simply howled.

It was my good fortune that Nurse Cullen was not present. The hair-cutting ceremony clearly was a hygienic measure. A 'nit' comb was considered an indispensable article of toiletry in many a poorer class home. I remember the one in our own household; it had extremely fine and closely-spaced steel teeth, which were guaranteed to rid the hair of the most elusive of lice. This should not be misconstrued as an indictment of the average working-class family's standards of hygiene, but rather as an indictment of society in general, which did little or nothing in those days to help repair the causes, such as the primitive sanitary and bathing facilities. What chance of remaining sweet had my furnace-stoking father, for example, who came home from work to a house equipped with one cold-water tap?

The fourth stage of initiation was the most humiliating and painful one of all. For us, it was not just a matter of asking permission to go to the lavatory. Instead, we had to visit the lavatory at regularly appointed hours: and we queued up for it. This system persisted throughout our two infant school years. As yet unversed in the art of queue jumping, I once failed to hold myself in control, much to Nurse Cullen's anger. My punishment was a severe caning on my bare bottom, administered in the presence of the whole of House Forty by that otherwise perfect and understanding infant school headmistress, Miss Isobel Bateman. That 'whipping' as Miss Bateman termed it, still rankles, and not even the passage of 75 years has succeeded in eradicating the sense of injustice of it all. (I really must talk this matter over with my psychiatrist.)

My initiation virtually complete, I could now take stock of my surroundings. After the freedoms of life in the country — the lanes and the roads which in those days were safe for children to play in, the Chertsey Meads, the 'Rec', and the footbridge over the railway level crossing (where we would revel in the idea of becoming engulfed in the smoke and steam of passing trains) — the pocket-handkerchief sized area which constituted our playground proved to be one of the more upsetting aspects of my new life.

To the north was a high brick wall separating the Hospital from St. George Gardens*, to the east the hospital infirmary, laundry and swimming bath; to the south the boys' wing of the main building, and to the west the massive iron gates of the Brunswick Square exit — to us, the Brunswick Square entrance. And for the next few months what went on just beyond those gates — the coalman tipping his loads into the cellars of the fine houses, the arrival or departure of a resident's horse-drawn carriage, the nursemaid wheeling her charge, or maybe the LCC street cleaner wearing his traditional cockaded slouch hat — was to be the sum total of our contact with the now remote outside world.

So came to an abrupt termination the happiest of early childhoods. For it, Deo gratias.

Post-script:

We were given the sad news that one of our number, Herbert Mount, had died in the infirmary. It all started, apparently, with a tiny sore, which gradually spread over the whole of his body. Incidentally, this was to be the only death among the children during my eight and a half years at the hospital.

I became initiated into the intricacies of cat's cradle.

Miss Bateman announced to our especially assembled company that Britain had declared war on Germany.

At my asking, a boy named Cartmell would repeat over and over again the children's hymn —

>   Jesus bids us shine with a pure clear light
>   Like a little candle burning in the night
>   He looks down from Heaven to see us shine
>   You in your small corner and I in mine.

It was not so much the hymn that fascinated me, as Cartmell's funny little way of bobbing his head down and up every time he sang the name

* Formerly known as the burying grounds of St George Bloomsbury and St George the Martyr.

'Jesus'. I lay the blame for my ignorance on this score directly at the feet of my non-church-going foster-parents, who in all probability would have been as completely mystified at little Cartmell's head bobbing as was I myself.

Nurse Cullen on the other hand was a good church-goer.

FOOTNOTES TO CHAPTER 4

[1] D.M. Dyson, *No Two Alike* (London, 1962), p.43.
[2] Nichols and Wray, p.117.

5: *The Infant School*

Our House Forty days behind us, we were moved to the infant school, joining up with the seven- and eight-year olds from earlier intakes.

The school playground must have been one of London's most tranquil and beautiful enclosures. Its southern side faced the chapel, its eastern side the Mecklenburgh Square cul-de-sac (which balances symmetrically the Brunswick Square cul-de-sac), its western side the infirmary and grounds, and its northern side the hospital laundry and swimming bath. (The building which once housed the swimming bath is now occupied by the London University's School of Pharmacy.)

The playground was set in the midst of a fine group of plane trees. There was also one solitary ash tree encircled by a wooden seat, and a large, heavily-populated dovecote. Yet it all meant very little to any of us. At our tender ages, and in our peculiar set of circumstances, I am sure we would all gladly have exchanged this seclusion for some of the characteristic sights and sounds of the great city beyond.

A large room tiered at one end served the combined purposes of playroom, classroom and theatre. Even as late as 1914, it would seem that neither its structure nor its several functions had changed since Charles Dickens's visit to the hospital in 1853:

> 'Proceeding to visit the infant school, which was their future destination, we found perhaps a hundred tiny boys and girls seated in hollow squares on the floor, like flower borders in a garden; their teachers walking to and fro in the paths between, sowing little seeds of alphabet and multiplication table broadcast among them. The sudden appearance of the secretary and matron whom we

accompanied, laid waste this little garden, as if by magic. The young shoots started up with their shrill hooray! twining round and sprouting out from the legs and arms of the two officials with a very pleasant familiarity. Except a few Lilliputian pulls at our coat-tails; some curiosity respecting our legs, evinced in pokes from short fingers, very near the ground; and the sudden abstraction of our hat (with which an infant extinguished himself to his great terror, evidently believing that he was lost to the world forever); but little notice was taken of our majestic presence. Indeed it made no sensation at all.

'One end of this apartment being occupied by a grade of seats for the little inmates, is used as a convenient orchestra for a band of wind instruments, consisting of the elder boys.

'A new supply of toys had just been brought into the room; and, during this performance, the juvenile audience were vigorously beating toy drums, blowing dumb horns and soundless trumpets, marching regiments of wooden infantry, balancing swinging cavalry, depopulating Noah's arks, starting miniature railway trains, and flourishing wooden swords. They were all sensibly and comfortably clothed, and looked healthy and happy. They were certainly under no undue restraint. The only hush that came upon the cheerful little uproar was when the chaplain entered. He came to take out the first clarionet (and he laid his hand on the boy's shoulder in a friendly manner which was very agreeable), who had attained the maximum age of fourteen, and was that day to be apprenticed to a lithographic printer.'[1]

There was, however, one material change, for in my day, we no longer sat on the floor to be scattered with the little seeds of alphabet and multiplication tables; in the intervening years, some mundane person had broadcast some foreign seeds on the flower-bordered garden of Dickens's day, which had germinated and grown into a vulgar, but healthy, crop of classroom desks and forms. And there was worse to come; the money spent in the purchase of these foreign seeds must have reduced the toy fund to a state of permanent insolvency. The magnificent collection described so enthusiastically by Dickens was never in evidence, either in my day or in the days of subsequent generations of infant foundlings.

There were three classes, two of the three being taught simultaneously in the large room just described. Our three mistresses were Mrs Griffin, Miss Barker, and the headmistress, Isobel Bateman.

I retain three distinct memories of Mrs Griffin: one her gold tooth; the second, her enormous bun of auburn hair, which according to Isaac

Newton's law of gravity should have resulted in her eyes being raised permanently heavenwards (which they weren't); and the third, an incident involving myself. She and her husband (who taught in the boys' school) came into our playroom one day and called me out. I went forward, asking myself what on earth I had done wrong. Nothing apparently, for husband and wife went into earnest discussion regarding the shape of the back part of my head. They were, I suppose, amateur phrenologists — a queer hobby, I would say, for a husband-wife partnership. I heard no more about it.

The Griffins were not the only people to show an interest in this part of my body. Eight years later when I was convalescing in a hospital in Winchmore Hill, the ward sister (of whom more later) felt behind my ears, and made the gloomy prophecy to the effect that one day I would be 'a gouty old gentleman'. Her prediction (although I would not be so indelicate as to comment on the correctness or otherwise of the 'gentleman' part of her prophecy) subsequently proved itself uncomfortably near on target.

Miss Barker was the most forceful, or, if you will, the 'bossiest' of the three mistresses. During my time in the infant school she married, in whirlwind fashion, a member of the hospital's administrative staff. Her marriage was a tragically short one. Her husband, Mr Andrews, tall, good looking, and I believe, a lovable (if somewhat naive) personality — became caught up in the great upsurge of patriotism which swept England following the outbreak of the 1914 war. Answering Kitchener's call, he volunteered for service in the army, and was commissioned as second lieutenant. He was killed in action in his very first battle. 'And who dies fighting has increase' would have made a befitting epitaph.

The undeserved humiliating experience I suffered at the hands (or rather at the cane) of Miss Bateman notwithstanding, I soon learnt to love her. Short and dumpy, feet permanently pointing to the hour of 10 minutes to two, a wealth of silvered hair, and neck encircled with the then fashionable black velvet band, she endeared herself to us all, for she just radiated happiness.

As yet, we were apparently considered too young to attend services in the chapel, so Miss Bateman, perched on her high chair, would conduct her own Sunday services. Almost without exception, her weekly reading from the Bible was Psalm 103 —

> 'Bless the Lord, O my soul; and all that is within me, bless His holy name.'

Although not going along wholeheartedly with verse 5 (which told us that the Lord satisfied our mouths with good things), Miss Bateman's regular readings of this psalm left their permanent mark on me, for to this day its message continues to fill me with an inward and spiritual peace.

Miss Bateman's choice of text for her sermons was no less consistent, and more often than not it was based upon the quality of unselfishness. Unfortunately the message was largely lost on us, simply because she never explained the meaning of the enormously long word 'unselfishness' and we were all too timid to ask her its meaning.

Letters were now beginning to arrive from our respective foster-parents, which would be read to us by Miss Bateman. (None of us received letters during our House Forty period, a predetermined policy on the hospital's part to allow the healing properties of time to take effect.)

Sometimes my father wrote the letters, but more often than not it was my mother who applied herself to this duty of love.

Her letters were so stereotyped that to this day I am able to repeat her opening and closing clauses:

> Dear Bar,
>
>   I now sat down to pen these few lines to you, hoping as they finds you in the same state of health as it leaves me at present.
>
>   Your Dad, brother Bill, Aunt Lil, Uncle Harry, Mimey Paine, Miss Williams, Miss Bixley, Lizzie Miller, etc. etc. send their love, as does your loving mother,
>
>   Fanny Mills.

My parents would sometimes enclose a dahlia bloom from grandfather Mitchell's garden (my mother's father), together with a number of penny stamps which would be credited to my savings account. When I came to leave the infant school, my savings amounted to 6/5½d. I quote this simply as proof of my foster-parents' generosity, for in those years, 6/5½d was a no mean sum of money for an eight-year-old.

The first visit from my parents took place in the September of 1914. Although supposedly a happy event, for me it became the cause of yet another emotional upset. As my parents appeared at the playroom door, I broke down once again and howled.

Although, naturally, I looked forward immensely to the periodic visits of my parents, and was never again to experience quite so great an emotional upset, in retrospect I find myself questioning whether it would not have been more sensible and humane had the initial break between foster-parents and child been made final and complete; for none of us I would say became so hardened or so indifferent as not to be deeply affected by these periodic leave-takings.

I would imagine, for example, that this same feeling of homesickness, depression (call it by what name you will) must strike into the heart of the most hardened convict, when it comes time for him to farewell his visitors and return to his cell. For however kind the staff at this early stage of our schooling, the hospital was just one large cell.

Like most foster-parents, mine would arrive laden with 'stuff' (foundling children's term for goodies) and toys. Our names would be pencilled on the eggs they might bring, which we would have in addition to our usual tea meal of a hunk (literally) of bread, margarine, and watered-down milk. (The tell-tale evidence here was the pale blue appearance of the milk around the basin's edge.)

And as though they had not done enough, my parents would give us (my elder foster-brother and myself) some money.

Before leaving Chertsey almost six months earlier, I remember having set my heart on a clockwork aeroplane in Stott's shop. In later years I discovered that my mother had asked Miss Stott to put it aside until such time she could afford it. She produced it on her first visit.

Coming to visit us involved all foster-parents alike in no small personal sacrifice. Setting out on the 7.19 am workman's train, my parents would arrive at Waterloo Station an hour or so later, which left them with about six hours to while away before the official visiting hour of 2 pm. They would first breakfast in a modest eating-house hard by the Union Jack Services Club in Waterloo Road, and then wander down the 'Cut' behind Waterloo Station to do their shopping.

I can imagine nothing so exhausting for a country-bred woman than to be walking the streets of London for anything between five and six hours and carrying a progressively heavier shopping bag. Little wonder in later years when musing over these excursions, she would complain of arriving home feeling 'fair knackered'.

I was to see my father very few times again after the September 1914 visit. Herrings's Iron Foundry was soon to switch over to manufacturing munitions and father was not allowed even the odd day off. Our mother continued to visit us regularly in the March, June, September and December of each year (the March and June visits coinciding respectively with my own and my foster-brother's birthdays). By 1918 the number of her foster-children at the hospital had doubled from two to four. * Yet 'mum' continued to 'come up' as regularly as ever, even though by now she was widowed. Her straightened circumstances compelled her to take in an increasing number of foster-children (not exclusively foundlings) who were now her sole means of support. Her son, who by then had been conscripted into

---

* Her death notice which appeared in the *Surrey Herald and News* of April 16th 1937 reported, 'in her time [she] had brought up twenty-four foundlings'.

the Royal West Kent Regiment, was hardly in a position to give her very much help.

Our school curriculum (if I may accord it so dignified-sounding a term) was virtually the same as that of the usual elementary infant school. It did, however, include one somewhat novel subject — darning. We were introduced to the art of darning our own socks early on in our infant school period, an art which we mastered with varying degrees of success. I became a good sock darner, and this stood me in excellent stead during the whole of my 40-plus years of an otherwise happily married life.

Young as I was, I soon discovered that there could be few discomforts in life greater than that caused by badly darned socks; for twist and turn one's toes and feet as one will, there is no escaping the hard little knots resulting from badly darned socks, which inflict upon the feet a form of refined, almost exquisite, torture.

In this case, Miss Bateman's moralising by way of her oft-repeated story of Mrs Be-Done-By-As-You-Did was hardly appropriate, for there was no guarantee of our receiving the same pair of socks once they had been laundered — nor for that matter, of our receiving the same of any other item of under-clothing. It behove all of us, therefore, boys and girls alike, to darn to the best of our limited abilities. Gloves did not create a similar problem, for the good reason that however cold it might be, they were not deemed a necessary article of clothing. Those children who possessed gloves had their respective foster-parents to thank.

Once we had reached standard 3, our spiritual pastors and masters decided, apparently, that we were now ready to receive the Word of God. And so scripture was added to our growing list of subjects.

The school chaplain was the Rev. H. S. Stork, a graduate of Cambridge. Surprisingly (or unsurprisingly perhaps), the subject of Mr Stork's first scripture lesson had nothing whatever to do with the Word of God, but with the middle finger of his left hand. He must have come to realise early on in his position of school chaplain (he was elected to that office in July 1898) that however absorbing his lessons might be, to a class of seven-year-olds, the story of the finding by Pharoah's daughter of the infant Moses was far less interesting a subject than that of a hand consisting of $3\frac{1}{3}$ fingers and a thumb.

And so he anticipated our otherwise certain spate of nudgings, whisperings and giggling, by relating to us the story of its missing two upper joints. It was the result of a threshing machine accident when he was a youth in his native Yorkshire. Thereafter, he would come into the class-room with his left hand already buried deeply inside his trouser pocket.

Mr Stork was the hospital's most commanding personality, and insofar as it affected the children, its most influential figure — the illustrious role of governors notwithstanding.

While we were as yet considered too young to attend services in the chapel, during my two years in the infant school there were two exceptions to this rule, one a notable exception.

It was a custom of the Foundling Hospital to hold daily services throughout Holy Week, when the children would sing *The Story of the Cross.*

The custom dated back to 1784, when a committee meeting in the March of that year resolved that the Reader should perform Divine Service each morning in Passion Week at 11 o'clock, 'As such a Sense of Religion will be thereby expressed as well becomes the Governors of a Charity established amongst others for the Purpose of training Children in the Paths of Religion and Virtue, and which will show the Public their Attention to this very important part of their Trust'.

Unlike Sunday services which were attended by the general public, Holy Week services in my day were for staff and children only — hence the inclusion of the infant school.

Older ex-foundlings may like to be reminded of two of the melodies of *The Story of the Cross,* whose words largely escape me:

The notable exception was a performance of *Messiah* by the Huddersfield Glee, which made the pilgrimage from Yorkshire in order to perform the oratorio amidst surroundings wherein the composer had identified both himself and his work so intimately.

We were told before going into the chapel that the performance would be attended by the then Prime Minster, David Lloyd George, and although neither his name nor his position meant anything to me (or indeed to any of us) I well remember the audible whisperings of the audience as he walked to his seat.

As to my reaction to the performance itself, dearly would I like to impress readers with proof of my youthful musical precosity. Instead, alas, I must abjectly confess that *Messiah*, judged the world over to be Handel's greatest work, to me meant precisely nothing. No scales fell from my eyes, I do not recall the *Hallelujah Chorus* exciting every nerve in my young body, nor did I find myself going limp when chorus and orchestra united in those three fervent and final *Amens*. Sad to relate, my *Itchy-Koo* and *'Enery the Eighth I am* style of musical background persisted stubbornly in standing in the way of my understanding.[2]

Our dormitory was reached by our first passing through one of the senior girls' wards (as we called them), when more often than not, its 40 or so occupants would be in varying stages of undress. I suppose this wholly new experience must have aroused our curiosity — in a nice way, naturally. Perhaps it was a case of over-sensitivity on the girls' part of their burgeoning womanhood, or maybe of their non-*chic* lingerie. Whatever the cause, we were instructed in venomous, hissed whispers to keep our eyes averted, which forever after we did; for the senior girls were frequently entrusted with the task of 'minding' us during staff mealtimes.

Likewise, our meal tables were situated at the far end of the girls' dining hall. This room occupied the same position in the east wing of the hospital as the court room and picture gallery occupied in its west wing. Rectangular in shape, the dining hall's main structural features were its lofty ceilings and its spacious windows.

In view of its spaciousness and graceful design, in the November of 1756, a General Committee Meeting ordered 'That the Girls' Dining Room be particularly appropriated to receive all whole length Portraits, which have already, or may hereafter be given to this Hospital'.

By my day all these artistic refinements had long since disappeared. Their places had been filled by whole length, varnished boards, headed LEGACIES, 'with the names of benefactors' (as Dickens saw them) 'set forth in goodly order like the tables of the law'. Exactly.

The substitution took place some time during the 19th century, although the reason behind it is not clear. Whether it was that the authorities gave up in their attempt to 'instil into these barbarians respect for fragile canvases'[3], or whether some stern 19th century patriarchal governor deemed it more fitting that charity children should be constantly reminded of their lowly state, is not recorded. What is known, however, is that whereas the 18th century foundling girl could gaze upon some superbly executed portraits of her benefactors, her 19th century counterpart must forever gaze upon the faceless caricatures of her benefactors, in the form of column upon column of meaningless and probably long-forgotten names, and equally meaningless column upon column headed £ s. d. The exchange symbolised the substitution of the real horse of the 18th century by the 'iron horse' and all that went with it — the spirit of laissez-faire, the industrialisation, the newly opened avenues to individual wealth (and individual misery), the smoke and the grime, and the consequent rape of the English countryside — (in short, the intensified Worship of Mammon) — of the 19th century.

Base ingratitude on our parts though it may have been, I think I can speak for the whole of my generation when I say that however well-intentioned the architect of the exchange may have been, these legacy boards, duplicating themselves along the entire length of both girls' and boys' dining halls, to us meant precisely nothing. For all we knew (their significance having never been explained to us) they may well have been the Tables of the Law. Fortunate were the girls who faced the window side of their dining hall.

We were given two outings during my two years in the infant school, both of them romps over Hampstead Heath. On the first of the two outings I recall our climbing to the Heath's summit, a pleasure denied us on the second outing, as the hill's summit now bristled with anti-aircraft guns. It was one of the earliest signs for us that the war was in progress.

Our games were improvised, as we had none of the equipment which is now a standard feature of the children's playground of today. In his book *Opening Bars,* the author, Spike Hughes, has this to say concerning the improvisatory nature of the games we played:

> 'Lionel's flat looked over the Foundling Hospital and the antics of the "Fondlings" in their playground afforded an interesting study of child-behaviour. The Fondlings (they were never known locally as anything else) played games which bore little relation to those played by other children — strange variants of tig and hopscotch, games with stick and ball which, like the uniform they wore, can only have had their origin in the eighteenth century. They

> also presented first-rate instances of the spontaneity of motion peculiar to children, who stand still one moment and dart off to some distance point at full speed the next.' [4]

'Here one minute, gone the next' for many years was to be one of the patterns of my own life-style.

Our favourite game, naturally enough, was playing at soldiers. A regiment of khaki-clad soldiers had taken over the area of ground between the chapel and our playground and we came to learn their drill and parade ground terms which we incorporated in our less grim war games. Another sign of war was the observation balloon which hovered above our playground presumably on training flights.

Items of war news were now being given us by the mistresses. We were told of a great Allied victory at sea in the sinking of the German raiding cruiser, the *Emden*. We were taught by rote the names of the Allies —

Foundling girls at play. ▼

England, France, Belgium, Russia, Serbia, Japan, Italy — in that specific order. Miniature replicas of their respective flags were pinned up on classroom blackboards and on other strategic places. We were taught a new hymn (not in the *Foundling Collection)* which years later I identified as being No. 595 in *Hymns Ancient and Modern* to a tune by the most eminent music theorist of the day, Ebenezer Prout:

> Holy Father, in Thy mercy
> Hear our anxious prayer
> Keep our loved ones, now far distant,
> 'Neath Thy care.

I suppose I must have been regarded by Miss Bateman as a promising pupil, for shortly before I was due to leave the infant school she sent me over armed with a number of my work books to a Mr Gray, who taught standards I and II in the boys' school.

It was during the spring of 1916 that our infant school term came to an end. I am able to fix the timing of our move to the boys' school with some degree of accuracy, for I was a lowly member of B.4 (the youngest boys' ward) when we were told that Lord Kitchener had been drowned at sea. During the same year we were told there would be an extra hour's daylight; they called it Daylight Saving. This new measure meant little to us, for there was no concession to the time of our going to bed, which remained somewhere between 5.30-6.00 pm — certainly no later. The only difference daylight saving meant to us was lying awake for an hour longer, listening to the dull thuds of the staff's tennis racquets. And as the ward nurse's cubicle was at the far end of the ward, we had no opportunity for window-gazing or chattering amongst ourselves to help while away the long waking hours.

One cheering thought was that we could look back upon our scholastic achievements in the infant school with a justifiable pride. The little seeds of alphabet and multiplication table which had been broadcast among us had all borne fruit. We had learnt that the five 'fowls' were a, e, i, o and u; that never must we trust the printed word (verse v of Psalm 103); why Cartmell bobbed his head down and up at the name of Jesus; and the art of darning our own socks. We mastered the names of the Allies, and were able to recognise their respective flags. We were taught to respect the natural modesty of the female sex — or else. For my own part, I formed the conclusion that in terms of intrinsic musical worth, *Itchy-Koo* and *'Enery the Eighth I am* were infinitely superior to *Messiah*.

In short, we had laid successfully the foundation stones of a formal education.

FOOTNOTES TO CHAPTER 5

[1] *Household Words*, pp.51-52.
[2] I must own to a memory slip here. The performance took place not during my Infant School years, but in the December of 1917. It was attended by Mr and Mrs Lloyd George and Miss Lloyd George. The soloists included the then celebrated soprano Agnes Nicholls, and the no less celebrated bass, Robert Radford.
[3] Benedict Nicolson, p.33.
[4] Spike Hughes, *Opening Bars* (London, 1946), p.251.

6: The infirmary

Each child was given a wicker basket into which he placed his neatly folded day clothes before climbing into bed.* On one occasion (when I would have been between seven and eight years old) an observant ward nurse noticed me bending over my basket in obvious distress. I was suffering from another of my now all-too-frequently occurring headaches. She took me to the infirmary, where I became an in-patient — the first of only three times during my eight years at the Foundling Hospital.

As I recall it, the care and attention was excellent. The discipline among the staff, right down to the wards' maids, was firm. The high standard of care and discipline was due entirely to the person in charge, Sister Cleeve. She symbolised the non-emotional, but splendidly efficient and dedicated nursing sister of that era. Autocratic in manner, aristocratic in bearing, next to the school chaplain, I would say that Sister Cleeve was the school's most commanding personality. Her rapid, staccato, manner of speaking placed an unreasonable demand upon the person she might be addressing. Likewise, her well-nigh indecipherable style of handwriting could well have passed for an a-systolic cardiogram.

She insisted upon the highly-polished infirmary floors being strewn with used tea leaves, as a precaution against dust-pollution; and that children entering the infirmary must do so on tip-toe. So far as the boys were

---

*In 1840, The Report of the Special Committee recommended 'That in order to obviate the present unhealthy and uncleanly habit of the children in the disposal of their clothing when taken off at night, a basket be provided for each child, similar to those used at the London Orphan Asylum'. And also, 'That all the wooden bedsteads be disposed of and replaced by iron bedsteads, and that every child have a separate bed'.

concerned, this was a fair enough restriction, for the impact of a pair of boy's steel-tipped 'Blucher' boots on the infirmary's stone-floored, high ceilinged corridor would scarcely have been consistent with the deathly silence of the place.

It was the first time since my Chertsey days, now some two years behind me, that I was to enjoy sliced bread, against the hunks that normally were doled out to us.

In my final year at school, I became 'headmaster's boy', and one of my duties was to collect and deliver Sister Cleeve's mail. This was placed in a despatch case by the gate porter, who locked it with his duplicate key. A strict ritual was observed. I would be expected to stand to attention, salute, and hold the despatch case waist high (Sister Cleeve's waist, not mine) for her to unlock, and remove her mail. This part of the ritual completed, I would give a further salute, execute a military-style about-turn, and make my exit. This would sometimes take place without a word being spoken on either side, for early on I learnt not to speak to her unless I was spoken to.

All this is a far cry from the schoolboy of today, who expects to be saluted rather than salute; who expects (even demands) as of right, to sit on school (and later, on university) committees, and deliberate upon such matters as staff appointments and promotions, curriculum, and the business in general of running a school or a university. I do not suggest that the Sister Cleeve style of discipline is necessarily a good example to go by. What I do suggest is that the pendulum has taken so violent a swing as to make all too large a proportion of today's youth impatient of any form of discipline whatsoever.

In our situation, we were expected to address with respect the most menially employed servants, from 'Bruno' Bruns (the hospital's Pooh-Bah, whose duties ranged from gate porter to emptying the summer camp latrine buckets) to the newest-joined scullery maid. I do admit that this sort of discipline tended to give us over-exaggerated ideas of deference towards our elders, but looking back on it all, I would say that in the end we lost nothing substantially by it.

Like all truly big personalities, Sister Cleeve could, and occasionally (but only occasionally) would, unbend a little. In the great influenza epidemic of 1919, when certain of our dormitories were converted into temporary sick-bays, she would make a break in her official ward-rounds to entertain us with her special brand of card tricks. And when Walter Crossley became a long-term infirmary patient (we never discovered the nature of his complaint), Sister Cleeve came as close as her position in the hospital and her self-imposed code of discipline would allow, to adopting him, unofficially, as her own son. * This mother-son relationship continued long after she had retired to her native Cornwall.

Outwardly severe, she commanded our respect, but never gave us cause to fear her, which is more than could be said of the school doctor. Had a portrait been painted of Sister Cleeve, the artist could hardly have overlooked her most characteristic pose, of hands held limply in the manner of a child imitating a dog begging for favours.

In sharp contrast, the school physician, William John Cropley Swift MRCS was a martinet. His almost brutal manner of barking at us, together with his cold, aloof manner, invited neither our respect nor our affection. His stentorian bellow, amplified several times over by the resonant properties of the infirmary's corridor, turned his throat examinations into something of a legend. These performances were not unlike the one-time popular military band 'Echo' serenades:

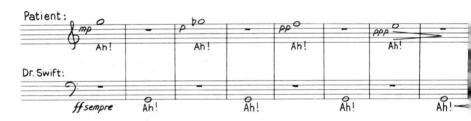

His fierce manner of barking at us (and his bite was no worse than his bark) coupled with his built-in look of haughty condescension, were at times quite frightening. I remain convinced that it was only out of respect for his own particular medical specialisation that he stopped just short of scaring every one of us, boys and girls alike, out of our very lights and livers. By comparison, Dr Milsome, the 'bleedin' butcher' of Chertsey, was nothing worse than a meek and accommodating herbalist.

Even so, during the Swift-Cleeve era, the children maintained a remarkably clean bill of health.

The infirmary was not equipped with an operating theatre, which meant that cases requiring surgery were sent to one of London's public hospitals. I was singled out for having my tonsils removed; why me, I never discovered.

---

* Children having normal family backgrounds could find it difficult to understand the degree of affection in which many ex-Foundlings hold their old school. The late Walter Crossley's is a case in point, for in his Will he bequeathed the bulk of his estate (some £138,000) to the Thomas Coram Foundation.

I was simply sent for, and told of the impending operation. Although regarded today as a minor and perfectly straightforward operation, in those days, removal of one's tonsils could be a barbarous affair. I was taken by Sister Cleeve to St. Bartholomew's Hospital, and straightway exchanged my school uniform for a linen overall and linen cap to match — in themselves hardly a pre-op. tranquilliser for a nine-year-old. Once on the operating table, what looked like a lint pad was held some few inches above my nostrils to receive the drips from the chloroform bottle. The stench was nauseating, reminding me of my father's toe amputation.

Upon coming round, I found myself lying on a long bench, alongside some other young patients, who presumably had had similar operations. I proceeded to vomit what at the time seemed to me like quarts of blood. Once the vomiting ceased, I changed back into my school clothes, and accompanied by Sister Cleeve, walked to the hospital gates where we waited for the porter to summon a taxi. I was taken back to the infirmary and put straight to bed. I cannot help but compare these primitive methods with some plastic surgery I received 30 years later. I was anaesthetised whilst still in my own bed, and 'came to' after each successive operation still in my own bed.

I never discovered how the few candidates singled out for circumcision came to qualify for that operation. Sister Cleeve's indecipherable lists (which sets me musing as to the possible number of boys during the Cleeve regime who were given false tip-offs) would be read out in class, the boys named returning to the fold a week or two later, with their respective penises now resplendent with finely-fashioned bowler hats (as foundling boys termed them). We were not aware of the surgical term for this particular operation for when Mr Stork guided us through the Collect, Epistle and Gospel as set down in the *Book of Common Prayer* for *The Circumcision of Christ,* he evaded the issue, telling us, simply, that circumcision was 'a form of cutting'. Even so, from his obvious awkwardness of manner, and although we were unable to guess just what it was, we sensed that he was withholding from us the vital facts of the business.

Newly-circumcised boys never showed off their 'bowlers' to other boys — however persistent they might be; for there existed among us a curiously inherited prudery which tacitly outlawed any form of sexual exhibitionism. The only case of nude exhibitionism I recall came from a boy named Foster, who when undressed ready for bed, delighted in striking the classical pose of Mercury after Giovanni Giambologna. For the traditional modesty-leaf, Foster would substitute his scrotum, into which he would tuck his you-know-what. Under these conditions it is a moot point as to whether Foster's behaviour could have been regarded as cheap exhibitionism, or as a manifestation of a latent artistic talent. It may well have been Foster who gave the Daimler car people their inspiration for the traditional decorative radiator cap. Incidentally, Foster was the most graceful diver I have ever seen in action, and to please me, he would execute dive after dive in our swimming bath.

When Dr Swift and Sister Cleeve retired, they were followed respectively by Dr Fairlie and Sister Tudor. Dr Fairlie (who lived in one of Mecklenburgh Square's graceful and exclusive residences) attained overnight popularity with the children by reason of his novel (to us) prescription for influenza — a generous supply of oranges for sick and well alike. A quietly-spoken Scot, Dr Fairlie was the very antithesis of his fiery predecessor. Of Sister Tudor, I can write only with affection. She had none of the aloofness and severity of Sister Cleeve, and although never an in-patient during her time as infirmary sister, I would say that life as an in-patient under her care must have been as relaxed a mode of living as could ever be devised. Bless you, Sister Tudor, wherever you may be.

I did become a regular out-patient. Once a headache struck, I was sent to the infirmary and given the stock prescription. This consisted of a generous dose of a purgative which masqueraded under the pleasant, but misleading, name of Rhubarb and Soda (even so, a vast improvement over my mother's liquorice powder) to which was added, I suspect, some aspirin; for within a miraculously short time the pain had disappeared. An hour or so's relaxation on the infirmary's leather-covered couch, and back to school — until the next time.

Judged by today's standards, the dentistry as we knew it was equally as primitive and no less barbaric than the tonsils' operation. The school dentist was a Mr McKay. His drill was pedal-operated, rather after the style of the crofter's spinning-wheel of his native Scotland. Fillings and extractions alike were, of course, done without anaesthetic of any kind. Children who suffered extractions were given the dubious privilege of having bread-and-milk for their next few meals.

7: Segregation

To me, it will forever remain a cause for wonderment that the governors should have allowed the building of the chapel to take precedence over the addition of the eastern (girls') wing. So scared must they have been of bastard begetting bastard, that they drew up in the earliest days of the hospital, stringent regulations aimed at bringing about the total segregation of the sexes:

> That the Boys be kept separate from the Girls and never permitted to have any Intercourse together, either in their employment, Dieting, or Diversions!

And as if they had not made their point sufficiently clear, the governors supplemented this with this quaint, but redundant, regulation:

> The Girls are to be kept in Wards, entirely separate from the Boys . . . They are always to be apart from the Boys, and are to be attended by the Nurses of their Wards.

These regulations meant that not only were the children denied all contact with the world outside the hospital gates, but denied also the most harmless of boy and girl relationships within them.

In the main, these restrictions were still in force in my own day. Admittedly, it was no longer necessary for ex-foundlings to seek permission before entering the hospital, and occasionally the boys (but not the girls) did rub shoulders with other children, such as visiting sports teams from other London schools. These isolated exceptions apart, we continued to be cooped up like chickens, we did not associate with other children, and continued to be virtually cut off from the strange outside world which lay beyond our few sequestered acres.

During our two years in the infant school, we had enjoyed mixed schooling; but once we were drafted to the 'big boys' and girls' schools, segregation of the sexes became total.

Apart from the annual Christmas party, when boys and girls 'danced' around the Christmas tree in formations of something like six or eight abreast with hands linked behind their backs in the manner of children playing at teams of horses, and a steamer trip at the 1919 Henley-on-Thames summer camp, for the remaining years of my stay in the hospital, the two sexes lived their respective lives in splendid isolation.

By day, we were divided by the 'road' which separated the girls' and boys' sides. These 'sides' included our respective playgrounds, playrooms, dining halls, classrooms, and of course, our wards (or dormitories).

We were separated in the chapel by the organ loft; at confirmation and holy communion by the division in the altar rail; at summer camps by the different days of the week allotted for our respective shopping expeditions and country walks. Foster-parents with children of both sexes were required to divide their visiting hour between boy and girl.

We were further separated by day by our own inner awareness of the thousand pairs of eyes which never relaxed their vigilance; and by night, by the hidden but uncomfortably close presence of our nurses, who slept in cubicles at the end of each ward. A transposition of Francis William Bourdillon's lines:

> The Night has a thousand eyes,
> And the day but one.

into —

> The Day has a thousand eyes,
> The night but one.

would be an apt summary of the situation.

Perhaps the most absurd aspect of the segregation policy was its application to male and female twins, who, having been reared in the same foster home for the first six years of their lives, found themselves unnaturally separated from the age of eight onwards.

Apart from the two exceptions I have already given, I think I can claim that during the six-odd years I was in the boys' school, I was not to engage a girl in conversation for the space of one single minute.

I suspect that many of the end results of the hospital's policy of segregation would be sufficient to assure their respective psychiatrists an annual trade-in of their Bentley, Jaguar or Rolls Royce cars.

Yet, even before we came to understand in our vague, ill-informed way of what was what (or, if you will, the dawn of our sexual awakening) we were wont to indulge in the innocent pastime of declaring our love for one girl or another. Segregation notwithstanding, we devised a subtle method for conveying written declarations of unrequited love.

Both sides of the 'road' were lined with concrete pillars, relics of the hospital's earlier days when the approaches to the main building were lit up by oil lamps. The boys used these pillars as wickets. A bowler would deliberately offer the batsman the most simple of full-tosses to be slammed clean over to the girls' side. The fielder (the go-between) would chase the ball like mad (after giving it a few seconds' start) and at the appropriate moment execute an adroit exchange of billet-doux for ball. As in those days cricket for girls 'simply was not done', our protestations of unrequited love failed to draw sympathetic response. At no time in cricketing history, not in the respective hey-days even of Spofforth the Demon Bowler, or body-liner Bill Bowes, was the game so fraught with peril. To my knowledge this ruse was never discovered, but even now I shudder when I think of the frightful consequences which assuredly would have followed at headmaster 'Digger' Holgate's hands had it been detected.

Only once was the subject of sex broached, during our preparation for confirmation when candidates were counselled individually by the school chaplain. The procedure was for boys to go into a classroom one at a time, where the chaplain would already be seated. "You look into the fireplace, Nalden, and I'll look out of the window." During the course of the 'sermon' we were advised not to play with young girls' bodies. And that was it.

As may well be imagined, the cumulative effects of all this were hardly helpful in our subsequent lives. The unnatural restrictions manifested themselves in varying ways.

Until well beyond my teens I still fondly believed that woman was born with a built-in halo. When disillusionment ultimately set in, its effect was devastating. I was to learn the hard way that to defeat the deadly combination of women's wiles and men's weakness, I must rid myself of what George Bernard Shaw described as 'sex partialities and their romance' and learn to regard women not as the Unattainable Ideal, but (Shaw again) as 'the female of the human species, and not a different kind of animal with specific charms and specific imbecilities'.

For years to come I was shy and painfully awkward in female company. But behind this shyness there forever lurked a dangerous capability of falling in love with any young and not so young woman who might come along. And it may well have been my own erstwhile plight that accounted for the advice my son David alleges I gave him before his leaving home for study overseas — "Remember to clean your teeth regularly, and remember also that every woman you may meet is out to marry you."

Percy Buck in his admirable *Psychology for Musicians* proposes that if you wanted to reform a drunkard, any psychologist would tell you it would be misguided strategy to route him on the way home from the factory down streets where there were no public-houses. Rather would you map out a route which contained as many public-houses as could be found. He continues: 'You may suppress, but cannot eradicate a tendency by destroying its scope of action; in all probability it will, during its temporary restraint be merely accumulating force and momemtum for an ungovernable outbreak when the opportunity occurs.'[2]

Would that the hospital had adopted this philosophy; for it would have provided against the boys having to learn the 'facts of life' from the sordid cross-talk of the barrack room, and the girls from the furtive whisperings of the servants' hall.

Even so, in retrospect, we can hardly blame the Foundling Hospital for our abysmal ignorance in these matters; for not so many years had elapsed since the protest burning by the Bishop of Wakefield of a copy of Thomas Hardy's *Jude the Obscure*. And we may be tolerably certain that this same good bishop would hardly have selected as his sermon text Bernard Shaw's plea on behalf of the *Old Maid's Right to Motherhood*. It was not so many years thereafter that a titled woman in her brave (and ultimately successful) fight to establish the legitimacy of her child, was to ruin herself financially, to be pilloried by the gutter press, and cruelly tormented by the 'Charing Cross Road Boys' song hit of the 1920s, *Whose Baby are You?*

Sex education had about as much chance in my day of finding its way into the school curriculum as had the unexpurgated edition of T.H. Lawrence's *Lady Chatterley's Lover* into an SPCK recommended reading list.

Although, as I have suggested, these unnnatural restrictions manifested themselves in varying ways, let me make it plain that homosexuality was not among them.

FOOTNOTES TO CHAPTER 7

[1] William Maitland and Others, *The History and Survey of London from its Foundation to the Present Time* (London, 1756), Vol.II, p.1302.
[2] Percy C. Buck, *Psychology for Musicians* (London, 1946), p.19.

8: *The boys' school*
Wards

Once settled in the boys' school, we soon assimilated new words and expressions, which, like certain of the games we played, and the uniforms we wore, dated back probably to the 18th century.

One of these words was 'glish'. The term implied a state of joyful anticipation — perhaps a boy's foster-parents were 'coming up' (another of our quaint terms), or maybe the approach of the annual summer camp. To 'glish jolly thick' implied a state of supremely joyful anticipation. This expression was used on the rare occasion only, for the good reason that our monotonous day-to-day, month-to-month, year-to-year style of living gave us little to glish jolly thick about. Should a boy be in a sulk, or was angry, he had 'got monk'.

'Would you like to come on my mate' was the expression used when one boy extended the hand of friendship to another. Should the friendship break down, one of the disaffected parties would inform the other 'I've sacked you off my mate'. 'I'll rush you' implied a threat of physical assault. The potential aggressor, naturally enough, would first be confident of his superior physical strength before issuing his threat. Our equivalent for 'running the gauntlet' was the 'bull-fight', a form of punishment reserved for the most extreme cases of offence against society. The traditional arena for bull-fights was the senior boys' washroom, where the hapless offender would be flailed unmercifully with knotted towels and 'dobbed' by nail-brushes.

The expression 'fit' and its variant 'twit', referred to an act of homosexuality. (There is scarcely need for me to explain that it could hardly refer to an act of heterosexuality.) 'So-and-so was caught having fit' was our manner of expressing it.

As I have already said, although our unnatural mode of existence manifested itself in different ways, homosexuality was not among them — or very rarely so. When we remember how rife this practice is alleged to be in British public schools, foundling boys' comparative blamelessness on this score becomes the more surprising; for at least the public school boy can, should he choose, mix freely with the opposite sex. If any set of conditions was devised (even though unconsciously) to encourage this unnatural form of behaviour, then those conditions surely were ours. Should, on the rare occasion, a boy be caught 'having fit', he would be accorded the foundling boys' own peculiar form of charivari, which was a prolonged vocalising on a monotone of the vowel 'e'. It was an expression of derision mingled with disgust. What is more, for the remainder of his time in the school, an offender was never allowed to forget his misdemeanour.

There were several reasons for our glishing at the prospect of leaving the infants' for the boys' school. Insofar as it affected me personally, I would be reunited with my foster-brother; for although we had been in the hospital together for two years, the fact of our being in different schools (he being in the boys', and myself in the infants' school) automatically precluded our meeting each other — even when visited by our foster-parents.

We were now free to go to the 'yard' (lavatory) whenever we wished, instead of at prescribed intervals. No longer would we be subjected to the indignity of sitting on communal three-abreast-type lavatories, nor to the consequential indignity of being stared at by the queueing children.

We were allowed to use knives with our meals, and henceforth were held responsible for making our own beds, cleaning our own boots, and keeping our clothes brushed.

Greatest glish of all; we would be going into long trousers, irrespective of age or height. Our new uniform comprised a 'bum-freezer' jacket and pocketless trousers (made from a thick, dark-brown woollen material), red waistcoat, white starched collar, black bow tie, and 'blucher' boots, which of course gave rise to the most obvious of schoolboy jokes and pranks when the German warship of that name was sunk by the Allies. Our jackets and waitcoats boasted six brass buttons apiece, each of them bearing an embossed figure of a lamb holding in its mouth a 'Sprig of Thyme proper'.

All six waistcoat buttons had to be fastened, but a quaint custom ordained that the jacket's top button only be done up.

The girls' uniform was similarly coloured, their high-necked brown dresses being trimmed at the top by a band of red braid, thus matching the brown-red colour scheme of the boys' uniform. Their lace-up boots were certainly more elegant and stylish than the boys' ugly steel-studded bluchers. On Sundays the girls' off-white calico aprons would be exchanged for spotlessly white 'Tippets and Aprons' (an innovation of the year 1793), and the elbow-length sleeves of their dresses trimmed with white bands of the same material. All this was set off by a quaintly designed white bonnet, exclusive to girls of the hospital. Their hair, which was worn in plaits during the week, fell loosely down their backs. The overall effect was charming.

An unsuccessful attempt was made in 1922 to replace our 18th century uniforms by a style of dress more in keeping with the times. Boy and girl models wearing the new creations entertained the governors to a specially-mounted fashion parade. But lurking in the background was the formidable figure of headmaster 'Digger' Holgate, who had already chosen me to appear before the governors (as boys' representative) to make an impassioned plea for the retention of our 18th century uniform; and as he had briefed me well in advance in what I was to say, the victory for preserving the status quo was his and not mine.

This was not the first time that tradition (whose survival is dependent upon the good-natured tolerance of reality) succeeded in winning its battle for survival; for in the January of 1813, a group of would-be reformers were out-voted in their proposal to change the style of the boys' uniform. On that occasion it was resolved 'That the Present Dress of the boys be continued and made in future by St George's, Hanover Square, Day School of Instruction and Industry'. This resolution was supplemented by an order for 'a hundred and fifty suits of brown cloth with red waistcoats at 17s 6d. each'.

We now had to adjust to the idea of our sleeping in all-boys' wards. Boys' and girls' wards were numbered respectively B1, B2, B3, B4, and G1 to G4. The youngest boys (i.e. the eight-year-olds) started off in B4, and arrived in B1 by about their 13th year. The girls' system of ward numbering reversed this procedure, the youngest girls starting in G1 and progressing to G4.

Being a member of B1 carried with it a certain social cachet. All new arrivals were given to understand that they must consider themselves privileged visitors for their first six months in B1. Once out of the visitor stage, a boy could acquire a 'lacquey', who would be drawn from one of the junior wards. A lacquey's duties might include cleaning his employer's boots, brushing his clothes, tidying his locker, and parting what little hair the school barber 'Daddy' Clapp, of Marchmont Street, left him to part. We all made for Mr Clapp junior's queue, as his father enjoyed the well-earned reputation for tugging at our hair in most unmerciful fashion with his (obviously blunt) hand clippers. During the war years we had no option but to submit ourselves to Daddy Clapp's rough usage, as his son had been conscripted into the Cycling Corps, one of the most hazardous of hazardous war occupations. It was said of the Cycling Corps that the seats of their trousers were the last portion of that garment to show signs of wear — the outside of their trousers' seats, that is.

Lacqueys could not expect to be paid for their services in cash, but a generous employer (provided he were sufficiently strong willed) would pay in kind by foregoing his nightly supper of a hunk of dry bread and cheese, which he would leave to mellow over-night in his playroom locker. The lacqueying system was, of course, strictly unofficial, and although the masters could hardly have been otherwise than fully aware of the practice, they chose to wink a blind eye at it.

In return for services rendered, a lacquey would look to his employer for protection against bullies, and for a generous 'tip' (generally 2/6d) when he left school. I was once lacquey to 'Block' Burnley (so nicknamed by reason of his outsized, square-shaped head), who was both regarded and feared as the 'strongest' boy in school. In return for my cleaning Block's boots, brushing his hair and his clothes and bowling cricket balls at him, I was guaranteed complete immunity from the attentions of school bullies.

The relationship between employer and lacquey was generally based on mutual friendship. Should the relationship become strained the senior would 'sack' the junior 'of' his lacquey. But as being given the sack resulted in a lacquey being deprived of his pre-breakfast bread and cheese, his physical protector, and his two shillings and sixpenny terminal gratuity, it behoved him to 'keep on his employer's lacquey'.

My own lacquey was a gentle, unassuming boy named Walter Odell. Like other lacqueys, he looked to me, as his employer, for my supper bread and cheese. He knew better, however, than to look for me for protection against bullies. I just was not good at that sort of thing (the sight of other boys' blood making me feel physically sick), and so from an early age I judged it more prudent and less painful to resort to diplomacy in place of fisticuffs.

Walter was not destined to live long. I hesitate to say which circumstances were the more tragic — those surrounding his unwanted coming into this world, or those surrounding his untimely leaving of it. He was 'placed' in the army shortly after his 14th birthday, and was killed in action in World War II.

The more aggressive bullying B1 types need only yell 'second, third and fourth wards brush!' to be surrounded in Lilliputian fashion by a host of terrified 'bottom yarders'* (as opposed to the B1 elite, whose social status elevated them to the 'top yard') duly armed with clothes brushes. It was not solely a matter of pride or vanity in seeing that one's boots were cleaned and clothes brushed; for Captain Coram help the girl or boy who arrived for the morning drill parade with unbrushed clothes or dirty boots. I shall write about our drill parades later: for the moment let me explain that they were held between 9.00 and 9.30 daily (Saturdays and Sundays excepted) and commenced with an inspection by the drill master. To have one's name taken for untidy appearance meant, for boys at any rate, the cane for sure.

Wards B2, B3 and B4 were supervised by nurses who slept in partitioned cubicles, equipped with a 'spy' window. B1 was supervised during my time by 'Digger' Holgate, who with his wife occupied the flat adjacent to it; so that whereas a constant vigil was maintained in the junior wards, things were somewhat more relaxed in B1; certainly more relaxed, apparently than the atmosphere in Digger's flat.

Each ward slept somewhere between 50 to 60 children. The following account (taken from one of the Journals of *The Old Coram Association)* was given by a boy who left the hospital in 1911. It gives a humorous if somewhat pathetic insight into what might be expected of a boy ward assistant, and serves further to underline what I have already written concerning our abysmal ignorance in matters relating to sex:

> 'It started in the second ward under Nurse Wood. I was the tallest boy in the ward so I was chosen to walk up and down the ward and ensure that all boys kept their feet at the bottom of the bed and all boys went to sleep. When all boys were asleep I had to sit in front of the fire at the feet of Nurse Wood, who would hand me the top of a cottage loaf with plenty of butter and cheese. Being tall also got me the job of Band Sgt. [Sergeant] at the School although I was by no means the best musician. The Band Sgt., strange to say, had the job of sweeping and dusting the Band room on Wednesday afternoons. The Band room was on the girls' side. I used to leave the door ajar to allow my sweetheart to enter; she would help me with the work, then we would sit and talk. On one occasion Mr Neil [Neal] the head gardener, came in and asked what we were doing here. We said we were cleaning the Band room. "You are not doing anything wrong, are you?" It was a long time before I knew what he meant.'

---

* 'Yard' was our term for lavatory.

I very much doubt whether Harry Neal reported this incident — he was far too tender-hearted a person to do a thing like that.

The walls of our wards were hung with prints as perpetual reminders, presumably, of England's past deeds of glory. There was *The Meeting of Wellington and Blucher after the Battle of Waterloo, The Death of Nelson, The Sinking of the Troopship Birkenhead,* and others depicting various actions of the Boer War. The exchange of the Hudsons, the Highmores, the Wilsons and the Hogarths which once graced the girls' dining room walls for this style in art, was symptomatic of the difference in outlook which marked the 19th century Governor and Guardian of the Foundling Hospital from his 18th century counterpart.

During the week the beds were covered with red counterpanes, which were adroitly exchanged for white ones on Sundays, when wards, dining halls, and picture gallery were open to the public following morning service.

Although I cannot speak for the girls, we boys judged it prudent to be no less wary of ward nurses than of our masters; for nurses were equipped with a well-stocked personal armoury of retaliatory weapons. They washed our faces, they bathed us; they tied our 'bows' (ribbons) before Sunday morning chapel service; they supervised evening prayers, and, most potentially deadly weapon of all, they doled out our food. In short, they held us at their mercy in rather too many ways for our comfort.

Nurse Bayfield, a jolly extrovert, was just right for the youngest boys in B4, as was 'Goosey' Gosden for the 11-12 age group in B2. Goosey's affected look of haughty disdain notwithstanding*, she was loved by all who passed through her ward. But there was one nurse who deliberately set out to make the children's lives a sheer misery, and in this she was eminently successful. With one curiously solitary exception, I feel I am not being in the least uncharitable when I say that she was detested by every one of us. Indeed, one could well imagine her echoing the sentiment expressed by Mrs Deborah Wilkins when that otherwise good woman was requested by her master to take care of the bastard child, Tom Jones — 'Faugh, how they stink! They do not smell like Christians'.

As summer camps approached, members of B3 would chant in a sing-song manner among themselves:

Six weeks' time we shall be
Out of the hands of Nurse Dovey
Five weeks' time we shall be
Four weeks' time we shall be
and so on, down to zero.

* 'I s'pose yer fancy yerselves bein' inspected by a Dook' — a reference to an inspection by the hospital's president, the Duke of Connaught.

This particular nurse delighted in thinking up various types of sadistic punishment. One of these was to have the victim (clad only in nightshirt) face the dormitory wall, and with a boot loaded on each of his hands, extend his arms above his head. Timely taps on his elbows indicated that the arms were not sufficiently extended.

Another punishment was what we called 'soap-nose'. Soap-noses were administered at the bedtime face-washing parade. She would work up a really good lather on her flannel, and without prior warning, proceed to regale her victim with an account of his misdemeanours, forcing the soap hard up his nostrils at the same time. Nurse Dovey never reported a boy for using bad language. Instead she would deal with the offender herself, using the good old-fashioned, time-honoured 'cure' of scrubbing his tongue, again with a liberal application of soap.

Yet another form of punishment was to make us repeat the whole of our prayers, including the special war-time *Long Prayer* as we called it. The novelty of this particular weapon lay in the fact that unlike the more fortunate Christopher Robin who knelt at the foot of his bed, we Infant Samuels knelt some three or four feet in front of our beds on the bare, generously-nailed floorboards, which may, or may not, have dried out from the same morning's scrubbing. The next time you say your prayers, I suggest you try out this Infant Samuel position for yourselves, promising not to cheat either by opening your eyes or shortening your normal prayer session (minimum time, 10 minutes). The wonder of it is that this form of punishment (sufficient in itself to undo all the good work of the school chaplain) did not turn the whole lot of us into a bunch of practising young heathens.

Vain young gentlemen that we must have been, it was common practice for us to crease our trousers by placing them between the bottom sheet and mattress of our beds. Nurse Dovey frowned upon this practice. She would sometimes see us tucked snugly in our beds before giving the order "Get up and stand at the foot of your beds." She would then strip the beds down (all 50 of them) and do her damndest to humble our pride and lower our morale by throwing offenders' trousers on to the floor, and erasing their creases with the soles of her shoes. Such was her mentality.

But it was at the midday meal that she brought to bear her most powerful weapon, when she by-passed a miscreant's plate in the matter of second helpings, or 'extras' as we called them. That rare phenomenon, a smile on her face, in all probability was not a smile at all, but a sudden paroxysm of wind. Clearly, she was the embodiment, the very re-incarnation in fact, of the 18th century parish nurse.

Following her retirement from the hospital she married a foundling old boy (many years her junior). This act made her calculated bestialities towards the children entrusted to her care the more difficult to understand. Likeable person that her husband was, it is to be hoped that his marriage did not subsequently rob him of the distinction of being 'the one curiously solitary exception' to Nurse Dovey's beastliness; that he was not required to repeat his prayers, forgo 'extras', or walk the streets wearing uncreased trousers; for lumpy though Nurse Dovey was, I could not quite see her permitting hubby to defile the sanctity of their marriage bed with pairs of his trousers — Sunday best, or no Sunday best.

Boys in B3 looked forward no end (glished jolly thick in fact) to Wednesdays, for this was Nurse Dovey's night off duty. Her duties for that evening of the week were carried out by Sarah James who, incidentally, was the one and only member of staff whom we presumed to address by her first name — a tribute to her lovable nature. Sarah was the tiniest gnome of a woman (well under five feet tall), with a swarthy complexion, matching eyes, iron-grey hair, and bird-like features. With Sarah in charge, we could release the tensions, pent-up emotions, and frustrations which had built up in us over the previous six days. Her oft-repeated threat "I'll throw my shoe at you — I'm a good aimer" never failed to provoke a concerted roar of laughter, and caused us to play her up all the more; for we knew that never, never, would Sarah report a single one of us. In return, she gained our loyalty and affection. Should we have reason to suspect a master in the offing (boys at either end of the ward acted as spies on Sarah's duty evenings) the word 'Skit!' would be passed down the ward, and within moments, silence would reign supreme.

Each ward had it's quota of 'wet-beds'. These unfortunate children were made to suffer the double indignity of segregation (they slept in specially constructed canvas beds at the far end of the ward) and washing their sheets under the gaze of the remainder of the ward. Yet two of the 'wet-beds' of my own age group were outstanding in the classroom. Walter T . . . (whose porridge-stained jacket took on the appearance of a highly-polished suit of mediaeval armour) was claimed by his natural mother, who in the intervening years had married a successful man of business. Walter went on to enjoy a more extended and liberal education than he would otherwise have had. How we all envied him his civilian suit, his new home-life, and his potentially brighter prospects in life. The second of the two 'wet-beds', Benjamin M . . . became the editor of an overseas' newspaper.

I well recall that December night in 1919, when the whole of us in B2 lay awake, turning restlessly in our beds, and daring to look out of the ward windows in the hope of sighting the promised *Daily Express* maroons.

'Wireless' (radio) was yet to find its way into British homes, and so the *Daily Express* promised it would send up green maroons should the reigning British heavyweight boxing champion, Joe Beckett, win, and red maroons should France's Georges Carpentier be the victor. Red it was. Joe Beckett was to suffer the double humiliation of being KO'd within seconds of the start of round one, and of being caricatured by Joe Webster of the *Daily Mail* as being fast asleep on the floor, curled up in that 'Good-night Daddy' position. Still, in our view, that served Joe Beckett right for KO-ing our hero Bombardier Billy Wells in the fifth and third rounds respectively of their 1919 and 1920 fights at the old Holborn Stadium.

Ever a practical joker, I recall one jape which misfired badly. It happened when I was a member of the B1 elite. The editor of some popular comic (most likely *Boys Own Paper, Comic Cuts,* or *Merry & Bright* — for by then I had outgrown *Chicks Own, Rainbow,* and *Tiger Tim's Weekly)* invited his readers to 'try this trick on one your little chums'. The idea was to wait for one's little chum to go to sleep, and then cause water to drip slowly on to his forehead. 'Next morning', claimed the editor, 'when you ask your little chum what he dreamt about, he will tell you of his being caught in a violent thunderstorm'. My chosen victim was Tony Farrell. Whether he was an exceptionally light sleeper I cannot say, but it took only a few drops to waken Tony thoroughly, who let go at me with such uninhibited invective as to wake the whole of B1 and bring an enraged 'Digger' Holgate storming in from his adjacent flat to discover what the pandemonium was all about. That night I lay awake for a long time, composing in my mind a strong letter of protest to the editor, which I knew would never slip through the school censorship. The exercise at least served the purpose of keeping my mind off other things.

Some years later Tony and I were chatting together in our common barrack room. Tony said to me "You know that every one of us is a bastard, don't you?" I had to admit that I was not aware of the fact. I suppose I would then have been 15 or 16 years old.

Tony left school at 14 to enlist in the Royal Artillery (Mounted) Band, which was stationed at Aldershot. He started off as a cornet player, but later changed over to the french horn, developing into a moderately accomplished player. Finally he changed over to percussion and became an excellent timpanist and percussionist. Tony was to die in the Cambridge (Military) Hospital, Aldershot, at the absurdly young age of 23, following a series of unsuccessful operations to remove a stomach ulcer. I visited him shortly before his death to find him genuinely distressed. He had received a sharp rebuke from his ward sister for daring to show interest in the way she was dressing his wound. Such was the great divide in those days which separated a member of the exclusive Queen Alexandra's Imperial Military Nursing Service from the rude soldiery.

There was a pathetic sequel to Tony's death. An advertisement giving Tony's true name, together with the name given him by the Foundling Hospital, appeared in the *Unclaimed Wills* column of the *News of the World*. The amount involved was some £200. From this advertisement it could only be assumed that the hospital had failed in its attempt to trace his natural mother.

The Girls' Dining Hall, John Sanders, 1773.

9: The boys' dining hall

Situated immediately below ward B2 was the boys' dining hall. We sat at four long tables, and on four proportionately long wooden benches. There was a division in the centre of the dining hall, sufficiently large to accommodate the boys' brass quartet, which accompanied the singing of grace both before and after the midday meal on Sundays, and on the occasional weekday. I stress 'both before and after meals', as the school bandmaster, Mr Cawley, was forever fighting a valiant, but foredoomed, rearguard action to prevent the quartet playing for grace after meals, on the grounds (so he claimed) that their instruments were slowly, but effectively, becoming clogged with particles of food.

Foundling boys and girls of my own generation may care to be reminded of two of the graces, as I recollect them:

of Thy mer-cies we par-take, Bless us Lord for Jes-su's sake May our bod-ies strength-ened be,

And our hearts re-joice in Thee. A - men.

Looking back, it would appear to me that the dining hall was especially designed with a dual purpose in view; as a place for our bodily, and for our spiritual, sustenance; or put another way, a place in which we might not only eat and drink, but reflect long and often upon the lowliness of our estate.

Those boys who sat facing the 'wall' (as opposed to the 'window') side of the dining hall were forever confronted with what in Dickens's eyes resembled 'Tables of the Law'.* These were imposingly large varnished boards headed 'Legacies' which set out the names of the hospital's many benefactors, together with the date and the amounts of their respective benefactions. They made for frightfully dull reading; and having no option but to face them, three times daily, for some eight-and-a-half years ($365 \times 3 \times 17/2 = 9307\frac{1}{2}$, not counting those extra days for leap years), meant that when it came our turn to leave the hospital, we had come to accept without question the fact that our very existence had been dependent wholly upon the charity of others.

The pity of it was that the terms of certain of these bequests were not afforded hanging space, if only for the diversion they would have created from the persistent dullness and gross insufficiency of our daily fare; for then indeed would we have perused with rather more relish than was usually our wont the provisions relating to the benefactions of William Williams Esq., who in 1759 bequeathed his property in Jamaica to his trustees 'to sell the same, together with all and every the Negro, Mulatto, and other slaves whatsoever to me belonging, with their future offspring, issue, or increase, and to pay the net proceeds to the Treasurer of the Foundling Hospital'.**

* See Page 73-74

** These yielded to the hospital £ 5563.

William Williams Esquire's next bequest was of somewhat less generous a nature —

> 'Item, I give and bequest to that most abandonedly wicked, vile, detestable rogue and imposter, who hath assumed, and now does, or lately did go by the name of Gersham Williams, pretending to be a son of mine, one shilling only, to buy him an halter, wherewith to hang himself, being what he hath for a long, long, very long while past merrited and deserved from the law of the hands of the hangman, for his great and manifold villainies.'

And the long, long, interval between the finishing of each meal and the reciting of the final grace would have become far less tedious had we inscribed in front of us the history of the bequest made by one Omychund, a native merchant of Calcutta. He bequeathed the sum of 37,500 current rupees in equal division between the Foundling and Magdalen hospitals. The dramatic touch surrounding this particular legacy was that not even the combined efforts of Warren Hastings, the Governor-General, and other Indian officials could persuade Omychund's executor, the wily Huzzorimal, to part up with anything but a fraction of the 37,500 current rupees.

So it meant that the boys who faced the 'window' side of the dining hall were that much more fortunate in that they were less bored.

But whichever side one faced, there was no escaping the several quotations from the Holy Scriptures, which were inscribed on the impost of each of the ceiling's cross-vaults:

> The fear of the Lord is the beginning of Knowledge.
> The eyes of the Lord are in every place, beholding the evil and the good.
> For I was hungred, and ye gave me meat
> I was thirsty, and ye gave me drink;
> I was a stranger, and ye took me in
> Naked and ye clothed me.

These several claims to charitable acts, with ourselves the beneficiaries, were fair enough. But never could I for one go along with the angry reproof:

> Go to the ant thou sluggard;
> Consider her ways and be wise —

for remembering that we darned our own socks, cleaned our own boots, made our own beds, fetched and carried our own food from the kitchens, washed and cleaned our own crockery and cutlery, scrubbed our own wards and dining hall, swept and tidied our own playroom, rolled our own cricket-pitch, carried coals from the basement up to staff-rooms which were located on the second and third floors — considering we did all these things, the rebuke appeared a trifle unmerited, and a little unkind.

And our being counselled, 'Remember thou thy Creator in the days of thy youth' appeared faintly absurd, especially when taking into account the hospital's painstaking efforts to suppress all clues as to our respective creators.

The sombre tone of these exhortations was hardly relieved by a further set of plaques bearing the names of old boys killed in the South African War.

Then there was a photograph of a tablet bearing the legend 'Greater love hath no man than this, that a man lay down his life for his friends.' The inscription read:

Wm. Clark
Mark Healy
Wm Barnes
Drowned at Aldershot 4 June 1912 while doing their duty, the two former lost their lives in trying to save their comrade.
19th Hussars

Mark Healy was a foundling old boy. The memorial tablet itself is mounted on the northern wall of All Saints Church, Aldershot.

In happier vein was a photograph of the school's cricket hero, Philip Crompton. Photographed in 'white ducks' (which were worn by the 1st XI when playing visiting elevens) and holding his bat at the classic 45 degree tilt, Crompton was so honoured in recognition of his feat of scoring 103 and 115 not out against our most formidable sporting opponents, the Orphan Working School!

In common with most other aspects of life at the hospital, mealtimes were disciplined affairs. We paraded in company formation before each meal in the playroom and from there marched into the dining hall. The procedure from then on was regulated by a series of taps from a gavel: tap (mark time); tap (halt); tap (face inwards); tap (hands together); tap (say grace); and so on. Apart from these gavel-taps, the only other distinguishable noise during meal-times was that created by the munching of 200 sets of young jaws. Talking was strictly forbidden.

The meals were plain. A typical breakfast would consist of four hunks of bread steeped in a basin of milk. This would occasionally be varied with bread and margarine or dripping.

During winter months, breakfast consisted of porridge and milk.

Dinner (served, naturally, at midday):

Sunday,	Roast lamb, potatoes, and 'dough-cake'.
Monday,	Meat pie.
Tuesday,	Beef, potatoes and cabbage.
Wednesday,	Lentil soup.

Thursday,   Sausage batter.
Friday,   Steamed suet pudding with jam or treacle.
Saturday,   Rice pudding
(The suet and rice puddings served on Fridays and Saturdays were not the second, but the sole course.)

There was a time when the Tuesday meal consisted of sweetened rice pudding and herrings — the two courses being served in that order!

In summer, a cold meat meal would be supplemented with lettuce, invariably the cos variety. (Cos lettuce has a quite distinctive flavour of its own, and as a keen all-day-Saturday gardener, I always make a generous sowing of this variety. I do not follow the English gardeners' practice of tying up each lettuce in order to blanch its leaves; terribly un-British on my part, but life is just too short.)

The tea meal basically consisted of bread and margarine, supplemented occasionally either by jam, treacle, or that wartime refuge of the destitute, honey-sugar.

As wards B2, B3 and B4 were bundled off to bed shortly after the tea meal, supper (which consisted of a small hunk of dry bread and cheese) was served to Bl only.

It was, of course, purely fortuitous that the one and only two-course meal of the week should be served on Sundays, which happened also to be visitors' day.

For 364 days of the year potatoes were served in their jackets, the lone exception being Christmas Day. At breakfast on Christmas Day we would be greeted by a lavishly decorated dining hall. So lavish were the decorations that the ceiling was scarcely visible. The traditional Christmas Day dinner of roast beef, unjacketed potatoes and Christmas pudding would be supplemented with assorted fruits and a cracker apiece.

On Epiphany Sunday, the dinner meal would be supplemented by 'Epiphany Cakes' (iced sponge cakes), and a Sunday or two later by 'Shape Cakes'. These latter were ginger-bread biscuits 'shaped' after various animals, hence the foundlings' traditional name for them. Those boys whose job it was to lay our dining room tables could be forgiven for seeing to it that their own personal shape cakes were elephants and those of their 'sacked mates', mice.

And as in England the cuckoo is the harbinger of spring, so in the Foundling Hospital pea-soup, traditionally served to us on Ash Wednesday, proclaimed that Lent was in the air.

Lent is the season in the church's year when all good Christians practise some form of self-denial. They could hardly dock our already meagre food ration, and so as a gesture of collective self-denial, the boys were deprived over the ensuing 40 days and 40 nights of their starched collars. Next to ill-fitting footwear and badly darned socks, let me assure you there can be no more barbarous form of torture than a badly-frayed, heavily-starched, collar chafing at one's neck. (Our solution to the problem was to moisten the offending edge with an over-generous supply of spittle.) From which it follows that the awful solemnity of the season was somewhat lost on us.

The only meal of the year which boasted eggs on the menu was Good Friday dinner, when we were served with one hard-boiled egg apiece. Curious to relate, although we were all virtually egg-starved, it appeared every boy's ambition to be able to boast an egg harbouring an embryo chick. I myself never realised that ambition, but I can vouch for it that a number of other boys did.

Charter Day was celebrated by a whole holiday and Christmas pudding with the midday meal. This custom dated back to 1747, when a meeting of the general committee on November 17th of that year resolved 'That on the 17th October yearly the Children in this Hospital have a Holiday and Roast Beef and Plumb-Pudding for Dinner being the Date of the Charter'.

Our meatless days were not the result of the wartime government's decree that there must be one meatless day per week in all British households.[2] Rather were they the legacy of a hospital rule of 1790, which decreed that 'three "meagre days" should follow, every week, the day when meat was given'.[3]

Although the term 'meagre' was no longer in current use, I think it fair to claim on behalf of my own generation that with the possible exception of Christmas Day, every day to us was a meagre day (particularly when the German U-Boat offensive was at its height), for never were our schoolboy appetites really satisfied.

Most girls and boys, I suppose, pass through a phase of being acutely sensitive; acutely sensitive (for example) when kissing their parents in the presence of other children; acutely sensitive when he or she imagines him or herself to be the centre of discussion. It is, of course, all part of growing up, of a developing personal awareness.

In my case I developed early in life the habit of blushing furiously. One day a boy named Mortlock (who knew the distress this habit caused me) came to me in great excitement, to let me know that he had read (most likely in a Religious Tract Society or an SPCK publication) of a cure for blushing. 'Keep your mind pure', the writer claimed, 'and your habit of blushing will leave you'. It hardly helped; for all it did so far as I was concerned, was to implant firmly into Mortlock's mind that I constantly

Sunday at the Foundling Hospital, H. Townley Green, 1872

harboured 'impure' thoughts. My reaction, understandably, was to colour up.

For the sensitive foundling girl and boy this Sunday dinner meal could be a distressing and embarrassing experience; for as I have said, Sunday was visitors' day.

Grace having been sung to the accompaniment of the brass quartet on their professionally-polished instruments, a tap by the gavel denoted that we sit down. The moment we sat, boys would commence piling salt, not on to their plates (which had yet to be brought round) but on to their hunks of bread. It was a practice which embarrassed me greatly. Visitors would wander freely around our tables, pointing out a squint-eyed boy here, or maybe twins there. Should I sense that I was being singled out for discussion, I would blush most furiously.*

This weekly intrusion on our lives was considered by some of us as an affront (even though unintended as such) to our personal dignity — however tender our years may have been. Those responsible for allowing this practice to take place were so insensitve themselves apparently as not to realise that, unlike the inmates of London's Zoo, who revel in seeing visitors at feeding times, we did not. We learned to suffer indignities at masters' and ward nurses' hands in the seclusion of the classroom and the dormitory, but the Sunday peep-show I for one could never stomach.

My own generation found this unpleasant aspect of our day-to-day existence no more easy to accept than did the children in Hannah Brown's day;** and to suggest, as did one Sunday visitor, that 'The children seemed quite unconscious of the spectators who came to stare at them whilst they ate their Sunday dinner',⁴ betrays a mentality as insensitive and purblind as the mentalities of those who were responsible for having us exposed to this weekly humiliation.

All situations are relative, and we should have been grateful, I suppose, that we were at least spared the even deeper humiliation perpetrated on our 18th century counterparts by those sensation-seeking Londoners who derived some curious kind of pleasure from gaping at the children once they were in bed, and, no doubt, rather more than ready for sleep.***

---

* It is ludicrous enough to observe Ladies on Sundays going round the dinner-tables of the children, picking out the "aristocratic faces!" (*Observations on the Foundling Hospital* by 'One who has made the Foundling Hospital the study of his Life, and who lives but to promote its advancement.' — c. 1850, p.40).

** In those days the Chapel was crowded with a fashionable congregation, who, after the service, thronged into the dining hall, to see the children eat! We grew to hate our Sunday dinner-time, and as some of us grew older, we left our dinner untouched on Sundays. *(The Child She Bare,* pp. 20-21)

*** The Committee having been Informed That several Persons came to see the Children after they were in Bed, which disturbing their Rest. Resolved That the Bell be rung for the Children in this Hospital to go to Bed at Seven in the Evening and the Wards to be cleared and locked up at half an hour after Seven, and no person is to be admitted into the said Wards after that Hour. (Gen. Cmmtte. Minute, May 21, 1746).

One manifestation of our being subjected to this weekly torment was, of course, that we came to accept ourselves as some sort of inferior beings. Inferior, for example, to the headmaster's daughter, Iris, whose ambitious mother would recite to some of the more senior boys the ever-expanding list of Iris's acquisitions and accomplishments — the City of London School; the new Steinway grand; the violin lessons under the German professor ('F sarp dearie, F sarp') at the Guildhall School of Music; the French lessons, the German lessons, and so on and ad infinitum, ad nauseam. How could any one of us ever expect to aspire to her exalted social position — let alone beg her hand in marriage?

Another of its effects was to implant into certain of our number a shyness when sitting down to a meal with our 'betters'. I recall two instances of this. Three of us were 'selected' by the headmaster to have afternoon tea with a Mrs de Bergh and her young daughter who lived at Brockham Green, the site of our 1920 annual summer camp. We were all completely tongue-tied, and too shy to eat. The second occasion was when Dick D... and myself were invited by Mrs Betts (wife of one of the Foundling Estate architects) to afternoon tea in her flat at 39, Mecklenburgh Square. (This house was destroyed by bombing in the 1939-45 war.) The same thing all over again — we were both tongue-tied, and too timid to eat.

But the greatest joke of this particular comedy came when Mrs Betts (then a young bride and new to the scene) enquired genteelly and in all seriousness as to whether we took milk and sugar with our tea. Bitterly do I look back upon my dismal failure to do justice to these two tea-parties, for I count them as two of life's missed golden opportunities. The very memory of them still rankles, and never fails to arouse in me retrospective pangs of wolfish hunger. Even so, when the Mrs Betts episode comes to mind, I cannot restrain myself from emitting a hollow laugh. Did we both take milk and sugar with our tea!

I would say that this particular aspect of life in the Foundling Hospital, the Sunday dinner meal, implanted in our minds a far greater awareness of the 'lowliness of our estate' than did the dining hall's mosaic-like 'Tablets of the Law', and all the exhortations from the Holy Scriptures combined.

Here is a description of our dining hall customs as seen through the eyes of Dickens:

'Although we inspected the school-rooms, the dormitories, the kitchen, the laundries, the pantries, the infirmary, and saw the four hundred boys and girls go through the ceremony of dining (a sort of military evolution in this asylum), and glanced at their school life, we saw nothing so different from the best conducted charities in the general management, as to warrant our detaining the reader by describing them.'

'Of the appearance, food, and lodging of the children any of our readers may judge for themselves after morning service any Sunday; when we think their objections will be limited to the respectable functionary who presides over the boys' dinner, presenting such a very inflexible figure-head to so many young digestions, and smiting the table with his hammer with such prodigious emphasis: wherein it rather resembles the knock of the marble statue at Don Juan's door, than the call of a human schoolmaster to grace after meat.'[5]

After allowing for the possible replacement of a set or two of knuckles for the marble statue's right hand, and for the fact that the Thor-like hammer blows were now administered by the school's tallest boy who took his cue from the presiding master's nod of the head, so far as my own generation was concerned, matters had not changed since Dickens's day.

What an enduring pity it is that Dickens did not record any instances of the liberalising effects of his novel of 14 years earlier. I mean, whether any of the 400 Foundling Hospital Oliver Twists, shielding themselves behind the great man's august presence, had the temerity to ask their own Mr Bumble for more.

FOOTNOTES TO CHAPTER 9

[1] Another of London's Charity Schools, erected at Hoxton in 1760.
[2] This decree inspired the writing of what was perhaps the most puerile effort of Britain's otherwise rich output of wartime songs:
> My meatless day,
> My meatless day,
> I aint gonna eat
> Any sort of meat
> Any sort of meat
> Meat, meat, meat, meat,
> I'm thin and pale
> For want of ale, etc.
[3] Nichols and Wray, p.144.
[4] Sophie Cole, *The Lure of Old London* (London, 1921), p.120.
[5] Dickens, *Household Words*, pp.52-53.

10: Domestication

As I have said, once in the boys' school, we were held responsible for cleaning our own boots. An ill-lit basement room was set aside for this purpose. The bootroom was also witness to many a black eye, 'blood-nose', 'thick-ear' and loosened tooth, as traditionally it was the arena in which boys settled their disputes.

In the bootroom were a number of 'pairs' (boot brushes). We cleaned our boots on wooden blocks each measuring about 12 cubic inches, into which was let an oblong cake of Day and Martin's Blacking. Some of the older, more affluent, and appearance-conscious boys disdained using Day and Martin's (on the grounds that it cleaned, rather than polished, one's boots), and so purchased their own tins of Wren's, Cherry Blossom, or Nugget boot polishes.

Adjoining the bootroom was a pitch-black recess, the 'stoke-hole'. The more gullible of us were led into believing that this was a 'snake-hole', and during our initiation period in the boys' school, some of us walked in genuine fear of certain bigger boys' threats to cast us into this black abyss. Even my own foster-brother and his friend, the otherwise lovable Oxley, terrorised me in this manner.

Once a boy became a member of B1 he could expect to be allotted some kind of domestic work. It might be assisting ward nurses to bath their young charges, scrubbing wards or the dining hall, setting out and clearing the dining hall tables, carrying the food from the kitchens and returning any 'orts' to the 'piggy', sweeping and tidying the playroom, cleaning B1's dressing and shower rooms, and so on. The worst fate that could befall a boy was to be given the job of washer-up, and this for several very good reasons. The scullery was on the same basement floor as the bootroom, and reached via an iron staircase. Every piece of crockery and cutlery (which was piled into great wicker baskets) had to be carried up and down this staircase, which stood in sharp contrast to the fine wooden balustrades leading up to the dormitories. Repeated use over the years by thousands of foundling washers-up had given the iron stairs a smooth, burnished surface.

The main hospital staircases were so planned that one could stand on the basement floor, and looking up, see the third floor ceiling. This meant that there were no barriers to obstruct the passage of sound. Reverberate freely it did, when for example some unfortunate washer-up, laden with a basket of crockery, came to grief on the iron staircase. All those within earshot of the sickening crash of crockery would take up the cry 'Count the Lambs!' — for it was only by piecing together the crests that the full extent of the breakages could be determined. Each piece of crockery bore the hospital crest, a Lamb, carrying in its mouth a 'Sprig of Thyme Proper'. (A 'Sprig of Mint Proper' might have been rather more appropriate.)

And as though the double humiliation of breaking a load of crockery and suffering the jubilant whoops of 'Count the Lambs!' were not sufficient punishment in themselves, the unhappy victims of these accidents were required to make good the damage.

By now, my readers may be wondering how we came by the money we spent on our Cherry Blossom Boot Polish, Solidified Brilliantine, twopenny boxes of Coconut Oil Shampoo (which in our ignorance we used as hair-cream), our *Nelson Lee's, Sexton Blake's, Magnets, Gems,* twopenny bars of Sharp's Kreemy Toffee, Seebackroscopes (one of the *Magnet's* special offers to its readers of which I took advantage), photographs taken in cowboy attire at The Fancy Dress Studio in Tottenham Court Road, bars of Fry's Cream Chocolate, comb-and-mirror sets, and the rest.

The answer is simple; with one notable exception (the steward's boy), it came from two sources — from our foster-parents, and/or from our efforts as domestic workers. The maximum rate of pay for washers-up and scrubbers alike was 4d per month. This meant of course that it needed only one major accident to put a washer-up in the red for the remainder of his time in the hospital. It was one of the very good reasons for the unpopularity of this particular chore. Other reasons were the sheer physical demands of the job; for although there were two tubs, with two boys at each tub, washing up for some 200 boys three times a day throughout the whole year was no sinecure. The scullery also housed the knife-cleaning machine. Five or six knives at a time were inserted into the machine, which was fed with a black, abrasive substance whose trade-name was Wellington

Powder. Too enthusiastic a turn of the handle would cause the machine to jam, which was another sure method of mortgaging one's pocket-money.

Menial though they were, these tasks, after all, simply prepared the girls for their future roles as domestic drudges, and the boys for their barrack-room fatigues, which masqueraded under the curious but imposing name of 'Interior Economy'.

I was fortunate in my not being made a washer-up. During my first year in B1 I was made a ward boy, whose main duties included sweeping those parts of the ward which were not due for a scrubbing, and scrubbing those parts which were not due for a sweeping. For scrubbing purposes, each ward was arbitrarily divided into 'sides' and a 'centre', these being further subdivided. A section would be scrubbed on each weekday, so that a ward would emerge at the end of a week with a completely scrubbed face. Should a boy decide to give his patch a particularly good scrub, he would 'tug it' — another of our exclusive expressions.

Why these wards should have been scrubbed from end to end each week I could never fathom, for never were we permitted to enter a ward other than in rubber-soled slippers into which we changed before going to bed. During the winter months the boards were never given a proper chance to dry out, as the only heating in the wards (a solitary coal fire) was monopolised by the nurse, who, suitably screened off from our vulgar gaze, would sit roasting herself in front of it until her own bed-time.

Ward scrubbing was done before breakfast, and would take an hour at the very least, as some 50 beds had to be trundled out into the centre of the ward, and re-aligned once they had been trundled back again.

The plum jobs which fell into the laps of the fortunate few, to the envy of the less fortunate many, were 'boys' to staff members, such as master's boy, steward's boy, plumber's boy, and so on. These jobs carried with them all manner of perks and privileges. The weekly perk for the steward's boy, for example, was a generous allowance of sugar and raw cocoa, which he would sell to other boys (who devoured the mixture in its raw state) at one penny per spoonful; rank profiteering maybe, but a regular and lucrative source of income to salt away for spending money at summer camp and at Christmas. Masters' boys were the most privileged and coveted jobs of all.

Perhaps their greatest privilege was that of being allowed out on errands. It meant that on production of a signed pass for each separate errand, a master's boy was free to venture out into the dazzling world beyond. This privilege (with one exception) was extended to masters' boys only. The one exception concerned boys who wished to be photographed, when a special pass would be issued. Few boys opted to be photographed in school uniform, preferring instead to be taken in one or other of the fancy dresses supplied by the photographer. Easily the most popular get-up was that of cowboy, replete with cocked six-shooter, lassoo, ten-gallon stetson, check-shirt and what Damon Runyon would describe as 'pants with hair on', and mounted on a life-sized wooden horse; but as the photographer posed his young sitters with the muzzle of the gun resting on the forearm of the hand which held the reins, stylistically the overall effect resembled Dick Turpin rather than the intended Buffalo Bill.

Mistresses' 'girls' were never allowed outside the grounds.

I became one of the privileged few, first as boy to Mr Gray, and then as boy to the headmaster, Mr Holgate.

My duties as Mr Gray's boy included cleaning his shoes, carrying his daily allowance of coal from the basement to his third-storey sitting room, clearing and re-setting the fire, tidying his rooms, fetching his supper from the school kitchens, and singing to his piano accompaniment current song 'hits' which were reproduced each week in one of the popular Sunday papers.

Any master who valued his self-esteem would leave for his boy at least part of his nightly supper (usually the second course), which is the reason why Mr 'Fishbones' Chubb, the hospital architect, was rated among the boys as a poor employer, because (legend had it) he made a practice of devouring every particle, fishbones and all. Mr Gray was particularly generous in this respect, so that for the first time since my Chertsey days (which were now some six years behind me), I came to re-discover the forgotten flavours of pink and chocolate blancmange, jelly and custard. Fetching Mr Gray's supper was by no means the end of the story, but simply its beginning; for the duty cook more often than not would let masters' boys loose on anything in the kitchen that might be lying around; and egged on by the cook, we would stuff to our hearts' and stomachs' content.

Mr Gray was something of a sweet-tooth, and one of my more pleasant and rewarding errands was to purchase his chocolates, which I did from Fuller's Southampton Row Branch. This meant a chocolate of my own choice being popped into my mouth by the Fuller's assistant, and another on my return by Mr Gray himself.

Long before I became his boy, I knew Mr Gray to be fond of me. On one occasion, when I was about eight or nine years old, he lifted me up in his arms, a rare and I would say, dangerous, departure from the undemonstrative attitude of the staff in general. It was not without reluctance therefore that I left his service to become Mr Holgate's boy. This position carried with it additional duties and additional pay. In the matter of supper left-overs, when it came to chocolate blancmange, Mr Holgate would quip, "I won't tell you what it looks like, but you can have it" —

hardly a stylish introduction by one's headmaster to a pre-breakfast appetiser.

As Mr Holgate's boy, one of my duties was to awaken him at six o'clock each morning by tapping on his bedroom door. I would then make him (and myself) a cup of tea, over which he would ruminate (even addressing the occasional remark to himself) in his dressing room. This room (for whose cleanliness and general tidiness I was responsible) was situated at the far end of B1 ward on the second floor. But the gas-ring for boiling the kettle was on the third floor, immediately outside Mr Gray's bedroom. Whether it was occasioned by pique on his part at being deprived of his trained and trusted boy by Mr Holgate, or whether by my own lack of elementary diplomacy in not pouring him an 'early morning cuppa' from 'Digger's' pot, I cannot say; but whatever the cause, Mr Gray was forever upbraiding me on the grounds that the bang emitted by the gas-ring at 10 minutes past six sharp each morning rudely awakened him from his sleep.

Another duty, and one which I enjoyed more than any other, was that of exchanging staff members' books at the now defunct Mudie's Lending Library. Mudie's stood at the High Holborn end of New Oxford Street. At the time, I was going through a violent Scarlet Pimpernel phase, and Mr Holgate would allow me to include the odd Orczy novel on his reading list. Some members of Mudie's staff, knowing my passion for Orczy, made me a semi-formal presentation of some of the Baroness's novels, but not without first checking on those that I had already read! And it was by the odd interpolation into Mr Holgate's list that I came to read A.S.M. Hutchinson's classic *If Winter Comes* and F. Anstey's *Vice Versa*. It was not until I re-read these books later in life that I came to discover the depth of poignancy in the former, and Anstey's delightfully original sense of humour in the latter.

Another worthwhile errand was to collect Mr Holgate's morning and evening papers from the newsagent's shop, which before Hitler took a hand in things, stood a little way up Lamb's Conduit Street, almost opposite The Lamb public house.* The moment I re-entered the hospital gates I would be surrounded by a mob of boys eager to learn Kent's and Surrey's close of play scores. The news-agent, Mrs Charles, a bespectacled, kindly-faced, rotund lady in her middle-60s probably, might well have been author Richards's prototype for his creation Mrs Mimble of Greyfriars School Tuckshop fame.

* Geoffrey Fletcher in his fascinating book *London Overlooked* upholds *The Lamb* as possessing 'one of the finest Victorian interiors in London. Comfortably padded and buttoned settees line the wall along one side, blending to perfection with the brass-railed, cast-iron tables, the legs of which are ornamented with figures of Britannia. Above are rows of Victorian and Edwardian stage celebrities, faded but choice, and eighteenth-century engravings, including one of the benevolent Captain Coram.'

One of my regular errands was to the Holborn branch of Dunn's Hat Shop, where I would take a staff member's silk top-hat for steaming and polishing. The cost of this service was sixpence.

Each Saturday morning I had the job of cleaning Mrs Holgate's brassware fender, tongs, poker, kettle hob and the rest. For this I was paid sixpence per cleaning. I would shop at Staples of Lamb's Conduit Street for her greengroceries, at Uglows of Red Lion Street for her bread, and at the Institute for the Blind in Tottenham Court Road for Mr Holgate's special brand of canes. I had good reason for looking forward to shopping in Uglow's Bakery, for the beautiful assistant, a Miss Hurst, never sent me away without a selection of Uglow's newly-baked buns.

Perhaps the most mysterious errand I ever ran was to Chapman's, whose grocery, wine and spirit shop (which also housed a post office) stood on the corner of Lamb's Conduit and Great Ormond Streets. I was sent there by Mr Moffit, the hospital porter, for a bottle of whisky 'as a little surprise for the missus'. It cost 18/6d. Looking back, I still find it astonishing that a shopkeeper should allow a schoolboy of 14 to take away a full bottle of whisky, with no questions asked. I need scarcely add that Mr Moffit did not ply me with the Fuller's Chocolate Shop style bonus.

Immediately outside Mr Moffit's lodge was an asphalt pavement, with a steepish incline, which we turned to good use during the winter months. Should a sharp frost threaten, either Mr Moffit or 'Bruno' Bruns would douse the asphalt with buckets of water. By morning there would be an excellent 'slide' and although not exactly a St Moritz, it gave us a run of 30 to 40 yards.

Dear old Moffit had good reason for being grateful to the hospital for taking him on the staff; for a hospital porter (whose sole duty it seemed was to open and close the hospital gates for visitors and trades-vans) must have been the only type of employment he was capable of doing. His manner of hobbling painfully along on his heels, together with his gnarled hands, told their own sad tale. But the boys' version as to how he came by all this was something quite different and far more novel. We believed (and in all sincerity) that in his youth Mr Moffit had been a keen huntsman and that his misshapen hands were the result of his thrusting them down the foxes' throats as a preliminary to turning them inside out. I strongly suspect that this story was put in circulation by Mr Moffit himself.

Other errands took me to Bearus's, who repaired our watches at special discount rates — or so he said.

It was by running these errands that I came first to know, and then to love, this fascinating corner of London — Lamb's Place, with its charming 'Rebecca at the Well' marble drinking fountain, over which the statue of

Captain Coram appeared to be keeping permanent watch; Kingsway, the site of the old Stoll Theatre and the Holborn Stadium in which Billy Wells and Joe Beckett clashed for the British heavyweight title; Southampton Row, where the old Premier Hotel offered its guests the luxury of a turkish bath; where Pitman's College offered its famous course in shorthand and typing; and where one chemist's window made a special feature-display of Dr Scholl's famous cures for 'Corns, Callouses, Bunions and Fallen Arches', Sloan's ('Every picture tells a story') Liniment, Reudal Bath Salts and Kruschen Salts.

I once tried a packet of his Kruschen Salts, and although I followed the directions implicitly ('Take as much as will lie on a sixpence'), they did not give me 'That Kruschen Feeling'. In fact, apart from the most obvious of the manufacturer's claims, they fell woefully short in all others; for I did not feel like vaulting over my bed at 6 am; I did not romp in such games as leap-frogging over the backs of six-footers; I did not see the promised return of my once-rosy cheeks (apart from blushing); and they did not cure my headaches, which was my sole reason for my purchasing them.

Then there was Doughty Street, where once lived Charles Dickens, and 'the greatest of English wits and the most humourous wit in English', the Rev. Sydney Smith; Great Ormond Street, Bloomsbury in general, and Holborn, where I once saw the thrilling spectacle of a fire engine drawn by a team of six greys at full gallop; and it was in Holborn where on many occasions I suffered a self-inflicted form of refined torture by window-gazing in hopeless longing at Bassett-Lowkes's model trains.

I delighted in wandering down to the Thames Embankment and returning by the single-decker tram which emerged from its mole-like burrow at the Kingsway — Southampton Road — Bloomsbury — Theobald's Road junction.

Some few years later I paid many a visit to Theobald's Road because of its association with Samuel Coleridge-Taylor's early childhood. I was then going through an intense, but short-lived, Coleridge-Taylor phase. It was for this same reason that I visited, and continue to visit when in England, Sir Arthur Sullivan's statue at the foot of Savoy Hill on the Thames Embankment; for I regard the comic operas of Gilbert and Sullivan as one of England's great art treasures.

To these shopping expeditions I owed my newly-acquired sense of freedom (stifled since my Chertsey days), a keen sense of observation and appreciation, and my awakening to the vibrancy of a big city — all rich experiences which dear little Chertsey could never have given me.

And I came to love both Mr Gray and 'Digger' Holgate.

FOOTNOTES TO CHAPTER 10

[1] Hesketh Pearson, *The Smith of Smiths* (London, 1948), p.100.

11: Masters

When I joined the boys school in 1916, the headmaster was Mr Overton. Patriarchal in appearance, sporting a beard, stiff shirt-front, butterfly-wing collar and benign in speech and manner, he managed to maintain a tight disciplinary control over his 200-odd young charges, and still be revered by most of us.

A system was in force whereby a monitor (senior boy) could report a junior for acts of misbehaviour such as being out-of-bounds, talking during mealtimes, and petty offences of a similar nature. Caning sessions were in the nature of a ritual. They were carried out in front of the whole school during the post-tea-bedtime period.

Monitors would 'bring out' the offenders, and recite their misdemeanours to the headmaster.

Mr Overton backed up his monitors by caning all those who were 'brought out'. But he tempered the severity of each punishment according to the type of offence. Caning could vary from one lethargic tap on the behind (in effect a reproof for the over-zealous monitor) to so mighty a series of wallops as to have earned even the great King Solomon's unqualified approval.

Having been warned in advance that we were to be 'brought out', we would 'pack-by'. Our favourite 'pack-by' material was *Chums,* mainly because of its superior area of coverage and its adjustable thicknesses. Packing-by was not merely a matter of stuffing paper down one's trousers, but was an art in itself. Only a tyro would have been so naive as to pack-by with the stiff cardboard cover from a bound volume of *Chums,* for a boy has yet to be designed with a rectangular-shaped bottom.

So it never reduced itself to a question of the amount of paper one could safely use, for we knew only too well that none of the masters was so tone-deaf as not to be able to distinguish aurally between *Chums* and bums; and a boy suspected by a master of packing-by would be told to unpack, when the caning would start again from stroke one.

Mr Overton was never known to be defeated by a boy at chess, and few boys emerged wholly unscathed from his 'underarm twisters' at the wicket. Whether it was the combination of beard and stiff-fronted shirt, or his undoubted prowess as a chess player, it was accepted by the boys that Mr Overton was by far the wisest teacher on the staff.

He did not rely solely upon corporal punishment as a corrective; rather would he 'let the punishment fit the crime'. An example of this centred around a boy who stole into the steward's office, which was, of course, strictly out-of-bounds. As the boy was leaving the office, he spotted Mr Overton walking in his direction, but who, by a stroke of good luck, was engrossed in his book — or so it appeared. Ducking back into the steward's office, he hid underneath the cloth-covered table. To the boy's consternation the door opened and Mr Overton (recognisable by his button-up boots no doubt) sat himself at the table and settled down to reading his book. It was a Sunday afternoon. After about an hour, he gently lifted the table-covering and said to the boy, "I think you had better come out, or you'll be late for chapel."

We were all genuinely sorry when out of the blue he announced his pending retirement. A pall of gloom settled over the whole school following his departure some few days later. This was not out of veneration for the departing head so much as out of fear and terror of his likely successor, 'Digger' Holgate, whose Saturday evening caning sessions had already established themselves as terrifying experiences for victims and onlookers alike.

In all truth, 'caning sessions' is putting it charitably, as they were virtually floggings*. In this he was the true and undoubted heir of Dr John Keate of Eton, who 'flogged more than eighty boys on the same day, 30 June 1832'. When roused to anger (which was often) he could take on a fearsome appearance. Angry eyes like burning coals set deep in lunar-like craters,

---

* In disciplinary matters such as canings, a child's sex counted for nothing either in Hannah Brown's day, or in my own: 'When the writer was old enough to enter the Upper School, she can remember seeing girls cruelly beaten ... it seemed as though it was done to crush their spirit. I used to thrill with admiration for them: they would not flinch, and the sickening blows descending on the open palm was terrifying to witness. When they turned from the teacher's desk to come back to the class, I saw their faces as pale as death, black shadows round the nostrils and under the eyes and corners of the mouth. And their eyes were wonderful! I did admire them, because they wouldn't cry . . . I was standing in the playroom one afternoon, when I saw one of my companions being belaboured across the shoulders: a very common occurrence. I could hear the woman saying to the child, "I'll teach you to go to the Infirmary and shew your bruises to the Doctor." ' (pp. 35-36, 74-75.)

a sort of Malcolm Sargent handsome-ugliness (but missing out rather more than Sargent on the handsome aspect), hair brushed back in a severe middle parting, an habitual frown, redeemed only by a wide generous mouth. As for the remainder of his body, I can only conjecture that it was normally proportioned; but as his trousers were generally hitched up just that much too high, and his jackets cut just that much too low, it appeared that lengthwise his torso gained at the expense of his legs.

Gone were the lethargic, token-gesture taps of the Overton era; 'Digger' would listen attentively to the monitor's evidence and then pronounce the sentence "Bend down and take six of the best." (He was nicknamed 'Digger' after his constant preocupation in 'digging' at his rectum — probably to relieve an irritation caused by piles.) There were two periods in particular during my time at school when these caning sessions reached a state of unbridled ferocity never before witnessed. They were provoked by bicycles and bananas.

After the war, a firm named Hearn was permitted to store hundreds of surplus-stock army bicycles underneath the boys' side 'Arches' (the colonnades on the west side of Coram's Fields). We were given strict instructions not to go near them. But when the masters were safely out of the way (having a meal perhaps), the temptation became too strong for some. The combination of saddle-soreness and canings must have rendered some of the boys' bottoms indistinguishable from tenderised prime rump steak.

Then came a gift by the firm of Elders & Fyffes consisting of consignment after consignment of bananas, which again were stored on the boys' side, in the sports store, half-way along the same western colonnades. Although I steered clear of the bicycles, the bananas (a fruit whose flavour by now we had all but forgotten) proved just too much of a temptation.

But I was one of the lucky ones who was not found out; just as well, for I became caught up as it were in the sequel to the Elders & Fyffes gift. It was sort of inverted poetic justice. Mr Holgate chose two of us to meet one of the partners of Elders & Fyffes to tender grateful thanks on behalf of the children. Whereupon the partner concerned handed us each some half-dozen large blocks of chocolate, assuring us at the same time that the banana supply would continue — which it did. I should, of course, have been striken with mortification and suffered prickings of conscience, for at the time I was boasting red sergeant stripes on my right arm, a golden good-conduct stripe on my left arm, but none of the richly-deserved purply-green stripes on somewhere else. The whole incident was symptomatic of the charmed life that has always been mine.

On another occasion a group of boys was spotted by 'Bruno' Bruns talking to some of the infirmary maids. He reported it straightway to Mr Holgate, who immediately lined up B1 boys (the younger boys were already in bed) and held a roll call. This was considered the most heinous offence of all, and the boys involved were caned unmercifully. I do not know what action (if any) was taken against the maids concerned, but to be dismissed from domestic service without a reference in those days was a serious matter.

In more light-hearted vein was the case involving a group of boys who wrote and produced their own play entitled *Spies in Wartime*. They must have broken one or another of the hospital rules, for the complete cast was 'brought out' and made to re-enact the play in the presence of the whole school. (To those of you who become caught up in the Heredity v. Environment discussion, it may be of rather more than passing interest when I explain that the daughter of the author of *Spies in Wartime*, Josephine Tewson, is a well-known actress on British television.)

The play got under way in the usual tense atmosphere that attended caning sessions but ended in uninhibited merriment, in which even 'Digger' himself became caught up. It all started with Jansen, when he moved round the stage's perimeter, flapping his arms in penguin fashion, which synchronised with a curious clk, clk, clk, clk-ing noise of his tongue.

Mr Holgate: And what's that supposed to represent?

Jansen: I'm supposed to be clipping the hedge, sir, but secretly spying on the house next door.

Enter Oakley, crawling along on all fours and wearing a striped football jersey.

Mr H: And what are you supposed to be?

Oakley: A beetle, sir.

Jansen (interrupting): Excuse me, sir, he's misunderstood me, he's supposed to be the Beadle.

Loud laughter off stage, and a free pardon for the entire cast.

In fairness to Mr Holgate, I should point out that he was not alone in caning us. All masters used the cane, but he tried very much harder than the rest.

Our masters sadly failed to understand that a caning resulted in a rupture in our relationships, which at best were difficult to re-establish and at worst, complete and permanent. I know of one old boy, Harold T — now past 70, who continues to smart under what he considered to be the futility and injustice of it all.

As drill master, Mr Holgate was a martinet, threatening rather than promising, to make us "as 'smut' as the Guards". Not one, but numerous, press photographs of the children on parade afford proof that his threats were no idle ones. Never on parade without his drill-stick, he would double up and down the ranks when we were practising the march past in company column, landing a stinging whack on the calves of boys who might be out of dressing.

Although the girls were spared this treatment, they came under the same parade-ground discipline as the boys; they formed fours, slow and quick marched in open and close column, and repeated the same evolution over and over again until 'Digger' was satisfied.

Next to the banana and bicycle episodes, the morning drill parades gave rise to more canings than any other cause. The problem was the dangerous half-hour period between breakfast and drill, which we filled in with playing cricket or football.[1] Both sports left our boots (so carefully cleaned before breakfast) in a right mess. The bootroom being closed, the popular remedy was to polish them on the backs of one's trouser legs. Drill parades always started with an inspection by 'Digger'; some made it, others didn't. This was one of the many absurd aspects of life in the Foundling Hospital; to be compulsorily turned out in the grounds to play, only to be punished should one's boots become soiled in the process. Although we smarted under the injustice of it all, there was no appeal against it.

Next to the deadly Tuesday morning classroom readings from the *Second Book of Moses called Exodus* on the *Furnishing of the Ark of the Covenant and the Tabernacle,* the daily drill parade was the least palatable part of the curriculum, save only when the school band turned out. Having the band meant we would be marching and not executing everything at the double; and keeping in step from the drum beat and not from 'Digger's' monotonous "Lep, righ', lep. Lep, righ', lep."

In fairness to Mr Holgate, he was only carrying out what was, after all, part of his job. And we may forgive him his 'Smut as the Guards' threat, which was simply a legacy he had inherited from his 19th century counterpart:

"We thought," wrote Dickens, "when the male pupils were summoned by trumpet to the playground to go through their military exercises — which they did, their drill master assured us confidentially, in a manner that would not disgrace the Foot-Guards — we had traced the entire history of the connection of a blank child with the hospital." [2]

On the football field, Mr Holgate was a formidable fullback, and it took a goodly measure of pluck on the part of a boy in the opposing team to tackle him, so hefty was his charge. For these occasions, he wore what must have been his shortest pair of trousers, whose turn-ups barely covered the tops of his boots. I recall seeing him bat only twice, when I formed the

"As 'smut as the Guards' ". Prince Albert (later Duke of York and King George VI). The author is on the extreme right.

opinion that he was better at football than at cricket. In his first knock he scored one run, but in his second knock he was not quite so successful. Paradoxically he considered boxing a brutal sport, and never encouraged it among the boys.

I happened to attend the 1970 old boys' and girls' reunion dinner, when one of my own generation of foundlings described Mr Holgate as a sadist; and after what I have said regarding his savage caning sessions, it might appear a just description. My own personal contacts with him as his 'boy', and again after I had left school, lead me to suggest that this description was unjustified. In the days of his headmastership, caning was the accepted and normal method of punishment, whether in public or charity school; and the day when educationists were to prove King Solomon wrong was still in the far distance.

Mr Holgate shouldered an enormous measure of responsibility, including the placing of boys out in the world, the overall discipline of the boys' school, the planning and general running of the annual summer camps, maintaining the excellence of standards on the parade ground, and the more mundane duties such as ensuring that 'grease-pots' did not use hair-oil on the day they were being confirmed — "We can't send the Bishop of Willesden away with his hands reeking of your stinking stuff.''

"Some of you stink on the face of the globe" was a well-worn expression of his.

At times his anger was justified. How would you react, for example, should four boys, positioned at the four points of the compass, armed with a soup ladle apiece, take turns in bashing in the crown of your best bowler hat? (I was not one of them.)

I do believe that he cared for the boys far more than his gruff exterior and rough methods of handling us would suggest. During the 1922 scarlet fever epidemic, when large numbers of foundling children were sent to London fever hospitals, it was he who introduced the scheme for sending each child a luxury food parcel. And I do know that many an old boy would burden him with his troubles, with the certainty of receiving a sympathetic hearing. I recall this amusing exchange between one such boy (who had been apprenticed to the fishing trade in Grimsby) and Mr Holgate:

Mr Holgate: So you are finding things hard going?

Ralph D — r: Aye.

Mr H: I suppose 'Aye' means Yes?

Ralph D — r: Aye.

Mr Holgate's 'achilles heel' was his daughter, whom he worshipped. When his marriage finally broke down and his wife was given the custody of their only child, I suspect that there remained only his boys standing between him and utter dejection. It was little short of pathetic when he confided in me (a mere boy of 18), that since his separation he had been living on five shillings per week. And then he lost his beloved Iris in tragic circumstances.

'Digger' was no sadist; to me he was a lovable man, who was constantly weighed down by the twin burdens of responsibilities of office and domestic strife. If, as I suspect, his brutal caning sessions were simply an outlet for his frustrations, then our role of Balaam's Ass was not wholly an unrewarding one.

Even so, I feel bound to admit that insofar as these caning sessions affected me personally, each individual chastisement caused a rupture in my relationship with the master inflicting the punishment. And however strong may have been my affection for the master, it was a rupture which never quite healed. It was not so much resentment on my part against the punishment as such, as an inner rebellion, a smouldering sense of injustice, against my utter helplessness to make any form of appeal or complaint.

With the possible exception of the school chaplain, the person who was to have the greatest influence over my whole outlook and thinking was a master named Gray.

Wyndham Charles Gray joined the teaching staff in 1916, the year I left the infants' for the boys' school. Like other members of the teaching staff, he held no university qualification, which in his case did not matter a rap, for he was an excellent teacher, wholly dedicated — to the point of being over-conscientious.

Fortunately for those he taught (perhaps better expressed 'for those fortunates he taught'), he was an exceptionally well-informed and interesting person. He would illuminate his classroom work with matter quite outside the narrow limits of our elementary school-type education — the newly-developed art of invisible mending; the opposed beliefs of East and West concerning the doctrine of re-incarnation; the Jess Willard - Jack Dempsey heavyweight championship fight; the personal sorrows of William Cowper; the epic stories of the British destroyers *Swift* and *Broke* and of John Travers Cornwell VC the 16-year-old hero of the Jutland Bank battle, as he was posthumously styled; Ranjit Sinhji's wrist-work; Horatio Bottomley playing safe by denouncing a political opponent as a 'terminological inexactitudanarian' rather than risk calling him plain 'liar'*; and of Britain's youngest First World War brigadier, the 25-year-old Brigadier Bradford, who, before going in to what was to be his last battle, invited his men to join him in prayer, reminding them after Tennyson,

More things are wrought by prayer
Than this world dreams of.

And there were his blackboard demonstrations of soccer tactics (which, be it said, tended to overlook the fact that there was an opposition to be reckoned with); and should we meet the name Cholmondeley, to pronounce it 'Chumley.'

"I put it to you, that if the name 'Cholmondeley' is pronounced 'Chumley', then 'Bolmondeley' would be pronounced 'Bottomley'.'' (This drew from us a prolonged 'eeee' of feigned disgust; it was started by the more alert few, and spread in a mounting crescendo through the entire class.)

It was these, and a whole host of other seemingly irrelevant topics; the Ingersoll Watch Company, Messrs Negretti and Zambra's barometers, and

---

* The term may have originated with Winston Churchill when as Under-Secretary of State for the Colonies he launched an attack in the Commons in 1906 against exploitation of migrant Indian labour: 'It cannot in the opinion of His Majesty's Government be classified as slavery in the extreme acceptance of the word without some risk of terminological inexactitude.'

Wyndham Charles Gray   **Galatea Thorpe**

so on, which went to illuminate what would otherwise have been just another dull, routine classroom lesson. It was because he was never dull, and because he was never plain factual, that he appealed to us as an interesting teacher.

He was an ardent believer in the British Empire, and would have been at one, I am sure, with Lord Beaverbrook's 'Empire Free Trade' movement. (For all I know it was he who posed for the picture of the *Crusader,* which for many years was emblazoned in red on the front page of the *Daily Express;* but the helmet's lowered visor made positive identification somewhat difficult.)

"Now, boys, everything you see on this map of the world which is coloured red, is yours. Young, New Zealand is yours; Nalden, India is yours; Jennings, Australia is yours; Derwent, Canada is just as much yours as it is mine," and so on.

Ungrateful though it may appear, and Mr Gray's boundless enthusiasm notwithstanding, we were not very impressed. I do feel we would have shown more enthusiasm for our newly-discovered affluence had the end product of Canada's vast wheatfields, for example, been rather more in evidence on our dining tables; for seldom, if ever, were our animal appetites satisfied.

In the classroom, Mr Gray would not suffer fools gladly: "Open up your Catechisms. Now, I'll put the questions, and as I call on you, read the answers."

W.C.G.: "Strutt, what is your name?"

Strutt: 'N or M, sir.'

W.C.G. "You silly little chump! You know jolly well your name isn't N or M."

Strutt: "That's what I thought, sir, but that's what it says here."

We were then given an explanation of the italicised N and M, which, incidentally, was to prove our second and final Latin lesson, our first coming from Mr Overton: "If you fail to put dots after £s.d. I shall feel compelled to call you Little Silly Dunces."

Nor would Mr Gray allow ensemble class reading to degenerate into the type of sing-song associated with the village school:

Class: 1. "Lord, who shall dwell in Thy tabernacle; or who shall rest upon Thy holy hill?

2 Even he ...."

W.C.G.: "Stop — that won't do at all. In verse I you are asking the Lord for answers to two questions, and jolly searching ones at that. Even the Lord must be given time to think out His answers. Now start again, and when you come to the end of verse I, make a pause, and count one, two, three, four to yourselves."

Even so, no amount of cajoling, threatening or pleading on his part succeeded in toning down the belligerent manner in which we recited the Catechism lines —

'and by God's help, so I WILL'.

And during the period of the Elders and Fyffes banana bonanza, he had the good grace not to flicker even so much as an eyelid when we recited the vow 'To keep my hands from picking and stealing'; for he was only too painfully aware (as, in a different sense, were we) that that was the one Catechismal vow which we had decided among ourselves temporarily to suspend.

In some ways we dreaded canings from Mr Gray rather more than from Mr Holgate. It was not so much the relative severity or the number of strokes given, but the part of our anatomy on which the cane fell. Whereas Mr Holgate favoured caning us on our behinds, Mr Gray chose to cane us on the outstretched palms of our hands. And it hurt — particularly in cold weather when not a few of our hands might be chapped, or chilblained, as very often they were.

A further disadvantage of being caned on the hand was that you could see each stroke coming; whereas when they were administered to the behind, as with a person about to be beheaded, none but a dolt would make matters worse by peering over his shoulder.

Teachers were required to teach two standards simultaneously. When I entered the boys' school, Mr Gray taught standards I and II, which were separated by a narrow aisle. The two classes read different periods of history; worked different types of sums; and were set different topics for essays — 'compositions', as we called them.

One of the few times the two classes met on common ground was for the bi-weekly religious instruction periods.

Morning prayers were held between the end of drill parades and commencement of lessons. Evening prayers were supervised by the respective ward nurses. Chapel services were held on Sunday mornings and afternoons, and on each week-day during Holy Week. In addition to all this, a minimum of two school periods per week was devoted to the Scriptures.

Each boy and girl had their own personal copy of the Bible, which was kept inside his or her classroom desk. We learnt to say by heart the Catechism, together with the Apostles' and the Athanasian Creeds, and of course, the Lord's Prayer. Although I do not claim that we read the Bible from cover to cover, nevertheless we did read through (almost word for word) the Pentateuch, and selected passages from the remaining books of the Old Testament. And in the New Testament we made a no-less thorough study of the four Gospels and the Acts of the Apostles. In addition, we read through certain of St. Paul's epistles and parts of the Book of the Revelation.

We were required to memorise passages such as the whole of Isaiah 53, various chapters from the Gospels (such as the Beatitudes from Christ's Sermon on the Mount, and St. John 15), and certain collects. We also memorised Psalms 1, 15, 23, 46, 103 and 121. And here Mr Gray impressed upon us not once, but several times, that W.E. Gladstone's command of the English language, together with his great powers of oratory, were due in no small measure to his learning by heart the whole of the Psalms of David. (I trace back the root cause of my personal limitations in these two respects, command of the English language and powers of oratory, to my learning by heart but four per cent of the Psalms of David.)

On one occasion we were tested on our knowledge of Biblical history by Governor Percival Etheridge. "And what are the names of the three men in the Bible who committed suicide?" was one of his questions. To this day I still fail to appreciate how knowledge of the fact that Samson, Judas Iscariot and Ahithophel committed suicide, assisted in any way our otherwise carefully guided spiritual development.

With this sole reservation, I look back upon our Biblical studies, not excluding even the *Furnishing of the Ark of the Covenant,* as perhaps the most important aspect of my early education.

As I have said, Miss Bateman had already shown Mr Gray some of my work, and it was on the strength of this, I suppose, that he advanced me straight into standard II.

He did not remain with the two lowest standards, but moved up progressively through standards III and IV to V and VI, where he stayed. The higher standards, VII and X VII, were taken by Mr Holgate.

In our very first year with Mr Gray, he adopted a group of us, which he named his 'six'; and as he moved up, he contrived somehow to take his 'six' with him. So that apart from his 'six's' final two years, the whole of its schooling came under Mr Gray's tutelage. However well-intentioned, the disadvantages of this system are plain, the main one being that we were seldom exposed to other teachers' minds and methods. Even so, I have never harboured any regrets on this score, so excellent and inspired was Mr Gray's teaching.

Our syllabuses were virtually the same as those prescribed for any elementary school — reading, writing, arithmetic, history and geography. Reading included a group of poems such as Keats's *Endymion* (the first six lines only of Book I — 'A Thing of Beauty is a Joy for Ever'); William Blake's *The Lamb;* Alfred Noyes's *The Call of Spring;* R.L. Stevenson's *When I was sick and lay a-bed;* patriotic poems such as Alfred Noyes's *A Song of England*;* and Walter Scott's *Breathes there the man with soul so dead;* and verses from now forgotten 19th century poets, such as Eliza Cook's *Springtime.*

Our prose readings included easily digested stories from Dickens, a moralistic version of *The Mutiny on the Bounty,* whose last seven words were 'Sin always brings misery in its train', the whole of Palgrave's *Golden Treasury,* and Wolsey's farewell speech from *Henry VIII* (our one and only meeting with Shakespeare).

The only full-length book we read in class was Walter Scott's *The Talisman,* which we voted mighty dull. We decided among ourselves that there was more action on the first page of a *Magnet,* a *Gem,* a *Nelson Lee,* or a *Sexton Blake* than there was in the whole of *The Talisman.* There probably was, but it was not until some decades later, when I discovered Scott through certain of his *Waverley Novels,* that I came to realise how thoroughly misguided were our schoolboyish ratings of his work.

---

* This and other patriotic poems were a special feature of World War I Christmas pantomimes, and were the cause of many a tear-moistened eye.

No science subjects or languages were taught, and even the teaching of English grammar was kept down to the barest minimum. We learnt that a verb was a 'doing' word; that 'and', 'but', 'so' and 'or' were conjunctions; the meanings of such terms as 'noun', 'pronoun', 'adjective', 'subject', predicate', and that was about it. It meant that we were incapable of parsing a simple sentence.

Serious instruction in any of the art forms — painting, drawing and music — was virtually non-existent, so the few who happened to possess an innate talent for such as drawing and painting were left to develop it as best they could. Music was limited to those fortunate enough to be elected to the chapel choir (signified by a lyre worked in gold thread and worn on the right arm of jacket or frock), or the school band. And when I once had the temerity to ask Mr Miles (an articled pupil of the chapel organist, Dr H. Davan Wetton), whether he could arrange for me to be taught the piano, he simply refused to take me seriously. (I was to be refused a similar request some few years after my leaving the hospital.)

It was during my last year at the hospital that the chaplain purchased a gramophone. He would entertain the senior boys (and presumably senior girls) of an evening with records such as Dame Clara Butt singing *The Hills of Donegal,* and Kreisler playing Drdla's then-popular *Souvenir.* ("I fail to understand how he can play two notes simultaneously" was Mr Stork's bewildered reaction.) Here and now, I make the abject confession that our undisputed favourite was neither Dame Clara Butt nor Kreisler, but *The White Hope* featuring comedian Harry Weldon. Harry was upheld as the 'White Hope of British Boxing', and his oft-repeated invitation 'Any ladies?' never failed to provoke a great deal of merriment among us.

In passing, I wonder just how many of us at the time appreciated the sheer physical effort involved in carrying a 'table-grand' gramophone, plus a dozen or so 1920 wax-cylinder records, from Mecklenburgh Square to our third-floor classroom. I for one certainly didn't. Mr Stork's record sessions quickly established themselves as the most 'glishfully' anticipated event of the week.

Limited though our education was, we were neither more, nor less, fortunate than the hundreds of thousands of other elementary school children. The well-intentioned British Government's Education Act of 1944 was still a quarter of a century away. And less than three decades earlier, we had the enlightened, but lone voice of George Bernard Shaw publicly ridiculing an English nobleman because of his reactionary views on education for the masses:

> "If the scheme [weekly orchestral concerts] does not pay at first, it should be taken over by the County Council, which could meet

the loss by at once confiscating the entire property of the Duke of Westminster, as a judgement on him for signing a petition to prevent the schools of London being provided with pianos, on the ground of 'extravagance'. If this thrifty nobleman were worth his thousand a day to us he would long ago have put a Steinway grand into every Board School in London at his own expense.'"[3]

And later:

"Some day I shall enlarge on the respective shares of the school time-table allotted to music, and to the comparative unimportant and revolting subject of mathematics.'"[4]

But, I repeat, his was a lone voice.

No homework was set us, and we sat no public examinations. We were thus automatically debarred from professions requiring matriculation for entry. The loss to the nursing service alone of some excellent potential material was but one consequence of the 18-19th centuries' orientated thinking on the part of successive Foundling Hospital governors: it was a mentality which set out deliberately to deny equal opportunity to the less fortunate strata of society; an excellent breeding ground in fact for the Judes of this world. This is not an expression of personal bitterness, but simply the plain facts of the matter.

In my own case, particularly as one of the favoured 'six', I had excellent reason for being grateful to Mr Gray for giving me the best that could be extracted from the narrow limits of the elementary schools' syllabus.

Once a year, the whole school was inspected by a Mr Winter, a London County Council Inspector of Schools. He was appropriately named, for to us he appeared a somewhat dour, cold personality, whose sole reason for visiting us year after year seemingly was to correct our pronunciation of the conjunction 'and'. "Bread 'nd butter, not bread and butter", he would say. He was at least sufficiently realistic not to use by way of example "Strawberries 'nd Cream", or "Jelly 'nd Custard".

Boys in each class sat three abreast, so that a double class would sit in horizontal rows of six to each row. Mr Winter would set each vertical row a written test on a different subject, which might be history, arithmetic or poetry. Some few days before his visit Mr Gray would rehearse us in examination-room tactics. "Now, Morley, history is one of your weak subjects; so should your row be set history, dodge down underneath the desk — make a pretext of dropping your pen or something — and change places with Parker."

'Greylegs' as we called him (not openly, naturally) was a man of great compassion and understanding. Some time after I had left the hospital, I happened to enquire of him the whereabouts of a boy who only too clearly was destined to become one of life's unfortunate misfits. It transpired that the headmaster had experienced the utmost difficulty in placing him out in the world, so unfitted was he for employment of any kind. Mr Gray repeated to me the jubilant headmaster Holgate's remark, "Well, we've managed to get him off our hands at last." Mr Gray's reaction was, "That's all very well from Mr Holgate's point of view, but what about the boy — what's going to happen to him, I wonder?"

When he retired from teaching he continued to take a very real and active interest in the welfare of old boys and girls through his work for the Old Coram Association, so that he served the hospital in one capacity or another from the year of his appointment to his death in 1968 — a total of 52 years.

I am inclined to consider it a pity that we are denied opportunity of reading our own obituary notices, and overhearing our own funeral orations; for many of the departed would learn straight from the mouths of erstwhile friends and foes alike (and with no small degree of astonishment to the deceased themselves) of a whole host of hitherto unsuspected qualities of character, which but for the occasion of their passing on, would have received either grudging acknowledgment or no acknowledgment at all.

Wyndham Charles Gray was in no need of such obsequies. Nor was there need for the preacher at Mr Gray's memorial service to have proceeded beyond the opening sentence of his valedictory address —

> 'Well done, thou good and faithful servant; enter thou into the joy of thy Lord.'

Apart from Messrs Holgate and Gray, my acquaintance with our masters was come by outside the classroom. There was Mr Morley, possessor of a fine tenor voice and an even finer leg-glide, which, I suspect, he borrowed from the acknowledged master of that particular stroke, Prince Ranjit Sinhji. He was a man of extreme moods, hateful, hot tempered and lovable by turns. He would charge into a ward with the ferocity of a goaded bull, belabouring boys right and left for petty offences such as talking or being out of bed. With that over and done with, he would melt, and enter into detailed reasons as to why it was considered good style in dress for a man to wear old brown shoes but new black shoes, yet never the other way round.

His end was tragic. While yet a young man well within his 30s, he attempted to 'doctor' himself by applying his smattering of medical knowledge (acquired during war service with the RAMC) to clear up a blood disorder. Mr Holgate warned him of the folly of it, but too late. He died within a few days of being admitted to hospital.

And then there was 'Trolley' Wheeler, tall, handsome, possessed of a natural debonair manner which Tom Walls himself (whom 'Trolley' was not altogether unlike) might well have envied. The Fifty Shilling Tailors's obese dummy exemplifying the firm's boast 'Size No Object' excepted, the gents' tailor's dummy tends to fit into one of two categories — the over-handsome moustachiod dummy, and the no less handsome clean-shaven dummy. 'Trolley' fitted into the former category, and indeed might easily have been the prototype model for some exclusive West End tailor, such was his manly appearance. His most prominent feature was his magnificent Roman nose ('beak' we dubbed it) which he acquired, so the story went round, by his diving late one evening into an empty swimming bath.

Little wonder that we linked his name romantically with the girls' games mistress, the beautiful Irene Cissy Carter. (I became the envy of the other boys when she once handed me a telegram to dispatch.) She compared more than favourably with Sir Percy Blakeney's divinely beautiful, but perfectly stupid, wife Marguerite (in my imagination, of course). Time was to prove that any romance there may have been between 'Trolley' and Irene Cissy existed but in our imaginations.

'Trolley' was the complete extrovert. His walk to the wicket was the signal for the bowler to position as many fielders as he could safely spare deep on the boundary. I remember him stopping a bowler during his run-up, and turning to a group of spectators calling out, "Bunny" (his boy, Warren), "please run up to my room and fetch my cap — the sun is blinding me". A piece of pure exhibitionism, no doubt, but this was part of the essential 'Trolley'.

It was during 1919 that we lined the City of London streets to see the Foot Guards' victory march. Men who had been 'demobbed' went back into uniform for this very special occasion. Corporal Wheeler was one of them, by virtue of his war service with the Grenadier Guards. We became hoarse from cheering the seemingly endless marching columns of fours, but even so, managed to raise our loudest 'Hurrah!' for our very own 'Trolley', who responded in his uninhibited style, cocking a snoot at Guards' discipline, and acknowledging our cheers by waving to us with his free right arm.

He was certainly something of a hero to the boys, and rather too much of a good thing to last. He resigned from the staff to join the City of London Police. There remains one last incident to relate. In characteristic 'Trolley' manner, he once held up a particularly busy flow of city traffic to allow a solitary pedestrian to make his crossing with dignity. The person so privileged was our school chaplain, Mr Stork.

It was 'Trolley', I'm sure, who inspired the phrase 'London's Policemen are wonderful'.

FOOTNOTES TO CHAPTER 11

[1] For these unofficial 'pick-up' matches as we called them, we played with rag balls which we made ourselves. The core would be a stone, around which was wound strips of rag. The outer calico cover (which was sewn on) came from odd strips given us by the crippled seamstress, Miss Phillips, and the tailor, Mr Danvers.

[2] Dickens, p.52.

[3] George Bernard Shaw, *Music in London, 1890-94* (London, 1949-50), Vol.I, p.143.

[4] Ibid., Vol.II, pp.99-100.

12: The school chaplain

The demolition of the old Foundling Hospital buildings in 1928 attracted an army of memento-hunters — I was one of them.

I was offered what the caretaker falsely claimed to be the keyboard of Handel's organ; but as my place of residence at the time was hardly compatible with such a priceless *objet d'art,* I declined his world-shaking offer.

You see, alongside about 25 other young men, I was then in residence in an Aldershot Garrison Camp barrack room — hardly the ideal setting for the museum-piece the caretaker claimed it to be. Instead, I settled on a crested salt-cellar (the crest depicting our old friend, the Lamb Argent holding in its mouth a Sprig of Thyme Proper), and a hymn book. I have since lost trace of the salt-cellar, but still have the hymn book; and this, together with a plaster-cast of a cherub's head (one of several which once adorned the chapel), I count among my most treasured possessions.

The hymn book, or to give it its full title, *Hymns and Anthems sung in the Chapel of the Foundling Hospital,* is a copy of the 1874 edition. This particular copy could not have been in general use, but belonged most probably to a member of staff; for meticulously recorded alongside each of the hymns and anthems are the several dates on which they were sung. The earliest recorded year is 1884, and the latest 1921.

One of the most heavily scored hymns is No. 101:

'Put thou thy trust in God,
    In duty's path go on';

Those who were foundlings between the years 1892-1925 will know the reason for this particular hymn's popularity — it was Mr Stork's favourite hymn, and served also as the text for many of his Sunday afternoon sermons.

The simple, unequivocal beliefs embodied in the words of this hymn were his beliefs. In turn, he communicated these beliefs to successive generations of foundlings in an equally simple but extraordinarily convincing manner. And it can be no coincidence that the Roll of Honour, 1939-1945 (which is appended to each issue of the Journal of the Old Coram Association) should be headed, 'In Duty's Path Go On'.

Mr Stork was a man of great stature, in both meanings of the word. Over six feet tall, and proportionately broad, he cut a fine figure of a man. Add to his natural height an extension of a further 15 or so inches (brought about by his top hat), plus a commanding personality, and you arrive at a man ideally cut out to carry out the complex task of moulding the minds and everyday lives of a heterogeneous collection of about 4-500 parentless children; for it was he, more than any other, who exerted the strongest and most enduring influence over the children's daily lives.

Mr Stork was born about 1860, and appointed school chaplain in July, 1892; an office he held until 1925 when he resigned to take up the living of St. Mary's Church, Stone, near Kidderminster. He died in 1952, thus living well beyond his 90th year. Were I asked the secret of his great age, which until near the end, when arthritis set in, was attended by robust health and physical fitness, I would answer — 'Mens sana in corpore sano'.

In my day, although turned 60, he took part in the boys' cricket and football matches. Many a time do I recall seeing him on a Wednesday afternoon, attired in clerical garb and about to go out, succumbing to a boy's entreaty to keep goal. Some 15 or so minutes later he would reappear dressed in baggy trousers, sweater and his favourite deer-stalker hat, to take up his traditional position (between the sticks). Clearly, it was all part of a pre-determined object lesson of his in the quality of unselfishness; for he need not have routed himself through the hospital grounds at all.

Our cricket and football matches consistently attracted a large crowd of onlookers which pressed itself against the railings on the pavement in Guilford Street. During one of these football matches when, in a characteristic manner, he was pacing up and down the goal mouth, he was highly amused to overhear one particularly vociferous spectator yell to another "and there's their parson, jazzing between his two sticks as usual".

On the cricket field, he transplanted from his native Yorkshire all those dour, stubborn tactics traditionally associated with the annual Battle of the Roses. He played with a straight, unspectacular bat, and bowled a straight and equally unspectacular ball, aimed always at the batsman's leg stump. He was a most difficult batsman to dismiss, and in his cricketing hey-day must have broken the spirit of many a Lancashire bowler.

His golf was as unspectacular, but as safe, as his cricket; for his drive, though uninteresting to watch, almost always managed to find the middle of the fairway. Incidentally, I have never forgiven Mr Stork his unjustifiable and personally disparaging remark — "Look here, Holgate, why do persist in having Nalden as your caddie; he does nothing but chase butterflies." (This would have been at the 1921 Bracknell summer camp; Mr Holgate related this story to me some few years later.)

Every year Mr Stork wrote, directed, and produced a play exclusively for the boys to act. The scenery was painted by Mr 'Fishbones' Chubb which, because of its size, was hung during preparation on one of our playroom walls. The costumes were run up by the girls' seamstress, Mrs Arnold, who lost all her four sons in the 1914-18 war. The dominant theme of his plays during the war years naturally enough was patriotism; but with his young audience in mind, he had sufficient shrewdness to subordinate any such sentiment to the theme of the play itself. One such theme (which in World War II Mr Punch satirised under the general heading 'Wartime Weaknesses') was the German spy. His production for the year 1917, described on the programme as 'A Further Short Play of the War', was entitled *Somewhere in France,* and Mr Chubb's backdrop for the scene of that name added just the right touch of poignancy — the broken and scarred tree-stumps, the waterlogged shell craters and the trenches. The programme carried on its cover a verse from Kipling's poem, *For All we Have and Are:*

There is but one task for all — For each one life to give;
Who stands if freedom fall? Who dies if England live?

In this same play (much to the boys' delight) the Germans managed to plant one of their spies into the very grounds of the Foundling Hospital. The part of the spy, Wilhelm Kluck, who enlisted in the 7th Middlesex Regiment (the Bantams) under the false name of William Clark, was played by my dear friend, Ted J... . The stage fight (in which Kluck, as would be expected, came off worst) developed into something rather more realistic than was intended by the producer or realised by the audience; for Ted emerged from it with a nasty cut, blood streaming down his face. Thus the burnt cork he was given to blacken his eye became somewhat redundant.

Mr Stork's plays, a subtle blend of story and moral, were simply an extension of his own teachings. 'My left hand represents the story, and my right, the lesson. Clasp both hands together and you have a parable.' And thus with his plays.

The only play in which I was given a part was a Christmas fantasy, into which characters from favourite fairy stories were cleverly interwoven. Taking advantage of a pair of identical twins, Mr Stork could not resist the opportunity of introducing Tweedledum and Tweedledee. The play opened with a prologue, introducing three boys, all too aware of their grown-up status, and pooh-poohing the land of make-believe:

1st Boy: I don't believe in Father Christmas.

2nd Boy: Neither do I — nor in those Fe-Fi-Fo-Fummers either.

Father Christmas: So they don't believe in me?
                        Well, Well! (waving his magic sleep-bringing wand)
                        They must be taught, they ... must ... be ... taught.

Father Christmas (Mr Morley) then went on to sing the popular, but hardly seasonal, ballad, *Because*. The author's wit was sometimes a concession to the grown-ups.

Prince Charming: (addressing the Ugly Sisters)
                        Avaunt! And quit my sight!
                        Let the earth hide thee!
                        Thy bones are marrowless, thy blood is cold;
                        Thou hast no splendour in those eyes which thou dost glare with.
                        Hence, horrible shadows!
                        You secret, black and midnight hags,
                        Unreal mockeries,
                        Hence!

1st Ugly Sister: (Margery) What disgusting language.

2nd Ugly Sister: (Gertrude) One would think we had come to Billingsgate.

And in the scene when the Ugly Sisters are dressing for the ball:

Gertrude: Marg! Will you wait a minute whilst I put on my Kalinsky Model fur set.
                        (To audience) Nine, nineteen, six, Marshall and Snellgrove!

Marg: I wish you wouldn't call me 'Marg'. A most disgusting name, and full of very odious associations.
                        (A sly reference to the wartime substitution of margarine for butter. The 'best' people would admit to using margarine for cooking only.)

Another sequence involved a group of scalp-hunting Indians, who were seated around a fire, hungrily eyeing two captured white men being made ready for the pot.

Indian Chief:	And to celebrate this great event, you shall all have jelly for your tea.
Indians in Chorus:	Hurroo!
Chief:	Followed by buns!
Chorus:	B a l f o u r ' s ?
Chief:	Aye! Balfour's!*
Chorus:	Hurroo!

Although these deliberately absurd incongruities went over our heads, they appealed to the grown-ups.

I was cast in the role of Red Riding Hood, and as late as 1947 (the last time I was to see Mr Stork) he related to the assembled company at the inaugural dinner of the Old Coram Association an incident which took place at the conclusion of the play's first performance. It appeared that a very serious young man in the audience approached Mr Stork with: "I would very much like to meet that young lady [Red Riding Hood] so perhaps you would be kind enough to arrange an introduction." Such was the sheer artistry of our make-up team.

The plays were written out by Mr Stork in his own stylish longhand. A cyclostyled copy was given to each performer, who undertook not to divulge any word of it to boys outside the cast.

I would say that he had even less time for the 'Hun' of 1914 - 18 than had Nelson for the French. He lectured us not once, but several times, on the heroism of Nurse Edith Cavell and upon the brutality of her execution; and he echoed and re-echoed in classroom and pulpit the Belgians' rallying cry, "Remember Louvain!" He explained to us in simple and understandable terms the enormity of Roger Casement's crime; and when an outburst of patriotic fervour moved the British Government in 1917 to change the name of the Royal Household from the House of Saxe-Coburg-Gotha to the House of Windsor, Mr Stork started a similar (but unsuccessful) campaign to have Mecklenburg and Brunswick Squares renamed.

His undisguised hatred of the Huns notwithstanding, as a member of the local company of Volunteers (who drilled in our grounds on Saturday afternoons) he confessed to us his abhorrence of bayonet practice, even though it involved no more than bayoneting a truss of straw.

---

* A reference to a local baker's shop where Mrs Stork purchased her cakes.

He abhorred all forms of cruelty to animals. I recall an incident at the 1918 camp which was pitched in Shardeloes Park on the estate of Sir Walter Tyrwhitt-Drake. A team of men armed with shotguns was picking off rabbits as they scuttled out of a wheat field which was being harvested. As each rabbit turned its death somersault, a cheer would go up from the boys. Mr Stork walked up and down pointing out to us the sheer inequality of the battle. And at a later camp a group of senior boys was taken 'fox-cubbing'. Mr Stork was the only absentee from the male members of staff.

Incidentally, this proved to be my first and last experience of blood 'sports'. The hopelessly unfair odds, the spectacle of the master's neck and surrounding veins swelling to bursting point as he directed the blasts from his horn almost literally into the hounds' ears, the unbridled savagery of the hounds at the kill, and the sickening stench of the little victim's blood (which remained in my nostrils for months) were all so revolting as to cure me forever of following this brand of 'sport'. *

> Twould ring the bells of Heaven
> The wildest peal for years,
> If Parson lost his senses
> And people came to theirs,
> And he and they together
> Knelt down with angry prayers
> For tamed and shabby tigers
> And dancing dogs and bears,
> And wretched, blind pit ponies,
> And little hunted hares.
>   Ralph Hodgson

Although he was not versed in the art of string-pulling, Mr Stork would, I am sure, gladly have acted as Heaven's Bell-Ringer.

It was characteristic of the man that he should name his dogs after two of the Evangelists, Mark and John, and should jestingly rebuke his wife Alice (whose love of birds and animals equalled his own) for preparing an obvious surplus of communion bread.

He attended all our summer camps, when he assumed the double role of executive and spiritual head. It was he who drew up the Detail for the Day, mapped out and headed our 'long walks' (as opposed to 'town days' which meant only short walks), and supervised the general pattern the camp

---

* My son David once had hanging on his bedroom wall a Thelwell cartoon of a hunt in full cry, but in reverse order. The field was headed by the huntsmen, followed by the hounds, then the fox, and bringing up the rear was an infuriated bull. Mr Stork would have loved it.

should take. At the same time he never was so preoccupied as not to find time to fly his giant-sized box-kite. Having had children of my own, I hesistate to say whether this was for the children's amusement or for his own.

When in my early 40s, I took on the conductorship of a youth orchestra of 80 players, continuing in the position for the ensuing 23 years. It was during my last few years with the orchestra that I became more and more conscious of the gradual but every-widening gap between our respective ages — between the average age of the players (which, because of the annual turnover, remained at 18) and my own which, try as I would, refused to stand still.

At some point in his career, Mr Stork must have experienced this same feeling; but the ever-widening gap between his and the children's ages notwithstanding, his unerring faculty for entering into a child's mind accounted in large measure for his hold over us. It accounted for the success of his annual plays, for example. It accounted for the stimulation we derived from his conducted tours of London's historic buildings, such as St. Paul's Cathedral (where, with us, he climbed the great flights of stairs to the Dome and Whispering Gallery), the Tower of London, the British Museum and Westminster Abbey. And it was befitting that he should lead us past the body of the Unknown Warrior as it lay in state in Westminster Abbey.

Nor did his advancing years weaken his sense of fun. I should know, for I was once the victim of his good-natured brand of humour.

In 1921, the school cricket team had a bumper season. It won every one of its 'outside' fixtures and so headed the championship table. To celebrate this, the First XI was taken by Mr Stork to Madame Tussaud's. I was included in the outing by virtue of my position of official scorer. (Although I never made the First XI, I once scored 73 runs for the Second [or was it the Third?] XI against Brockham Green Boy Scouts.) As we entered the exhibition, Mr Stork called me out of line. Holding his forefinger to his lips (a characteristic 'hush' pose of his) he pressed a coin into my hand and whispered, "Nalden, would you kindly get me a programme?" The programme-seller was seated at a table, with one side of her face resting in her cupped hand. She appeared to be completely absorbed in her reading, which was aided by the light of a table lamp. Timidly, I asked her for a programme. Clearly, she was too absorbed in her reading to have heard me. I asked a second, and third time, but still no response. Plucking up courage, I touched her lightly on the shoulder, but again no reaction. I was by now blushing to the roots of my hair, and turning to Mr Stork in a mute appeal for guidance, I came face to face with the spectacle of the boys trying desperately hard to suppress their giggles. Mr Stork himself was shaking visibly with uncontrolled mirth. It slowly dawned upon me exactly where I was.

In June of the same year, Mr Stork took a party of us to Lords Cricket Ground to see a day's play in the England v Australia Second Test Match. That was the year when the Australian team lost only two of its 38 matches, and retained the Ashes by winning three, and drawing two, of the test series. But then England was without its Hobbs, who was out of cricket for most of the season — much to we 'Surrey-ites' ' dismay. The Australian team was captained by Warwick Armstrong (at 22 stone, the heaviest test cricketer ever to have been exported by Australia), and included the great pace bowlers Gregory and McDonald, the 'googly merchant' A.A. Mailey, and wicket-keeper W.A. Oldfield.

It was the test match in which the great left-handed all-rounder, F.E. Woolley (who played for Kent) was out within five runs of a century in his first innings, and within seven of it in his second innings. We saw him batting in his second innings, look nervously at the scoreboard at 93, and then — out. Sorry as I was for Woolley, I was even more sorry for the Gloucestershire player, Dipper. Dipper was chosen for his qualities as a batsman, but clearly not on the strength of his fielding. With each muffed take, a particularly vociferous critic (who was sitting near us) would angrily yell, "Stick 'im in the nursery 'nd chuck pom-poms at 'im!"

Other of England's players were the test series' two captains, the Hon. L.H. Tennyson (a nephew, I think, of the poet), the immaculate J.W.H.T. Douglas (who I seem to remember was drowned in a North Sea crossing), Surrey's great wicket-keeper, Herb Strudwick ('Struddy' to the crowd), and 'Patsy' Hendren of Middlesex, who was probably the most popular and entertaining cricketer of his day. 'Patsy' was certainly not selected for the England XI on the strength of his looks. Once, when fielding close to the boundary, a spectator complimented him with "Well fielded, monkey-face." To which Patsy retorted, "Me monkey-face? You wait till you see ---'s face when he comes out to bat."

Mr Stork had prepared us for this match in no less diligent a manner than he had prepared us for confirmation. He regaled us with the names and deeds of past cricketing giants such as W.G. Grace, Victor Trumper, Spofforth, 'Ranji', Jessop, C.B. Fry and the rest, and impressed upon us the sanctity of Lords Cricket Ground — the Mecca of cricketers and followers of the game from all over the world. Imagine his disgust, therefore, when a nearby party of schoolboys started vying with each other as to whose cork, from their shaken-up stone ginger-beer bottles, could hit the pavilion roof with the greatest force.

In those days, amateurs were distinguished from professionals on scoreboards and in the press by the inclusion of their initials — J.W.H.T. Douglas, P.G.H. Fender, against plain Hobbs and Sutcliffe. They were allotted separate dressing rooms, and all county and test match elevens were captained exclusively by amateurs. I believe it was the *Daily Express* which struck the first blow at the roots of this antiquated social distinction by announcing its intention of prefixing all cricketers' names, amateur and professional alike, with their initials. It was an English County XI which brought to light the most odd double-barrelled name I ever encountered — the name being Rought-Rought, which, to say the least, had a decided ring of in-breeding about it.

Although it deviates from the main story, I must relate the anecdote of how a New Zealander dealt with a somewhat similar case of class-consciousness. The small North Island township of Kerikeri had managed to attract as permanent residents a posse of retired British Army officers, Colonial Service administrators, and planters. Within the course of time, a plate appeared on one resident's gate announcing (let's call him) Brigadier-General Knatchbull-Taillyour. The plate was smartly removed, so the story goes, when some few days later a plate appeared on a near neighbour's gate announcing Lance-Corporal Stiggins, Royal New Zealand Artillery.

To return, those were the cricketing days when such tactics as body-line bowling, bouncers and leg-theories had yet to be introduced; when Somerset's wicketkeeper, the Rev. A.P. Wickham, could testify that in Dr Grace's mammoth innings of 288 runs (incidentally his 100th century in first-class cricket), the great W.G. allowed only four balls to pass his bat. A far cry from today's all-too-familiar commentary 'outside the off-stump — no stroke'. The very fact that over a half-century later I can recall those 1921 test match incidents points to it as being one of my childhood's dream days. It was.

Once a week, Mr Stork took each class in scripture. These sessions were not straight-out readings from the Bible. Instead, he would select a small group of boys and allot them characters. Scriptural stories thus developed into embryonic plays. As producer, Mr Stork himself would demonstrate the action, as for example, St. Paul appearing before Agrippa:

> And Paul said, I would to God, that not only thou,
> but also all that hear me this day, were both almost,
> and altogether such as I am, except these bonds.
> (Acts. Ch. 26, v.29)

At the words 'except these bonds', Mr Stork would move as though attempting to extend his arms heavenwards, to be sharply reminded by his shackled wrists of his prisoner status.

He enjoyed the joke as much as any of us when a boy named Rowlands, in reading aloud the 1st Psalm, recited in somewhat desultory fashion:

> But his delight is in the law of the Lord: and in his law will he execute himself day and night.

I would hesitate to ascribe to Mr Stork the epithet 'popular'. He was somehow too large a personality to be termed that. One could not imagine his being out to court popularity. He would have been the first to warn us that the person who courts popularity runs the very real risk of winning his fellows' contempt.

I see him now as the greatest single influence in the hospital, as a man who would not yield an inch were a principle involved, no matter how severe the pressure, and how illustrious the opposition (and there were some illustrious personages on the board of governors).

A fitting epitaph might have been 'He loved the children, who in turn loved him'.

The Foundling Hospital Chapel, John Sanders, 1773.

13: Services in the chapel

I found in a diary I kept at that period an account of a Sunday morning in the Foundling Chapel. I wrote:

> The iron gates opened at 10.30 and I climbed with many companions up dark passages into the gallery that runs round the chapel. Soon the children trooped in — all in order, looking neither to the right nor the left, every little boy in a short jacket and red waistcoat, with a starched Eton collar; every girl in a black dress and speckless white apron and white cap. On both sides of the organ they ranged themselves — below the girls with a mistress, and behind the boys with a master. I saw no signal, but there must have been one, for suddenly every small bullet head bent forward and touched the wooden rail in front, and every spotless apron covered every spotless face, and every girl too leant forward, face in apron, apparently to pray for God's blessing on humanity in general and foundlings in particular.

> Meanwhile the body of the church was filling up with a well-dressed crowd, intent on watching the rows of children, all appearing at a distance as alike as layers of matches in a box of Bryant & May's. If we looked further we saw differences; there were foundlings with glasses, there was even one foundling who smiled, and some who wore a red badge in token of their superior behaviour and their function of keeping the less well-behaved in order. "Terribly alike, they are," I whispered to my neighbour — a man with a fair moustache and kindly foolish face. "Oh yes,"

he said, "just like a lot of soldiers, aren't they?" "Yes" I said, "ghastly, isn't it?" But he only looked astonished.

Then came hymns, and three hundred small voices sang of 'the home for little children, beyond the bright blue sky'.

(Kingsley Martin, Father Figures, pp. 150-1)

The hospital organist in my day was Dr H. Davan Wetton, who held office from 1892 until April, 1926. He presided at the organ on the occasion of the farewell service in the chapel in that year, when the crowd who wished to gain admission equalled those witnessed at the performance of *Messiah* in the days of Handel.[1] A native of Brighton (where he was born in 1862) Dr Wetton became in turn acting organist of Wells Cathedral, and assistant to the organist of Westminster Abbey, a position he held for 15 years. Dr Wetton was an articled pupil of Sir Frederick ('Westminster') Bridge. He took the degree of Doctor in Music at the University of Durham, known at one time in musical circles as 'the poor man's university', being one of the few universities to open its doors to external students.

Dr Wetton was never otherwise than charming, affable, and impeccably groomed. On Sunday mornings he would arrive for the eleven o'clock service dressed in full morning attire, with top-hat and spats rounding off his extreme ends.

His genial suavity, with its suggestion of an easy-going manner, went together with his fixed smile through tightly-closed lips. He walked with a slightly rolling gait, a characteristic of his particular brand of self-assurance. This outward display of self-confidence he managed to infuse into the children's choir, so that he could always expect a ready response and full co-operation.

At the same time the boys would sometimes take advantage of his apparent geniality, and rag him unmercifully. He once threatened to report a boy named Morton. "What is your name?" he demanded as angrily as his normally unruffled calm would allow. "Dryon, Sir." "What a curious coincidence, Dryon; I'm a Wet'n and you're a Dry'n." Such flashes of anger were rare and short-lived, and his oft-repeated threat to report a boy never did materialise.

When I first entered the ooys' school, the children's choir for Sunday morning services was augmented by a professional mixed choir, made up of two women's, and two men's voices. It meant that the children, ably led by the solo quartet, were able to participate in anthems and settings of the *Te Deum, Jubilate* and *Benedictus*.

My sole recollection of this group's contribution is the bass duet from Handel's *Israel in Egypt* which, like a great deal of other music sung in the chapel, had a habit of cropping up at regular intervals. The boys looked forward to this particular anthem in 'glishful' anticipation, regarding it as a good morning's entertainment. Straightway let me confess that the reason for its popularity was not a musical one.

When singing this aria, the two male singers in the quartet inserted an aspirate among the vowel sounds ('the intrusive h'), so that instead of coming out like this (which normally it would have done):

the intrusive h' technique resulted in its coming out like this:

It was just as though the two bass singers were enjoying a huge and immensely funny joke between themselves. That we should be expected to adopt our 'inchurchiest expression' (to borrow a Shavian phrase) whilst listening to the Brobdingnagian chuckles of the 1st Bass being replied to by the gargantuan chuckles of the 2nd Bass and vice-versa, was expecting just that little bit too much of a bunch of otherwise angelic-faced chapel-disciplined schoolboys. Our furtively-exchanged glances and barely suppressed sniggers were hardly a compliment to the composer, who, after all had been our greatest benefactor. But I'm not so sure that the great Handel himself would not have chuckled at the comic effect produced by the intrusive H in this particular aria. It need only to have been performed with the basses wearing Old Testament costume (for *Israel* like other of Handel's oratorios is little removed stylistically from his operas) to have been uproariously funny. For days after each time it was sung, the boys' playroom would resound with 'The Lord is a man of War-haw-haw-haw-haw-haw-haw-haw' etc. And so it became a matter of deep regret to us all when in 1917, exactly 90 years after its establishment, our professional choir was abolished.

Happily, the disbanding of the special choir did not affect our singing of anthems, which we loved doing. The boys' favourites were *Let the bright Seraphim* and *O had I Jubal's lyre,* which traditionally were sung on the two Sundays preceding our departure for the annual summer camp. Other favourites with us were Mendelssohn's settings of Psalm 121, *Lift thine eyes,* Isaiah 60, vv. 1,2, *But the Lord is mindful of his own,* Handel's *Waft her Angels,* and *How beautiful are the feet of them that preach the Gospel of Peace,* and the same composer's *Angels ever Bright and Fair.*

When singing this anthem, we supplemented the text with an interpolation of our own:

It was one of several gunnery terms we had picked up from the Royal Artillery who were then training in our grounds.

My own favourite anthem was Handel's *O Lovely Peace* from *Judas Maccabeus.*

At some time during his years as organist, Dr Wetton introduced the special carol services, when the chapel would be packed. For these services our choir would be supplemented by a small group of boy soloists, loaned for the occasion by James Bates (1856-?), Director and Founder of the London

College for Choristers, and acknowledged in his day as England's foremost trainer of boys' voices.

Yet who today remembers even the name James Bates? Pitifully few, I would say; such is fame, ephemeral and quickly forgotten. My personal yardstick for assessing the quality of voices trained by James Bates was a comparison of his results with the voice of Ernest Lough, whose recordings came out a year or two after I had left the hospital. My view then was that not a few Bates-trained voices were every bit as beautiful.

Beautiful though these carol services were, the service which made the deepest and most lasting impression on me was confirmation. My youthful impressions were probably emotional rather than spiritual. It may have been the solemnity of the occasion, or the moving spectacle of the children as they went one by one to the altar rail for the bishop's laying on of hands, or perhaps the subdued singing of the very beautiful confirmation hymn *Come Holy Ghost,* whose faintly modal harmonies fell so strangely upon our untrained ears. Whatever the reason, for me confirmation was the most impressive service in the Church's year.

A few days after being confirmed, candidates were invited by Mr and Mrs Stork to their home in Mecklenburgh Square — boys on one night and girls on another. These parties always commenced after dark, so that Mr Stork could assemble us on the pavement outside his home and give us an illustrated (and extraordinarily interesting) lesson in astronomy. By rights and intention this should have marked the party's climax, but it did not; for us, the climax came when Balfour's oven-fresh buns were produced.

The chapel organ stood in the west gallery, flanked on either side by the children. The youngest boys and girls were seated in the front row, and immediately behind them the very seniors, who by long-standing tradition took it upon themselves to prod the smaller children into action should they fail to sit bolt upright, or hesitate either to stand or sit at the appropriate times.* The north, south, and east wings of the gallery, and the whole of the ground floor, were allotted to the congregation.**

There were two pulpits (one really a reader's desk) which were occupied throughout the service by the school chaplain and the guest preacher. At

---

* Thus Hannah Brown's experience — 'The recollection of my first Sunday at Church is very vivid. What a terrible ordeal it was. The babies were placed in the first row of the Chapel — the bigger girls behind them: and, in those days, we sat the whole of the service through and were not allowed to move. As we were not able to keep awake, the big girls would thump us in the back every time we nodded, and punish us the next day." *The Child She Bare*, p.20.

** My own generation, mercifully, was spared the terrifying form of punishment meted out to our erring 18th century counterparts, girls and boys alike, when the recess on the north side of the organ was fitted up as a place of solitary confinement. Children incarcerated in this airless 'Dark Room' were restricted to a diet of bread and water. It was put into operation shortly following the publication of a pamphlet extolling the benefits of solitary confinement, the brainchild of that otherwise humanitarian-philanthropical Governor, Jonas Hanway.

morning service the preacher faced the congregation with his back to the children. Because of this, sermons were mainly lost on us.

By way of a diversion we would browse in furtive fashion through the *Book of Common Prayer,* whose opening three clauses of *A Table of Kindred and Affinity* seldom failed to spark off a spate of nudgings and sniggerings —

A Man may not marry his
1. Grandmother
2. Grandfather's wife
3. Wife's Grandmother —

for naive and uninitiated though we may have been, these solemn prohibitions appeared to us as something of a redundancy and quite comical.

The sermons were wholly lost on Dr Wetton who, borrowing a page from the illustrious Samuel Sebastian Wesley's book, invariably would disappear at the preacher's words "In the Name of the Father, the Son, and the Holy Ghost" to swing his legs back over the organ bench at the valediction in time (but only just) to accompany the amen.

The afternoon service was essentially for the children. The preacher now faced the children, with his back to the congregation. The theme of many of Mr Stork's sermons was based on the Parable of the Talents (Matthew 25). 'The higher you aim the higher you get' was a phrase of his which became as familiar to us as the words of the Lord's Prayer. And in the autumn of each year, when children of sufficiently ripe years were about to leave the calm waters of the hospital for the tempestuous seas beyond, Mr Stork would liken them to so many 'little boats about to leave harbour'.

We enjoyed having the occasional guest preacher, especially the Rev. Hall, who in his youth had been an amateur boxer. After regaling us with stories of his victories, he would come to the moral of it all (the part we enjoyed least); "I couldn't have won those fights had I not first trained my body. Neither will you win the Fight of Life unless you first train your spiritual bodies. And now to God the Father ... ."

And then there was dear old 'Dust Pan and Handbrush', a mumbling, but kindly old bore, even in the eyes of the children. "This great hospital was built patiently, brick by brick, and the little bits left over were swept up by dust-pan and handbrush. And so with your characters, which you must build up patiently bit by bit ... ."

The most solemn moment of the children's services (which even at my tender age moved me profoundly) was when Mr Stork announced the names of old boys killed in the War — 'Percy Alford, George English, Joseph

Furniss, Robert Oxford, Charles Daintree', with the roll continuing to lengthen as the war gained in ferocity and beastliness. We would stand, Mr Stork would face the altar, and Dr Wetton would play *The Dead March* from *Saul*. At these times an awesome stillness seemed to descend upon the chapel, the like of which I have never experienced since, not even during the silence on Armistice Day.

Uncharacteristically dropping his guard, Dr Wetton once bustled into a choir practice, excitedly breaking the news to us that he had submitted an entry for the Royal Air Force Official March Competition.* He composed a fine bracing tune, very much a product of the Dr Wetton of the ever-so-slightly rolling gait:

Fine march though it undoubtedly was, the entry submitted by Sir Walford Davies (later, Master of the King's Music) was adjudged to be finer still, and to this day remains the official march of the Royal Air Force.

It is unlikely that Dr Wetton's main source of income came from his Foundling Hospital appointment. Like most other church and cathedral organists,** he would have needed to supplement it by way of teaching, examining and adjudicating at music competitions.

One of Dr Wetton's pupils was named Griffiths. He was immensely popular with the senior boys, not by virtue of his prowess as an organist (which we were not in a position to assess, anyway), but because of his passing on to us his copies of the current week's *Magnet, Sexton Blake* and *Nelson Lee* library. All transactions had to be carried out furtively, as 'Digger' Holgate strongly disapproved of us reading 'blood and thunders'

---

* The Royal Flying Corps and the Royal Naval Air Service were united in 1918 into the independent Royal Air Force.

** The successful cinema organist of the 2nd and 3rd decades of the present century could earn more in a week than most church and cathedral organists earned in a year. I seem to recall Sir Malcolm Sargent turning down an offer of £ 7000 a year from the New Gallery Cinema, which would have involved him in some three or four personal appearances each day at the console of the cinema's 'Mighty Wurlitzer'. Perhaps it was that Sir Malcolm blenched at the idea of adopting the name Reginald, the 'in' name for the successful cinema organist — Reginald Foort, Reginald Dixon, Reginald New, Reginald Stone, and so on. 'Dr Reginald Sargent' doesn't sound right, somehow.

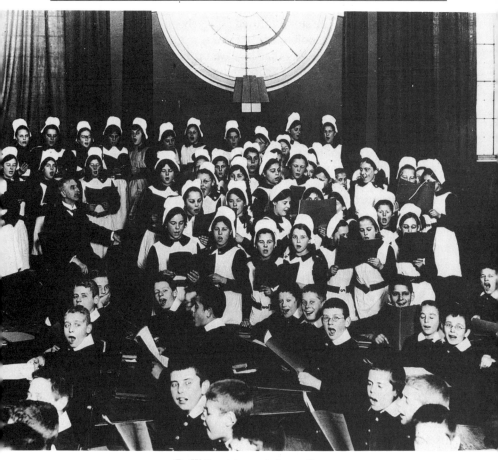

Dr Wetton takes a choir practice.

and 'penny dreadfuls' as he sourly termed them. We were thus inducted by Griffiths into the envied world of *Nelson Lee's St.* Frank's School as related by 'Tec Lee's resourceful schoolboy assistant, Nipper. We followed avidly week by week the swiftly declining fortunes of the Honourable Douglas Daryll Cyril Singleton, who but for Nelson Lee would have gambled away a personal fortune of £250,000; also the gourmandising feats of Fatty Little (the St. Frank's counterpart of Greyfriars's Billy Bunter), the sartorial elegance of Sir Montmorency Tregellis-West, who was forever screwing in his eye-glass; the caddish behaviour of Fullwood, Gulliver and Bell, three bounders of the Remove, and the blustering, belligerent, but lovable Handforth.

One of the *Nelson Lee* stories proved strangely prophetic. Jerry Dodds (probably the greatest schoolboy cricketer ever) was sent to St. Frank's from Australia. One condition was that he gave up his cricket; he was at St. Frank's for an English Public School education — not to play cricket. However, a series of good reports on his school work decided his father to lift the ban, when Jerry immediately set about sending at least five out of each six-ball over to (if not over) the boundary fence, so that he seldom left the crease before notching up a double-century. Less than three years after the appearance of this serialised 'yarn', 'Boy' Bradman (as one British newspaper dubbed him) entered into his long period of breaking the hearts of our British bowlers.

Simultaneously, Griffiths's generosity introduced us to life at Greyfriars School; to Mr Quelch of the Remove, to Billy Bunter, the fat Owl of the Remove, who, when not gorging, was forever yelling 'Leggo!', 'Yarooh!' and 'Oops!'; to Fisher T. Fish the dollar-minded American ('Yep! that's a deal'); to the Sixth Formers, Bullstrode, Wingate and Co.; to Coker of the Fifth, and to the friends of the Remove, Bob Cherry, Harry Nugent and Wharton; and to Timothy ('Admitted, my dear Sir') Tucker; to all those lavish midnight feeds in the dorm.; the strolling arm-in-arm around the 'Quad'; and the continual 'cutting' of 'prep'. And of course to the monocled dandy, Arthur Augustus D'Arcy (the swell of St Jim's), who had inherited the 19th Century cavalry officer's affectation of sounding R's as W's — 'I'm fwightfully sowwy dear boy'; and not forgetting the over-polite Hurree Jamset Ram Singh, the Indian student, and Mrs Mimble of the tuck shop.

I'm afraid author Frank Richards lost the confidence I had placed in him and ceased being one of my heroes when, many years later, I discovered his powerful drama (in which Bob Cherry was wrongfully expelled for allegedly stealing a chum's five-shilling postal order) to be a direct crib from the case of the Winslow Boy.

One over-zealous of our number came very close to ruining our literary diversions in the following manner. The back covers of boys' magazines displayed advertisements which were designed to appeal especially to their young readers. 'Boys!' (challenged one advertiser) 'Own your own Shocking Coil'; and another, 'Know what is going on behind as well as in front of you, with the aid of one of our world-famous See-Backcroscopes'; 'Superior Printing Outfits consisting of Letters, Points and Ornaments, a Typeholder, supply of Ink, Pad and Tweezers.'

But the advertisement which very nearly put paid to our arrangement with Griffiths took a somewhat different, and more generous line. 'All you need do is to fill in the coupon and post it to us together with a Postal Order for 1/6d. This is to cover the cost of despatching to you one of our world-famed 17-jewelled pocket watches, complete with second hand and luminous dial which is absolutely free. You must send now as we cannot possibly repeat this generous offer.'

Unfortunately for the boy who fell for this, the watch (which actually did arrive) was intercepted by 'Digger', who clearly smelled a rat. He read the firm's reply to the assembled school (we were in the dining hall) taking pains to expose the unhappy victim to public ridicule. "Dear Sir" the reply ran, "may we congratulate you upon being the possessor of one of our world-famed pocket watches, which, as you will see, is equipped with second hand and luminous dial. You will also see that the handsome chain in genuine EPNS is permanently attached to the watch, which, as an added service, we do as a safety measure for our customers' benefit. You will appreciate that we are thus unable to sell either watch or chain as separate articles. If you will therefore kindly remit to us the sum of 15/- for the chain, both watch and chain will become yours!' The watch and (permanently attached) chain were returned, and the embarrassed victim, who unwittingly had provided the school with its loudest laugh for many a year, was spared further chastisement.

Once I left school, I lost track of Griffiths completely. For all I know he may have become a famous church, or even cathedral, organist. But looking back on the whole episode of *Magnets, Nelson Lees,* and *Sexton Blakes,* I cannot escape the feeling that it was somehow an incongruity for a potentially serious musician to be so ardent a devotee of this type of literature. For let us be frank, Johann Sebastian Bach and Bessie Bunter (Billy's equally famous sister) were most queer bedfellows. But thank you all the same, Griffiths, for the happiness you brought us.

At morning service the first lesson was read by one of the governors, generally Governor Percival Etheridge. To the boys Mr Etheridge was distinguished from his fellow governors by the sheer magnificence of his chauffeur-driven Daimler, whose exterior had the appearance of wicker-basket work. His reading of the lessons was upheld by Mr Gray as a model of style and elegance, and he would exhort us to mould our own diction and mode of delivery on the example set by Mr Etheridge. Mr Gray's exhortations were tendered in all good faith, and for our good; so that it was singularly unfortunate when he once found himself caught up in a moral dilemma. It happened during one of our Tuesday morning Bible reading sessions.

"Open your Bibles to Numbers, Chapter 22. Each boy will read a verse out loud.'' All went well until we came to verse 30 —

> 'And the ass said unto Balaam, Am I not thine ass, upon which though hast ridden ever since I was thine unto this day?'

This provoked the whole class into synchronised laughter.

"How dare you, Willis! How dare you!" demanded Mr Gray angrily.

"Well Sir, you did say that we were to copy Mr Etheridge.'' Hence Mr Gray's moral dilemma; for Mr Etheridge pronounced the word 'ass' to rhyme with 'pass'.

The hospital's method of taking the collection was peculiar to itself. In its earliest days, four governors carrying white wands passed up and down the centre aisle of the chapel after prayers and just before the sacrament began, while a foundling boy and girl passed along each row with plates to receive the collection. In my own day, one of the hospital's clerical staff, attended by two of the boys, stood at the chapel entrance. The offertory plate was placed on a waist-high pedestal, and visitors were expected to make their contributions before entering the chapel. An exceptionally generous contribution would be acknowledged by the donor being escorted into the chapel by one of the boys, who would pass him over to the verger (presumably for extra special attention), although I could never bring myself to any definite conclusion as to what form this favoured treatment could take.

Whether boys were chosen for this duty by virtue of their alms-hungry looks, or as particularly piteous symbols of charity, I cannot say; but I myself held the position of chapel boy during my last two years at the hospital, and gloried in every moment of it. And summoning all the humility and modesty at my command, I make the confession that my angelic countenance and look of unsullied innocence was such as to have found its way into the deep pockets of the great Duke of Westminster himself had he been one of our chapel-goers.

I can only conjecture the reason for the hospital's quaint system of chapel collections. It may have been a case of twice bitten, thrice shy.

Numbers of bad halfpennies were finding their way into the collection plates, which prompted the committee, in the December of 1795, to notify people attending chapel that henceforth nothing less than a silver contribution would be expected of them. Even this could not have produced the desired effect, for two months later the committee decided to ban halfpennies from chapel collections. Some two decades later it was not bad halfpennies, but base coinage, which was finding its way into the collection plates. In 1812 this averaged £10 per month over the first five months of that year.

Of one fact I can be more positive; it is, that no dud halfpennies were passed during my two years at the chapel door; for how could anyone, even the most compassionless of mortals, have contributed anything less

Demolition of the Foundling Hospital chapel, c. 1927

than a fiver when beholding a face so full of human and alms-hungry appeal as mine?

In general, Sundays were pretty mournful affairs. Sport in any form was forbidden, so should it be fine, we would walk round and round the cricket pitch in little knots engaging each other in conversation. One particularly keen band member named Stanway solved his Sunday afternoon problem by pacing up and down the road on his own, mentally going through the 'fingering' of scales on his imaginary euphonium. When wet, we would be confined to the playroom, where we would sit on our lockers (which lined the playroom walls) reading the pamphlets supplied to us in liberal quantities by the SPCK or the Religious Tract Society, or playing chess and draughts.

The solitary exception was the Sunday before our annual summer camp. We named it Dolman Sunday. On that Sunday, both before, between and after chapel, small knots of excited, 'glishing jolly thick' boys would parade round and round the cricket pitch, discussing with each other their plans for camp, the amount of pocket money they had saved, how they planned spending it, and so on. Some boys would creep up behind others and attempt to 'Dolman' on them — that is, to overhear their plans. Anybody caught in so dishonest a practice would be sneered at as a dirty little Dolman, and remain socially ostracised for the remaining days before camp.

FOOTNOTES TO CHAPTER 13

[1] Nichols and Wray, p.232.

Mrs Alfred (Hannah) Betts (left) and the author, August 1923

The author in hospital camp uniform.

14: *Annual summer camp*

Once 'Dolman Sunday' was behind us, we counted the days remaining before camp on the fingers of one hand. It is difficult to put into words our feelings as each summer camp approached. By the time Dolman Sunday came round, we had been hemmed in on all sides for the best part of 11 months, our only live contacts with the outside world being the occasional outing (such as to a Christmas pantomime), the disagreeable personality of the man who delivered our bread ('Chibnall's Bread, Baked in Hot Air Ovens'), and the daily goings-on beyond those 100 or so yards of railings which opened up to us the vista of parts of Guilford and Lamb's Conduit Streets.

With the approach of each summer camp, we knew in our minds just what we were looking forward to — the train journey; the simple pleasures of a walk through an English wood; renewed acquaintance with the foxgloves and the wild strawberries; the lulling drone of bees and insects on a hot summer's afternoon; being let loose for an hour's spending spree in some quiet market town; the traditional currant bread for the Sunday tea meal; the exchange of our hot stuffy uniforms for khaki shorts and shirts, and our thick crested china for enamel-ware, which (to the temporary relief of washers-up) was 'Count-the-Lambs' proof; living under canvas for six whole weeks; the early morning combination of mist and dew which we came to recognise as being the harbingers of a fine day; the informality of the Sunday hip-bath and the outdoor games which commenced before breakfast and went on until dusk; the relaxed attitudes of the staff, and, for the occupants of ward B3, six glorious weeks free from the tyranny of Nurse Dovey.

It was considered a great privilege to be included in the camp advance party. This was made up of Mr Holgate (in charge), a few stalwarts from the maintenance staff such as 'Bruno' Bruns, and a few of the senior boys. The seniors' job was to have everything in readiness before the arrival of the main party, which meant three or four days' hard, but stimulating, work. It meant stuffing some 500 palliasses and pillows with straw, sorting the same number of kitbags and assigning them to their respective marquees, unpacking and washing a like number of enamel mugs and plates, helping erect the tents and so on.

Even though the work was rewarding in itself, the advance party's traditional reward was a 'spending' day in town; and this in addition to the privileged experience of enjoying the most carefree few days we had known since our admission to the hospital. Once the main party arrived members of the advance party let it be known, and in no uncertain fashion, that so far as they were concerned, camp had already come to an end; an utterly selfish, but understandable, attitude.

The daily morning prayer sessions were conducted by Mr Stork, who on these occasions did not intone them, but adopted a more intimate style, more as the father of a very large and young family — which he was.

We were now free to spend our accumulated year's savings when Mr Stork's 'Detail for the Day' posted on the camp notice board announced a walk to town. We made a bee-line for the things we had been deprived of for so long, the most popular of these being jellies, ice-cream, sweets of every variety and broken biscuits (a far more economical purchase than whole ones). Our good resolutions to eke out our purchases were soon broken, a goodly proportion of these being safely in our stomachs and on the way to being digested well before our arrival back in camp. Even jellies disappeared in this way, for in those days they were processed in the form of concentrated gelatine cubes, quite unlike the crystals of today.

One enterprising boy named Jimmy Deacon, determined to learn to play the piano (the total lack of practice facilities notwithstanding), blew most of his savings on a 'Teach Yourself' piano tutor. It included a full-length paper reproduction of a piano keyboard, which folded up in concertina fashion. Back in camp, Jimmy would 'practise' his scales and other technique for hours on end. My greatest school friend, Charles K..., blew a large part of his savings (2/6d to be precise) on a copy of *Love in Lilac Time,* a song which we had learnt from the previous year's Christmas pantomime.

The 1918 camp was pitched in Shardeloes Park, on the estate of Squire Tyrwhitt-Drake, just outside the lovely Buckinghamshire town of Amersham. Our walks took us to the neighbouring towns of Chesham and

High Wycombe — a stretch of about seven miles. I think the squire must have contracted polio, for he had a withered arm. So we were shown over the manor house by his son, when we were each given a tomato from the greenhouse, and a freshly-baked bun from the manor's own bakery. Our tour of the house took us through the billiards room, where Mr Tyrwhitt-Drake Junior, succumbing to our inquisitive entreaties, gave us a demonstration of the very game we were cautioned to avoid. The game of billiards, we were told, was the first step down the slippery slope taken by Hogarth's famous, or infamous, Rake.

The camp ended in near-disaster. The boys' tents were pitched on the periphery of the field, and sited under a belt of ancient beech trees. On the very last night, the whole camp was awakened by a series of ear-splitting crackles, followed by what sounded like a clap of thunder, reminding us sharply of the air raids which we had temporarily forgotten. One of the beech trees had come down and landed squarely on the senior boys' tent, injuring several boys, one quite seriously. Rescue work was carried out by the light of hurricane lamps, the injured being moved to the hospital tent, with the remaining occupants of the wrecked tent doubling up the best they could in other boys' beds.

The final day of all camps was wrapped in the deepest gloom; and the thought of having to readjust to the rigid discipline of our London home always was an upsetting one. Then there were Mr Stork's ill-timed quips such as "We'll all take a long walk to High Wycombe." Such quips were greeted with our sickliest of sickly smiles. Bad taste on Mr Stork's part, we voted it.

It will thus be appreciated that it was a particularly crestfallen procession which marched out of camp on the day following the accident. The mood of dejection was heightened by the monotonous tramp of 500 pairs of sullen feet, which normally would have been enlivened by the strains of the school band; but the casualties had put the band temporarily out of action. It was as though the whole camp had 'got monk', and I'll wager that the sight of our mournful procession as it approached Amersham Station was in itself sufficient to have sent the local undertaker into chaste ecstacies of delight.

The more seriously injured boy had already been earmarked for enlistment in the Band of the Royal Scots Greys. His enlistment was delayed until near his 16th birthday — an unprecedented age still to be 'hanging around' school.

The 1919 camp was pitched on Lord Hambledon's estate at Henley-on-Thames, and sited in a field opposite Statue Island, hard by the banks of the Thames. My friend, Charles K.... (ever a romantic) promptly fell in love with the Lord's ravishingly beautiful daughter Peggy. It led to Charles writing a short story in which he, naturally enough, was the hero, and 'Peggy Dearest' the heroine. The story involved our young hero in bouts of delirium and ghoulish nightmares (the direct result of his rescuing Peggy from drowning), which, by comparison, made the macabre dreams of the opium-eating lover of Berlioz's *Symphonie Fantastique* appear about as hair-raising as the Queen's tantrums in *Alice in Wonderland*. The ending of the story found the re-united lovers locked in fond embrace, 'the only witness to the scene being the sun which was sinking slowly in the west'.

The weather proved idyllic, and the riverside scenery, together with the constant movement of river craft of every description, provided for us a kaleidoscope-like interest the whole day long.

A special and personal treat came from Mr Gray, who rowed two of us from camp to beautiful Henley Bridge, capping the outing with a sumptuous afternoon tea, which we enjoyed in the dream-like setting of a riverside tea garden.

A frequent visitor to camp was a Captain Gribble, a resident of Henley, who had served during the war with the Royal Engineers. Captain Gribble assumed the role of camp entertainer. The camp piano was dragged out of the marquee into the open, when the captain proceeded to entertain us with songs, acting as his own accompanist.

His favourite song went something like this:

> The Boys will call me Aubrey
> When I'm in my Sunday clothes,
> The Girls will yell out 'Strawberry'
> Right under the tip of my nose, etc.

His particular brand of entertainment must have administered a nasty shock to the piano's nervous system, for its exclusive role hitherto was that of accompanying the hymns at Sunday services. But for us boys, it proved a pleasant way of idling away a drowsy summer's afternoon.

Just before setting out on one shopping expedition, we were all lined up and Captain Gribble moved slowly along our ranks, presenting us each with a newly-minted sixpence. To the onlooker it may have smacked faintly of charity; but charity or no charity, it failed to evoke the voice of protest from any of us, for the purchasing power of a sixpence in those days equalled three bars of Sharp's Super Kreemy Toffee, a pair of Phillips's screw-on rubber heels, one and a half Mars Bars, two to three pounds of broken biscuits, an Everready torch battery, one and a half Rowntree's jellies, one copy each of *Magnet, Sexton Blake* and *Nelson Lee* (or *Rainbow,*

Comic Cuts and *Bubbles,* should you be a Bottom Yarder*), a pound at least of apples, pears or plums, a tin of solidified brilliantine, and six penny, or three tupp'ny ice creams. With such a magnificently varied choice open to us, was it likely that any one of us would scream 'charity!'? Hardly!

The climax to the camp was a trip on the Thames in a specially chartered launch from Henley to Wallingford. It was also something of an historic occasion, for it marked the first time that boys and girls had shared an outing, and had been permitted to mix freely. Clearly, it was an economy measure, for never again during my time at the hospital was there any similar relaxation of the old 18th century rule relating to the segregation of the sexes.

All in all, I look back upon Henley-on-Thames as the most idyllic camp of all. Indeed, the year 1919 proved a happy one in several other respects, not the least being my advancement to ward B2; for it meant that I was out of the hands of Nurse Dovey for ever. The peace celebrations of July 19 were marked by a whole day's holiday, and although we were sad to see them go, the Royal Artillery vacated our grounds, which allowed the girls' playing area to be restored to its former condition. And in Guilford Street and Langham Place, the barrel-organs started up once again, churning out *When Irish Eyes are Smiling, The Bells of St Mary's* and *Roses of Picardy.*

The one ugly blot on the year was when we resumed wearing our starched collars on all seven days of the week.

For the 1920 camp we had a change of county, from Oxfordshire to Surrey. We camped on farmland adjacent to Brockham Green, to me one of England's loveliest and least spoilt of villages. The approach to the village takes one over a charming old bridge, which is so narrow as to restrict entry to the Green to all but the smallest of vehicles. It stands as a bastion, as though barring the way to the invasion of 20th century ugliness, which in 1920 was already on the march. Once the bridge bids you 'Pass, Friend' the village opens up in all its beauty. Its dominating feature, I suppose, is the church, which was built and dedicated in 1847 as a memorial to the work of Henry Goulburn (1786-1856) who was Chancellor of the Exchequer and Home Secretary. In the centre of the Green itself is the well, from which villagers once drew their water. The little general store, tucked away in the far corner of the green, was run by a Mr Sherlock, and later by his niece, Ida Sherlock, with whom (unbeknown to her) I promptly fell in love.

---

* One of our social distinctions. The upper set of lavatories were for the exclusive use of boys in B1 hence Top Yarders, a privilege they guarded jealously. All other boys, B2, B3 and B4, used the lower set, hence Bottom Yarders.

To complete the picture of this almost too idyllic setting in rural England was the village smithy, whose forge in those days was kept extremely busy.

A little beyond the general store was ivy-covered Elm Grove Farm House, and it was on this farm that our camp was pitched. Finally, there was the spacious village green itself which has been witness to many a delightful weekend game of cricket.

I am able to describe Brockham Green in such detail, as its quiet beauty lured me back for a short stay in 1931, and again in 1960 and 1970 when I was on sabbatical leave from New Zealand. And I still gaze nostalgically at the five snapshots I took during my visit of 1931.

Towards the end of camp, our school band gave a concert in the spacious vicarage grounds to an audience of parishioners. In his speech of thanks, the Vicar, the Reverend Cooke, expressed agreeable surprise that none of the local orchards had been raided. That year's Harvest Thanksgiving Service, and more particularly the Harvest hymn's lines —

　　　Behold the bending orchards
　　　With bounteous fruit are crowned.
must have taken on an added and more meaningful significance.

Indeed, so unsullied were our reputations that one woman, who owned an extensive orchard, invited a party of boys to take away as many windfall apples as our capacious laundry baskets could hold. As we were filling them, word was whispered round that our benefactress was an ex-convict. I should explain that the entire female members of our hospital staff sported literally masses of hair, which, after the fashion of the times, and with the utmost ease, could have nested a brace of young eagles. But this woman's hair was short; very short, in fact. We learned later that this was a revolutionary hair styling known as the Bob. The Bob, together with the short skirt and flat chest, were to become the distinguishing marks of the 'flapper' of the 1920s.

It was during this camp that I was selected to play for our Second XI against the Brockham Green Cubs, scoring those immortal 73 runs. 'Shhh', murmured Umpire Stork, 'You've never been seen with a cricket bat in your hand before, and you come out and score 73 runs.' At this distance of time, I can afford to be honest about it. The Cubs' bowling was so weak that not a few of their balls failed to travel the full 22 yards' distance. And so it was agreed that the Cubs borrow a couple of the opposition's bowlers (i.e. the Foundling boys' XI), when I was promptly dimissed LBW off a ball from one of our boys named Hilton.

The great craze in children's toys during that era was the Diabolo. This was a two-headed top which was made to revolve by means of a piece of

string attached at each of its ends to a stick (O.E.D. Diabolo = Devil on two sticks). The art of the Diabolo was not only to spin it, but to catapault it high into the air and catch it on the string on its return. Our most expert diaboloist could maintain an unbroken sequence of several hundred throws.

During the entire six-weeks' camp, the weather remained fine, for this was the year of the Great Drought, when not even the mighty *Daily Express* (whose gunners fired salvo after salvo of maroons at the blameless heavens) — when not even the *Daily Express* could intimidate the Almighty into turning on His Great Tap. The whole episode must be counted as one of that paper's more magnificent failures.

With the frightful spell of weather which dogged our 1917 camp still fresh in our memories, for us the unbroken spell of fine weather was just heavenly. But for the farmer and farm labourer the drought, which in some areas of England (such as the eastern counties) went on throughout the summer, proved disastrous. The Corn Act of 1917 which assured the farmer a guaranteed price was repealed within less than a year following its enaction. In some cases, the corn did not even come to ear, and resulted in many farmhands' wages being drastically reduced, or in their being laid off work.

Our shopping expeditions took us to the town of Dorking, which 'might be compared with a woman having plain features and fine hair — nothing much to look at, but surrounded by an aureole of beauty'.[1] Dorking was the home of one of England's foremost, yet retiring, composers — Ralph Vaughan-Williams. At the time his name meant nothing to any of us, and little then could I have imagined that one day I would be meeting R.V.W. on equal terms as fellow member of the war-time ENSA Music Advisory Committee.

Our 'Long Walks' took us to Box Hill (whose chalk shoulder was clearly visible from Brockham Green), and to the summit of Leith Hill and its well known landmark, the Tower. This was built in 1766, with the approval of Sir John Evelyn, by Richard Hull, 'so that the public might better enjoy the prospect from an elevation of one thousand feet'. At his own request, Hull was buried in the floor of the structure in 1772. The view from the Tower inspired one 18th century traveller to record, 'it is like a sight that would transport a Stoic, a sight that looked like an enchantment and a vision; ... you may behold the very water of the sea at thirty miles' distance, ... at that very time, by a little turn of your head, look full over Box Hill and see the country beyond it, and London; and over the very stomacher of St. Paul's at twenty-five miles distance, and Hampstead and Highgate beyond it'.

Acts of vandalism during the early years of the 19th Century led to the Tower's closure, and the filling in of its interior. It was not re-opened until 1864, when access to the top was provided by an exterior staircase.

The year 1920 ended on a note of personal sadness, for my foster-brother Henry and my friend Charles left school. Two more of Mr Stork's 'little boats' left harbour, and promptly ran into rough seas; for they both enlisted in the Band of the 9/12th Lancers, which at the time was stationed first, at Longford (of that county's name), and later at the notorious Curragh Camp, one of Ireland's worst trouble spots. For them it must have been a dreadful emotional upheaval, for I can think of no more violent transition than theirs. To have been uprooted from a sheltered, monastic-like, existence, and pitchforked straight into a hard-going, hard-riding, hard-swearing set of cavalry troopers (then on a semi-war footing) was a fate which neither of them merited. Both had just celebrated their 15th birthdays.

For the 1921 camp, we had a further change of county — from Surrey to the then sleepy market town of Bracknell in Berkshire.

It was at this camp that Mr Stork questioned my efficiency as a caddy. There were six in the golfing party, made up of my detractor, Messrs Holgate and Forbes, and their three boy caddies. We were driven to the Bracknell Golf Links in a horse-drawn trap by the camp-site owner's daughter, who herself lent a hand on her father's farm. The route to the links took us past 'Cause and Effect' (the *Green Man* pub, and the parish workhouse) and along a dusty highway known as Nine-mile Drive. The road being a fairly hilly one, at Mr Stork's suggestion we would all alight at the bottom of each hill and proceed on foot, out of consideration for the horse.

In those days, golf clubs were not identified coldly and clinically, as they are today, by means of numbers. Woods were identified as Driver, Brassy, Spoon and Baffy; and irons as Long-iron, Mid-iron, Cleek, Mashie and Niblick. The steel and aluminium shafted club had yet to be designed, so that all shafts were made of hickory. Neither had the plastic nor the wooden tee been thought of, so that when driving off, players would fashion their own tees out of wet sand, which was stored in boxes. They (or rather the caddy) would place a handful of sand on the ground and shape it to the required height with the aid of a contraption which was shaped rather like a double-ended candle snuffer, but which (like Mother Earth) was flat at either end. Automatically, one would stand well clear of the player driving off, for fear of being showered with wet sand.

The golf trundler had yet to be introduced, for the very good reason that it simply was not necessary, each golf club having its own pool of

caddies. Golf was still very much the prerogative of the well-to-do, and for preference, it was desirable that the Club Secretary be not below the rank of Brigadier (Retired). Plus-Fours made out of tweed constituted 'correct' golfing attire, until Burton's and the Fifty-Shilling (Size No Object) Tailor were so plebeian as to mass-produce plus-fours in materials other than tweed. As late even as the fifth decade of the present century, some English golf clubs restricted the 'Artisan Class' (as the clubs termed it) to limited set times of the week for play. Other clubs would not accept their green fees.

Etiquette on the course was observed as a matter of good breeding. A threesome (which had no recognised standing) automatically would give way to a two- or a four-ball match. Not that I am implying that the etiquette of golf no longer exists; for it does, as borne out by a notice displayed on the wall of the Auckland Municipal Course Club House at Chamberlain Park.

Notice to All Players

The Rules of the Course on the Board by the steps applies [sic] to you, and to everybody who uses this golf course.

No shirt or blouse	— No Play
No footwear	— No Play
No clubs	— No Play

No Argument.

I scarcely need add that the Chamberlain Park Golf Club Secretary (who formulated the above rules) is not a Brigadier (Retired), and further, that the rules' restrictive first clause relates to men, and not to women; for the topless female golfer has yet to make her appearance on this side of the world.

We were not paid a caddy's fee, but instead, were given a slap-up afternoon tea in the club house.

During this same camp, the Treasurer of the Hospital, Sir Roger Gregory, decided to pay us a visit, and two of us were chosen to meet him at Bracknell Station. Sir Roger must have expressed a wish that he should walk rather than be transported to the camp, for we were briefed to follow the route which would take us via the fields and lanes. We all stood in awe of this somewhat severe (and to us remote) personality, but on that day, at least two foundling boys had revealed to them an entirely different side to Sir Roger's make-up.

It soon became apparent to both of us that Sir Roger Gregory, solicitor and senior partner of the firm of Gregory, Rawcliffe & Co., Past Master of the Grocers' Company, a President of the Council of the Law Society, and a Justice of the Peace for the County of Kent, was at heart a simple man in one direction at least — his knowledgeable and deep-rooted love of nature. Our walk back to camp took on the character of a live lesson in nature study, which by the way, was our first, and last, lesson in that subject. Nothing escaped his attention, from the more obvious trees to the most shy and humble of wayside flowers.

The lesson would have been the more enjoyable but for Sir Roger's embarrassing way of pointing to every specimen he came across and questioning, "Now, can either of you tell me the name of that flower?"; for he above all should hardly have expected a pair of elementary-school children, living in the heart of London, to have been capable of distinguishing between an oxslip and a cowslip; or to have known the difference between the ragwort, the soapwort, the motherwort and the pink lousewort; or that there existed even such wild flowers as the asphodel and the sun-dew.

The only camp which could be counted a failure was that of 1917. It was pitched on a site near the little village of Hyde Heath, in Buckinghamshire.

Whether for reasons of economy or non-availability, the year 1917 was the only one when our tents were not hired from Thomas White's of Aldershot. It was a little ironic that in making this exchange of firms, we should have struck a particularly wet summer; for whereas Thomas White's tents never leaked, the new firm's tents leaked so badly that the suppliers came down and fitted them with double-ceilings. In solving one problem they created another, for the waterproof lower ceilings retained the drips from the upper ceilings, thus forming miniature duckponds.

Because of the atrocious weather, camp was extended by a further two weeks in the vain hope of an improvement. For ever afterwards, the name Hyde Heath was synonymous with cancelled shopping expeditions and sports fixtures, and with days and nights on end spent inside leaky tents.

The few walks we were able to go on took in Amersham, Chesham, and the two delightful Missendens, 'Little' and 'Great'.

And it was during this and the following year's camp (at Amersham) that our walks in the country took us through woods which were wall-to-wall carpeted throughout with foxgloves in such profusion of colour that even Harrod's carpets 'in all their glory were not arrayed like unto these'.

A few of our number were sufficiently foolhardy as to conduct experiments on themselves to test the alleged efficacy of the dock-leaf. The

test involved voluntary exposure to the stinging-nettle, and the immediate application of the dock-leaf to 'the affected part'. The result? 'Experiment not proven.'

Because of the atrocious weather, we thought ourselves hard done by. We were too young to take in what was happening on the Western Front; for it was the summer of the Third Battle of Ypres, known to those who took part in it as Passchendaele. The combination of the incessant rainfall and the failure of the drainage system which had been smashed to rubble by the intense bombardments had turned the battlefield into 'a desolation .... diseased, pocked, rancid, stinking of death: a gigantic monotonous wound.'[2]

Yet our combined war effort amounted to nothing more than that of grumbling at the weather.

The last camp I attended was sited near Bognor, which (on the credit side) had yet to be dignified by the cognomen Regis, and (on the debit side) had yet to see its sands gradually lose their commercially-publicised golden hue.

This particular camp could not have come at a more timely moment, for the closing weeks of the year 1921 and the early months of 1922 witnessed an outbreak of scarlet fever which quickly reached epidemic proportions.

An outbreak of diptheria had struck the hospital two years earlier, and in an effort to contain the disease, swabs were taken and 'positives' isolated from 'negatives'. This arrangement collapsed the moment one of the 'negatives' was re-diagnosed as 'positive'. Our reunion was celebrated by a cricket match, Positives v Negatives. The number of serious cases, mercifully, was small, so that our infirmary was well able to cope.

But the scarlet fever epidemic assumed such proportions as to expose the inadequacies of our infirmary when placed under real pressure. All cases were sent to various London fever hospitals, which marked an abrupt (even though temporary) end of our children's insulation against outside influences. I would not claim that we were a band of unspotted innocents, but as yet we were ignorant of the significance of certain 'swear words', and of course on all matters relating to sex.

After six weeks' absence, we returned to the fold, now in possession of somewhat more extensive vocabularies, plus some crude ideas on sex. It was as though the whole school had lost its virginity overnight in one mass rape. We were bound sooner or later to become exposed to the whole gamut of the 'facts of life', but the precipitate and crude manner in which we came by them revealed one of the more obvious weaknesses of our secluded system of living.

I myself was taken to a fever hospital in Tottenham and thence to a convalescent hospital in Winchmore Hill. Here I was made a 'ward boy' whose most important (and frequent) duty was to engage the ward sister in her favourite game of Halma. A fellow-patient named Rutty soon put me right as to the tactics I should adopt — 'Always let Sister Dore win.' His tip paid off handsomely. Put the other way round, I quickly discovered that a diplomatic loser was not nearly so liable to fall victim to Sister Dore's petty spite.

One of my weaknesses (or was it one of my strengths?) was my inability to provide a 'specimen' on demand, whether or not I had the necessary urge to do so. I blame myself in part for being so naive as to beat Sister Dore at Halma, but mainly do I lay the blame at the feet of the sister herself for my 'specimen-on-demand' complex which has continued to bedevil me ever since. Praise be that New Zealand nurses are more understanding. I discovered this when, as a patient in Auckland's Middlemore Hospital, I was due for one of a series of skin-graft operations. A 'specimen-on-demand' request threatened to deprive me of my usual evening's walk over the adjacent golf course. But I managed to solve what might otherwise have developed into an impasse in an entirely novel way, which allowed me both to deliver the specimen and to take my walk. However, when I returned to the ward, I was met by an abnormally sympathetic nurse. Placing a comforting arm on my shoulder she whispered, "You're not to worry, Dr Nalden, but tomorrow you are going to have a most serious operation; our surgeon is going to fit you up with a permanently built-in tea strainer."

And so it was that Bognor Camp, for most of the children, was virtually a convalescing period.

Apart from one notable exception (a boy named Galton), Bognor gave all of us our first glimpse of the sea. Galton had been sent to Margate for a prolonged stay for health reasons — a no mean tribute to the hospital's sense of its responsibilities towards its young inmates.

Camping by the sea proved a quite different experience from camping in the country; and for us a far more enjoyable and exciting one. First, there was the sheer novelty of exploring for the very first time the seaside pier and its side-attractions; of seeing for ourselves, for example, exactly 'What the Butler Saw'; of holding ourselves in breathtaking suspense as a scantily-clad female with an unpronounceable French name set fire to herself before executing her thrice-daily spectacular dive off the pier; of our gaping open-mouthed at a brace of British sun-blistered blondes as they paraded up and down the promenade; of our comparing the Cheshire

Regimental Band with our own school band; and our sea-bathing and fashioning castles out of sand.

All this, and more, was infinitely more exciting than building castles in Spain, walking for miles and miles down hot dusty country lanes, and voluntarily exposing ourselves to nettle stings.

We had fondly imagined that a seaside holiday meant sandcastling and swimming the long day through. We were in for a disappointment, for we had failed to reckon with a by-law which prescribed the compulsory use of bathing machines for changing in and out of one's swimming costume. And so like all other urban council disciplined holidaymakers, we bathed at fixed times, for fixed periods, and on a fixed part of the beach. In short, the freedoms which sea-bathers now enjoy had yet to be won, for in those days changing on the beach was a punishable offence.

However, some five years later, an angry crowd of holidaymakers, its patience exhausted, and stung to action by this same petty by-law which had them queueing for a bathing machine for anything up to two hours, defied authority (and convention) by a mass undressing protest on the beach. Their act of defiance sounded the death knell for the archaic monument to Victorian prudery — the bathing machine. Seaside town councillors mourned no doubt their consequential loss of income, but for holiday-makers it meant that from henceforth they could bathe where they liked, when they liked, and for as long as they liked. How they liked, had to wait a while longer.

It was at this very same seaside town six or seven years later that I was to fall a willing victim to a con man. He sold me a perfect-fitting bathing suit — which in those days covered the upper as well as the lower half of one's body — for the staggeringly low price of sixpence. It was still wet from the sea. When ultimately it dried out, the initials B.[ognor] U.[urban] D.[istrict] C.[ouncil] stood out in vivid white lettering against their dark-blue background, being clearly visible, I'll warrant, at 20 to 30 yards' distance.

When sadly it dawned, the final day of the 1922 Bognor Camp marked not only the last day of my last school camp, but the end of a series of dream-like episodes, whose like I was not to rediscover until 13 years later.

And then, a like episode became mine, or rather ours (Peggy's and mine) to re-dream all over again; a dream which went on and on, undisturbed, unruffled, for three rapturous years in the then captivating Channel Island of Guernsey.

Headed by our band, we arrived back once again in our London home. The massive iron gates facing Guilford Street were already open to receive their 500 unwilling guests. Standing beside his gates was dear old Porter

Moffit, greeting us as we marched through them with a wave of his poor arthritic hand.

FOOTNOTES TO CHAPTER 14

[1] J.S. Ogilvie, *A Pilgrimage in Surrey* (London, 1914), Vol.II, p.213.
[2] Sholto Douglas, *Years of Combat* (London, 1963), p.139. Quoted by Douglas from Cecil Lewis, *Sagittarius Rising*.

15: The Great War, 1914 - 1918

We became war-conscious in our infant school days, when the Army requisitioned an area of land adjacent to our playground for use as a parade ground.

It was in the early days of the war that an artillery unit took over the front part of our grounds for training. The girls lost their grassed playing area, which was ploughed up, and converted into a fenced-in riding school, complete (to the boys' delight) with jumps. They also lost their 'Arches', (colonnades) which were converted into stabling for the gunners' horses. And the 'Road', which served the boys as a football field come the winter, and as a number of cricket pitches come the summer, was taken over for a goodly part of each week by the artillery for gunnery practice and various types of manoeuvres.

In all this, the boys fared very much better than the girls, for their grassed cricket pitch, so lovingly tended, was declared inviolable and thus left severely alone 'for the duration'.

The gunners' grim war games became the basis of our war games. We learnt their gun-drill orders, such as 'Three rounds, Battery ... Fire!', 'Rear limber up', 'without drag-ropes — pre-peddervance' (without drag-ropes — prepare to advance).

We came to know the functions and duties of individual members of the six-man gun team — the loader, the breechcloser, the rangefinder, and so forth. And we took in how individual members of a gun team would be required to take over other members' positions, for German shells respected neither the person nor his gun position. We revelled in the sight of a battery in full battle order, the drivers mounted on their horses (six horses and three drivers to each gun team), and the gunners riding on the gun limber. A Lieutenant Lambert was one of our heroes, for not only was he young and handsome, but a fine cricketer to boot. A mighty six from his bat once hit a boy named Leigh square on his forehead, but as it was our hero who made the stroke, we all forgave him (except Leigh, of course).

Some boys preferred playing naval games. There was one boy named Carnegie who promoted himself over everyone else to the rank of Admiral of the Fleet, and insisted upon being saluted at all times and piped on board his flagship. (We learnt these terms from *Pears Cyclopaedia* and from old boys who were in the Royal Navy). I was a lowly crew member under his command when he decided to lead an expedition to the Dardanelles. However, after leaving school he beat his admiral's sword into a ploughshare when he was found employment as a farm-hand in the charming Surrey village of Brockham Green.

And then there were frequent periods of general excitement mingled with alarm, caused by horses breaking loose from their tethers and galloping wildly round the grounds, not bothering even to respect the sanctity of the boys' cricket pitch. When this happened, we were instructed never to run away, but to stand our ground and remain perfectly still. Although this advice proved effective (no child was ever kicked), this did not come easy to us; and let's face it, the whole lot of us (masters not excluded I suspect) were quite terrified.

We learnt about the progress of the War from several sources. From the *Daily Graphic,* which was posted each morning on our playroom wall, we became familiar with the various types of German aircraft, such as the deadly Fokker, the Gotha, the Focke-Wulf and the Taube. We read with pride the individual feats of heroism such as that of the lone fighter pilot, Lieutenant William Leefe Robinson, Royal Flying Corps, who won his VC by destroying a German Zeppelin at Cuffley, near Enfield in Essex. His plane, a BE2 C biplane, was capable of flying at the incredibly fast speed of 70 mph! And of Lieutenant R.A.J. Warneford, also of the Royal Flying Corps, who was awarded the VC for a similar feat. We were overjoyed when we read of the gallant German Baron Richtofen's last air battle, in which he was killed. [1]

On land, we were able to follow General Allenby's military victories in Palestine, culminating in the fall of Jerusalem and the defeat and expulsion from the Holy Land of the Turks. "Allenby", Mr Gray rather obviously pointed out, "has accomplished more than Richard the Lionheart." And we read of the cataclysmic collapse first, of Germany's allies, Bulgaria, Turkey, Hungary and finally, of Germany herself. One paper (I believe it

was the *Evening Standard)* carried the banner headline,
THE ELEVENTH HOUR*
One of our number, possessed of an analytic turn of mind for one so young, worked on the number 11, relating the sequence, the 11th hour of the 11th day of the 11th month (the time and date of the signing of the Armistice) to the Bible. The 11th verse of the 11th chapter of the 11th book of the Bible (Kings I) reads:

> 'Wherefore the Lord said unto Solomon, Forasmuch as this is done of thee, and thou hast not kept my covenant and my statutes, I will surely rend the kingdom from thee, and will give it to thy servant.'

Under the terms of the peace agreement, Germany was stripped of her colonies. For ever after, we regarded this boy as the wisest of us all.

A novel source of information relating to the War was a series of cigarette cards[2] issued by the makers of Players cigarettes, under the title, *Britain's Part in the Great War*. From these we learnt to recognise the different types of British aircraft, such as the Armstrong-Whitworth, Sopwith Camel, Bristol fighter, the Avro, Henry Farman, Handley Page and the de Havilland DH 4S. We learnt also the difference between the Dreadnought and Destroyer class of warships, and the role of the WAAC (Women's Army Auxiliary Corps). From Mr Knapp junior (the hospital barber's son) we learnt something of the dangers faced by the Cyclist Corps (pedal, not motor, cycles) running the gauntlet of enemy fire; and from *Pears Cyclopaedia* we learnt by heart (that is, if in our games we wished to qualify for promotion) the badges of rank from private to field marshal, and from able bodied seaman to admiral of the fleet.

A visiting army non-commissioned officer gave us a lecture on 'igh explosives'. (I well remember his demonstration of the correct method of lobbing a hand-grenade, and the traditional feed of buns which followed the lecture.)

Perhaps our most dramatic sources of information were Able Bodied Seamen Bowden and Langton (two old boys) who were on duty in their ship during the surrender of the German Grand Fleet to the Royal Navy in 1919. They held us spellbound (somewhat in the manner of Millais's *Boyhood of Raleigh)* as they related their experiences of that momentous day in Britain's naval history — of the tension, and the feeling of sheer physical and mental exhaustion, the result of remaining at action stations throughout the act of surrender.

---

* It was thus that "The Eleventh Hour" became the catch-word it now is.

But living as we were in the heart of London, our most vivid sources of information were the bombs rained down on us from the German 'Zepps' and aeroplanes, when we would exchange our warm beds for the cheerless 'vaults', as we called them. The first raid caused genuine panic. We were rudely awakened and told to go down to the vaults, which meant negotiating several flights of stairs from our top floor ward. On that occasion, we were not given time to dress, but ran, helter-skelter, down the winding staircase in our bare feet, clothed only in our calico nightshirts.

After that initial raid, evacuation of wards became a much more orderly affair; and when the Germans stepped up the intensity of their raids, we took to sleeping on our beds, fully dressed. Should there be air-raids on consecutive nights, the loss of sleep incurred would be made up by afternoon rest periods, with the consequential cancelling of lessons — a not unwelcome exchange for the average school child.

The vaults on the boys' side housed Mr Tite's engineering, and Mr Howland's plumbing, workshops. They were ventilated by means of iron grilles which were set at ground level. There were, of course, no floor coverings — just the bare flagstones. To while away the time, we sang songs we had picked up from our annual visits to the Lyceum and Drury Lane Theatres' Christmas pantomimes, and from neighbouring barrel-organs — *It's a long, long trail, Keep the Home Fires Burning, Tipperary, Take me back to dear old Blighty, Pack up your Troubles, Good-byee, don't Sighee, there's a Silver Lining in the Skyee, Fight, fight fight for Kitchener's Army, Mademoiselle from Amentieres,* and so on. On the domestic front, a song eulogising the reigning Prime Minister ran —

Lloyd George of Criccieth in gallant North Wales.

Where the Welsh lambs are swishing their tails.

And we sang *Roses of Picardy,* to which Air Marshal Sholto Douglas makes poignant reference in his *Years of Combat:*

Whenever I allow my mind to summon up thoughts of the Somme there are always recalled for me memories of the songs that we all sang in the first war, and they are memories that never fail to bring a lump into my throat. 'Roses of Picardy' is more than a pleasantly sentimental song to those of my generation; it evokes a poignant memory of the sight of columns of dishevelled troops, at times very muddy and torn, as they marched back from the trenches.

The remarkable thing about these First World War songs is that, unlike their Second World War counterparts, they remained alive, and continued to be sung for several decades following the war, finding their way into factory community-singing sessions during the years 1939-1945. One reason

for their undying popularity may have been that the First World War was very much an infantryman's war, and songs such as *Tipperary* and *Mademoiselle from Amentieres* were virtually marching songs. An analogy might be the Orange Party Song *Lilliburlero,* and *John Brown's Body* of the American Civil War.

Air raid warnings were given by the firing of maroons, which were similar in effect to Guy Fawkes Night rockets. The 'all clear' was signalled by boy scouts, who paraded the streets sounding the all clear call (which was the same as the army 'lights out' call) on their bugles.

And then, literally out of the blue, came the famous daylight raid on a Saturday morning in 1917, when for some unexplained reason we were not packed off to the vaults, but ranged along the wall (thus facing the window side) of the dining hall. We never discovered who was responsible for this arrangement. It was fortunate for whoever was responsible that there were no bombs around for their blast most assuredly would have cut us all to pieces.

One male member of the hospital staff who should have been on duty during this particular raid, was found hiding in the vaults. He was dismissed from his employment on grounds of cowardice.

Following the 'all clear' after one night raid, we were taken briefly into the grounds to see the sky, which was lit up for as far as the eye could see by a vivid orange-red glow, emanating from a fire in nearby Red Lion Street. The searchlights were still playing their own grim version of 'cat's cradle', and the occasional aeroplane which became caught in their converging beams was optimistically dismissed by our masters as 'one of ours'.

Playtime on the day after a previous night's raid was spent in looking for shrapnel, which generally was plentiful. As well as finding pieces of shrapnel, we came across some mysterious substance which looked like red jelly-beans. The story got around that they were poisoned sweets, dropped by German airmen.

Although certain neighbouring houses suffered some superficial damage, never once was the hospital itself hit.

The Germans' intensification of the submarine warfare brought England very close, literally speaking, to the breadline; but for us, there was little, if any appreciable cut in our rations, for obvious reasons. Mr Overton announced to the assembled school that in compliance with the Government's plea for personal economies, our white starched collars would be worn on Sundays only. It was our Lenten sacrifice all over again, but this time in permanency — at least for the duration.

Boys with relations in the Army — foster-fathers, foster-brothers and so on — proudly displayed the appropriate regimental badge, which they inserted in the second button-hole of their jackets. As we were permitted to use only this one button-hole, I alternated with the Royal Engineers' cap badge (representing my 'Uncle' Ernie who died in Italy of pneumonia) and a Royal West Kent's badge (representing my 'Brother' Bill, who in 1918 was called up for military service). By then my foster mother was widowed, and when her son received his calling-up papers, she followed him down to the Regimental Depot in Kent, where she stayed for a while. In later years, she recounted to me how she would conceal herself behind a tree on the parade ground so as to keep an eye on 'what them bleedin' brutes of drill-sergeants' were doing to her Willie.

She recalled how on one occasion, unable to contain any longer her pent-up emotion, she emerged from her hiding place to bombard the hapless drill-instructor with such a salvo of abuse as temporarily to halt the drill parade; whereupon one of Bill's squad-mates applauded her action with 'Good for you! Let 'im 'ave it Ma!' "And didn't I bloody well!" recollected Ma triumphantly. Willie managed to survive the war, and (more remarkably still) the tyrannical persecution of the 'bleedin' perisher' of a drill-instructor.

The rising cost of living, food rationing and general shortages notwithstanding, my foster-mother still managed to visit us at three-monthly intervals, and still managed to bring us a bountiful supply of confectionery and homemade cakes, which, I suspect, she was able to do only by depriving herself.

At the end of the war we were taken on one fine crisp winter's morning to see the thousands of captured enemy guns on display in Hyde Park. And during a period of a glut on the market, we came to re-discover the taste of real butter.

FOOTNOTES TO CHAPTER 15

[1] Baron Manfred von Richthofen was one of the great 'killer aces' of the 1914-1918 War. Up to when he was killed in the April of 1918, he had shot down 80 Allied aircraft. The day after his death, 'in a chivalrous gesture', a British pilot flew over Richthofen's base at Cappy and dropped a photograph of the 'Red' Baron's funeral and an explanatory note which read:
> 'To the German Flying Corps: Rittmeister Baron von Richthofen was killed in aerial combat on April 12, 1918. He was buried with full military honours.'

[2] Every boy's ambition was to collect a complete series of 'fag' cards, generally some 25 cards in all. This we accomplished either by swapping, bargaining, or by 'playing' one another for them in a game of our own devising, whose general principles were not altogether unlike those of the game of bowls. Our rules permitted the gumming together of some three or four cards, which we termed a Dobby, the equivalent of the jack in bowls. The Dobby was used for the opening 'flick', aimed at the centre spot in a chalk-drawn circle. The remaining cards were then flicked. The boy whose Dobby landed nearest the centre of the circle won the right to the first 'sweep' of the cards, claiming as his all those which found the inside of the circle. The Dobby's equivalent in our own brand of the game of marbles we termed the Fobber.

16: The school cap

Boys were fitted with forage-style ('fore and aft') caps, which were woven in the traditional reds and browns, and set off with two brass buttons at their helms, and the school crest on their port sides.

But for something approaching 350 days of the year our caps were kept under lock and key in a glass case which extended the full length of the platform (the traditional venue for caning sessions) in our playroom.

Wearing of caps was limited to two special occasions — for drill parades in the school grounds in honour of distinguished visitors, and for occasional outings, which amounted to some half dozen a year.

Most of our outings coincided with the Christmas season. One regular 'treat' was to be taken to the Lyceum, Drury Lane and Alhambra Theatres for dress rehearsals of their respective Christmas pantomimes. As we were given seats in the 'gods', it meant us standing in a queue for anything up to an hour before the doors were opened, frequently in bitterly cold weather. However, anticipating what lay in store for us, and enjoying meanwhile the novelties provided by queue-buskers (the violinists, cornettists, singers, one-man-bands, and the individual strongman acts) we came to regard the queueing as an essential part of the outing.

We were enchanted by the sheer magnificence of Cinderella's ball gown (never before having seen the like of it) and the splendour of her coach, which on one occasion was drawn across the stage by a team of white horses. And the elegant Prince Charming dressed in satin coat and knickerbockers (even though it struck us as something of a misnomer that the principal boy should in fact be a girl). We roared with delighted laughter at the spectacle of 'Little Tich' in his Puck-styled boots perched on a mechanically operated toadstool which carried him out of sight, now high above the wings and now through the stage trap-door.

Equally funny were the antics of the human horse. I have remained intrigued ever since, musing to myself on occasions as to the type of person who takes on the part of the horse's hind legs. I am now satisfied in my own mind, either that he must be cursed with so deep an inferiority complex as to conclude that no other type of employment is open to him, or that he is hiding from the law, or is permanently doubled up with rheumatoid arthritis. Whatever the motive, to me at any rate, it certainly seems a queer way of making a living.

To our delight, one pantomime featured the then famous *Daily Mirror* Pets — Pip (a dog), Squeak (a penguin) and Wilfred (a rabbit) whose adventures had long since become an integral part of our daily lives. Lest awkward questions be asked as to what the governors and guardians of we innocents' morals were thinking about in permitting us to read the *Daily Mirror,* let me hasten to explain that together with the now defunct *Daily Sketch,* the *Mirror* of the earlier decades of the century was calculated, nay, guaranteed, never, never, to 'bring the blush of shame to the cheek of modesty'. Not that page three of today's version of the *Daily Mirror* would either.

It was the pantomime that gave us our initial introduction to the orchestra; and the sound of an orchestra tuning-up has no less an exhilarating and anticipatory effect on me today as it had then.

And it was from the pantomime that we learnt the popular songs of the day such as *Love in Lilac time, I'm forever blowing bubbles, Swanee,* and

> K - K - K - Katey,
> My b - beautiful Katey,
> You're the only g - g - g - girl that I adore.
> Wh - when the M - Moon shines
> Up - upon the C - Cowshed,
> I'll be w - waiting for you at the K - K - K - Kitchen Door.

And it was at the pantomime that we were initiated into the world of 'blue' jokes. I recall one wartime pantomime audience roaring its vulgar head off with the minimum of coaxing from the stage at the lines

> We'll draw up our blinds
> And show our behinds
> When the day of peace is declared.

This was one of the ones which got away from the Lord Chamberlain's otherwise barbed hook.

And we came away from the pantomime with the naive belief that George Robey and Stanley Lupino must be just as funny in real life as they were on the stage.

As another 'treat' we were taken to a show featuring Sir Harry Lauder, who invited us to join him in singing his current hits, *I love a Lassie* and *You tak' the High Road and I'll tak' the Low*. On this occasion not only were we given seats in the stalls but presented with a handsome half-pound box of chocolates apiece, a personal gift of Sir Thomas Lipton. Sir Harry expounded from the stage on Sir Thomas Lipton's generosity, which in turn drew a prolonged round of applause from the audience, which in turn no doubt sparked off a prolonged demand from a newly-won-over posse of British housewives for Lipton's Tea. Be this as it may, forever afterwards I followed the fortunes ('misfortunes' is perhaps more apt) of Sir Thomas's 'Shamrock' series of yachts in their run of unsuccessful bids to wrest the Americas' Cup from the Yankees.

During the whole of my eight-and-a-half years at the hospital, we were taken to the cinema but twice only, when we saw *Pollyanna* and *The Mad King of Bavaria* — the queerest of bedfellows, I do agree. *Pollyanna* starred Mary Pickford ('The World's Sweetheart' as she was then known) and although the amputation of one of her legs still left Pollyanna with a not-to-be-sneezed-at 32" - 26" - 34" figure, the episode reduced not a few of us to tears.

Another Christmas-time outing was to the Scala Theatre to see a musical fantasy called *Fifinella,* a play which none of us pretended to understand. My sole recollection of the play is that it was punctuated throughout by a succession of apparently distraught, flimsily-clad females flitting across the dimly-lit stage and crying out as though in the final stage of distraction (and in the most perfect Cheltenham Ladies' College accent), "Fifinellah! Fifinellah!"

Again we were given seats in the stalls, but I suspect for a rather different reason; the play was taken off, so we were told, after a disastrously short run. And to add to our disappointment, Sir Thomas failed to cough up.

Then there was the charming presentation by Jean Sterling-Mackinlay in the Aeolian Hall, which consisted of a whole host of nursery rhyme characters. And although the 13 and 14-year-olds among us were inclined to sniff it off as kids' fare, had we been honest with ourselves, we would have admitted, however grudgingly, to the sheer artistry of the presentation.

All these were matinee performances. The only evening concert I attended was when I was taken (as 'headmaster's boy') by Mr and Mrs Holgate to hear their daughter Iris play a violin solo in a charity concert. On the day of the concert itself, I ran a special errand for Mrs Holgate. It was to purchase from kindly bespectacled Mrs Charles, the newsagent, some enormous number of copies of the *Daily Mirror,* which carried a photograph of Iris complete with violin whose caption read 'Iris Holgate, who is not yet nine, is to play in a concert' etc. etc.

The concert did not start until the hideously late hour of 8 pm, by which time the remaining 500-odd foundlings would already have enjoyed some two hours' sleep,

I was, of course, in no way qualified to assess the standard of Iris's playing, which, by the way, was hardly helped by the incident of her bow making contact with the stage curtain. So far as I was concerned, her performance served simply to deepen my already acute sense of inferiority and to re-emphasise the seemingly unbridgeable gap which separated children of her social standing from children of ours. She appeared as though endowed with all those things which we, not without envy, both lacked and coveted — an adoring father, a doting mother, a toy 'pom' dog, the luxury and comforts of a home, and a City of London/Guildhall School of Music education. Subsequent events (the final breakdown of the Holgate marriage, and the tragic circumstances surrounding Iris's untimely death) were to prove us wrong on all counts. It was to be many years hence ere I encountered by way of Lamb's essay *Chelsea China* the perfect antidote to that most human of human failings, covetousness.

An outing of a different kind was to hear the explorer, Sir Ernest Shackleton, give an illustrated lecture on one of his expeditions to the South Pole. During my years at the hospital we had several visiting speakers who expounded on such topics as 'The Evils of Strong Drink', 'igh explosives (already referred to), 'The Exciting Career of an army bandsman' (as against the dull life of a clerk in the City), and 'The Exciting Career of a city clerk' (as against the dull life of an army bandsman). Needless to say, the former lecture was given by an army bandmaster, and the latter by an accredited representative of the firm of I. & R. Morley, of Wood St, London, E.C.2. But by reason of its unflagging interest, its humour, and its ready appeal to his young audience, Sir Ernest's lecture stands out still as having been the most enjoyable and memorable of all.

And of course we were taken to the London Zoo in Regent's Park, and to the Bertram Mills Circus at Olympia, which turned me forever against all circuses and all zoos. That a lioness should be kept in permanent captivity, removed from the physical and mental climate into which she was born, and whose only form of exercise was in answer to her trainer's command, "Come on, Alice! Over the barrier!" — that these things should be perpetuated in the name of entertainment is to my mind an abuse of God's Order of Things. And the case against zoos is even more damning. That live fowls, rats and mice should be sacrificed (but not before being subjected to a prolonged and petrifying experience in the snake's cage) in order to sustain the inmates of the reptile house, is as revolting and barbarous a form of murder as any contrived by man.

> You think that life is nothing but not being stone dead ... to shut me from the light of the sky and the sight of the fields and flowers; to make me breathe foul damp darkness ... all this is worse than the furnace in the Bible that was heated seven times ... if only I could still hear the wind in the trees, the larks in the sunshine, the lambs crying through the healthy frost ... But without these things I cannot live.

> (G.B. Shaw, *St. Joan*)

It is not Joan's intention here to speak merely for herself, but to draw man's attention, surely, to the unhappy plight of all those living creatures, the innocent victims of the barbarous policy of indiscriminate captivity.

On the odd occasion, entertainments such as the Punch and Judy Show were staged in the hospital itself. Each year, for example, the hospital solicitor, Mr Gardiner, arranged for either a clown or a 'magician' (as we quaintly called him) to entertain us. For one of his tricks at least, the magician was assured of a prolonged 'Oooh!' from his young and naive audience. For a prop, he borrowed the school chaplain's silk top-hat, and without further ado, proceeded to break an egg into it. Five hundred pairs of young eyes simultaneously swivelled in Mr Stork's direction, who appeared to accept it all very unconcernedly, as though it were simply one of a top-hatted clergyman's occupational hazards. But when this same magician performed the same trick using the same top-hat (and probably the same egg) year after year, our devilish wish (had we searched the innermost recesses of our souls) was for the trick to come unstuck, with all its embarrassing consequences. But it never did.

Never were we given any form of musical entertainment, for the very good reason I suppose, that none of the staff being genuinely interested in music, the possible effect of a concert of worthwhile music on an audience such as ours never entered into their understandings.

Most of our outings were rather in the nature of sugar-coated pills, for inevitably they would be followed up by classroom essays on topics such as 'A Day at the Circus', or 'King George V's Drive through London'. This event, by the way, took place shortly after the war, and I recall that it was the tremendous ovation accorded His Majesty which drew from this somewhat remote monarch the almost pathetically moving comment that never before had he realised the degree of affection in which his subjects held him.

Which brings me to the subject of distinguished visitors to the hospital. Apart from Charter Day (October 17th) and Quarter ('Court') Days, the hospital flag was flown only on occasions such as these, distinguished visitors' days. The flag was emblazoned with the arms of the hospital, which among other symbolic figures (such as the inevitable naked infant) sported 'a terminal figure of a Woman full of Nipples proper'. (Hogarth's sketch depicted a woman with five such nipples).

In later life, I heard not a few old foundling girls and boys express their personal objections to this particular feature of Hogarth's design. I recall being present in 1947 at a meeting of the Old Coram Association Committee and hearing one particularly vehement committee member describe Hogarth's 'Woman full of Nipples proper' as 'downright disgusting'!

I personally could never subscribe to these views, remembering (as old foundlings should) the style in which Hogarth expressed himself, and the lifestyle of the period which he so thought-provokingly caricatured and portrayed.

We were visited, among others, by Queen Mary, the Duke of Connaught, and the Princes Albert and Henry (as they then were). Prince Henry wore the uniform of his regiment, the 10th Hussars, and Prince Albert the uniform of the then comparatively new Royal Air Force. Had these, and other illustrious personages, been even minutely aware of the intensive and exacting drill parades, inspections (which we dreaded), additional floor scrubbings and the rest which preceded their visits, they would, everyone of them, have spared us their calls, if only out of purely humanitarian considerations — for Digger Holgate's cane became the vehicle for the release of his own pent-up emotions, tensions, and fears as to what might go wrong 'on the day'.

Go wrong things did, but generally in circumstances which were quite unpredictable, as, for example, during Queen Mary's inspection. Following the final march past the saluting base, it was our custom to draw up in the familiar military 'square' formation in preparation for inspection and the distinguished visitor's address. We were instructed beforehand that should we be spoken to, we were to address men visitors as 'Sir' and women visitors as 'Madam'.

During our inspection by Queen Mary, she paused in front of a boy whose left eye was focussed permanently at an angle of some 45⁰. "How did you do that?" enquired the Queen as sympathetically as such formal occasions permit. "You see, Miss", came the reply, "it was like this; when

Prince Henry (later Duke of Gloucester) and the author.

I was young, my big bruvver 'it me in the eye with a 'ammer"; which was all very embarrassing, even though true, for some of us did tend to drop our aitches, and pronounce such words like 'you' as 'yer'. The story (a perfectly authentic one) was passed down from generation to generation of foundlings.

Paradoxically, those children, whose degree of maturity enabled them to sense shortcomings in others, felt almost sorry for Prince Albert (later Duke of York and King George VI) when he came to address us. At the time he suffered from an impediment in his speech, and on this occasion displayed a noticeable nervousness of manner. During the course of his address, we saw him edge closer and closer to our treasurer, Sir Roger Gregory, finally seeking Sir Roger's hand, which was readily proffered. To us, it seemed unbelievable that a person of such exalted rank should expose his woeful lack of self-confidence before so lowly an audience.

Life has since taught me otherwise, for I have on occasions heard of concert artists of the first rank who confessed to going though agonies of mind during the period immediately preceding a performance. Pity the person, such as a member of royalty, who perforce must go on with it, even though his whole being rebels against the very idea of publicity in any form.

It is surprising the number and variety of highways and byways through which the school cap led us.

17: The juvenile band

The Juvenile Band as it was originally styled, was formed in 1847.

I became a band cadet at 12 and came face to face for the first time with the most endearing and lovable of all the hospital characters, the school bandmaster, Mr Cawley.

Mr Cawley himself was a one-time inmate of the Foundling Hospital. He was born c.1856, and joined the Band of the Highland Light Infantry regiment at the age of 14½ — a comparatively late age for those times. He was promoted Band Sergeant, and entered Kneller Hall (the training establishment for military musicians) in 1886 as a student for bandmastership. He was appointed Bandmaster of the Royal Scots regiment four years later, and retired from the Army in 1897 when, I presume, he became our school bandmaster. He retired from the hospital in 1921, and died six years later at the age of 72.

Apart from an unfortunate nicotine-stained patch between his upper lip and nostrils, his long drooping moustache was of the same silvered texture as the few remaining hairs on his head. He was short and inclined to portliness. For his 'everyday' clothes, he clung tenaciously to the same frock-coat whose cut (and here we had those worn by the school chaplain and governors for purposes of comparison) and low-gloss finish on its lapels, dated it as a relic of a bygone age — probably 1897, the year of his discharge from the Army. It must be counted fortunate that his frock-coat hung below the knees of his trousers, for what portion of that garment did expose itself to view boasted no centre-crease, a lack which normally goes hand-in-hand with bagginess at the knees. Setting all this off were his two-textured (glace-

Programme

OF THE

FIRST CONCERT

PERFORMED BY THE

CHILDREN OF THE FOUNDLING HOSPITAL,

1st FEBRUARY, 1849.

IN COMMEMORATION OF THE ESTABLISHMENT OF

A JUVENILE BAND.

Under the Auspices, and with the Sanction of

CHARLES POTT, Esq.

TREASURER,

AND THE BAND COMMITTEE.

LONDON:

PRINTED BY

R. MACDONALD, 30, GREAT SUTTON STREET.
1849

The programme of the first concert of the Juvenile Band, 1849.

PROGRAMME.

PART I.

The National Anthem		Band & Chorus.
And the glory of the Lord.......	Handel.	Band & Chorus.
Their sound is gone out	Handel.	Band & Chorus.
The Heavens are telling	Haydn.	Band & Chorus.
He delivered the Poor that cried ..	Handel.	......Band.
Lord of all power and might	Mason.	Band & Chorus.
Sound the loud Timbrel	Avison.	Band & Chorus.
Lord of Heaven and Earth and Ocean .... }	Haydn.	Band & Chorus.

PART II.

March, from the Opera of "Norma,"	Bellini.	.........Band.
Come if you dare	Purcell.	Band & Chorus.
She wore a Wreath of Roses	Knight.	...Band.
Mynheer Vandunck	Bishop.	.........Band.
God bless thee, Queen of England..	Hobbs..	Band & Chorus
Life's a Bumper...............	Wainright.	.......Band
Bridal Polka	De L'Ambert.	...Band.
Britons, strike home	Purcell.	Band & Chorus.

NAMES OF THE BOYS COMPOSING THE BAND.

Name	Age	Instrument
Edward Luard............	14	E♭ Clarionet.
Matthew Pelham	14	
Edward Gardiner	13	
William Inwood.........	11	B♭ Clarionet.
Edward Bostock.........	11	
Charles Prior...........	14	
Samuel Edwards	11	
Stephen Quilter	11	Flutes.
Joseph Gubbins	12	
James Lockhart........	14	Cornets.
Samuel Fryer	12	
Charles Wilson	12	Trumpet.
Joseph Moysey	12	Horns.
John Underwood	13	
Richard Hopkins	12	Clavicor.
Augustus Brown.........	11	Trombones.
Edward Hughes	13	
George Taylor	12	Ophicleide.
Edward Sheppard	12	Sax Tubas.
John Cross	11	
Anthony Beattie	11	Drum.
Paul Arnold...........	10	Side Drum.
Benjamin Scarlett	11	Cymbals.
Thomas Mackay	10	Triangle.

kid and cloth) button-up boots, a butterfly-winged collar, dark tie, and stiff-fronted shirt with matching cuffs. It would be ungallant on my part were I to reveal what I now suspect, that his stiff-fronted shirt was in fact no more than a showy facade; I mean a dicky — one of the outward and visible symbols of working and lower-middle class respectability.

This shabby but dignified ensemble was marred by its wearer's disregarding one of the elementary canons (sartorially speaking) of good taste; that it is just simply not done to set off frock-coat, striped trousers, starched shirt, collar and cuffs with a trilby hat. But whatever Mr Cawley lacked in sartorial elegance he more than compensated for by his courtly old-world manner, his natural gentleness, and his very real interest in, and love of, the boys whom he taught.

He had an almost uncanny knack of divining the particular instrument to which each individual boy was best suited. He would take into consideration a boy's height, weight, tooth formation, the relative thickness of his lips (so that a boy with thick lips would not be given a small-cupped instrument), the size and shape of his jaw, and from these, determine the instrument to which he was best suited. Rarely was he in error. But before going into all this detail, he would first ask a boy his particular preference, and provided there were no serious obstacles in the way, such as a jutting lower jaw or prominent front teeth (which could prove a handicap to brass instrument players), he would allow a boy his choice.

Our band comprised flutes, clarinets, saxhorns, baritones, valved-trombones, euphoniums, basses (or 'bombardons' as we termed them), side drum, bass drum and cymbals. Mr Cawley taught the lot, with the violin thrown in for good measure. I believe that the early issue of the slide-trombone was replaced by its valved equivalent on account of the frequent 'buckling' of the former's delicate slide, the result of its being converted (so Mr Cawley once let out) into a long-range pea-shooter. This was effected by the simple expedient of removing the outer tube. The only member of the band who did not come under Mr Cawley's tutelage was the drum major, who was expected to teach himself the art of swinging, throwing and (hopefully) catching his mace.

Mr Cawley's own principal instrument was the clarinet, and he would remind us at least once per band practice that his virtuosity as a performer had been slowly but inexorably undermined by his 'chronic chest condition', which accounted for his characteristic Napoleonic posture of chin resting on chest and right hand tucked inside the fold of his frock-coat. We never took him very seriously on this claim, for on the numerous occasions when he demonstrated to us his undoubted prowess as a clarinettist, his 'old chest condition' miraculously cleared up, only to return the moment he handed the clarinet back to its owner, who, understandably, was reluctant to blow it.

He would regale us with gripping stories of his past triumphs — how on one occasion his own bandmaster promised him anything he cared to name should he 'bring off' a very difficult solo which he was due to play at an important concert. "Well, Cawley, what is it to be?" (which was his way of letting us know that all went well). Adopting a pose of abject humility, he told us his answer. "Just a cigar and a glass of whisky, thank you, sir." In the circumstances, our reaction was probably no different from that of any other collection of wolf-hungry institutionalised school-boys — 'What an opportunity missed!'

Impatient as we were to get started on our respective instruments, Mr Cawley explained in his gentle way the need for a basic knowledge of the rudiments of music. His opening sentences to each new class of cadets never varied —

> These five lines are called the stave; they are counted upwards. Between the lines are spaces; they are also counted upwards. We remember the names of the notes on the five lines because they stand for Every Good Boy Deserves Favour. We remember the names of the notes between the four spaces because they spell FACE.

Natural child psychologist that Mr Cawley was, he would reduce these blackboard lessons to a minimum, knowing full well our impatience to receive our respective instruments. I was 'put on' the cornet (which we pronounced cor*net*). My choice of this instrument may been influenced by the fact that it happened to be my foster brother's instrument. A more likely explanation lies in the axiom that as every private soldier carries in his knapsack a field-marshal's baton (so they are told), so every tyro cornet player carries in his band cardpouch the coveted prize of solo cornet, the band's principal position. The reigning holder of this exalted position (who in some ways is more important even than the conductor himself) lays mute claim to the dignity of his office by occupying (by tradition) the end seat of the inner-circle of players.

The importance of this position in 'brass' and 'military' bands alike may be deduced from the fact that at one time all solo cornet music was dignified by the addition 'or conductor'. This in itself was sufficient to place the holder of the office of solo cornet into a social class all his own.

And so on to the cornet I went, graduating from the blackboard (upon which Mr Cawley wrote out our 'fingerings') to Walter Morrow's *Cornet Tutor.*

Had I then known my G.B.S. as I have come to know him since, never would I have stated my preference for the cornet; for Shaw berates the cornet as 'a most fearful instrument, and one with which self-satisfaction is obtainable on easy terms. The vulgarity of the cornet is incurable. At its best — playing *pianissimo* in heavenly sweet chords scored by Gounod, or making the sword motive heard, in the first act of *Die Walküre* — it is only pretty.'

Even so, Shaw or no Shaw, and 'fearful instrument' notwithstanding, I was never to regret my choice. Once having 'learnt my fingerings', mastered a few (but only a few) major scales and satisfied Mr Cawley with a tune or two from Walter Morrow, I was admitted to the band proper, taking my place as a humble second cornet player.

Band practice was the one school session which never palled, and which sped by all too rapidly.

The music we played necessarily had to be simple, tuneful stuff. We did our best to interpret pieces such as *Killarney* (cornet solo with band accompaniment), *Glorious Apollo, Hail! Smiling Morn, Louis XVI Gavotte, The Village Blacksmith, Un peu d'amour,* Felix Godin's *Valse Septembre,* and *The Glow Worm* from Paul Linke's operetta *Lysistrata,* which probably netted for the Charing Cross Road Boys (who subsequently 'put a beat behind it' — their humane method of bringing the 'classics' to the world's untutored masses) a thousand times more in terms of hard cash than was netted by the composer himself.

To our lasting regret when war broke out, our favourite march *Under the Double Eagle,* was deleted from our repertoire because of its Germanic overtones.

The sole 'classical' piece in the repertoire was the march from Handel's opera *Scipio* (which we pronounced 'See-pee-o'). This march (our 'inspection' tune) was reserved for special parades such as those in honour of one or another of our distinguished visitors. We would repeat it over and over again as our DV moved through the ranks at something less than a snail's pace while the parade remained stiffly to attention.

Bearing in mind the strain this can impose on some constitutions, even on those of grown men, the wonder of it was that unlike H.M. Bateman's hapless guardsman, not once did any one of us, girl or boy, ever 'drop it'. We were trained to keep our heads still, our eyes fixed rigidly to the front, and never to raise or lower them. The result of this discipline was that the bigger boys had to rest themselves content with viewing nothing higher (or lower) than Prince Henry's top tunic button, with the smaller boys' viewing point moving progressively downwards.

This was our special version of Scipio:

The semiquaver runs are, of course, quite spurious; but having due regard for the pleasure these runs afforded our cornet players, I would say that Handel, beholding us from the tranquillity of his assured corner in the Elysian Fields, smiled his assent on each of the thousand-odd times we played them.

One of the band's duties ('pleasures' would be a more correct definition) was to provide discreet background music as the governors assembled for their Quarter Day meetings. These were known as Court Days. On these occasions Mr Cawley would exchange his everyday ensemble for a sober lounge suit. He would also use his highly-prized presentation baton, a fine silver-mounted stick in ivory, complete with laudatory inscription. For these and like occasions our instruments would be burnished by two professional polishers who were especially hired from an outside firm. Experience had probably taught the governors that although costing them money, this was cheaper in the long run than letting us loose on them.

The band had very few engagements outside the hospital. One novel engagement saw the band heading a procession of London schoolchildren and playing them to the appropriate railway station for the famous Barnet Fair. (The band excepted, our own children were not included in this outing, the fraternisation aspect probably being considered too dangerous.) The band's 'fee' for this engagement was free access to all the fun of the fair, in addition to a liberal supply of food, the like of which we had not tasted for many a year.

A special treat for the band was its annual outing to the home of our treasurer, Sir Roger Gregory, which was in Shoreham, Kent. We took our band instruments with us, for although Sir Roger blandly assured us year after year that the day was ours and not his, nevertheless he expected of us a specially prepared programme for the benefit of his family and a few invited guests.

On important occasions such as this Mr Cawley's final exhortation before bringing down his presentation baton was, "Now boys, don't get excited and lose your huds."

On one occasion, unfortunately, our solo cornet player, Tony Farrell, apparently did get excited, and did lose his 'hud'. He was playing the solo part of *Killarney,* and had managed to clear each successive fence beautifully until he came to the final one.

In his anxiety to pitch the 'top F ', the note upon which you might say hinged the band's good name and Tony's claim that he should, as solo cornet, be set above his fellow-bandboys; the sort of climax note (always provided of course that it 'comes off') which silences forever the mutterings and murmurings of those who question amongst themselves the solo cornet player's fitness or otherwise for so elevated and responsible an office — in his anxiety to pitch the 'top F', poor Tony over-reached himself, pitching instead a note known technically as the first valve's seventh harmonic which comes out as an out-of-tune A flat:

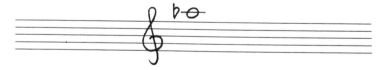

Once having alighted upon it, Tony had to hang on to it loud and long, the note being marked with a pause. Little wonder therefore, that the poor chap died at the unreasonably young age of twenty-three.

Whereas our reaction was to exchange sickly grins, the boys facing Sir Roger reported that he appeared not to notice that anything was amiss. Either this was an act of charitable diplomacy on Sir Roger's part, or, like his reigning sovereign (as it was alleged), he was tone deaf. Far be it from me to spin the fateful coin. Mr Cawley's reaction was "Sir Roger should never have allowed you to stuff your stomachs with strawberries mid-way through a performance and expect you to go on giving of your best.."

True to his declaration, "The day is yours and not mine", Sir Roger followed up our performance by taking us on a personally guided tour of his piggery. Insisting that "The pig is a clean animal," Sir Roger further insisted that we enter the sty and stroke each of the animals in turn. Base ingratitude on our part though it may appear, I am afraid we could muster but little enthusiasm for petting an animal whose delectable end-products never put in an appearance on either our breakfast, dinner or tea plates — nay, not even its trotters or its offal.

The return journey on this otherwise heavenly day (July 4, 1921) was marred by an item of bad news; for we gathered from the cries of London's newspaper boys that Georges Carpentier, whom we idolised even above the reigning British heavyweight champion Joe Beckett, had been knocked out in the fourth round of his world title bid by Jack Dempsey.

The school band, 1913.

The heavy hospital gates were opened up for us by dear old Mr Moffit in his slow, almost painfully laborious manner; he ventured the prophecy that next time we went to Shoreham, Sir Roger would probably be hiring for us 'one of them new Cherrybonks — so much more modern and comfy to travel in'.

At about the same time we came by another item of sad news, when Mr Cawley told us of his impending retirement. Those of us who were privileged to be taught by him were genuinely saddened. Game to the last, he stubbornly refused to admit to reaching retirement age, putting the blame instead on 'my old chest complaint'.

One of the school bandmaster's duties was to attend our annual camps, and in spite of his advancing years, Mr Cawley was sufficiently game voluntarily to join us on our long walks. On these occasions we took our lunches with us, and I recall Mr Cawley dutifully taking his place in the boys' queue and striking his pose of abject humility as he held out his opened lunch bag to receive the same rations as ourselves — a hunk of dry bread and cheese. It was characteristic acts such as this that endeared him to us.

It would be waxing rather too lyrical to claim him as being one of the musical influences in my life. (After all, how could he be with his *Hail! Smiling Morn* and suchlike?); nevertheless I do look back on him as one of my guiding spirits — a sentiment which I know to be shared by not a few contemporaries of mine. But however small his degree of influence

Foundling Hospital staff members — front row, l to r: Messrs Holgate and Overton, Rev. Stork, Mr Cawley (bandmaster). — back row, l to r: Messrs Wheeler, Hamer, Adams, Bruns.

may have been, his successor's was decidely less, for *Glorious Apollo* was deposed by *The Nigger's Birthday, Killarney* traded in for Louis Ganne's *Czardas,* and *Hail! Smiling Morn* retired in favour of:

It was as well that none of the governors and guardians of our morals took a peep over the solo cornet player's shoulder to have read that lot! The probable upshot would have been the sack for Mr Owen for attempted moral corruption, and the band marched forthwith to the chapel where it would have sung Hymn No. 179 from the Foundling Collection, *Oft in Danger, Oft in Woe,* recited the general confession, and been subjected to a homily by the school chaplain upon the temptations that were awaiting us in the wicked world beyond.

Now had Mr Cawley introduced to us a piece such as this, he would have explained it as a song about a little child asking its mother for maternal affection. Naive lot though we were, we were not quite so unworldly as to have swallowed that one — had he tried to put it across us, that is.

At about this time I was made a sergeant and awarded a good conduct stripe, two rare distinctions. And as though double honours were not sufficient in themselves, I was further privileged as a company commander to wear white gloves for all official parades. Beyond those distinctions, what more could a schoolboy of 13 wish for? Why! to become solo cornet!

After Mr Owen had been with us for about 12 months, Mr Holgate broke the news to me that bandmaster Owen was not at all satisfied with his solo cornet — which was me. Although this dealt my (probably far too puffed-up) ego a mortifying blow, I came to realise that Mr Owen was right; for my next bandmaster was even less complimentary on my prowess as a cornettist.

Here I make the plea that not until well into my teens was I able to sustain blowing my instrument beyond the first 20 or so minutes without becoming distressingly 'puffed out' and developing aching muscles around my mouth and cheeks. I recall some couple of years later when a pupil at Kneller Hall, my brashly accepting an engagement along with another cornet player named Green. This involved the pair of us heading a Good Friday Procession of Witness through the streets of Richmond. Our role was to give a lead to the procession's hymn singing (fee 10/-). Had it not been for Green's unflagging support, and for the homilies which were delivered at the several strategic stopping points (such as the Orange Grove Public House), the procession most assuredly would have sung their hymns unaccompanied. Neither before nor since have I prayed so fervently that the sermons be lengthy ones.

But to return to Mr Owen. One of his new-broom policies was to smarten up the brass quartet which accompanied the singing of grace on Sundays, which was also Visitors' Day. In place of playing first for the boys, and walking over the road to play for the girls, Mr Owen soon had us marching over with all the pomp, ceremony, solemnity and dignified gait of a Foot Guards' Colour Party. And the solo cornet player had to learn a new and involved technique for bringing in his three other players on the opening chord.

Mr Owen must have been an efficient bandmaster, for he brought the band up to a standard when it could present a programme in Bognor's promenade bandstand.

In part because of my stolen visits to the piano in one of our classrooms (a high-risk undertaking as it was overlooked by Mr and Mrs Holgate's private sitting room), but mainly through playing in the band, did I discover myself to be endowed with that most precious of musical gifts, and one which is bestowed so capriciously by the Muse Apollo, the gift of a good ear. This was paired in my case with the gift of a highly retentive memory. I discovered that I could pick out tunes and play them 'by ear'; — that is, without recourse to the printed score.

Although clear in its meaning, I have always considered the term 'playing by ear' a quaint, almost comical, expression. During the Second World War, I happened to be travelling from Chester to Oswestry where I was stationed. I was greeted on Chester railway station by our regimental physical training instructor. From his badly bruised and puffy face it was clear that he had been involved in a fight of some sort. He had; for on the previous evening he had volunteered himself as a willing contestant in a charity boxing tournament, and had taken a terrible hiding from that old Welsh 'pug', Frank Moodie, one-time British middle and light-heavyweight champion. In his day, Frank had the reputation for aggressiveness and hard hitting. And from his battle-scarred features it was clear that he himself had been hit hard and often in return.

"Maestro (as our P.T. instructor always addressed me), Maestro, let me introduce you to Frank Moodie, one-time British light-heavyweight champion," etc. etc. With introductions affected, our P.T. instructor proceeded to put on the gallant-loser act — "And Maestro, I'll tell you something else about Frank — something that'll interest you; Frank's not only a great boxer, he's also a fine musician — he plays the piano by ear." Hiding behind my superior rank of Warrant Officer Class I, but taking my life into my own hands all the same, I could not resist the rejoinder, "So I can see; from the look of it, Frank, I would say that you must have been a most assiduous pupil." When Frank's battle-scarred face puckered into a sort of twisted grin, I knew myself to be safe.

18: Careers

In my day the majority of boys were enlisted into army bands, with the minority (often through their failing to pass the army's medical examination) going into civilian employment of some kind.

The girls had no such gentle option. Almost without exception they followed in the footsteps of their long line of foundling predecessors by entering domestic service to take their respective places in the ranks of 'skivvies', as servant girls were derogatorily named.

The average young women of today's so-called 'middle and lower-class' parentage, have opportunities for education and employment denied to their counterparts of so very few decades ago. It cannot be easy for them to understand the humiliations to which the then domestic servant class was subjected. The young woman of today may be forgiven for finding it even more difficult to understand that the cheap jibes at these unfortunate servant girls' expense came in the main from the very people who were dependent upon them for their day-to-day living, and that it was these same people who were directly responsible for these unfortunate girls' so-called ignorance — in short, these girls' masters and mistresses.

Before entering domestic service proper, foundling girls were sent for a period of training to Roselawn, the hospital's own School of Domestic Economy at Chislehurst, Kent. Although their lives, albeit to a more limited extent, were still sheltered, they were quickly made to realise what the 'Game of Life' (as Mr Stork once put it) was all about. The school was supervised by a spinster who delighted in the unfortunate, but appropriately Dickensian, name of Sowerbutts. It would be but a poor imagination that could not conjure up to mind the foundling girls' metamorphosised version of 'Sowerbutts', especially her being the type of boss she was, apparently.

I have an account written by one such girl who went through Roselawn's six-month training course. This girl happened to be my favourite foster-sister Bessie Picton*. Bess became re-united with her natural mother relatively late in life, which led to her recording some of her early experiences for an English women's magazine.

* Bessie has since died.

My favourite foster-sister, Bessie Picton

Her account of Roselawn should be read in the light of the character and mental make-up of the girl herself. She was a high-spirited person, possessed of a tremendously powerful and ebullient personality which was forever seizing upon every new opportunity to make off with the latest bag of tricks at a time when the average person of her age would be thinking in terms either of retiring to a rest home or gravitating towards the grave. Had opportunity knocked at her door, she would have been equally successful and proficient as a headmistress (preferably of a boys' school) a politician (with nothing below Cabinet rank), a barrister, a horsewoman, a militant suffragette, a motorcar mechanic, or a mayoress; in short, the sort of extroverted, uninhibited personality which would have psychiatrists queueing in their thousands to draw the dole.

Here is Bessie's account of her Roselawn period:

"And now came the time to leave the home [the Foundling Hospital] I had known for ten years. At fifteen years old I was to go through those gates and earn my living; but first I must be trained to serve my betters, people who had been born on the right side of the blanket. Shall I ever forget those days of training. To every one of us who went there, it was hell. We had been sheltered at school, but now we went to a house in the country for training.

"I arrived on a bitterly cold day in February (by that time I had had my hair bobbed), and the housemaid's cap would just not stay on my curly top. I was put in a room to wait for the other trainees. It was Monday, washing-day, and in they came, girls I had known at school, wringing wet from washing. Two girls at one tub washed clothes, passed them to two girls at another tub, who passed . . . I think those clothes went through four or five different tubs. And then the girls came in to dinner (herrings); girls of fifteen who looked like tired old women.

"I sat with them, and everyone was watching. I couldn't eat a thing, and they knew; each one was waiting to pounce on my herrings. After dinner those girls started scrubbing wood — every piece of moveable wood, steps, rolling pins, boards, broom handles, brushes — you name it, they scrubbed it. By the time I left that place, I would have eaten herrings heads and all, and many, many times we have eaten all the raw vegetables — turnips, carrots, just leaving onions.

"I got up at six every morning, bitterly cold, and had to dress in servant's clothes. That cap! It was more often than not over one ear and the other ear was boxed because of it. And we scrubbed floors and rinsed them in cold water, and polished them. I remember the lino was blue, and every morning was the same. We cleaned windows, and washed and washed, and scrubbed, and cooked and served until I blew up and locked myself in a room and refused to come out. I cried and cried. They tried all they knew to get me out; in the end hunger won.

"Before I left that place, I wished I was dead. One thing I must say is that the head people knew nothing of this. I believe years later the 'House' was closed. I remember looking out of a window at some girls of my own age riding horses, and being caught. I got a beating, and was told 'How dare you look at young ladies. You are born to serve them.' Eventually I left that place to go to service, and ran away after a fortnight. But at last I began to earn my living at £1.6.8. per month."

Bess left Chislehurst during the July heatwave of 1928, when she wore "thick combinations, spencer, blue and white striped 'butcher's' petticoat, thick navy bloomers, grey whalebone lace corsets, navy serge dress (high neck and long sleeves), black woollen stockings, low-heeled shoes, grey winter coat and pink straw hat." *

Even now I find myself reflecting back upon the many sensitive girls who were subjected to this uncompromising method of initiation into the harsh realities of life; girls such as Curtis, Nelligan, Quilter, Aspinall, Longhurst, Vinal, Goodman, were all worthy of something rather better.

Although reputedly the stronger sex, our boys were in scarcely more enviable case. As I have said, the majority of us were destined to join service bands, irrespective of whether or not we were suitable material for this mode of life. The girls had it over us in that they at least were given a period of intensive domestic training. Boys were allowed one band practice per week, which was the extent of their pre-army training.

The worst aspect was the sudden uprooting, girls and boys alike, from their unnaturally cloistered existence and being plunged straight into entirely different modes of living for which they were all too ill-prepared. A case in point is that of Billy Strutt (of N or M fame). Billy joined the band of an infantry regiment, and within a matter of days of his enlisting, came back to visit the hospital, dressed in an absurdly ill-fitting infantryman's uniform. He had been given a few weeks' draft leave, pending posting to his band, which was stationed in India. Out of the kindness of her heart (or was it out of pity for Billy, who was one of her 'pets'?) Mrs Holgate

---

* Bess here is echoing the same sentiments precisely as those expressed by Hannah Brown a half-century earlier: 'When we arrived at the end of the railway journey it was pouring with rain, and the mud was thick on the ground, but the thing I was most conscious of was myself, and the clothes I was wearing, not because I thought I was looking nice, but that I knew the sight I was. One had not watched a hundred girls depart from the Institution and not learned that fact. So conscious was I of my appearance, and of the white cotton stockings, and elastic side boots, and long dress I had been put into, I would not hold it up — knowing I should feel a bigger fool than ever. One day the mistress told the nurse that she would like to pay for two seats on "the coach", so that she and I could go for a drive, but the nurse bluntly refused the offer, saying in front of me "that she would not be seen in my company, dressed as I was." I was such a specimen in my rig-out, so much so that the servants would refuse to accept tickets for concerts etc. if I were included.' (pp. 114-5, 136, 129.)

set to with her sewing machine, making the necessary alterations to his uniform so that he now at least looked the soldier.

In those days all Regiments of the Line consisted of two battalions — the 'Home' battalion and the 'Abroad' battalion. A 'tour of duty' (as it was termed) consisted of 21 years, so that a soldier who 'clicked' an overseas battalion might well serve the whole of his time abroad, which frequently meant India. And the band which Billy joined had many unexpired years of foreign service ahead of it before returning to home stations. And his was by no means an isolated case of its kind.

Another case concerned my elder foster-brother, and my closest school friend, Charles K . . . . Both had just passed their 15th birthdays, when together with two other foundling boys, they enlisted in the band of a cavalry regiment. Their regiment was stationed at Longford in Southern Ireland (as it was then named). The year was 1920, which marked the peak period of post-war unrest in that unhappy country. I am grateful to Charles for giving me this account:

"Immediately on leaving school, we went to Longford. We were virtually on active service — did duty soldiering, stables, stable guards, exercising horses, and lived in the most primitive conditions that I have ever experienced. It was an experience that made all else that was to follow a piece of cake.

"We had been enlisted for the 21st Lancers, which we discovered were actually in the process of being disbanded. Subsequently they were of course amalgamated with the 17th Lancers. One of us, Sam R- , was transferred to the 9th Lancers which was going overseas. The remaining three of us were left behind, and for three months were attached to the details of the 17th Lancers.

"Their Bandmaster did not want 'attached' boys, and so we were sent to the 12th Lancers (the 9th's sister regiment) which was stationed at Curragh Camp in County Kildare. The 12th Lancers was a crack regiment in every respect, and their Band, under Bandmaster Goddered, was absolutely first-class; but here again, as we were only attached to his Band, and not 'pukka' 12th Lancers, Goddered would not give us instruments. So we became permanent room orderlies, cookhouse orderlies, general 'dogsbodies', but attached to the Band for all other purposes, such as eating, sleeping and drawing our pay."

As Charles himself put it, "It was like being thrown in the 'Pool of Life' from the deep end."

Ultimately, the three boys were taken on the permanent strength of the 9th/12th Lancers. Following duty in Ireland came an overseas tour of duty which took them first to Egypt and then on to Trimulgherry in India. All this kept them out of England for the greater part of their army service.

Troopship conditions for 'Other Ranks' on the Middle and Far East runs were appalling. Sleeping quarters were ill-ventilated, over-crowded and insufferably hot. The common soldiery slept in hammocks which were hung so close to each other as to resemble a professionally-packed car park at the Twickenham rugby ground. And the very thought of the Port Said - Red Sea run (through the Suez Canal) with scarcely a breath of wind to bring relief from Scott's 'Burning Sun of Syria', or to dispel, even momentarily, the ever-present abominable stench (the romantic novelist's 'Mysterious Perfume of the East') — the very thought of this run in itself would have been sufficient to have caused the redoubtable Regimental Sergeant Major Brittain to wince.

These, then, were the sorts of conditions into which any foundling boy was liable to be catapulted.

It so happened that my school friend Charles was blessed with a magnificent physique, which was matched by an equally resilient and adaptable spirit. For example, while serving with his regiment in India, he established for himself a reputation as a formidable cross-country runner, thinking nothing of 20-mile training 'sprints'.

But for the boy who was not endowed with these faculties — a strong physique and an undaunted spirit — life could become, and frequently was, a living hell. There was little the faint-hearted could do about it, for as one old foundling boy put it, there was no one to whom we could turn — least of all the bandmaster. There was indeed one way out, and one only; he could purchase his discharge from the Army, provided he could save the stipulated purchase price of £35 from his pay packet of 7/- per week, plus his fare home.

The plain truth was that the misfit was trapped — hopelessly so. And although I would not classify myself exactly a misfit, nevertheless I did experience this feeling (of being trapped) on not a few occasions during my 26 years' period of army service. Yet my lot in life, when compared with the respective lots of many other foundling boys, was indeed a charmed one.

These are but a few of the manifestations of the hospital's well-intentioned but (some would say) misguided policies when placing out the children.

The question to be answered right now is, how did we act the parts in life for which we were intended? How did the girls measure up to the 'business of servants' and the boys to the 'business of the common soldier and the common sailor'? How did we act, we, who had been educated at a distance from all these objects?

I would say that we were all too near our individual selves to know the answers to these questions. So, instead, let us hear what one of our 'barrack-room mates' has to say on the subject:

"Most of our bandsmen had been in the army from the age of fifteen and had known only the care of orphanages. Most of them had the characteristics of institutionalised children, and despite their years of disciplining and dragooning in orphanage schools and foundling institutions, their faces would break into almost sheepish smiles if the slightest sign of kindness or affection was aimed in their personal direction. Then, anxious to reciprocate, like dogs licking the hands of their owners after being made much of, they would become embarrassingly grateful."[1]

It is interesting indeed at this stage of my life to see myself as others saw me. But — Oh! my! was I really like that? The answer on one count at least is an emphatic NO! Never will I admit to having the characteristics of a fawning dog.

I once came under the command of a gunner officer named Rogers. Major Rogers was a 'ranker officer', who had commenced his army career as a 'badgy' (an artillery trumpeter). "You know, Nalden," he once said to me, "you remind me of a bloody little terrier — you get your teeth stuck into something, and will you let go? Will you hell! You hold on to it to the point of making a bloody little nusiance of yourself."

Yes, I accept Major Rogers's description of me as being truer-to-life than Mays's depiction of the hand-licking dog type.

Placing us out into service bands may have been an easy and convenient way out for the hospital, but for the majority of foundling boys it proved no more than a temporary expedient, leading them, as it all too frequently did, up the blindest of blind alleys.

Once we became inured to our new surroundings, we discovered the army way of life as being every bit as sheltered (albeit rougher and more uncouth) as life at the hospital.

The set term of service in those days was for a period of nine years with the Colours (i.e. the Regular Army), followed by a period of three years on the Reserve. But the initial nine years with the Colours did not start until the recruit had reached the age of 18, when he officially began his 'man's service'. For the foundling boy this meant a minimum term in the army of some 12 or 13 years, which would have brought him up to 27 years old. What then? A soldier could opt to apply for his discharge, or to convert his three years' Reserve into Colour service. What then? He could again opt to leave the service, or soldier on to complete 21 years' 'man's service', which would qualify him for a pension of something in the region of £1 per week.

Then came the day of reckoning, for the temporary expedient, the sheltered life, had come to an end.

There used to be a long-standing and oft-repeated joke, which went something like this:

Sergeant: 'Why haven't you done so-and-so?'

Soldier: 'I thought . . .'

Sergeant: 'Shut up — you're not paid to bleedin' well think!'

The 'joke' carried with it rather more than a grain of truth, for any individuality and personal initiative the average recruit might have had at the time of his enlistment was ever in mortal danger of being well and truly suppressed. There was all too little opportunity for personal initiative, as I myself was to discover. Everything was laid on — food, clothing, accommodation, sport, the lot. And in one regiment in which I served, even the day of the week and the time when a soldier must have his bath was regulated.

Should one be posted from one unit to another, his route and train times would be worked out.

Shielded as he was from day-to-day struggles and decisions which are essential to life, and having one person to do his thinking for him, and another to make decisions on his behalf, the pre-war serviceman's greatest potential enemy lurked not on the battlefield but within his own self. His brain was in constant danger of becoming dulled, his mind stagnant, and his whole personality atrophied. All too often his off-duty horizons at best reached out no further than the local cinema and the local variety theatre (such as Aldershot's notorious 'Blood-Tub'), and at worst, Aldershot's 'Rat-Pit' and 'Bengal Tiger' pubs, or the wet canteen.

T.E. Lawrence (writing under the pseudonym of Aircraftsman Ross) expresses this particular aspect of service life in rather more stark fashion:

"The airmen of the future will not be so owned, body and soul, by their service. Rather will they be the service, maintaining it, and their rights in it, as one with the officers. Whereas we have had no rights, except on paper, and few there. In the old days men had weekly to strip off boots and socks, and expose their feet for an officer's inspection. An ex-boy'd kick you in the mouth, as you bent down to look. So with the bath-rolls, a certificate from your N.C.O. that you'd had a bath during the week. One bath! And with the kit inspections, and room inspections, and equipment inspections, all excuses for the dogmatists among the officers to blunder, and for the nosy-parkers to make beasts of themselves."[2]

The bandsman having his instrument to occupy his time was generally held (not least by himself) as being a 'cut above' the ordinary 'duty' soldier. Be this as it may, the position in which most bandsmen found themselves at the expiry of their army service was no different from that of the ordinary 'duty' soldier; for both were now faced with making the first major decision probably of their respective lives — in two words, 'What now?'

The reasons for the situation in which the average army bandsman found himself are not difficult to discover.

As a conservative estimate, I would say that during the second and third decades of the present century, even allowing for the fall of the 'Geddes Axe', there averaged about 6000 bandsmen distributed between upwards of 140 army bands. To this number must be added the three bands of the Royal Marines, the several naval bands, and the newly-formed bands of the Royal Air Force.

At the expiry of their respective periods of service, a few bandsmen at the 'tip' of this musical pyramid found their way into certain of our symphony orchestras.

One would have expected that these few, having succeeded in overcoming what to the majority of their fellow-bandsmen might justifiably have appeared as insurmountable odds, that these few would now be honoured for their hard work and enterprise; for to have graduated from the world of band arrangements of Tosti's Songs, of military marches, and of piccolo, euphonium and xylophone solos, to the world of Beethoven, Brahms and Bartok was no mean feat, surely. But not a bit of it! For a small minority of their newly-found colleagues, adopting a pose of confident superiority mingled with lofty disdain, let it be known (and in one instance to the world at large) that these outsiders' military band backgrounds must ever stand in their way.

Thomas Russell, for example, finds the average orchestra's first violinists "lovably childish", speaks of violists and double bass players as sharing a "serious turn of mind", and of the cellists, "smart clothes, a certain loquacity, and good looks [which] often endear them to the fair sex". He finds on the other hand that "trumpets, trombones and tuba represent, with a few exceptions, the soldier returned 'to civilisation' — and not liking it overmuch. They have little sympathy with what might be called 'modern' ideas, and secretly believe that a good dose of military discipline would do those unruly fiddle players a world of good. It is not for nothing that they play instruments which are meant to be heard, whose dominoes resound throughout London, and whose mistakes cannot be erased. Their views are direct and intransigent; argument and verbosity are for the less masculine departments of the orchestra. But they are as simple as they are direct, and their loyalty is easily obtained when they feel they are getting a square deal — even when, in fact, they are not.''

Russell goes on: "Players of the heavier brass instruments are rarely teetotal; they may go into training for an important season, but the deep sigh of relief when it is all over is usually the preparation for blowing the froth from a pint of beer."

Quite a character reference!

The ex-army french horn player comes off rather better:

"Although many of them [horn players] have spent part of their younger life attached to one of the leading Army bands, military life seems to have left no very deep mark on them, and their association with the colours has been more a stage in their career than an experience of its own. The very scarcity of good performers on this instrument has made it worth their while to buy themselves out before the stigma of the Staff band has become too apparent."[3]

My personal comment on this piece of arrant nonsense, this blot on an otherwise fascinating 'inside story of an orchestra', is that all too frequently has the military musician become the target of Russell's brand of cleverness. From my own observation of different orchestras' personnel, I would say that the froth blowing, the intransigence and the rest, are neither more nor less characteristic of the brass section than they are of any other section of the orchestra.

So much for the military musician who climbed to the tip of the pyramid.

The next layer down, embracing instrumentalists every bit as accomplished as those at the tip of the pyramid, but setting their sights in a different (and be it said more lucrative) direction, found their respective ways into London's most fashionable dance bands of the 20s and early 30s, such as those led by Jack Payne, Jack Hylton, Debroy Somers, Ambrose and Henry Hall.

Many of the third-layer players found their employment with ocean-going liners, receiving a wage of £16 per month, for which they were expected to do their share of general deck duties when not actually entertaining the passengers with their music. A few others found their way into the 'silent' cinema, and into Lyons Corner House orchestras. I stress 'the few', as positions for wind instrumentalists in those orchestras were relatively few.

Massed at the foot of the pyramid were those who had never entertained the idea of breaking into the ranks of the music profession; who recognised themselves as no-hopers insofar as a career in music was concerned. There they were in their thousands, aged somewhere between 27 and 40, awaiting their discharge from the Army, but knowing no trade of any sort. It is true that a scheme was introduced during either the late 1920s or the early 1930s which offered the soldier coming up for discharge a six-months' vocational training course; but with all the goodwill and diligence of application in the world, it is hard to see how those taking the courses managed to master, in six months, trades whose periods of apprenticeship were reckoned in terms of years.

And so for the majority of army bandsmen returning to civilian life, it meant at best employment in positions such as those of hospital orderly, Army Field Stores worker, shop assistant or low-grade clerical assistant; and at worst, common labourer. One bandsman I knew, who was worthy of something very much better, was compelled to take on the job of stoker on the steamer which plied between the Channel Islands of Guernsey and Sark. Another, with a somewhat more original turn of mind, became Official Rat Catcher to the City of Southampton.

This is what I mean when earlier I suggested that the hospital's policy of sending most of its boys into army bands was for them no more than a temporary expedient; a postponement of the day when the majority of boys would find themselves faced with the unenviable task of carving out a new career at a time when the average man of like age had long since been settled in some trade or business. Far better had we all been taught trades, however lowly, which would have stood us in good stead throughout our lives. As it was, not one of us had ever been afforded the pleasurable experience of handling either chisel, saw or plane, so that for us the poem we learnt to recite by rote —

Drive the nail aright boy,
'it it on the 'ead.

held no practical significance.

After all, Jesus Christ was a carpenter, and what was good enough for Him, surely, should have been good enough for us.

The relatively small number of boys who for one reason or another did not join army bands were found civilian employment of some kind. Some went into clerical posts with City firms such as I. & R. Morley of Wood Street; and it certainly did not take some of their number long before they blossomed out in the City's regulation dress of sober serge suit, bowler hat, spats, and permanently-rolled umbrella. Two boys, Tillett and Dunster, were apprenticed to a commercial fishing company in Grimsby. Another boy, Ogden, after failing to make the grade as 'Buttons' in a London hotel, went to Westminster School — not, let me hasten to add, as a finishing school, but to wait upon his 'betters'.

Another boy, who showed exceptional promise as an artist, went farming in Canada. I well remember this same boy assisting Mr 'Fishbones' Chubb in painting the scenery for some of Mr Stork's plays. I remember him also for his exquisite water-colour of Westminster Abbey, which was officially 'hung' in our playroom. Yet another boy who was sent to Canada managed to work his way up from office boy into becoming chief editor of a Canadian newspaper. He was one of Mr Gray's 'Six'; and given the same opportunities which the English schoolboy of today accepts as part of his birthright, he would, I am certain, have carved out for himself a brilliant career in journalism.

No less brilliant was a boy named Tinley (another of Mr Gray's 'Six') who could have developed into as brilliant a mathematician as could M ... into a brilliant journalist.

It is a curious but sad fact that both these potentially brilliant boys should have been afflicted with a common weakness; they were both 'wet-beds', and because of this were made to suffer the daily humiliation of literally washing their dirty linen in public. This they did under the gaze of the remainder of the boys in their ward. One would have thought that the mental distress and physical discomfort occasioned by their affliction would have been regarded as punishment sufficient in itself. But not a bit of it. Even now I can hear Nurse Dovey snarling at them to 'get on with it'. There can be little doubt that the fundamental cause of the bed-wetting in both their cases was a psychological one, which today would be dealt with in a far more humane manner by a child guidance clinic.

I find it quite sad, even now, when I reflect back upon those things which might have been; the sort of careers our many bright young children might have followed had they been given opportunity of developing their natural and individual talents. Charles K ..., who showed a natural talent for writing and acting; Lidstone, Leigh and Furlong, three talented child artists; Buller, whose scientific preoccupation (through the medium of a weekly magazine) with the then newly-invented gadget known as wireless, filled us all with a 50/50 mixture of admiration and awe; Parr, who was forever designing something or other in that exquisitely-shaped handwriting of his; George Kemble, the pint-sized all-round sportsman; and not least, the many boys whose obvious musical talents should have found their expression through the medium of the orchestral, rather than the military band, background.

One can but lament, what a waste! What amount of talent there must have been which was never allowed to fulfil itself.

FOOTNOTES TO CHAPTER 18

[1] Spike Mays, *Fall out the Officers* (London, 1969), p.14.
[2] T.E. Lawrence, *The Mint* (London, 1955), p.196.
[3] Thomas Russell, *Philharmonic* (London, 1953), pp.105-9. Well do I remember at the time of *Philharmonic's* publication the furore created by Russell's remarks among the ranks of the staff bands' directors of music.

19: *Another three little boats*
leave harbour

With the Christmas of 1921 behind us, I became increasingly conscious
of the fact that I was soon to enter the year when (like lots of other 'little
boats' before me) I would be leaving harbour; for my 14th birthday and
our traditional school-leaving season were fast approaching. A further year
at school would have placed me well beyond normal school-leaving age.
I recall the case of only one boy leaving school at the relatively late age
of 16, and that due to the injuries he sustained in the 1918 summer camp
tragedy when he was pinned beneath one of the great branches of the fallen
beech tree.

For me, the year 1922 hardly got away to a promising start, for on
February 6th I went down with scarlet fever. I was sent to a fever hospital
in the London district of Tottenham N.15. After four weeks there, I was
transferred to a convalescent home in Winchmore Hill, where for the first
time since leaving Chertsey I knew what it was to eat, and eat, and eat
until I could take in no more. Plain, wholesome food it is true, but the
out-of-door activities in the hospital's playing fields gave one the sort of
appetite which would disgust the sensibilities even of a newly-weaned puppy.

On the day of my discharge, I was handed back my fumigated Foundling
Hospital uniform, to be surrounded by a puzzled, rather than an admiring,
group of ward sisters, nurses and fellow patients. Clearly, they had never
seen anything quite like it; a boy of 13 dressed in long trousers (minus turn-
ups) a bum-freezer jacket with the top one only of its six brass-crested
buttons being fastened, this revealing a bright red waistcoat, which in turn

sported a further six crested buttons, but these all fastened. And as though this were not enough, there were red sergeant stripes and a lyre woven in gold on the right sleeve, and an inverted gold stripe on the left sleeve — the ensemble being topped off with an Eton-style collar, black bow, and a forage-style cap, carrying the school crest and a further two brass buttons.

And yet I was not unduly sensitive regarding the curiosity my clothes aroused, which was more than I would be able to admit to when faced with a similar situation in an army barrack-room some 10 months later.

Once back at the Foundling Hospital, I was admitted straightway to the infirmary's isolation wing, as a precaution I suppose against the possibility of infecting other children. The point I am leading up to is that I must have missed a good two months' schooling — scarcely a matter for deep personal regret to the average schoolboy. Being in my final year, I was automatically in Standard 'X-7', where little serious work was carried on anyway.

When the scarlet fever epidemic had spent itself, the whole school was assembled and told in no uncertain terms that all letter-writing to hospital staff members and patients alike must cease forthwith. We were not told why. And so we returned once again to our previous state of splendid isolation from the strange, busy world which continued to go its own way beyond those massive iron gates.

And then came the summer camp at Bognor, which, as I have already said, gave all of us our first ever glimpse of the sea.

Back from camp, I found myself in for the happiest of happy surprises — nomination for the highest award of the year, the Presentation Watch. It had been the custom each year for two children (a boy and a girl), to be awarded a medal apiece, known as the Robert Grey Prize. In 1921 the headmaster's wife conceived the idea that the award should be in the form of something more practical; and as this thought came from the headmaster's wife and not from the headmaster himself, the school authorities readily took the point and substituted Mrs Holgate's suggestion of a watch in place of the hitherto traditional medal.

The girl nominated along with me was one Maria Kenny. On the day of the presentation I was instructed to change from boots into rubber-soled slippers, as the ceremony was to take place in the Court Room, whose highly polished wooden floor registered its silent disapproval of having its surface exposed to the ravages of a pair of hob-nailed, steel-tipped boots. The presentation took place during a Court Meeting, an awesome gathering of our Governors and Guardians which struck instant fear into my already fluttering heart. Here I must confess to the truth, which is that every alternate flutter at least was occasioned by my close proximity to Maria, whom I had secretly worshipped (albeit at a distance of never less than 100 yards) for a very long time. (My repeated efforts, once I had left school, to strike up a friendship with Maria — or 'Grace' as she herself preferred to be called — met with as many rebuffs. It was all very hurtful.)

In my own case, unfortunately, the substitution of watch for medal was not to prove itself the practical solution for which Mrs Holgate had battled. Whether from over-frequent succumbing on my part to the temptation of reading the engraving on its inner case, or whether from some quite different cause, the unhappy fact remains that no watchmaker has ever been able to put it into going order. And perhaps I became a little over-sensitive when each successive watchmaker would shoot at me either a patronising, or an arch look, and murmur, 'Mm — good boy, eh?' For engraved on the inside cover is 'The Robert Grey Prize for Good Conduct. Charles Nalden, 1922.' Inset in the presentation case is a portrait of the donor, bearing the legend, 'The "Robert Grey" Prize. Governor 1878. Treasurer 1892-1914. He loved the children.'

And so there the watch remains — still in its red silk-lined case, its hands stubbornly refusing to budge this last half-century from their comfortably embedded 5.45 setting. 5.45 am or pm? I cannot say; memory has closed that particular door.

Maria Kenny's life turned out to be a sad one. She was one of two privileged girls who managed to escape the close-meshed net of domestic service, and instead, was trained at the hospital's expense as a Norland Nurse. One day, in an unguarded moment, her little charge was attacked while asleep in its pram by an Alsation dog. From that day on Maria's life developed into one unbroken sequence of admissions to, and discharges from, mental hospitals.

As explained earlier on in my story, one of my duties as Mr Holgate's 'boy' was to knock on his bedroom door somewhere around the hour of 6 am daily and have ready for him a cup of tea, over which he would meditate (constantly muttering to himself the words 'I dun'no') in his dressing room. This room was an L-shaped affair, which allowed each of us to take his tea out of the view of the other — a not-altogether bad arrangement from both our viewpoints. On one such morning, he suddenly snapped out of his reverie with "Oh! Nalden! I've managed to fix you up with a job. You are going (not, mark you, 'how would you like to go') you are going into the offices of a woollen factory in Yorkshire, with the prospect, one day, of becoming manager yourself." I replied, simply, "Thank you, sir" — for we all came to accept such news of our prospective careers in the same unemotional, unquestioning manner in which we accepted all else in our lives. And so I resigned myself to office life in a

Yorkshire woollen factory, although (ungrateful though it may appear) I cannot recall experiencing at the time any feelings of personal elation at the glittering prospect of my occupying, in God's good time, the manager's chair.

It must have been some few weeks later, and in the same early-morning-cup-of-tea setting when Mr Holgate casually informed me that the Yorkshire job was off, and that instead, together with another boy, Ted Parker, I was to go into the firm of I. & R. Morley of Wood Street, City. I recall thinking to myself that this was a better prospect than the Yorkshire position, for I would now be near my old school and (more attractive still) my old Chertsey home.

But the wheel of fate was to take yet another turn, and yet another, before finally pointing its finger at what was to be my ultimate destiny. In just as casual a manner as though nothing had preceded this, his latest proposal, Mr Holgate broke the news that the City job was off, and that I had been accepted into the Band of His Majesty's Regiment of Royal Artillery, Woolwich. Had this newest proposal materialised, it would have meant my taking far smaller a step into the unknown than had I stalked the Yorkshire Moors or walked the streets of the City of London; for two of our old boys had joined this band as far back as 1912, of whom one, Dick Escott, was already well known to me.

Yet again, it was not to be, for Mr Holgate broke the news to me that this latest prospect was 'off'. Although he gave me no reason, my own private guess at the time (although I had no proof of this) was that my prowess (or my lack of it) as a cornettist had gone on before me to reach the musical ear of the then Director of Music of the Royal Artillery Band, one Captain Stretton. Recalling (as at the time I remember doing) Mr Holgate's remarks of some few months earlier, I knew Bandmaster Owen's opinion of me as the band's solo cornet to be a remarkably low one.

Just as surely as the cuckoo is a harbinger of the English spring, so to Foundling band boys was the visiting army bandmaster a harbinger of the English autumn. And just as surely as the cuckoo, once it has mated, changes the notes of its call from the plaintive interval of a minor third to the more sexually satisfying interval of a major third, so too did these visiting bandmasters, once they had accomplished their respective missions, relax their hitherto taut lips into a teeth-baring, happy 'Got you!' smile.

Each successive autumn would witness a steady stream of these bandmasters plying between Mr Moffit's gate and our band practice room. They were simply following in the same footsteps and bent on the same mission as that of their illustrious predecessor of some three-quarters of a century earlier, Bandmaster Charles Godfrey, of Her Majesty's

Coldstream Guards. Expressed less romantically, these well-dressed and sometimes expensive-looking gentlemen were driven by the harsh realities of Service life which bade them populate their bands or perish.

Their business techniques were remarkably little removed in style from those of the slave marketeers of early Rome, from whom I vow they could have traced their descent. Indeed, I'll swear to it that on one occasion when we were lined up for a looking-over by one of their number, I heard fall from his saintly Gregorian lips (so faintly as to be almost inaudible), "Non Angli sunt sed angeli."

When years later I myself became a bandmaster, I found myself faced with the stark truth, that in order to recruit a boy for one's band, one simply had to be prepared to grease the palm of the school bandmaster, whose best boys went, understandably I suppose, to the highest bidder. This was by no means always the case; knowing, for example, Mr Cawley's deep and genuine affection for his boys, I cannot imagine his having resorted to this practice. And the first and (as it was to prove) the last time I tried it myself, I was gently rebuked by the school bandmaster concerned with "Thank you very much, Nalden, but my school pays me a sufficiently high salary." The bandmaster's name was Lovell, and it was no coincidence that he should have named one of his marches *The Triumph of Right.*

Bandmaster Underwood walked into our bandroom during one of our practices. He stood listening for a while, and then made a discreet withdrawal with our own Bandmaster Owen to a far corner of the room, becoming engaged in what appeared to us a deep and earnest conversation. Mr Owen then beckoned me over and asked of me would I like to join the Band of the Cheshire Regiment. Whether he (Mr Owen) was unaware of Mr Holgate's intelligence concerning the Royal Artillery (Woolwich) Band, or whether he was endeavouring to circumvent that intelligence with a counter-offer of his own, I never discovered. It has been said that none is so bold as the naturally reserved man who, in a moment of confidence, throws his reticence to the winds. Surprising myself even, I gave a firm "No thank you sir." Mr Owen proceeded to caution me as to the great opportunity I was throwing away; but some inner strength came to my rescue, enabling me to repeat, "No thank you sir."

It was the first time that anything quite like this had happened to me. It was not to be the last time, whereby some hidden hand, some powerful force, intervened on my behalf when I found myself standing alone and unsure of myself at life's crossroads. It remains true that ultimately I did join an army band; but as subsequent events over the years were to prove, it was a band whose conditions of service, and whose direct bearing on my post-army career were such as to become the means of opening up

opportunities which neither would, nor indeed could, have come my way
had I joined the Band of the Cheshire Regiment.

It becomes scarcely necessary for me to record that upon hearing my
polite but firm "No thank you sir", the cuckoo reverted to his plaintive
call of a minor third, and my would-be employer adopted a facial expression
quite unknown to Alice's Cheshire Puss.

Going back a year to 1921; there came into our bandroom one day a
dapper little man, with a closely-cropped moustache, just as closely-cropped
hair, and a smile which revealed a gold tooth. There and then, he contracted
with Mr Cawley to take five of our boys in one fell swoop. He was
Bandmaster Thomas James Hillier, of the Royal Artillery (Mounted) Band,
whose permanent station was Aldershot. Returning once again to 1922;
when I learnt from Mr Holgate of yet another placing out (the Royal
Artillery Band, Woolwich) falling through, it was with a sense of elation
that I received the news from him of my being accepted into the Royal
Artillery (Mounted) Band under Mr Hillier; for in all, this band boasted
having seven foundling boys in its ranks. And there was another, and
scarcely less important, cause for elation — being a mounted band, its
members wore riding breeches and spurs, against the dull puttees and
trousers of the Woolwich Band musicians. I had already travelled a fair
distance — from the prospect of sitting on an office stool in Yorkshire
to the now-assured reality of sitting on a horse in Aldershot.

The reader need express no surprise when I say that I had emerged quite
unscathed from a number of situations which could have resulted in a whole
series of emotional upsets; for as I have already said, our acceptance in
general of this sort of thing was simply a manifestation of the discipline
to which we had become inured. It taught us to accept everything that came
our way as inevitable consequences of our respective lots in life — accepting
everything, questioning nothing, blaming nobody.

It was Max Beerbohm who wrote "the advantage of a public school
education in the bad old days was that, after it, almost anything that befell
one seemed an easy option." So too with our particular style of upbringing;
for after eight years of being bred in an atmosphere of strict isolation from
the outside world; after eight years of being bred in an atmosphere of
servility, after eight years of being liable to receive a caning for the most
trivial offence, of stopping dead in one's tracks (no matter what game or
occupation one might be engaged in) to stand stiffly to attention in
deference to a passing governor; of undertaking without question every
menial task demanded of one, from carrying a master's coals from the
basement to his third-floor sitting room, to floor-scrubbing, dish-washing
and the rest; after eight years of all this and more to find oneself destined

on one day to work in a woollen factory and on the next to enter an army band, took no learning, no process of mental re-adjustment at all. For we came to accept every day-to-day happenings as inevitable.

And so it came about that along with two other boys I was to join the Royal Artillery (Mounted) Band, which would thus bring to 10 the number of foundlings in that unit.

One of the foundling chapel vergers told me what a lucky young fellow I was — "Seven bob a week and all found — what more could a young fellow like you want. Wish I had had a start in life like that!" I am sure that these sentiments represented to him the truth.

Upon her learning that I was to join the Army, Mrs Betts's reaction (so her husband later told me) was to have a weep. And Mr Morley cold-comforted me by pointing out that "Aldershot is at least a little better than that terrible Tidworth Camp."

It was on Tuesday, October 31st, 1922, that Mr Holgate took the three of us to the London Army Recruiting Centre — a grim, soulless, frightening, 19th century barracks of a place, which made our own buildings by way of comparison appear to exude a warmth and friendliness such as we had never before realised.

First, we were ordered to strip, stark naked, for our medical examination. It was all so puzzlingly impersonal. One at least had been consciously aware of Sister Cleeve's aloofness of manner, and of Dr Swift's bark, but the army doctor who examined us registered just nothing. Everything was coldly formal and mechanical — "Cough" — "Take in deep breaths" — "Raise your right knee, now your left" — "Read these letters" — "Stand on tip-toe".

It was all as clinically statistical as my 'Description on Attestation':

Name: — Nalden, Charles.
Age on enlistment: — 14 years, 230 days.
Complexion: — Fresh.
Eyes: — Grey.
Hair: — Black.
Height: — 4 ft. 11½ inches.

This part of the enlistment process over, we were next ushered into another room, and each handed a copy of the Holy Bible. "Clasp the Bible between the forefingers and thumbs of your left hands; now lay your right hands on the cover."

Having satisfied himself that we were duly impressed with the awful solemnity of the vows we were about to make, the recruiting officer told us to repeat after him, phrase by phrase, the *Oath of Attestation:* "I, Charles Nalden, do solemnly promise and swear that I will be faithful, and bear true allegiance to His Majesty King George V, his heirs and successors, and that I will faithfully serve in the British Army, and that I will loyally observe all orders of His Majesty, his heirs, and successors, and of the officers set over me until I shall lawfully be discharged. So help me God.''

We had now been 'sworn in', and at the same time had bound ourselves in solemn contract to His Majesty King George V, from which (short of purchasing one's discharge) there was no possible loophole of escape. The contract was infinitely more binding and inescapable than that of marriage; for to desert one's wife was not regarded as a criminally punishable offence. But to desert from His Majesty's Forces in those days led automatically to trial by court martial, followed by a stretch in that grim and dreaded military prison to which few returned for a second dose — the notorious Aldershot 'Glasshouse'.

After being sworn in, we were taken to a third room, and ordered to step forward as our names were called to receive our first week's pay. Phew! None of us ever before had handled quite so large a sum at one time. "Lucky young fellow — seven bob a week, and all found.'' How very right the verger had been!

On the morning of the following day we were given permission to make our rounds of the hospital at will in order to make our fond farewells. My own round took in the kitchen, whose staff members had always given me a bit of anything that might be going when I went there to collect the masters' suppers. This visit, by the way, produced the very thing I had hoped it would produce — fortification of the inner man in preparation for the swift-approaching ordeal. Mrs Betts loaded me up with a parcel of goodies, as did Mrs Holgate. One of our number was permitted to spend some little time with his twin sister, Fanny.

Mr Holgate reminded us that once fitted out by the Army, we were to return our school uniforms, except our boots, which we were permitted to keep.

Later that same morning we were summoned to secretary Nichols's office, in which all departing foundlings were officially farewelled.

The traditional form of farewell, which held good through the greater part of the 19th Century, was to present the departing foundling with a parchment proffering him this advice:

"You are placed out Apprentice by the Governors of this Hospital. You were taken into it very young, quite helpless, forsaken, poor, and deserted. Out of Charity you have been fed, clothed, and instructed; which many have wanted.

"You have been taught to fear God; to love him, to be honest, careful, laborious, and diligent. As you hope for Success in this World, and

Happiness in the next, you are to be mindful of what has been taught you. You are to behave honestly, justly, soberly, and carefully, in every thing, to every body, and especially towards your Master and his Family; and to execute all lawful commands with Industry, Cheerfulness and good Manners. You may find many temptations to do wickedly, when you are in the world; but by all means fly from them. Always speak the Truth. Though you may have done a wrong thing, you will, by sincere Confession, more easily obtain Forgiveness, than if by an obstinate Lie you make the fault the greater, and thereby deserve a far greater Punishment. Lying is the beginning of every Thing that is bad; and a Person used to it is never believed, esteemed, or trusted.

"Be not ashamed that you were bred in this Hospital. Own it; and say, that it was through the good Providence of Almighty God, that you were taken Care of. Bless him for it.

"Be constant in your Prayers, and going to Church; and avoid Gaming, Swearing, and all evil Discourses. By this means the Blessing of God will follow your honest Labours, and you may be happy; otherwise you will bring upon yourself Misery, Shame, and Want.''

This form of farewell no longer held in my own day. Even so, we had been made no less conscious than had our 19th century counterparts of the immovable boundary line which defines Right from Wrong; no less conscious of the solid Virtues of Truth, Honesty, Industry and Sobriety, as of the squalid Vices of Lying, Cheating, Slothfulness and Incontinence.

What our own peculiar style of upbringing had failed to achieve, or put the other way round, what it had managed to instil into every one of us (albeit unintentionally), was a sense of inferiority, which in turn made us unsure of ourselves.

Looking back upon the whole scene, I feel bound to say, and this without malice, that the 18th Century hospital regulation which ordained 'that the Officers of the Hospital do often remind the Children of the Lowness of their Condition and that they [the children] ought to submit to the lowest Stations', even in my day was still strongly ingrained within the system; too strongly for it to have shown any signs of its dying even slowly.

For example, saintly man though he was, and I do not say this unkindly (for I loved him dearly), had the school chaplain known when baptising me that he was holding in his arms a future Doctor of Music, university professor, and CBE, then I remain convinced that in deference to the above regulation, he would have dropped me, head first, on to the chapel's uncompromising 18th century stone floor. Mercifully, he must have taken for granted that he was bringing into the Anglican faith just another little soldier boy of the future — which I suppose he was.

During our eight years in the Foundling Hospital (the Henley-on-Thames river outing and the closely-supervised annual Christmas Tree parties excepted), none of us had enjoyed the company of the opposite sex of our own respective age groups for the space even of one minute.

I scarcely need say that the effects of the system were potentially damaging.

In her recently published account of the Foundling Hospital*, Ruth McClure admits to finding herself unable to arrive at conclusive answers to such questions as the extent to which a foundling's early history marked his or her personality; as to whether foundlings wondered who they were and how much it mattered to them. Were the adult foundlings ashamed of their origins and eager to escape and deny them?

Set against this negativism the author becomes more sure of herself when she writes: "On the whole, however, there is a strong probability that the Foundlings suffered no great psychological damage."[1]

As one who went through the whole gamut, I can but comment that there can be no such generalisation on fundamental issues as these.

As Ruth McClure herself well knows, many foundling old boys and girls continue to attend Coram, and Charter Day, reunions. On the other hand I know of others whose devastating experiences of life in the London Foundling Hospital determined them never again to go near the place.

As to wondering who we were, and how much it mattered to us, we have only to recall the case of the young ex-foundling boy who in 1974 perched himself on the roof of the Coram Foundation building, threatening, unless told his 'natural' mother's name, to hurl himself to his death — and this in full view of the Queen who was visiting the institution.

And what of the foundling girl who consistently refused her fiance's proposals of marriage unless and until she was given information relating to the circumstances of her birth?**

Many another foundling has felt no less strongly about the system, but has managed nevertheless to give vent to his or her smouldering resentments in less spectacular fashion. I quote my own case.

It was c.1950 that I wrote to secretary Hardy Nichols seeking information regarding my true parentage. In refusing me the information, Mr Nichols cosily suggested that today's society had become far more liberal-minded on the illegitimacy issue. The manner in which I released my own decades-old tensions was to follow this up by making strong representations to the secretary that the 18th century rule which safeguarded the identity of the

* *Coram's Children*
** Information given me by a former secretary of the Coram Foundation.

mother be repealed. (I was later told by my old master, Wyndham Charles Gray, that it was efforts such as mine which led in 1953 to foundlings being furnished as of right with the shortened form of birth certificate — but in their foundling-bestowed names.)

It is as well perhaps that I never sought actual reunion with my mother, for, as one former secretary of the hospital put it to me: "Someone is bound to get hurt."

Ruth McClure questions were foundlings ashamed of their origins and eager to escape and deny them? The plain commonsense reply to this is that no foundling ever need be ashamed of his origin for the very good reason of his having had no say in the matter of his entry into this world. On the other hand, human nature being what it is, and having ingrained within it, as it does, those deep-rooted traits of mischief-making, sanctimoniousness, hypocrisy, and the most woeful of all human failings, that of deriving some warped kind of pleasure from the misfortunes of others — is it to be wondered at that we illegitimates are not exactly bursting to proclaim to the world our origins?

A further difficulty experienced by many a foundling arises from the attitude of the marriage partner. Some partners are easy about it but others quite the reverse. Some partners will accompany their foundling spouses, quite unconcernedly, to foundling reunions, whereas others, intentionally or otherwise, will embarrass their partners by their persistent refusals to attend.

In my own marriage the matter was never discussed, and it was not until my children were well into adulthood that they were given the facts of my origin.

Again speaking for myself, for the greater part of my life I found it difficult to mix easily. I was awkward in company, and particularly so when in the company of my own sex. I was long tortured with feelings of inferiority, especially when coming into contact with people who had enjoyed superior educational advantages: all symptomatic of the effects which boarding schools are liable to have on young boys.

Then again, throughout the course of my life the consequences of my beginnings have had the annoying habit of surfacing periodically, only to land me in some embarrassing situation; for example when required to furnish particulars of my parents for the marriage licence, the passport, the insurance policy, and the rest. And worst of all the simple question "Are both your parents still living?" It was as though Mr Weller's charity boy was forever lurking around the corner ready to chuckle at my discomfiture.

Paradoxical though it may sound, this lack of faith in myself was dispelled in part through the influence of a person whose lack of faith in his own self was more deep-rooted, I suspect, than was my own. On the day I was leaving the Royal Artillery Band to enter the Royal Military School of Music (Kneller Hall) on a studentship for army bandmaster, Mr Hillier counselled me to think seriously in terms of taking the university degree of Bachelor in Music. "Whatever else you do," he said in his quiet way, "you must not make the same mistake that I made, in thinking that you cannot do it." Mr Hillier had passed all but the final examination; in this, he had failed once, and made no further attempt.

A deeper and more abiding faith in myself was brought about by the untiring ministrations on my behalf by my wife Peggy. Her faith in me and in what she felt I should be able to accomplish never faltered. In good time, by dint of persuading, cajoling, and as I termed it teasingly 'Lady Macbething' me ('Infirm of purpose! Give me the daggers'), she managed to succeed in convincing me that my early upbringing need not stand in my way.

We were farewelled by being presented with a Bible (which I still have), a prayer book and five shillings, which for most of us represented the total sum of our worldly possessions.

But not at this point of time, even on the very eve of our final departure, were we acquainted with the reason for our being admitted to the Foundling Hospital. We thus left the institution in the same state of blessed ignorance as that in which we had entered it some eight years earlier.

Between farewells and departure, not a few of the boys (including some from whom we would have expected rather more self-control, such as bullies), broke down and wept. For some reason or other, none of our trio did that. And neither did the abrupt severance from the place I had come to love involve me personally in anything like the desperate emotional upheaval caused by my equally abrupt severance from my foster-home of eight years earlier. But I do not deny that I was heavy-hearted.

Mr Gray was given the duty of piloting us out of harbour. The great iron gate was opened for us by dear old Moffit, who enclosed each of our hands in turn within the grasp of both his own poor misshapen hands as he wished us 'goodbye and good luck'.

We walked the length of Guilford Street into Southampton Row, where we caught the No.68 bus for Waterloo Station. It was a characteristically cold and wet November's afternoon, but once we became caught up in the non-stop bustle and excitement of one of London's great railway termini we were not conscious of the weather. As we were waiting for the Aldershot train to draw in, I found myself envying a young porter, who was whistling as he went cheerfully about his duties.

Unlike the three of us, who were about to step into the unknown, he at least knew where he was going.

After explaining that we would be met at Aldershot station by a group of our own old boys, Mr Gray continued to chat on any and every subject short of that which lay immediately ahead of us. Just as well attempt to console a person recently bereaved; for although in common with most other of our boys we had 'glished jolly thick' for the day when we would be leaving school, stranded as we were at that particular moment in time in a sort of no man's land, our faces must have told a quite different story. Even so, whatever the state of our feelings, I'll warrant that Mr Gray's heart was a good deal heavier than any of ours.

He remained standing on the platform until the train pulled out. We lost sight of him as the train rounded the familiar bend, to speed on its course through Vauxhall, on to Clapham Junction — strangely symbolic of life's 'Clapham Junction' which we choose to call the 'cross-roads of destiny'.

So came to a close the happiest of blank childhoods.

FOOTNOTES TO CHAPTER 19

[1] Ruth McClure, *Coram's Children* (Yale, 1981), pp.236, 243.

PART II
BITTER

The Royal Artillery (Mounted) Band, 1922. Author at extreme left of front row. Bandmaster Hillier, sixth from left in second row.

20: His Majesty's Royal Artillery (Mounted) Band

As soon as the train drew out of Waterloo station we opened the food parcel Mrs Betts had packed for me. There was really little else we could do, for being in the same boat as it were, we were of little comfort to each other. Arthur N . . . 's case was perhaps the most pathetic, for he had left behind his twin sister.

Once safely in the train it was the practice of some foundling boys to cut off any badges of rank they may have had, such as sergeant and good conduct stripes. It did not occur to me to do this. It was an oversight on my part that soon I was to regret.

It was at either Woking, Brookwood or Ash Vale station that we were joined by a gentleman who sported a full handsome moustache (of the style that must have given the 19th century inventor his inspiration for the once-popular moustache cup), set beneath a fine patrician nose. He asked us where we were bound for. We told him, whereupon he produced from his waistcoat pocket a french horn mouthpiece. "This is one of my instruments," he explained to us, "my other is the harp." A curious coincidence, for these ultimately were to be my own instruments.

As we approached Aldershot station, Mr Buckmaster (for that was the gentleman's name) pointed out to us our future 'home' in Waterloo Barracks East.

We were met on the station by a group of ex-foundling boys who escorted us to the barracks.

I think we were all fearfully nervous of entering the barrack room. I certainly did not wish to be the first one to go in. One of our ex-foundling boys, E.L., took me gently by the arm and led me in. We were introduced to Bombardier Claude Ward who was NCO i/c Boys' Room. He allotted us our beds.

I then started to take in the room into which were crowded (and I mean crowded) about 15 other boys.

Waterloo Barracks dated approximately from the Crimean War period. Just outside the door was a raised concrete slab upon which once reposed the night bucket. The whitewashed walls were of rough, unplastered brick. Each window was guarded with full-length, prison-like iron bars, which ran horizontally. We could hardly not have compared the state of the floor with the spotlessly clean ward floors we had just left behind, for it was plain filthy — stinking filthy.

There was a good reason for this. Writing on barrack room conditions during the first quarter of the 19th century, Fortescue mentions 'instances of rooms 32 feet long, 20 feet broad, and 12 feet high, where twenty soldiers ate, drank, slept, and did everything but drill'. Apart from the fact that the space between our beds was some 30 inches against their five inches, barrack room conditions in my day had not altered from those described by Fortescue; for our barrack room likewise was a multi-purpose affair. In it we had our meals, received religious instruction at the hands of the army chaplain, took 'rudiments of music' lessons from Bombardier Flux, horse-played around, and slept.

The room was lit by means of two gas jets, which more often than not gave out the barest flicker of a light, for the boys were forever breaking the delicate gossamer-like mantles. The normal method of extinguishing the gas was for a boy to stand on a form, and pull the 'off' chain. But on Friday nights when the forms had been scrubbed in readiness for the next morning's room inspection, the method then was for the tallest boy to take a running jump and hope for the best. This, and the horse-play, were the main causes for gas-mantle breakages.

The total furniture consisted of two tables, which were set on iron trestles, and two forms. The beds puzzled me, but I did not have the temerity to ask whether we were expected to go to sleep in a horizontal position; for the overall length of each bed was only about 34 to 40 inches. An hour or two later the mystery solved itself when a series of ear-piercing screeches (which were not unlike the sound of a London tube-train grinding to a halt) revealed that the beds were telescoped affairs, becoming normally-sized once the lower half had been pulled out. Three ugly brown coir mattresses ('biscuits' in army parlance) added up to one whole mattress, and I swear the rock-hard pillows had less 'give' in them than their marble counterparts upon which repose the heads of sculptured, arms-folded knights who lie peacefully at rest in our ancient cathedrals.

Above each bed was an iron rack to which was attached a wooden shelf. The rack was used for storing our 'best' uniforms, 'Wellington' and jack boots (which at all times were required to be immaculately arranged), and the shelf for our crockery, cutlery, shaving gear and the like. Stored underneath each of our beds was a kit box, in which we kept our cleaning materials, and what few of this world's material goods we possessed. In one corner of the room stood a collection of brooms, long-handled 'dry scrubbers', mops and hand-scrubbers. A solitary wall cupboard was used for storing what left-overs there may have been from the previous day's bread and margarine ration. It was, of course, usually empty.

The only alterations that had been made since the barracks were built (that is, within about 75 years) were the addition of gas-lighting and the substitution of a water-flushed urinal for the night bucket.

The night urinal was encrusted with a foul-looking, evil-smelling, deep-brown scaly substance, the accumulation of years. Its state was such that nobody would enter it in his bare feet. (Some year or two later a newly-appointed NCO i/c boys had us clean it with undiluted spirits of salts.)

The lavatories proper were situated outside, at the rear of the band block. I shall not attempt to describe them, as even at this distance of time the very thought of their primitiveness stirs up in me feelings of nausea.

Ablutions were carried out in the washhouse, which was adjacent to the urinal. There were no wash-basins, but one long slate slab, which was served by some three or four cold water taps. There were no facilities for heating water, either in summer or winter.

There were no baths in the block. We were expected to take weekly baths (at our own expense) at one of the numerous soldiers' homes. The Percy Illingsworth Institute (the 'Pip-I') at the top of Gun Hill offered you a bath for sixpence, and the Rotunda in Aldershot town itself, one for eightpence. Some of us felt the additional twopence to be worthwhile, as the Rotunda not only cleaned their baths with Vim (against the paraffin used by the Pip-I) but also allowed one unlimited hot water (which the Pip-I did not). And neither was one expected to hand in one's cap as a deposit on a towel.

There was one curious incongruity. High up on our barrack room walls were some old prints of grave-looking, spade-bearded gentlemen who belonged clearly to some bygone age. The only names I can now recall are those of Byrd and Palestrina. Some short time later we were made to lower them to eye level 'as' (so it was explained to us) 'they are all part of your musical education'.

A military band arrangement by Gordon Jacob, *A William Byrd Suite* (which came out a year or so later) did nothing to endear us to the spade-bearded gentleman of that name. Besides to us boys it seemed a bit sloppy having to play a piece called *Jhon come kisse me now*.

On my first evening in the army, my ex-foundling friend E.L. took me to Aldershot's Theatre Royal which was staging *The Walls of Jericho*. Our seats in the 'gods' cost us threepence each. (E.L. has yet to repay the threepence he borrowed from me.)

Both the Theatre Royal and the Aldershot Hippodrome and the several cinemas held two 'houses' on each night. We went to the 'first house' which emptied out somewhere around 7.45 pm. Except on the occasion of Iris Holgate's concert, never had I been out so late.

Once we returned to barracks the air became rent with trumpet calls — First Post (9.30 pm), Last Post (10 pm) and finally Lights Out (10.15 pm). Harsher and more strident than the blare of the trumpet was the follow-up of the Duty NCO's voice "Get them bloody lights out!"

That night I cried myself to sleep, albeit silently.

We were roused next morning by the 6 am Reveille call, and at daybreak were mustered on the barrack square for what was to be the first of our daily foot-drill parades. All this was carried out without even so much as an early morning mug of tea (known in army circles as *Gunfire*) for breakfast was not 'dished up' until a couple of hours later.

Shortly before the daily band practice was due to commence, the three of us were called out by name and marched into Bandmaster Hillier's office.

In the office were two army blanket-covered trestle tables and a glass-doored bookcase, whose learned tomes some few years later I was permitted to browse through at leisure. The collection included the six-volume *Oxford History of Music*, *Grove's Dictionary of Music* and a number of other scholarly books on music. One such book was W.G. Whittaker's *Bach's Cantatas* which some few years later was to be pressed into my hand by Bandmaster 'Tim' Hillier himself. I still have it, and it still bears the stamp Royal Artillery (Mounted) Band, Aldershot.*

---

* The Band just failed to celebrate its centenary. It was formed in 1887 and disbanded in 1983 as a result of the Thatcher Government's cuts in defence expenditure.

Seated at one of the tables was Mr Hillier, and at the other Band Sergeant-Major G.W.E. Soars (or 'Gee-Whizz' as we called him).

It came naturally to us to stand stiffly to attention, for our Foundling Hospital training had taught us at a very early age that particular basic principle of behaviour.

Both Messrs Hillier and Soars remarked what a fine trio of boys we were, and went on to wish us a happy life in the band. Tim was a dapper, well-groomed man, with the then army style of closely-cropped hair, and an even more closely-trimmed moustache. (The wax-ended moustache, although occasionally to be seen on the odd 'old sweat', had long since been deprived of its former unchallenged fashionability.)

I noticed that when Mr Hillier smiled he revealed a gold tooth, which determined me upon having at least one of those for myself one day. (I recalled Mr Gray's telling us of the world heavyweight boxing champion Jack Johnson, who, he alleged, sported a whole mouthful of gold teeth.)

Strangely enough, 'Tim' did not appear at all at his ease, for he was shuffling about in nervous fashion until it came time for us to be marched out. His nervous manner rubbed off on to his fox terrier Scamp, who would snap even at the hand that went to feed him.

In later years I was able to assess the man. He was highly nervous, quite unsure of himself, and certainly not the army type. I think he must have been brought up in an orphanage, for when sympathising with a band member who had lost his mother, he consoled him with "Perhaps you should consider yourself fortunate in having known your mother."

Mr Hillier was born in 1879, and enlisted as a boy in the Royal Artillery Band, Woolwich. He entered Kneller Hall c.1907, and was appointed Bandmaster of the Middlesex Regiment which was stationed in India. He once related to me the story of his arrival in India. His band sergeant greeted him with, "Thank God you've come, sir." The reason for this emotional outburst soon became clear when Tim's commanding officer greeted him with "Well, Mr Hillier, you are here; but let me tell you at once that I don't like either bands or bandmasters."

It was only those people who really knew 'Tim' who would have understood the effect that this boorish form of introduction would have had on him. 'Tim' must have led a thoroughly miserable existence in India, particularly during the hot season, when married men's families were sent up to the hill stations, leaving their spouses to sweat it out on the plains. Hillier put it to me thus: "I had to choose between frequenting the sergeants' mess which I loathed, or sitting in my room all day on my own. I chose the mess."

He was later appointed to the Royal Artillery (Gibraltar) Band, and finally to the Aldershot Band.

A serious, scholarly musician, 'good at paper work', Band Quarter-Master-Sergeant 'Perce' Rudd once described him to me. At the time I joined the band, he already had passed the University of Durham's first examination for the degree of Bachelor in Music, and had had his musical 'exercise' accepted (which in those days preceded the second written, or 'final' examination). He went up to Durham to sit his finals in 1923, failed, and never again attempted it. This in itself gives a penetrating insight into his make-up — his utter lack of self-confidence which was not helped by his exaggerated idea of what he thought to be the civilian graduate's musical superiority.

His conducting was wooden and uninspired; not because of his lack of musicianship, but because of a natural diffidence which caused him to shrink from any form of limelight. Even though he maintained a firm disciplinary control over the men in the band, on the rare occasion when he attempted to create a spirit of bonhomie by cracking a joke, his sallies, more often than not were greeted with a stony silence, for he did not have the personality to put the joke across, however witty it may have been.

Tim nursed an almost obsessional fear of horses, which was not lessened when once he was thrown by Kitty, the most gentle of our band horses. He loathed having to take any form of disciplinary action against us, and he had a strong aversion to the army system of punishment known as 'jankers' (confined to barracks).

Many a time did we hear Bill Soars complain testily: "What's the use of running anybody up in front of Mr Hillier? The only action he takes is to pat the offender on the back with 'Naughty boy! Go and practise your fiddle'." This was very true, for Tim's view was that the band as such stood to gain far more from a boy who was engaged in doing a bit of extra violin practice than from one who was marching aimlessly round and round the barrack square carrying a full kit on his back (for that was one of the 'Janker Wallahs' punishments).

Tim had two daughters, Madge and Gladys. I once fancied myself in love with Gladys, and she with me. This led to our meeting in secret in a quiet lane that ran behind the Aldershot Parish Church Hall. We kissed, but decided there and then that the whole business was too risky. Even so, in later years when I was a student at the Royal Military School of Music, Kneller Hall, Gladys was not averse to offending her fiance (his name was Padgham) by sending me the more successful of the two cakes she had baked. Apart from one chance meeting which took place after the war, I lost sight of her for ever.

'Padge' who later married her, became town clerk somewhere in the north of England. Gladys thus considered herself as belonging to a somewhat superior class socially to her sister Madge, who meanwhile had 'married into fish', as she (Gladys) put it; meaning, a man who had a fishermonger's business in Dover. (I christened them 'the Dover sole-mates'.)

Mr Hillier was to exercise a profound effect over me, for although my behaviour sometimes angered him (such as my high-spiritedness which I was apt to turn on at the inappropriate moment) he never ceased to give me guidance, and this right to the end of my army service, when he himself had long since been retired. His own tastes in music rubbed off on to me. Fate already had taken a hand in the shaping of my destiny. It was to continue to do so.

After the interview we were issued with our instruments, mine being a brass cornet. We were then directed to the band room, where an orchestral practice was already in progress. The walls of the practice room were hung with portrait prints of the better-known composers such as Mozart, Beethoven, Mendelssohn and Wagner. Hanging immediately above the fireplace was a picture of the band taken in 1906. Each member was represented by his own individual portrait. The centre portrait was of Henry Sims, who was appointed to the mounted band in 1887, thus becoming its first bandmaster. The profusion of gold braid which adorned his jacket, coupled with his dictatorial, bullying manner, led to his being christened by his men 'The Golden Pig'.

Army bands of those days fell into one of two categories — staff bands (which included Foot Guards, Household Cavalry, Royal Artillery and Royal Engineers), and line bands (which included all other cavalry and infantry bands). The main difference between the two categories was that whereas line bands were moved every three years or so from one garrison town to another, and from one part of the then far-flung British Empire to another, staff bands enjoyed permanent 'home' stations.

Most musicians who belonged to a Royal Artillery band, or to the Band of the Royal Engineers, were 'double-handed'; that is, they played both a stringed, and a wind, instrument. These bands were thus able to boast an orchestra and a military band.

Mr Hillier had little, if indeed any, patience with the military band, so that the order almost invariably was "Turn in — Strings."

When we three arrived, the orchestra was practising for its annual November concert which was held in the Aldershot Hippodrome. These concerts were in aid of the Royal Artillery Association. We were overawed by the very size of the band (which numbered about 60 or 70 players), by the spectacle of a full orchestra, and in particular by the size of the string basses, which we had not seen before. The music being rehearsed included Dame Ethel Smyth's Overture *The Wreckers**, Dvorak's *New World* Symphony, and (!) a cornet solo, which was W.H. Squire's *Mountain Lovers.*

At the climax of his cornet solo, Bombardier Tommy Band 'fluffed' his top C, blaming it on the dry condition of his throat.

Ever after, liquid refreshments were served during the interval, free of charge. Also, ever after, the grateful gunner-musicians' toast at these concerts was 'Raise your glasses and drink to Tommy's top C'. I suspect the whole episode was a put-up job, a clever ruse, on Tommy's part. Tommy Band later became caught up in the dance band craze which swept England during the 1920s. He purchased his discharge from the army, and joined one of London's leading dance bands which played for regular dancing sessions in the Covent Garden Opera House.

Only a few of the boys were considered sufficiently advanced to play for this particular Hippodrome concert, among them being Boys 'Winkle' Goddard, an outstandingly gifted violinist who died when only 27 years old, and Horace Barker, a no less outstandingly gifted trumpet player who ultimately was to become one of London's leading orchestral trumpet players.

The remainder of the boys were employed on general fatigue duties which included the loading and unloading of the band's music stools, stands and the more cumbersome equipment, and as programme sellers. It was at this concert that I was initiated into the typically characteristic (but downright dishonest) bandboys' 'racket'. The price of programmes ranged from one shilling in the stalls and circle to sixpence in the pit, and threepence in the 'gods'. At the conclusion of the concert, stalls' programme sellers 'bought' some of the unsold programmes from the boys who were selling them in the cheaper-priced seats. The buyers' price, naturally enough, was something less than one shilling per programme. All stood to make something, the only loser being the Royal Artillery Association.

The reader by now may have noticed something unusual about my memoirs — the omission (a deliberate one on my part) of a well-tried, albeit worked to death, aid to the literary style of the day. I mean the relative absence of swear words in general, and the total absence of the famous

---

* Some three decades later, a romantic nostalgia led me to choose to conduct this overture with the New Zealand Symphony Orchestra. Its composer was one of the pioneers of the women's suffrage movement, her extreme form of militancy earning her in 1911 a two months' prison term. She may well have inherited her fighting spirit from her gunner-officer father, General J.H. Smyth.

four-letter word in particular. In common with every other novelty such
as long hair and beards for men, short hair and denim trousers for women,
and the baubles that hang suspended from the necks of the two sexes alike
— in common with every other novelty, when everybody does it, it remains
no longer a novelty — or as W.S. Gilbert more aptly puts it, 'When everyone
is somebodee, Then no one's anybody.' So that the person who craves to
be regarded by his fellow creatures as an eccentric must set out again on
some other tack. But in this one instance, I am bound to use the famous
or infamous (depending upon the way you regard it) four-letter word; for
in no other way can I bring home to the reader the sort of brutal shock
to which the young army recruit was liable to be exposed.

The then army education system allowed for four certificates of
education known as third, second, first and special certificates. Within less
than a week of our enlistment, we were marched in company with other
of our boys over to Waterloo Barracks West (which accommodated the
Royal Horse Artillery), there to be prepared for our 'thirds' as we called
them. The class included a number of men, many years our senior.

The instructor was Chaplain to the Forces, the Reverend 'Paddy'
Yelverton, a tall, slim man with fair hair and 'A pair of blue eyes'. I believe
he was in fact of Nordic parentage. I later learnt that he was a morose
man, although he never gave us that impression. Our natural shyness led
the three of us to sit right at the back of the class. Mr Yelverton started
with a roll call — "Percy" — "Sah!", "Wylie" — "Sah!", "Wyndham"
— "Sah!", "Polkinghorn" — "Sah!", "Nalden" — "Yes, Sir". At this, the
whole class turned round, and one of their number, disregarding the
presence of Mr Yelverton, bawled out, "Christ! One of them's a fucking
sergeant." You may well imagine the effect that this produced on me, a
14-year-old boy, less than a week released from as cloistered an existence
as any that could be devised. The incident had a terribly levelling effect
on me. At school I had been the equivalent of head boy; at that moment
I became something rather less than nothing. Even a worm has the god-
given escape route of a hole into which he may crawl. I looked appealingly
to Mr Yelverton, and I vow that I saw a flash of anger cross his face. "Men,"
he said, "you may smoke. Boys, as it is a cold day, you also may smoke."
(Army regulations forbade boys to smoke.)

We were to meet Mr Yelverton on the Friday afternoon of each week
for religious instruction. These classes were held in our barrack room.
Invariably the chaplain brought with him a bag of buns. Friday was the
army's traditional pay day, and the traditional tea-meal for that day of
the week consisted of bread and margarine, cheese and onions; not spring
onions, but the large, raw, Spanish variety. Mr Yelverton shared our tea-

meal with us, munching away at his raw onion as though he really was enjoying it. He had a standing arrangement with his wife, no doubt, that they slept in separate houses on Friday nights.

I would say that the Reverend Yelverton was one of the finest, if not the finest, preacher ever to have mounted the pulpit steps in Aldershot's All Saints Garrison Church. Forceful, forthright, no nonsense, he would hit out fearlessly at anybody and everybody, with little regard for the sensibilities of the officers and their 'ladies' who sat immediately beneath the pulpit, should he feel morally justified in so doing. He was my first army hero, and to this day I continue to revere his memory.

But the event which brought home to me in brutally realistic fashion the fact that I really was in the army, came a few days later, when the entire regiment (including the band) was drawn up on the barrack square in one vast hollow formation.

One of our musicians had been court-martialled some time before our joining the band. He was now to hear the court's findings and sentence which, in keeping with the code of army discipline of the times, were to be read out in the presence of his unit. The three of us stood at a window, looking down upon this awesome, almost frightening, spectacle. I recall the wave of pity that the prisoner's thin, wan face aroused in me. He was pronounced 'guilty', and dismissed the service. I never saw him again, and never did I discover the nature of his offence.

Over the years I have amassed quite a collection of musical dictionaries, including of course, *Grove's*. I shall shortly be disposing of those which are now out-of-date and replacing them with up-to-date editions. But one dictionary which measures four-and-a-half inches by three inches, *A Dictionary of Musical Terms* by Jeffrey Pulver, I shall be keeping. Its back inside cover bears the official stamp of the Royal Artillery (Mounted) Band, and its front inside cover the inscription, 'R. Davies, Dec.4th, 1918'. I have kept this book for well over half a century in memory of the musician who was subjected to this quite unnecessary indignity. The punishment that he had already received (the anxiety of waiting) and the additional punishment that he was due to receive, which I believe included a period of detention in Aldershot's dreaded 'Glass-House' prison, in themselves surely should have been quite sufficient.

Shortly after this episode we were issued with our kits, an eagerly awaited event. The kit comprised two or three of everything — two tunics, two pairs of Bedford-cord riding breeches, two pairs of boots, three army 'grey-back' shirts, ditto socks. The issue did not include the refinement of a suit of pyjamas, so that we were obliged to sleep in the same under-garments that we had been wearing during the day. What I would like to write about is the boots — for when issued with those, our eagerness lost something of its original thrust. They were brown boots, not the type that one purchases from the shoe shop — dear me! No! — but brown, untreated (raw) leather. It was our chore not only to blacken them, but also to rid them of their natural oil, which we did by a process known as 'boning'. It was a long, heart-breaking process, for until every drop of oil had been extracted, it became impossible to work up a polish.

Each new boy was given 10 shillings which was to be put towards the purchase of a 'posh' superfine-cloth cap, and to having his riding breeches 'taken-in' — that is, so shaped that the arc-like bulge at the thigh tapered off to a tight fit at the knees. Our breeches were fitted with leather knee-grips, which were to be 'blancoed' with the Field Artillery regulation colour, *Pickerings 53*. Once, or at most twice, a week was all that was necessary for this to be done, provided one moistened the blanco with milk, because of its adhesive properties. And so on the Saturday afternoon of each week we took our enamel drinking mugs to Moys's Corner Store, there to receive in them one ha'porth of milk.

A boy would regard it as a matter of regimental pride that he discard his issue cap-badge and replace it (at his own expense) with one fitted with a superimposed gun-wheel which actually revolved.

Our kits included a cut-throat razor and a shaving brush; but as all enlisted boys were still some years removed from the need to shave, the razor more often than not was used for sharpening pencils. I once had a piece of indelible lead land fairly and squarely in one of my eyes. Painful though it was, far worse was the journey I had to make on foot to the army eye specialist, whose surgery was some three miles away in North Camp.

Once the novelty of tasting such foods as eggs, bacon, salmon, liver and custard had spent itself, I came to realise that plain though it had been, our Foundling Hospital food was more wholesome and more appetising than the army fare. And in a roundabout way it was the poor quality of the food which became an instrumental factor in bringing home one's lack of power, for there was nobody, it seemed, to whom appeal could be made. I quote two instances of this.

Our pre-breakfast riding drill parades left us ravenously hungry to the point that the amount of food allowed us never wholly satisfied our animal-like appetites. One of our number (then recently turned 18 years old) asked Bill Soars's permission to see the bandmaster. Permission was granted. It was a ludicrous sight; a well-over-six-foot tall soldier holding in his hand a plate upon which was reposing one tiny rasher of frizzled-up bacon.

"With respect, sir," asked Jerry Cox of Mr Hillier, "do you consider it fair for a man of my size to be expected to do a full morning's practice on this?"

"Well, I agree, it certainly doesn't look too much, Cox."

And there the matter ended.

On another occasion we deputed Tony Farrell, as senior boy, to ask of Bill Soars that he take a look at one of our dinner meals whilst it was still unserved in its army 'dixie'. It was a foul-looking mess consisting in the main of great hunks of fat swimming in a pool of semi-congealed grease. (Until such time as we had our own band dining-hut, all meals were carried from the cookhouse, which was about 200 yards across the barrack square. Meals were lukewarm at best by the time they reached us.) Bill came in, bent down, and took a sniff. "Lucky boys! I wish my wife would sometimes serve up this sort of thing to me."

Again, there the matter ended, for unlike most other army units, we had no officer of the day looking in at meal-times with his lethargic, "Any complaints?"

A 'boy's' pay was seven shillings per week, from which two shillings was deducted. This ostensibly was a compulsory savings scheme; but in reality those who imposed it knew full well that a peremptory order on their parts such as "Get yourself a new tunic", or "Get yourself a new something else" was the equivalent of a sure-fire COD order.

It remained true that every soldier did receive a monthly clothing allowance, but with as many as three different uniforms to maintain (a re-gold-braiding of a blue tunic alone could account for the best part of two months' clothing allowance), this allowance was barely sufficient.

We were by now in the swing of the band's regular routine, which went something like this:

6 am	Reveille, followed by an hour's foot-drill or horse-riding.
7.30-9 am	Breakfast, room and uniform cleaning. (Our clothes and boots would be rendered particularly grimy from the flying dust of the indoor riding-school.)
9-12 noon	Full Band practice.
2-3 pm	Young Hands' practice.
5-6 pm	Boys' practice.
10.15 pm	Lights out. (Boys were required to be back in barracks no later than 9.30 pm.)

After the religious instruction period, the remainder of Friday afternoons would be devoted to the cleaning of our barrack room. This process went under the curious name of 'Interior Economy'.

We were each allotted a different task. Forms and tables had to be scrubbed, windows cleaned (rendered difficult on their outsides by reason of their iron bars), table-trestles, fireplace, and iron coal bin black-leaded, the hearth and its surround whitewashed, and the entire floor scrubbed. It was either 'wet-scrubbed' on hands and knees (no hardship to foundling boys who already were practised hands at that particular art), or 'dry-scrubbed'. This latter was carried out by means of ground brick dust or sand and heavily-weighted 'dry-scrubbers' which were attached to over-long handles.

We three foundling recruits once found ourselves faced with the task of having to wet-scrub on our own the entire barrack room. Room NCO Claude Ward, who broke the news to us, was most apologetic; and rightly so, for he knew the three of us to be suffering from the effects of a recently-administered vaccination. It was a bitterly cold December's day, and raining into the bargain. To his credit, Claude had one of the boys build up a massive fire for us.

It so happened that one of the musicians, a Sergeant Foskett, had died suddenly, and at a comparatively early age. It must have been his widow's wish that he be buried at Brookwood Cemetery, which was two stations up the line. As we were the only band members not to be included in the funeral parade, it devolved upon us to get to and have the room scrubbed for the Saturday morning's room inspection. My own arm had swollen to something approaching double its normal size and was agonisingly painful. It severity was such that never again during my army service was any subsequent vaccination to 'take'. My *Soldiers Service and Pay Book* records against the vaccination entry for 22 February 1932, 'N.Taken'.

Military funerals were depressing affairs, very nearly as much for the bandsmen who headed the procession as for the mourners. And as though the mournful strains of Chopin's and Beethoven's funeral marches were not in themselves sufficient to create an atmosphere of brooding and melancholy, all drums were muffled and dressed with black crepe. A further depressing feature was the riderless horse with the dead soldier's jack boots attached to the stirrups, but in reversed position, so that their toes faced the horse's croup.

I recall one such parade being held up for a considerable time in the pouring rain outside the gates of the Aldershot Military Cemetery because of the late arrival of the officiating army chaplain. Even the mourners (who presumably were too poor to be able to afford a carriage) were subjected to these deplorable conditions. I recall also the wave of indignation which swept through the entire band at the cavalier treatment meted out to the mourners.

When Bombardier Claude Ward married, his place as NCO in charge of boys was taken by 'Porty' Prior, a well-fed, Falstaffian looking man who relinquished his comfortable 'diggings' in Mrs Green's home (both married and single men were permitted to live out of barracks) for the dubious double advantages of wearing a Lance-Bombardier's stripe on each of his sleeves, and a little extra band pay. 'Porty' immediately set about putting some ideas of his own into practice. One of these, as I have already said, was to have us remove the Crimean crusts from the night urinal. Another was to establish a room fund to which we were all compelled to contribute. The main object of this fund was to purchase occasional luxury items of food which otherwise we would not see, and extra coal for the fire. In this way, we were able to return our thanks to Mr Yelverton by putting on a pre-Christmas leave banquet in his special honour. One of our number was pledged not to use his pre-banquet issue of clean sheets, so that we were able to boast white 'table cloths' for the occasion.

'Porty' put a further idea of his to us — would we prefer to have our potatoes peeled, rather than have them cooked (as they were) in their jackets? Our reply was a unanimous 'Yes!' Our initial enthusiasm waned somewhat when we learnt that we must peel them ourselves. As the band block accommodated 60 or so men, comprised of musicians, boys and drivers (who groomed our horses), we found ourselves faced with the nightly task of peeling enough potatoes for that number.

We took it in turns, pair and pair about. Our method of peeling gradually developed into the simple formula of four sides, top and bottom, so that the potatoes came out either as square or rectangular in shape. We fell into the trap of our own springing, for lurking in the background was one Sergeant Stan Morrish, who having been primed of this, had been keeping a weight check on the peeled potatoes and the potato peelings. The latter, it was disclosed, far outweighed the former. Our game was up; and so a goodly part of our room fund balance went as payment for the estimated potato poundage which had been sacrificed to our brief excursion into cubist art.

My life was now beginning to take on a regular pattern which was no different from that of other of our boys. Like them, I would supplement the midday meal by going over to the NAAFI* and filling up with a cup of tea and two of their vanilla slices (5d). After the 5-6 pm Young Hands' practice, again like the other boys, I would go to a local cinema, winding up (when funds permitted) with a sixpenny fish-and-chip supper; for no food was served in barracks after the 4 pm tea meal. I recall vividly the

---

* Navy Army and Air Force Institute.

unsettling effect that some of the more romantic films had on me; for the juxtaposition of the luxury homes and the opulent style of living depicted on the screen (which we accepted as a reflection of real life) and the harsh realities of the barrack room, was altogether too incongruous.

An unwritten, but strictly-enforced, barrack room Sunday afternoon rule (which applied throughout the army) was 'In bed, or out of barracks'. Like most other boys I chose the former alternative, for practising our instruments on a Sunday afternoon being taboo, what else was there for us to do, apart from wandering aimlessly around the near-deserted streets of Aldershot town?

This then, went to make up my average day.

The next important event to come round was the band's annual Christmas leave. Although the distance from Aldershot to Chertsey is only 19 miles, I had not visited my foster-mother since my enlistment. There were reasons for this. In the first place there was no such thing as weekend leave for boys, as Sunday church parade was compulsory. (Weekend leave for boys began mysteriously to creep in when Bill Soars's own son Dick joined the band. It was as barefaced a case of nepotism as any ever devised either by Bill himself or by any other dad.) In the second place, no soldier was permitted outside the area of the Aldershot Command without a signed pass; and as yet still a 'rookie', there was no chance of my being allowed that concession.

It seemed that leave would never come round, but it did. Back once again in Chertsey after an unbroken nine years' absence, nothing appeared very much changed. The gentle Miss Williams was perhaps a trifle more hard of hearing, and her moustache (which tickled my cheek as she bent down to kiss me) may perhaps have turned slightly more grey. The lovable Miss Bixley's raven hair had lost none of its beauty and lustre, and Mr and Mrs Butler, who were some few houses removed from our own, had increased their family to well over double figures. Mrs Stott was still serving in her shop, the Misses Mallom and Bungard still teaching at Stepgates School, and Mr Tuffnell still playing 'The Old Year out and the New Year in' on his cornet at the corner of Station Road and Queen Street.

Neither did I detect too great a change in my foster-mother's appearance. She was still kindness itself, and soon re-introduced me to the delights of her cooking. It was only under pressure from me that she would accept any money for my keep. It was clear that she had suffered great hardships, but owing to the generosity of grocer Townsend (who magnanimously elected to wipe off a long-standing and obviously irrecoverable debt) she was able, but only just able, to get by.

In order that she might make ends meet, my mother had taken in a 'lodger' named Bert Fuller. Bert's bicycle carried a board which solemnly warned the Chertsey townsfolk to 'Repent, for the Day of Judgement is Nigh at Hand'. Bert worked in my uncle Harry's rag and bone shop and supplemented his weekly wage by carrying out some mysterious deals in rabbit skins (which involved his making some no-less mysterious bicycle trips to Uxbridge) and by using my mother's house as an agency for his vinegar-vending business. In this he somehow managed to undercut the local price by exactly 100 per cent and still make a profit.

I sometimes shared the front room's double-bed with Bert and would be lulled to sleep by his droning the general confession, the Lord's Prayer, and the odd bit of unaccompanied hymn singing. Thanks to my army religious instruction classes, I was able suitably to impress him by explaining the absence of door handles and knockers in Holman Hunt's *Light of the World,* a copy of which, as I said earlier, graced one of the front bedroom's walls. I thought of him as being a very holy man, but mum sized him up as 'a bleedin' ole 'ippercrit'.

I explored all over again my childhood haunts, the 'Rec' (Recreation Ground), the Pound Pond hard by Stepgates School, the gypsy caravan site and the Chertsey Meads.

I spent a few days of my leave with Mr and Mrs Betts in their lovely Mecklenburg Square flat. Mrs Betts offered to take me to see Jose Collins in *The Last Waltz* which (I seem to remember) was being played at the old Aldwych Theatre. I chose instead to see Mr Stork's annual boys' play. However, I did go with them to see *Charley's Aunt* and also Seymour Hicks who was playing in *The Private Secretary. Charley's Aunt* has remained a favourite with me ever since.

Returning to barracks was a mournful affair, for I was dreadfully homesick. After a taste once again of home comforts, the return to the squalor of the barrack room sent me into a fit of deep depression. And although I did not experience the pangs of homesickness again quite so forcibly, I never really found the re-adjustments to army life come easily. To deepen the general gloom, 'Greyie', one of our two barrack room cats, decided to die.

The year 1923 got under way as though it was going to be no different from 1922 — but it was. In the first place, the three of us were permitted to practise with the full band more frequently. Individual tuition was given to newly-joined boys by the band's more senior and advanced players. My teacher was Bombardier Tommy Band of 'Top C' fame. My lessons went something like this: 'Play me the scale of C major' (clink, clink). 'Now play me its relative minor, harmonic form' (clink, clink). 'Now its melodic form' (clink, clink, clink). The 'clinks' came from a shove-ha-penny board. It was all very unfair and unprincipled. I soon formed the opinion, rightly or wrongly, that Bombardier Band had taken a dislike to me.

I had sat and passed my 'third' in the December of the previous year, and was now attending school for my 'second'. This examination included a course in elementary map reading, and it was this which sent me exploring some of the surrounding countryside; for romantic names such as Normandy, Christmas Pie, Ash Church and so on determined me upon discovering these places for myself. I was once making for Ash Church choosing a cross-country route, when a farmer warned me that I was trespassing on his land. "And did I see you eyeing a girl a few minutes ago?"

"No, sir!"

"I should hope not at your age. Now be off with you!"

It was from that time that I came to discover myself as being something of a 'loner', as I would be quite happy in wandering off for extended walks on my own. My eyes were reopened to the beauties of the English countryside — beauties which have held me in their spell ever since. But more of that later.

And then I discovered Miss Daniel's Soldiers' Home which was at the top of Aldershot Town. Here at last was an opportunity to fulfil a long-cherished ambition — that of learning to play the piano. I approached one of the voluntary workers who agreed to give me lessons. The only snag was that each of her short lessons was followed by a long prayer session. My teacher was a religious crank possibly, but I still remember her as a woman of character, and clearly a woman of some breeding. I made but little progress, due to the fact that the piano was almost always in use.

It was singularly unfortunate that Bombardier Band should come into the home one evening (presumably for a cup of tea between his two cinema 'houses') to catch me playing the harmless game of bagatelle. "Have you nothing better to do, Nalden, than waste your time on this sort of thing?" he asked. I was too timid to explain to him the main purpose for my being in the home — to practise the piano.

Whether or not he passed on this information to Mr Hillier I never knew. What I did know was that shortly after this incident I was told to report to the bandmaster's office. A grave-looking Tim told me that I was making no progress whatsoever. "I don't know quite what to do with you other than send you to Kneller Hall on a pupil's course."

"Yes, sir." What else could I say?

I would have liked to explain the reason for my lack of progress; that I tired so easily as to be unable to sustain practising my instrument beyond a few minutes at a time. But overawed as I was by his rank, I remained silent.

Kneller Hall, or, to give it its official title, The Royal Military School of Music, enjoyed (and probably still does enjoy) a world-wide reputation as a first-class training establishment for army musicians. Yet by implication, Mr Hillier clearly looked upon it as a place whereby he could rid himself, if only for 12 months, of his disappointments such as myself. The simple explanation of this was the personal feud which existed between himself and Lieutenant H.E. Adkins, the then Director of Music, Kneller Hall.

Adkins did not subscribe to the theory of the staff-band musician being a 'cut above' his line-band counterpart. And it is significant that during his 22 years as Director of Music, not one bandmaster who had had a staff-band background ever made commissioned rank. I know that I would have become the first such person to have broken through this barrier, had not events taken the dramatic and wholly unforeseeable course that they did. But this came many years later.

Without doubt, Hillier's staff-band background was one factor at least that stood in the way of his promotion to commissioned rank. Then again, their personalities were as far removed, each from the other's, as they possibly could be. Tim, the introvert, the nervous, retiring scholar; Adkins, the brash extrovert, who would, had he been afforded opportunity, have beaten Barnum and Bailey all hands down at their own game.

Little snobs that we were, we in our 'superior' staff bands were prone to look down upon our line-band counterparts as soldier-musicians. In turn line bandsmen jeered at us as being musicians only, who could not distinguish between a rifle's butt and its barrel. There was more than a grain of truth in this. Lieutenant Adkins was out, clearly, to put a stop to this army-style nepotism which favoured the staff-band musician over his line-band counterpart. Hillier in turn showed a marked preference for musicians who had enlisted as boys directly into his band over those who had transferred into it from some line band.

And so I was simply a pawn in this soldier-musician version of the game of chess.

On the day of my departure for Kneller Hall, which was in the October of 1923, Mr Hillier talked to me in his office. "You must not be afraid of the director, sonny." (It was the first time he had called me that.) "He looks a very fierce man, but you'll be alright."

As I related earlier in my story, I was routed via Ascot, simply to meet the condition laid down by *King's Rules and Regulations* that a soldier travel by the cheapest route. It saved His Majesty (who I seem to remember had his daily dozen 'Natives' despatched by special courier from Cornwall) the sum of fivepence. Not knowing that I could surcharge my ticket, I travelled via Ascot at the cost of several wasted and tiresome hours.

At Twickenham station I joined up with a group of boys and men who, like myself, were heading for Kneller Hall. Loaded as we were with our kit-bags and the rest, we decided between us to hire a horse-drawn cab, thus arriving in style.

I was allotted a bed in room 10. Eight years later, when I re-entered Kneller Hall as a student, I was allotted the same bed in the same room.

My 'passing-in test' came a few days later. Hillier was right. 'Adko' was indeed a fierce-looking man. Already in the process of developing a Kiwi Dark-Tan complexion, he sported a ginger moustache which was waxed at both ends. This in turn was set over a pair of thin, tightly-drawn lips which when parted revealed an array of fang-like teeth. These he would bare as the band under his baton built up to a *fortissimo*.

He had a wide, backward-sloping Danton-like forehead. I recalled Baroness Orczy equating this shaped forehead with cruelty, hence my description 'Danton-like'. His hair, like his moustache was ginger. But the most frightening aspect of his make-up was his *pince-nez* style eyeglasses, which appeared to exaggerate the Reynard-orientated inwards slant of his eyes. To cap it all, he had a decided advantage over me in height, leaving me well over 15 inches further away from heaven than was he himself.

Once out of uniform he was devoid of any dress sense. Until well into the 1920s he was still wearing patent leather cloth-uppered button-up boots with his trousers hitched at half-mast as though in permanent public mourning. He no doubt would have continued wearing these outmoded clothes had not commandant Colonel Gregson of the Grenadier Guards, ordered him to up-date himself and to get his hair cut.

After testing me on my scales (which I knew thoroughly) we came to the sight-reading test:

"Not very good at that, are you, boy?"

"No, sir."

"Very well. That is all."

"Yes, sir."

It was merciful that neither Adkins nor myself could foresee the events of some two decades hence; for we both were to figure in the greatest drama in the history of military music.

I passed my entrance test. My foundling friend, E.L., who was sent to Kneller Hall some few weeks later, failed to pass in. Apart from the fact that it was considered a personal disgrace to be RTU (Returned to Unit), E.L's failure to 'pass in' widened more deeply the Adkins-Hillier rift; for

I believe the incident resulted in a first-class row between them. Insofar as promotion was concerned, Hillier henceforth was a doomed man.

I think I have already made it plain that I had a great deal of time for Tim Hillier. Even so, I must state that never should he have sent either E.L. or me to Kneller Hall at so young an age. The great majority of pupils were young men, and therefore so much more mature and better equipped to accept what the institution had to offer. Yet Tim continued to do this; and what is more, once a boy returned from Kneller Hall, one could safely bet on it that Tim would undo any good the course may have done by changing him over to some other instrument. Thus I was changed over to the french horn; Bill Walden-Mills* (a fine french horn player) to the trombone; Fred Goddard from the cornet to the euphonium, and so on.

The course itself consisted of weekly instrumental lessons, instruction in elementary harmony and aural training, and lots and lots of practising with the full band which numbered well over 100 performers. Of this number, about 30 were classified as 'students', that is, those who were undergoing a three-years' bandmastership course, and the remainder as 'pupils', whose course was for one year.

I found myself therefore as being somewhere around 14th principal second cornet, which was indeed a great comedown; for back in Aldershot I had, after all, been fourth principal second cornet.

"Is your name Hitch?" I asked of one student during a band practice.

"Yes,'' came the good-humoured reply.

"Well, sir, Bombardier Band wishes to be remembered to you.''

"Oh! Thanks!"

Johnny Hitch was one of the most outstanding students ever to have passed through Kneller Hall. He was gifted with an acute sense of 'perfect pitch', and was a fine french horn player. He also made a reputation for himself by consigning Adkins's bicycle to the Kneller Hall lake — and leaving it there to rot. That was in 1923. Over half a century later I received a copy of an article from the military *Fanfare Magazine*. It was written by Lieutenant-Colonel Rodney Bashford, a past Director of Music, Kneller Hall:

'The lake was where the students and pupils courted their girl friends, rowing or punting them to the secret places under the willows or to the remoter reaches where it vanished into Spooner's nursery. To me, a lad,

---

* Following his discharge from the army, William Walden-Mills played 1st violin in the Royal Philharmonic Orchestra. He later joined the music staff of Norfolk County Council. In 1954 he emigrated to New Zealand, eventually becoming National Music Advisor to the Education Department. He was awarded the OBE in the 1982 New Year's honours list.

it was a mysterious place . . . choked with old cardholders, stands, folios, and the Director of Music's missing bicycle — as was discovered when it dried up later.'

Exactly two decades later I too 'courted' my 'girl friend' by this lake. She was later to become my wife — but not until I had atoned for the following incident.

We had wandered down to the lake, Peggy looking very beautiful in her simple white ballgown. The lake, the surrounding woods, the distant bark of a dog, and the pale light of the full moon, all conspired to present as romantic and idyllic a setting as Cupid himself could ever devise.

"Darling," I whispered in Peggy's ear.

"What is it, Charles?"

"I have something to say to you."

"Oh! Charles dear, what is it?"

"It is something very wonderful."

"Yes! but what is it?"

"So wonderful!"

"Well, please tell me what it is."

"To think . . . "

"Yes?"

"To think . . . that today . . . I shot a bogey-four at number five — you know, the hole we call the Frying Pan."

Boys were still required to attend religious instruction. The Kneller Hall chaplain at the time was the Reverend Webb-Peploe. During the whole of his chaplaincy there I recall his developing three themes, and three themes only — the evils attendant upon stealing, cadging ('Givus a fag') and 'self-abuse'. A very different kettle of fish from Mr Yelverton, whose humane approach was mingled with the warmth of compassion. This man on the other hand regarded us obviously as the dregs of society, whose thoughts and ambitions reached out no higher than to petty thieving, preying upon one's fellows, and indulging ourselves in sexual satisfaction in its crudest form. Never surely was a salary earned more easily and less deservedly. He made no impression upon me whatever.

Webb-Peploe's successor was the Reverend Simmons, whose owlish appearance was not unlike that of a semi-weight-watching Billy Bunter. He held the view that religious instruction should not be restricted to boys, but open to men who should feel free to attend if they so wished. Curiously

Above: The Royal Military School of Music (Kneller Hall).
Below: The lake, Kneller Hall.

enough, Adko, who was up to all of our tricks (having once been a band-boy himself) readily agreed to this proposition.

I well recall the first turn-out for Mr Simmons's class. Men volunteered by the dozen — clearly out to dodge band practice, which admittedly could be a tiring and frustrating business, and in particular, when Student Pomphrey was on the rostrum; for we were never allowed to complete a bar without his stopping to correct us.

Suddenly, and without warning, Adko appeared on the scene accompanied by Band-Sergeant Allsebrooke, a great strapping well-over-six-feet-tall cavalryman. ("I like you, Nalden" he once said to me, "I like all men who ride horses.")

"Take down all the men's names, Allsebrooke," ordered Adko. "Now men," he went on, "as you are all so earnest in your religious devotions, as I see you are, I shall arrange for you to attend Sunday church parades for the remainder of your days at Kneller Hall."

The boys made up the soprano section of the chapel choir, irrespective of whether or not their voices had broken. This meant the majority of us having to sing in a falsetto voice, and it may be the root cause of my innate dislike of counter-tenors. Ever since my Kneller Hall choirboy days, the very sound of a counter-tenor voice causes my own throat muscles to suffer in sympathy.

Chertsey was now relatively close, being a mere 10 or so miles away. I was thus able to go over there by bus on Saturday afternoons, returning to Kneller Hall in time for the Sunday morning church parade. And then Mrs Betts bought me a bicycle which made my foster-home even more accessible.

An indication of the rate at which commercial traffic has increased its speed since those days — I was able, with no difficulty at all, to keep abreast of the passing lorry, secure a hold on its tailboard, and be towed from Staines to Hounslow.

I was once waiting for the Chertsey bus, when a car drew up. "Where are you making for?" asked the driver, who was a man in his 40s or thereabouts. When I told him, he said "Jump in, and I'll drive you part-way there." His intentions soon became apparent, for by no means was he the first so-inclined gentleman that I had encountered. "We could go out for some lovely drives and I know of a nice tea-shop where I could take you. Would you like that?"

"Yes, please, sir," I replied.

"Good, give me your name, and I'll write you."

"Yes, sir. My name is Frank Allesbrooke."

Naturally I had no means of discovering whether Allsebrooke subsequently heard from this man, and if so what were his reactions. At the same time, I have created and re-created in my own somewhat vivid imagination how Allesbrooke would have behaved had their meeting taken place. The imaginary picture of 'Allse', every one of his 72-odd inches a military man, driving out to some 'nice tea-shop' becomes all too silly.

The then Kneller Hall Commandant was a Colonel John A.C. Somerville, a humourless man, the possessor of a pair of insolent upper-class eyes and whose face appeared to have taken on a permanent look of haughty condescension mingled with a lofty disdain. He was the type of commanding officer that the army bandmaster dreaded more perhaps than any other — the type who considered himself (mistakenly) a musician. I recall Colonel Somerville's attempt to sing Schumann's *Die Beiden Grenadiere* at one of the winter concerts. "As I do not have a copy of the English translation," he announced to us in his humourless flat tone of voice, "I shall sing it in the original German — Nach Frank-reich zogen zwei Grenadier," — which of course helped no end our understanding of Heine's lines.

It sometimes happens that an interpretation of a dramatic song can be much too funny to be taken seriously. This was one such instance, when pathos degenerated into bathos.

We all dreaded in particular two parades which he himself attended — church parade and pay parade. We could hardly help but commit to memory this oft-repeated church parade dialogue:

"Why have you not polished your boots?"

"But I did clean them, sir!"

"I repeat, why have you not polished your boots?"

"But I swear, I did clean them, sir."

"I said 'polished', not 'cleaned' — there's a difference between the two. Take his name, Sergeant-Major."

My own dread of his attending pay parades arose from quite a different cause, for it was at these parades that he checked up on each individual pupil's salute as he stepped out of line to draw his pay. Having one's name taken meant an extra saluting drill parade on the following Saturday afternoon — for Saturday afternoons were observed as half-holidays. Knowing this, we put everything we had into our individual salutes. But the commandant was not the sort of person to be so easily satisfied. As well may be expected, staff-band musicians (excluding those belonging to guards' regiments) were sitting Aunt Sallies.

It so happened that the Colonel must take it upon himself to attend the one pay parade in the year that I personally wished him least to attend

— the day before the Oxford-Cambridge boat race. I had bought myself a small road map, as I had intended cycling to some part of the course.

Never have I forgiven, and never shall I, forgive Somerville.

It was part of a student's training in those days that he prepare and deliver a lecture on a subject of his own choice before an audience made up of pupils and students, whose attendance was compulsory. These lectures would be attended by Colonel Somerville who, at the conclusion of the talk, would make public his comments and criticisms.

Student Jones had elected to lecture on 'Ancient and Obsolete Musical Instruments'. At the end of the lecture the commandant took the unusual step of congratulating the lecturer on his scholarship, on the depth of his research, and on his initiative in his choosing so remote a subject.

> Student Jones has given us a most stimulating lecture, and has described to us in extraordinary detail many instruments which I must confess are quite new names to me. Congratulations, Student Jones. You have indeed set a very high standard.

Once the commandant had left the room and was presumed safely out of earshot, a tremendous roar of uninhibited laughter went up from the student members of the audience; for Jones, ever a practical joker, had prepared just nothing. His lecture had been purely extempore, with his inventing the name and description of each 'ancient' and 'obsolete' instrument as he went along. The whole 'lecture' had been one gigantic hoax, and its object (that, I believe, of taking a rise out of Somerville, whose *Bach Choir* background he had rammed down our throats) achieved.

In later years, one student who was present (George Smith) told me that sitting through one hour of this farrago of nonsense, without daring even so much as to smile (for Colonel Somerville always positioned himself at the back of the tiered class-room) was sheer torture.

A picture which was displayed prominently on one of the walls interested me greatly. It was a group photograph (c.1860) of Kneller Hall's foundation professorial staff. One name I recognised was that of Lazarus, acknowledged in his day as England's leading clarinet player. I recalled Mr Cawley regaling us with stories of Lazarus's feats as a clarinettist ('playing passages that even I, boys, experienced difficulty in playing') and of his preserving a clarinet reed for a year or more by his soaking it in oil. Another name was that of Sullivan. This was Sir Arthur Sullivan's father, who taught the brass bass instruments. He was also Bandmaster of the Royal Military College (Sandhurst) Band. But more of this later.

A soldier could not rise to the army's highest non-commissioned rank of Warrant Officer Class I unless he possessed the First Class certificate of education. To be without this qualification meant automatic exclusion from Kneller Hall's course in military bandmastership. I decided therefore that I must 'go for my First'.

Our instructor in education was 'Nick' Carter, a fine teacher who gave us a sound preparation. The set books in English for that particular year's examination were Kinglake's *Eothen,* Dickens's *A Tale of Two Cities,* and Sir Arthur Conan Doyle's *The White Company.* The book I enjoyed reading the most was *The White Company;* for at the time I was too immature to take in the deeper meaning of either *Eothen* or *A Tale of Two Cities.*

I still nursed a desire to play the piano, so throwing caution to the wind, I wrote Mr Hillier asking whether I might take it as a second study. A peremptory reply addressed to No.1055004 Boy C. Nalden written not by Mr Hillier, but by Sergeant-Major Soars, informed me that my request had been turned down. No reason was given. So that closed the door until the year 1946, when, rather belatedly, I took it up on my own accord.

I awoke one morning to find myself covered in a mass of ugly white weals, which caused me to itch most terribly. In addition I felt headachy and sick. Room Corporal 'Jock' Perrin, who must have noticed my distressed condition, was kindness itself. He told me to remain in bed, while he looked for the Orderly Student, who happened to be my cavalry friend, Frank Allsebrooke.

"Do you think you know what is wrong with you, Nalden?"

"No, sergeant."

"You haven't been going with a woman, have you?"*

"No, sergeant."

He told me to join the morning's sick parade. Getting to Hounslow Military Hospital meant some two to three miles' march, which was how 'walking patients', however ill they might be, got there. (I can recall only one case of a patient travelling to Hounslow Hospital by ambulance. He was a pupil who clearly was in great agony through his inability to pass urine.)

One strange symptom regarding my own complaint was that when ultimately I arrived at hospital, the main area of the rash had moved from one part of my body to another. The Army Medical Officer diagnosed it as urticaria, or nettle rash as it is more commonly known. The patient in the bed next to mine appeared to be shivering violently. Remembering my scripture reading classes under Mr Stork, I thought it must be the sick

---

* There was little likelihood of our concealing the symptoms of VD for we were subjected to the indignity of being lined up each month for 'short arm' (penis) inspection by the Army Medical Officer. Not a few of us resented the implication, but there was nothing we could do about it beyond continuing to chafe under the indignity.

of the palsy. But it turned out to be a recurrence of malaria which he had contracted while soldiering in India.

A legacy of my particular illness was that for several years afterwards I was unable to eat a banana without re-activating the symptoms.

Following my discharge from hospital I was excused all duties for some days. One of these free days happened to be a Wednesday. I thought I would like to hear the Kneller Hall Band's afternoon concert. I decided to stand as far away as I was able, so as not to be seen. But I was soon spotted, and by Adko himself, who called me over. "I want you to go into Hounslow and buy a chicken for Mrs Adkins. And make certain, boy, to prod it with your finger to see that it is tender." From this I concluded that they had been caught unawares by some unexpected guests. (Twenty-one years later I was accompanying Adko on an inspection tour of Scottish regimental bands. "I want you to go into Edinburgh and buy me a crab. You must ask for a cock crab, and give it a good sniffing over to see that it is fresh.")

The great British Empire Exhibition was held in 1924 at Wembley, whose famous Stadium was erected for the purpose of staging the more massive of the Exhibition's attractions. The full Kneller Hall Band was engaged to participate in the opening ceremony, which was to take place on St. George's Day (23 April) in the presence of His Majesty King George V. In addition, Lieutenant Adkins was commissioned to assemble and rehearse a Massed Military Band of 600 performers, whose members were to be drawn virtually from every regiment of the British Army. The massed bands were to be augmented by a further force of 400 drummers and pipers.

The early months of that year were devoted almost exclusively to practising for the Exhibition. Certain of Britain's then leading composers were invited to write special music for the occasion, which was published by the firm of Hawkes Ltd 'In Commemoration of the British Empire Exhibition 1924'. Vaughan-Williams wrote his *Toccata Marziale* for the occasion, and Gordon Jacob made an arrangement for Military Band of *A William Byrd Suite*. Dame Ethel Smyth came along to supervise a rehearsal of the overture to her Opera *The Wreckers* (I recall her demanding 'longer' and 'still longer' pauses in the *Chorale*); likewise Gustav Holst to supervise the rehearsal of some movements from his *Planets Suite*, which also had been arranged for military band.

And to Kneller Hall came Sir Edward Elgar to rehearse us on the music with which we were to accompany the singing of the massed choirs. This included *It comes from the misty ages* from his own *Banner of St. George*, and of course, *Land of Hope and Glory*. From the moment he mounted the rostrum, Sir Edward assumed an air of military-style authority, commanding us to throw out our chests and 'stand upright, like soldiers'.

I decided there and then that I did not like this man Elgar, even though he may have been a knight and the composer of one of our Foundling Hospital marching tunes which we knew as *Land of Hope and Glory.*

Another person who came to Kneller Hall to rehearse a specially-composed work was Lieutenant B. Walton O'Donnell*, who at the time was Director of Music of the Deal Division of the Royal Marines. He came along to rehearse his finely-written *Songs of the Gael* which was to prove itself one of the most popular (if not the most popular) piece played by the massed bands. Young though I was, I thought I saw in Lieutenant O'Donnell a fine musician and an equally fine man. As a musician he stood head and shoulders above all others who participated in the massed bands' several performances, not excluding Lieutenant Adkins himself. He became my second military hero, and remained so. So much did I admire both the man and the musician (albeit from afar off) that later I was to inscribe on the title page of my Doctor of Music exercise, 'Dedicated to the Memory of B. Walton O'Donnell'.

The thousand-strong corps of military bands, drummers, and pipers were assembled for rehearsals some two weeks or so before the Exhibition's opening date. These were held on Hounslow Heath — hence the coining of the term, I suppose, 'Blasted heath'.

For me, playing in the massed bands meant a further demotion; for I now found myself as something like 30th principal second cornet (I believe the array of second cornet players added up to just that number).

The whole vast exercise was placed under the direction of Lieutenant Adkins, who was to receive a personal fee of £2000, as against the average bandsman's fee of something like £10. But War Office intervened and had Adkins's fee reduced to one of £800. With it, Adko bought himself his first-ever car, and his wife Ada appeared even more expensively dressed than ever.

St. George's Day turned out to be a most beautiful English spring day. Tens of thousands of people packed the stadium for the opening ceremony.

Massive displays of pageantry such as the one we witnessed here have a humbling effect on me. It is on occasions such as this that the Lord Mayor, a lion in his own city; the Bishop, the revered Pastoral Father when moving about in his own see; and the Duke's Lady, the respected hostess extraordinary when within her own castle, must all revert for the moment into becoming plain men and women, and no different from those in the

---

* There were three brothers O'Donnell — Percy, Rudolph and Walton. At one stage the three of them simultaneously were Directors of Music of the Plymouth, Portsmouth and Deal Bands of the Royal Marines — a unique triumvirate.

'madding crowd' which mills around them. It is the same with Death. And yet, like the firmament on a still cloudless night, the splendour of pageantry seldom fails to move me.

For Elgar, to whom the peace and beauty of the countryside meant so much, and who during these years 'wanted to be away from London "for a long time" '*, the whole business connected with the opening of the Exhibition must have been a depressing experience —

> "The rehearsals," he told Lady Stuart, tried his patience, "overwhelmed with etiquette and red tape . . . The K. insists on Land of Hope and there were some ludicrous suggestions of which I shall tell you — if ever we meet. But everything seems so hopelessly and irredeemably vulgar at Court . . . I was standing alone (criticising) in the middle of the enormous stadium . . . 17,000 men, hammering, loudspeakers, amplifiers, four aeroplanes circling over etc. etc. — all mechanical and horrible — no soul and no romance and no imagination."*

Adko's persistent presence can hardly have acted as an emollient on Sir Edward; I recall one press report which spoke of 'the man in military attire who appeared to dog Sir Edward in his every step'. The reporter was correct in what he wrote, for Adko just would not let go.

Neither would I let go once I came to know and revere Elgar's music.

Almost half a century later, I was invited by Radio New Zealand to conduct its symphony orchestra in a programme of my own choice. After a great deal of soul-searching, I decided to submit the title of one work only — Elgar's *Second Symphony*. I had already conducted his *Enigma Variations* with the symphony orchestra.

It was only when I came to make a close study of the score of the symphony that I began to realise what a truly great man Elgar was. To me, the closing pages of this work's final movement are among the most movingly beautiful, but at the same time the saddest, in the whole range of musical literature. For beneath the richness of these pages' harmonies and the opulence of their orchestration, there lies a saddened Elgar. It is as though Elgar the visionary is looking wistfully over his own shoulder to a style of living, to a sense of security, that his England never again was to know. These final pages are Elgar's personal farewell to the burgeoning age of Edward VII and to the blue, cloudless skies that England never again was to see.

---

* Quoted from Michael Kennedy's *Portrait of Elgar,* 1968.

Sospiri

It so happened that my own Royal Artillery Band was playing in the Exhibition grounds during this same period. Naturally, I went along to see everybody. Mr Hillier said, "We are expecting great things of you when you return to us. You know that we are losing Sergeant Band? We look to you to take his place."

Phew! Short though the interview was, it was sufficiently long to set me ill at ease; for I knew (and Hillier himself should have known) that the very thought even of my taking over Tommy Band's position of 'solo cornet' was quite ludicrous.

Back once again at Kneller Hall, we started rehearsing for the approaching outdoor concert season.

Concerts were given on successive Wednesdays, the final one of each month being billed as a 'Grand Evening Concert'. A grand concert would end with one of three flogged-to-death old war-horses, namely, Eckerburg's *The Battle of Waterloo*, Kappey's *Episodes in a Soldier's Life*, or the *1812 Overture*. It did not matter a great deal how or what we played when it came to the respective final sections of these pieces, for we were drowned by the firing of miniature cannon, rockets, and the sound of Adko's voice bellowing at us to follow his 'buddy beat'.

But I suspect that it was the simulated battlefield atmosphere which was created by the mingling in equal parts of the cannons' cordite fumes and the carbide-acetylene gas given off by the huge lamps which illuminated the bandstand that lulled our audiences into accepting that they had indeed been given more than their full money's worth.

Rehearsing for these concerts could be sheer torture. These went on for some six hours each day. The bandstand was exposed to the full glare of the sun, and we were not permitted to sit. These attendant discomforts became even more exaggerated when the old wooden bandstand was pulled down in order to make way for a concrete one; for the heat of the concrete drew one's feet terribly.

Adko himself would sit at the far end of the lawn in a garden chair and under the shade of the trees. He gave his instructions through a megaphone, which I might add, was a quite unnecessary piece of equipment. And then there was his shrill whistle. Ask any army musician who went through Kneller Hall during Adko's regime and he will tell you that his whistle (which was a signal for us to stop playing) could be heard above the band, even when all 160 of us may have been playing fff. And this is no exaggeration.

"Adko would just not let go." Sir Edward Elgar conducting the Massed Choirs at the opening of the British Empire Exhibition, 23 April 1924.

It was immediately following Wembley that the source of a private income which hitherto I had enjoyed suddenly dried up. Student Willcox gave me the sack from being his batman for my alleged neglect of his person and equipment during the Wembley engagement. This left me the poorer by half-a-crown a week, which represented a 26.84 per cent cut in my weekly wage, for I was still on 'boys' pay' of seven shillings per week. 'Polly' Willcox later became Director of Music of the Irish Guards, and after he retired, Bandmaster of the Ford Motor Company's Brass Band. 'Polly' was a most likeable person, but he had to be admired and had to receive adulation. He was, I believe, Queen Elizabeth the Queen Mother's favourite Guards' Director of Music. 'Polly' could be forgiven therefore were he perhaps a trifle conceited. Once he had taken over the Ford Motor Company's Brass Band, the saying went around (so I was told), 'Ford's also make cars'.

It was during this same year that I was to experience the second of my 'all-time lows' (my first all-time-low being when I returned to army life after my first Christmas leave).

It happened when I was Duty Bugler. Both the Orderly Student and the Duty Bugler were required to sleep in the guardroom (a temporary wooden hut affair) during their respective periods of duty. This was to ensure that they were on call for the full 24 hours of a day.

Wednesday was observed as a half-holiday — a misnomer if ever there was one, for the only period we escaped was the 7.30-8.30 pm harmony class. The Orderly Student during my week as Duty Bugler was 'Taffy' Roberts of the Royal Welsh Fusiliers Regiment. (He succeeded Adkins as Director of Music, Kneller Hall, in 1943.)

It was about 10 pm that Taffy spotted some pupils, who if not exactly drunk, were, shall we say, decidedly merry. He placed the whole lot of them under close arrest, which meant their spending the night in the guardroom. Not content with this, the over-zealous Taffy ordered me to accompany him on a snap tour of the pupils' barrack rooms, when he placed a few more under close arrest. I well remember Pupil Reid of the King's Royal Rifle Corps being ordered to leave his bed (into which he was snugly tucked up) dress, and repair forthwith to the guardroom. (Reid's arrest was quite unwarranted, I thought.)

I slept that night surrounded by a regiment of semi-drunks, who, curled up as they were in just their blankets, took up every available inch of the guardroom's floor space. Even to this day do my nostrils sense the foul smell of their combined beery breaths, and my ears detect the disgusting belching noises that appeared to go on spasmodically throughout that long night.

Following this episode, I asked Student Louis Pay, the then Band Sergeant, whether I might be exempt Duty Bugler, on the grounds that I was unable to blow the calls sufficiently loudly. Pay patted me on the shoulder in paternal fashion, remarking, "You must tuck a lot more army duff into that stomach of yours, Nalden; you certainly look as though you could do with it." And with that he struck me off the Duty Bugler roster.

My then innocent-looking face was to bale me out from many a similar situation and from many a tight corner. It was not for nothing that I managed to go through a quarter of a century of army service without one single day's CB (Confined to Barracks).

The Cornet Professor was Charles Leggett, a brilliant instrumentalist, who in his hey-day was a household name throughout the military band world. Himself a Scot (he always addressed me as 'laddie') Mr Leggett was formerly solo cornet of the Band of the Scots Guards. (He later became solo cornet and deputy conductor of the now long-defunct BBC Military Band.)

Being the only cornet professor, his teaching roll was a great deal longer than that of most other professors. Even so, at the end of a long day's teaching, the last pupil to go to him could expect to enjoy a lesson no less stimulating than that enjoyed by his earliest pupil; for the man was as indefatigable as he was conscientious.

Charles was strong in his dislikes, and made no bones about them. "Offenbach may have been a brilliant composer of light operas, but he was a mean man, laddie." And when Kneller Hall underwent a radical character change, from being a purely teaching institution into becoming commercial-engagement orientated, Charles said to me (this, some decade later when I was a student), "This once-great institution is now run for the benefit of one man, laddie — one man, laddie." At the word 'one' he would waggle violently his index finger so close to my nose as to make me flinch. He was possessed of the most remarkable tooth-formation that I have ever seen. (This gave him a perfect embouchure for his instrument.) "Never would I have suffered the agonies I have gone through in the dentist's chair, were it not for my profession, laddie."

It was characteristic of the man, that with the thousands of London's residential streets open to him, he should have chosen to live in Melody Road. He always claimed that were he to be parted from his beloved cornet for even one week, he would die. He entered hospital during my final year as a student (1935) and after being in there for a week, did just that — died aged 60.

As my professor, it was his duty to evaluate my year's work and record this on my Pupil's Certificate. "It would be unfair of me to give you too high a grade, laddie, as your bandmaster may come to expect too much of you.''

My Pupil's Certificate reads:

> This is to certify that No.1055004 C. Nalden of the Roy.Arty.(!) Mounted Band has undergone a course of instruction on the Cornet and has attained a Good degree of Proficiency as a performer thereon.
>
> Charles Leggett, Professor of the Cornet.

Kneller Hall,
17th October 1924.

It was during our end-of-course examinations, more especially in harmony and aural, that I came to realise Mr Hillier's mistake in sending me to Kneller Hall at so early an age. I then came to realise that I was far too young to have benefited fully from what the course had to offer.

I recall the aural examination as going completely over my head; and yet by then I was aware of the fact that potentially I had a 'good ear'. I do not record this in any spirit of boastfulness when I add that nine years later when I sat my Kneller Hall Examination for Bandmastership, I topped both the harmony and aural examinations. My examiners in those subjects were Ernest Read (Royal Academy of Music) and Professor C.H. Kitson. I simply quote these facts in order to underline Mr Hillier's questionable policy in sending all too many of us to Kneller Hall at all too early an age.

Prize day arrived, with Colonel Somerville making the speech. After assuring the pupils that we carried a field-marshal's baton in each of our individual knapsacks, he went on to exhort the students once they had become bandmasters, to "stick to your Bach, and stick to your Beethoven". Adko gave the speech in reply. After reminding us how fortunate we were in having a musician for a commandant, Adko went on to echo the colonel's laudable exhortation. But once the colonel's Kneller Hall command had lapsed (when he retired to the seclusion of his estates in Ireland whose soil became the more enriched by the multifarious bulbs dutifully dug up and sacked by Kneller Hall gardener Attwell), the respective commands of Brigadiers Bach and Beethoven also lapsed, their successors in office being Jack Payne and Debroy Somers; for with Somerville now safely out of the way, Adko could afford to take his tongue out of his cheek.

Speech-making now over, the prize-giving ceremony got under way. Adko was then the only army musician to hold the Bachelor in Music degree. This degree was considered so great a hurdle as to merit the institution of a special prize for award to the student who was considered nearest to attaining that distinction. In that year it went to Student Jarman who must have been Buster Keaton's prototype; for never was he seen to smile. (Some few years later I asked Bandmaster Jarman to coach me in harmony, which for a limited period he did. Not the least enjoyable part of my lessons with him was the occasional glimpse I got of his ravishingly beautiful wife.)

My name was read out. I walked down the room's tiered steps, clicked my heels together, saluted . . . .

Up to that moment the proceedings had been attended with a dignity and decorum that would have graced a royal Levee. But as I made my salute the entire assembly released its Somerville-imposed inhibitions by letting itself explode into one great shout of derisive laughter. It was the second time during my up-to-then brief military career that I was to envy the worm his hole; for I had yet to learn that NEVER, NEVER, should a soldier salute unless wearing his cap. My shocking faux-pas constituted a resounding victory for the hundred or so 'line' bandsmen who were present; and at the same time served to uphold their claim in far more convincing a manner than any verbal argument, that artillery musicians simply were not soldiers. H.M. Bateman was then in his hey-day. What a pity (for him — not for me) that he was not present; for 'The Soldier who saluted without his cap on' would have made an hilarious Bateman cartoon.

I left Kneller Hall to return to Aldershot on 20 October 1924.

What had I accomplished? Apart from rubbing shoulders with musicians from many other army bands, sitting for my 'First', thwarting the ill-intentioned plans of the kindly gentleman who invited me out to tea, and of course winning a prize — apart from all this, practically nothing I'm afraid.

On the day after my return, I was ordered to report to the Bandmaster's office. Both Hillier and Soars were sitting at their respective desks.

"Well, Nalden, and how do you think you have progressed over the past year?" asked Tim.

"I won a prize sir!"

"Bravo, boy! Bravo!" interjected the man who would have liked to be boss but wasn't.

"What prize was it you won," asked Tim.

"Third Prize for religious instruction, sir."

At this point the interview came to an abrupt end.

I still have that prize in my possession. It is a book called *The Stories of Wagner's Operas* by J. Walker McSpadden. The Introduction points out —

This book is directed primarily to the needs of young people, and is sent out to them in the hope that sometime they may hear the dull booming of the Rhine about the Gold, the magic fire as it sweeps to encircle the sleeping maiden . . . .

The only dull booming I recall hearing on that particular morning came from Bill Soars's stentorian voice, which rapped out "About turn! Quick march!" A more appropriate command would have been "About turn! Slow march!" — to the *Funeral Music* from *Gotterdammerung*.

Some short time after this I must have given Bill Soars cause for administering to me a severe rebuke. His closing (and exact) words were "and you've come back from Kneller Hall a big disappointment and a failure. March out!"

Eleven days after my rejoining the band, the result of my 'First' came through — I had passed. Mr Hillier (so I learnt from the Band Clerk, Bombardier 'Dick' Thairs) declined to present me with my certificate, even though I happened to be the first band member to have passed what we knew as the 'new First' (revised syllabus). And yet in the previous year my 'Second' had been presented to me by the person who had signed it, Lieutenant-General Sir Philip W. Chetwode, General-Officer-Commanding-in-Chief, Aldershot Command. Such was the extent of Mr Hillier's disappointment in me. The one senior band member who did congratulate me was Band QMS 'Perce' Rudd. "I sincerely hope that one day it will be the means of unlocking all the doors you wish to be unlocked," said Perce, wringing my hand at the same time.

I resented deeply what I felt to be the cavalier treatment meted out to me by Messrs Hillier and Soars. Soon I found myself reverting to my former life, by doing exactly as the other boys were still doing — reading Edgar Wallace 'thrillers', going to revues at the Aldershot 'Hipp', to local cinemas, and to bed on Sunday afternoons.

I began to patronise one particular cinema more and more frequently, as to become perhaps its most regular patron. Moreover, admission for me was free. It came about thus.

About the time I returned from Kneller Hall, the job of Office Boy became vacant. The office boy's duties were to keep the office clean and tidy, sort the band mail, do the odd bit of office work, such as making out the Christmas leave passes (which earned him a 'tip' or two from the more generous types) and listing our married men's children's names in connection with the annual Christmas tree party. (I still remember 'Jammy' Sowden's sequence which ran — Winifred, Freda, Olive, Maud, Alice and Joan. 'Jammy's' excuse for this little brood was that both he and his wife were determined upon having a boy. In no other aspect in his mode of living did 'Jammy' display such unwavering resoluteness.)

Coming to those free cinema seats. One of our senior NCOs (who for reasons of security and good taste shall remain anonymous) had regular employment in the cinema orchestra (these were still the days of the silent film). A married man, he had also built up for himself a full circle of women friends, so that, at whatever seaside resort the band might be playing, he could always rely upon receiving an affectionate and loving welcome. He kept up his correspondence with them throughout the non-seaside-touring winter months, their replies being addressed to him c/o the band office.

I gained free entry to the cinema by taking him his letters which had arrived by the afternoon post. The cinema's uniformed commissionaire was never really happy about this arrangement, but I always managed to argue my way past him by stating the truth, that I had been instructed by — — to deliver to him personally his afternoon mail.

"Never, never, never, take letters to my home" was — —'s oft-repeated caution to me.

With one obvious exception, this proved itself a happy arrangement from all viewpoints — from that of its main architect, from that of his several strategically-placed women friends and from my own; for this Bottom Office Boy's 'perk' tided me over a full year, from early 1925 until 1926, when I entered upon my 'man's service' and so relinquished my office boy's job.

My office boss was Bombardier Dick Thairs, who was given the job of Band Clerk solely on the strength (perhaps I should say on the weakness) of his suffering from piles, which to say the least made horse riding hardly a comfortable pastime.

It was Dick Thairs more than any other person who helped me shape my moral being. It was Dick who taught me to honour a contract; who insisted upon my being punctual, being completely unequivocal in my replies*, and upon my investing what small savings I was able to make in 4½% War Savings Certificates. ("When you grow older you must put your money into bricks and mortar, as I have done," advised Dick. Most probably I would have heeded Dick's advice had I not come out to New Zealand, where it is rather more appropriate to put one's money into weatherboards and corrugated iron.)

Dick soon had me playing my trumpet in his own *Felix Dance Band*, of which he was pianist and business manager. By his seeing to it personally that I banked some of my dance band earnings, I was able to purchase

---

* "Don't let me hear you say 'I might' ever again. It is either 'I will' or 'I won't!'."

a trumpet of my own and rig myself out with a second-hand dinner-jacket suit from Madam ('Ma') Hart's of Camberley. ('Ma' Hart's, a time-honoured institution, was the trading centre in which impecunious Sandhurst cadets 'flogged' their anything and everything, from tennis racquets to pairs of shoes; and where impoverished persons like myself did their shopping.)

Throughout the whole of this year, and indeed well beyond it, Dick took it upon himself to supervise my development, thus guiding my transition from the ex-schoolboy stage to young manhood. And for that I have never ceased to be grateful.

Mr Hillier's profound disappointment in me notwithstanding, on 10 November of this same year (1924) he gave me my first paid Band engagement — The Lord Mayor's Show.

Ceremonial and all that

This perhaps may be the right moment for me to write about our musical duties.

Our official duties included playing as a mounted band (that is, playing our instruments when mounted on horseback)*, and playing as a straightout military band, or as an orchestra.

Mounted band involved us in duties such as the Lord Mayor's Show, the Aldershot Tattoo and the Royal Military Tournament.

'Dismounted' band duties included our playing for church parades, military funerals, Officers' Mess 'guest nights', Officers' Club cricket matches, Officers' Club afternoon tea concerts, regimental sports, point-to-point races, the Army Cup final (which put paid to our Easter Bank holidays), Old Comrades Association reunions (which likewise put paid to our August Bank Holiday Mondays) and so on.

Then there were several types of paid engagement which included playing at seaside resorts, church fetes and garden parties, when a small string orchestra was used. In addition, individual musicians were permitted to accept engagements such as playing in cinemas, theatres, cafes, at masonic and sports' club dinners, and of course, dances.

---

* The most unusual (and colourful) mounted musicians surely were the two in the service of the Indian rajah who in the 1930s placed an order with the English firm of Boosey and Hawkes for a piano which was to be especially shaped so as to fit on the side of his elephant. Sensing a pachydermatous-sized order no doubt, the enterprising (and appropriately-named) firm persuaded the rajah into having not one, but two pianos, pointing out to him the two-fold advantages of a more balanced appearance and a more extensive repertoire. However, I am unable to verify the alleged sequel that the rajah himself insisted upon playing the Primo part of Brahms's Opus 56B.

The Mounted Band

Before one could participate in mounted band duties, he had first to graduate through the riding school. Riding drill was taken either by Sergeant Stan Morrish, or by Bombardier Fisher, an army 'rough-rider', and a man's man if ever there was one. (Fisher once classified me as a rough rider, but applied the adjective in a quite different sense.)

In the early stages riding instruction was given in the Artillery Riding School, an enclosed great barn of a building where constantly flying dust penetrated one's eyes, nose, mouth, everywhere, as its soft peat-like foundation was never damped down. Having graduated from the riding school, we were taken to an outdoor 'manage' as we ourselves called it. Within our own exclusive little circle it was known as the 'dust-hole'.

During the early stages of our training we were permitted full harness, i.e. saddle, reins and stirrups. But once progress was established we shed our saddles and stirrups, leaving us equipped only with reins. The final stage ordained that we let go of these and fold our arms when taking a jump.

A frequently given order would be 'Ride — Halt! Dismount! Change horses one up.' This taught us to become accustomed to the idiosyncrasies of horses of all types — horses with 'hard' mouths, horses with 'soft' mouths, placid horses, nervous horses, horses with 'easy' backs, and horses with 'razor-blade' backs.

Should you care to simulate the feel of riding bare-back on a razor-blade backed horse, I suggest that you bump up and down for an hour non-stop on, say, the slender arm of a wooden chair. Like us, you will soon be seeking relief first in your left, and then in your right, cheek; for dead centre will long since have become so tenderised as to arouse in your local butcher a lively commercial interest. (One of the arts of horse-riding, military fashion, is to 'grip' the mount's side with one's knees. Stirrups tend to make one careless of doing this, hence our being compelled as part of our training to ride without them. The one way to circumvent the effects of riding bare-back on a razor-blade backed horse is to 'rise' up-down-up-down in rhythm with the trotting motion of the horse; and this can be done only by gripping with one's knees. Riding at either a canter or a gallop is a far more comfortable affair; for the technique here is to remain motionless.)

During our riding school days we were never permitted to wear spurs. A good riding instructor would demonstrate to us that neither the spur nor the whip need be applied to make a horse respond to its rider's bidding.

The pleasures that go with horse riding do not become apparent until such time as the rider has gained full confidence both in himself and in his mount; for any sign of nervousness or hesitancy on his part will transmit itself to the horse. It took me two years before I attained complete confidence, when riding became an eagerly anticipated pleasure (except when Tim Hillier headed the ride, for then we never got past the 'gentle trot' stage). Before my own confidence became established, I was thrown on more than one occasion. My horse, a skewbald, was named 'Angel', a misnomer if ever there was one. The moment Angel sensed the beginning of what might develop into a general stampede, she would bolt. I had neither the technique nor the confidence to hold her in check.

I acknowledge that the tough training we received in the riding school proved itself one of the factors of army life which saw to it that I did not develop into a namby-pamby; for otherwise I might well have become just that. Instead, the training became a vital factor in my then-developing manhood.

The only instrumentalists who were exempted from playing in the mounted band were players of 'double-reed' instruments, oboists and bassoonists.

The pride of any mounted band is its drummer; or rather, the combination of drummer and drum horse. The drum horse carries a specially-constructed pair of timpani, which are strapped on to each of its sides. Because both the drummer's hands are in use, he must guide his horse by means of foot-reins, which are attached to his stirrups.

The mounted drummer in my day was Tony Farrell, who, as I said earlier, was an ex-Foundling boy. The drum horse's name was 'Margot', whose appearance was very similar to that of the cream and white palfrey upon which rides the beautiful blonde princess of fairy-tale land. Margot became the subject for a specially-commissioned 'portrait' which was hung in the bandmaster's office. Margot's successor was 'Prince', a handsome stallion in cream and brown. The combination of Tony Farrell and Margot was one of the more spectacular sights of the Aldershot Tattoo, the presence of the various other cavalry drum-horses notwithstanding.

One of the occupational hazards with which the mounted musician is faced is the unexpected and sudden toss of his mount's head; for should he be playing his instrument he is liable to sustain some nasty damage to his teeth. One of our horses, 'The Rat', a highly nervous creature who (as I myself discovered) was quite unfitted to be a band horse, had the nasty habit of doing this, until ultimately checked by the addition of a martingale to his normal accoutrements.

For the 1924 Lord Mayor's Show we travelled to London by train, our horses and drivers (grooms) being accommodated in separate carriages of their own. We were accommodated in the Household Cavalry Barracks, which brought home to us, and that forcibly, how very much better off were the Guards in matters relating to army rations.

On the day of the show itself, we mounted our horses at approximately 8 am, and apart from a brief rest near the Guildhall (when we were served a cold lunch) we remained in the saddle virtually the whole day. And it would so happen that I was suffering from one of my special brand of headaches, which was made all the more agonising by the busby that was stuck on my head. An artilleryman's busby is an uncompromising piece of headwear, its inner 'core' being made of unsoftened leather and I am told that in weight it exceeds the bulkier-looking guardsman's 'Bearskin'.

I have quite forgotten exactly the amount of money that engagement was worth, but never was a fee so hard-earned. For example, we were treated to a bit of good-natured but potentially dangerous hooliganism from a group of London University students who did their best to unsettle our horses (and so unsaddle us) by pelting them with pebbles. But in this they were 100 per cent unsuccessful.

The Royal Military Tournament

In 1925, we were 'clicked' as one of the duty bands for that year's Royal Military Tournament, which was staged at Olympia.

In addition to our own special 'turn' which was to parade around the arena as a mounted band, we were required to provide music for certain of the tournament's display items such as the navy's tug-o-war contest. In other words, our role was not unlike that of the circus band, but not nearly so well paid, of course. (We only received an additional clothing allowance.)

I recall the final dress rehearsal. We remained seated in our saddles doing simply nothing for close on two hours, during which time the officer-producers went into conference. With the lure of London literally on our doorstep, it took only a bit of fidgeting on our horses' parts to set tempers fraying.

Our sleeping accommodation was the most crude of its kind I had as yet encountered. The whole of Olympia's upper floor was equipped with three-tier wooden bunks, each army unit being separated from the other by a piece of hessian. This meant that an area which normally would have accommodated, say, 20 men, now slept 60. Olympia's grand hall, some two and a half acres in extent, is covered in by 112,500 square feet of glass roofing. Directly beneath this were our sleeping quarters. We had to rely solely upon skylights for our supply of air, which never was anything but foul. This decided many of the men upon sleeping outside on the roof.

I'll warrant that Olympia has never quite rid itself of the stinks deposited there at its opening show in the December of 1886, when the French artists of the Paris Hippodrome brought over 250 performing animals. Some cocktail!

We derived but small comfort from the liberal supplies of sample tubes of Kolynos toothpaste which were freely distributed by a bevy of girls dressed in the then Kolynos coloured (yellow and green) crinoline frocks; or from the generosity of Messrs Bovril Ltd. whose prominently-slung banner made the proud boast 'Bovril is supplied to all competitors here' — which was true, provided one was up at some ungodly hour of the morning to receive it.

Some of us were ordered by Bill ('Get your hair cut') Soars to do just that. I recall being down literally to my last shilling, which was the charge exactly for a hair-cut in a nearby barber's shop, against the fourpence we paid back in Aldershot. But I had no option other than to have it cut. With the cutting process over, the barber proceeded to light a wax taper.

"Singe, sir?" (I had never been addressed as 'sir' before.)

"No thanks!" (thinking of the extra cost).

"Promotes the growth of the hair, sir!"

"No thanks!"

"I think you should have it singed (sssss) sir; fine head of hair like yours, sir (sssssss); pity not to take proper care of it sir (sssssssss)."

More in panic than anything else, I won this round by going on the offensive in blowing out his taper.

"Shampoo, sir?"

"No thanks!"

"Very refreshing, sir."

"No thanks!"

"What about a little astringent lotion, sir? Wonderful as a hair conditioner."

"Yes, thanks!"

"That'll be one-and-ninepence, sir."

"But I've only got a shilling."

"Well, (pointing to his *Scale of Charges*) there it is, (no 'sir' this time) Astringent lotion, 9d."

"I'm really very sorry, but I've only got a shilling."

"Next time you'd better read the scale of charges before having your hair cut."

There and then we parted company for ever, with no 'Good day, sir' on his part, and no 'Thanks very much' on mine. I had unwittingly inflicted on him a two-fold besting, for London barbers, I came ultimately to learn, looked for a tip as of right.

The Aldershot Tattoo

The Aldershot Tattoo marked the nadir in the calendar of the Aldershot Command soldiers' a-Christian year.

Massed mounted bands rehearsals which were held on Aldershot's famous Laffan's Plain would drag on interminably while tattoo producers went into one of their frequent and prolonged huddles.

I recall one of these rehearsals taking place on an especially hot summer's morning. One particularly foul-mouthed Cavalry Trumpet-Major brought the entire mounted bands to heel by his abusing them with a string of oaths and expressions the like of which I had never before heard. 'Nobby' Allsworth who was riding next to me muttered in a hoarse whisper, "Charlie! I bet you half-a-dollar that that bloke gargles every morning with lavender water." I would like to think that he did; for even now I am liable to find myself giving an involuntary shudder when contemplating upon what his flow of language might have been had he not so tempered it.

The thrilling spectacle of the tattoo itself bore no relation to what went on behind scenes. We mounted our horses each evening at 7 pm for inspection by the Band Sergeant-Major. We would then proceed from barracks to the tattoo ground in time for the 8 pm start which was signalled by the firing of a rocket. And there we became stuck for the next four hours with virtually nothing to do beyond giving our own 'turn' which might go on for some 20 or so minutes. We could not return to barracks for we were required (as were all performers) to form part of the final tableau.

Should it rain, our jack-boots trapped the lot. Unless one took it turn and turn about with some other band member in minding the other's horse, one had to become reconciled to the company of one's mount for the whole evening; for to allow your horse to break loose was liable to be viewed as a punishable offence.

The huge marquee which served as the troops' canteen was as sordid a place in which to while away the waiting hours as anything ever devised. The heavy smoke-laden atmosphere provided just the right setting for the several Crown and Anchor 'schools' which operated until broken up by the 'Red Caps' (military police).

I myself managed to avoid using the canteen in a novel way. Normally, some of us would have taken a sandwich pack; but the difficulty here was the complete lack of facilities for carrying any extraneous article, even one as small as a book. From the year 1929 until I left the band for Kneller Hall, I was permitted to live out of barracks for health reasons. My good landlady, Mrs Barnes, would pack me a substantial supper, majoring in tomatoes, of which she knew me to be over-fond. But where to put it? Why! Of course! Within the ample cavity of my busby!

All went according to plan until Band Sergeant-Major Perce Rudd's inspection. "Nalden, your busby is perched too high on your head. You should have learnt by now that . . . the . . . hair . . . of . . . the . . . busby . . . should . . . be . . . on . . . a . . . level . . . with . . . the . . . eyebrows." By the time Perce had finished ramming it into its regulation position, I could do nothing about it but ride to the tattoo ground with this mess of squashed tomatoes trickling idly through my hair and down to the back, sides, and front of my head.

One tattoo found the Massed Bands of Infantry saddled with a particularly nasty spot of work of a sergeant-major. Traditionally, the massed bands were headed by the Drum Major, who in turn was followed by the Sergeant-Major i/c Massed Bands. On this particular tattoo, next in line after the sergeant-major was the Royal Warwickshire Regiment's mascot, a gazelle. It was led by two orderlies, one on either side.

The long-awaited moment for revenge came. The gazelle by nature is a shy, nervous animal, and the Warwickshire's regimental mascot was no exception. He would become so frightened by the glare of the searchlights and the noise issuing forth from the thousand or so instruments of the massed bands as to require the maximum amount of effort on the part of the orderlies to keep him in check.

Biding their time, the orderlies waited until the bands were making their exit from the arena, when they both deliberately let go their ropes. The frightened animal leapt forward butting the Sergeant-Major clean over the arena's touchline.

My friend George Savage (who was the then Warwickshire Regiment's Bandmaster) told me the sequel; how next morning the two orderlies were hauled up in front of their grave-faced commanding officer.

"I hear that you failed to control the mascot at last evening's tattoo?"

"Yes, sir, but it was an accident, sir."

"Must have been bloody funny! Wish I had been there. Case dismissed!"

We would arrive back in barracks from the tattoo certainly no earlier than 12.30 am for 10 to 12 consecutive nights.

I believe all profits went to military charities; but this charity brat cannot recall himself as ever becoming one of the tattoo's objects of charity.

Officers' Mess duties

I think it fair to claim that in my day the military band's everyday function was to provide background music which was heard, but seldom listened to. Some years later, when I was Bandmaster of the Royal Artillery (Portsmouth) Band, I decided to put this long-held theory of mine to the test.

My band was playing for a regimental cricket match. I decided to use the occasion for rehearsing a programme we were due to broadcast from the BBC. Following that, I rehearsed some new music, stopping the band to practise some of the more difficult passages, and so on. At the conclusion of play, I was thanked officially for the 'most enjoyable afternoon's music you have given us'.

One of the greatest farces musically speaking was our playing at Officers' Mess dinners. Our band served the Royal Artillery Officers' Messes at South Camp (our own unit), North Camp, Deepcut, Blackdown, Ewshott, Bordon and Longmoor. The band was either screened from the diners by means of heavy floor-to-ceiling curtains or placed in a room apart; so that we would forever be playing to an invisible audience. For 'away' messes (that is messes other than South Camp) we were paid the sum of fivepence 'supper money', which fell short of the minimum local charge for a fish-and-chip supper by one penny. So far as I personally was concerned, the most frustrating aspect of these Officers' Mess duties was not connected at all with the music but with the delicious and tantalising smells which wafted from the kitchens.

As a dinner progressed and the various courses' respective wines flowed, so the diners' conversation grew more noisy and their behaviour more boisterous. Towards the end of a guest night dinner, the diners' and the band's roles would have become reversed, with the diners providing the background noise, and the band the audience. And yet each Officers' Mess insisted upon having a supply of commercially-printed programmes which were proof-read most carefully by the band librarian.

At the appropriate time, speeches were made and toasts proposed. 'Stick to your horses, gentlemen' was the theme of one after-dinner speech; but the speaker was either too drunk or too inarticulate (or both possibly) to get very much beyond that most laudable exhortation. Each repetition of his exhortation was applauded by the thumping of fists on the table, which in turn caused wine glasses to execute a giddy dance of their own.

It was not until after a guest night dinner that the band's presence became apparent; for it was then that the officers came to realise that we were there. The younger officers would then crowd themselves into our curtained-off space and proceed to coax Mr Hillier into giving them some current musical comedy hits. Mr Hillier was far too unsure of himself to do otherwise than oblige; furthermore, there was no escaping this at South Camp, as the band's music library was housed only about 100 yards away. And so it frequently happened that the 'extras' would drag on longer than the official programme itself.

The final act in these farces came when it was time for us to return to our barrack rooms, which might be as late as 11.30 pm. But as Lights Out would long since have been sounded, we were obliged to find our way around the barrack room (stumbling over the odd kit box en route) either by the flicker of a match or in total darkness.

I hazard a guess that not for one moment would the British soldier of today tolerate like conditions, and rightly so. But then in those days we accepted them, admittedly with a great deal of grumbling, but without question or even resentment; for numbed sensibilities, like numbed fingers and toes, are not susceptible to pain.

The paid engagement

There was no grumbling here.

Seaside engagements were generally popular with the band, for although we gave at least two, and sometimes three performances on all seven days of the week, we had time still for sea bathing, playing on the local clock-golf course, and enjoying ourselves generally. Moreover, these engagements got us away from the barrack room for sometimes as many as eight weeks of the summer.

We generally found seaside landladies to be a kindly lot, even though their 'stone's throw from the sea' claim would at times have severely tested the skill of a New Zealand surf-casting champion. And those landladies who did look after their guests could have made very little profit out of them.

Each landlady would have her own personal set of rules, suitably framed, and displayed in a place of some prominence. One Bournemouth landlady went under the delightful, and somehow appropriate, name of Mrs Hipkiss. One of her more immutable rules read: 'Tea stains on the tablecloth will be charged for at one penny per stain.' On the final morning of our stay, one of our number reached for the tea-pot and proceeded to join up all the little stains into one big stain. Then making a mock bow to Mrs Hipkiss with all the grace and majestic dignity of the repertory actor, he proffered her the sum of one penny. I cannot recall the sequel.

Another form of paid engagement was the stately country house afternoon garden party, whose death knell was sounded by the new-style cocktail party of the early 1930s. A small orchestra of 10 to 12 players was the normal complement for this type of engagement.

It was pathetic to see some fawning young curate (whose living it would seem was at the grace and favour of the garden party's hostess), spend his entire afternoon in running to and fro with glasses of iced coffee or cups of tea for My Lady's fine friends. Poor sycophants! how I used to pity them their lots in life!

I once spotted the Foundling Hospital architect, Mr ('Fish-bones') Chubb at one of these deep-in-Hampshire garden parties, but although our eyes met in mutual recognition, he appeared not to notice me.

Musicians in general, but clarinet players in particular, will appreciate this anecdote. At one of these garden parties we were playing a selection from *La Boheme*, which on the edition we were using was given its anglicised title, *The Bohemians*. A portly dowager-type peered over the shoulder of our clarinet player (a dour Yorkshireman named 'Nobby' Holdsworth) and positioning her lorgnette, enquired of Nobby: "Boheme?" Nobby swivelled round in his chair, and holding his clarinet up to the dowager as though for her inspection, replied: "Naw, ma'am, mine's a Clinton model; but I hawp to be changing over to a Boehm model shortly. You naw, ma'am, the change awver takes one a right good six month."

As I have already remarked, our musicians were permitted to accept permanent positions in Aldershot's local cinemas and theatres, provided these did not interfere with their official band duties.

I once deputised for Bill Wickens, the Aldershot Hippodrome's trumpet player. It was during that week that I came to see for myself the degrading conditions to which chorus girls were subjected. These poor wretches (there were about 12 in this particular show) were allotted one small and crudely-appointed dressing room, below stage, and completely airless. A thin wooden partition separated their dressing room from the band room, which, as may well be imagined, was peppered with peep-holes.

I recall the profound shock I received when I heard their swearing, for never before had I experienced anything quite like this coming from women. Condemned as these poor girls were to their nomadic-like existence, in and out of cheap lodging houses week after week, grossly underpaid and being taken for granted by any old 'stage-door Johnny' (such as our own local Sandhurst officer cadets) as fair game, was it to be wondered at that they should on occasions relieve their frustrations in the way they did?

I have always looked upon the year 1925 as marking for me the dawn of a new era. It was the year in which I began musically speaking to 'click' as it were. My sight-reading suddenly improved, and I found myself able to practise my instrument for progressively longer periods without becoming so distressingly fatigued. This in turn must have led to a marked improvement in my standard of performance, for my name was now beginning to be included in the lists of 'official' and 'private' engagements.

My first important (and most romantic) private engagement of the year provided me with a unique experience. A few of us were selected to assist in the very first Haslemere Festival, which was directed by the festival's founder, Arnold Dolmetsch. I will not pretend that I understood the strange idiom of a great deal of the music that was being performed. The Dolmetsch family seated in arc formation and playing on their various-sized viols presented a charming picture.

Should you have access to, say, the fifth edition (1944) of *The Oxford Companion to Music*, plate 171 (or the 10th edition (1970), plate 178), you will find a photograph of the Dolmetsch family which would have been taken around this same time. Note in particular the clothes that Arnold Dolmetsch himself is wearing. This was his dress style when he came to our barracks to supervise preliminary rehearsals. While his exclusive Haslemere audiences would come attired for the concerts in the 'vulgar diamond show' as Shaw once put it, Dolmetsch himself would come dressed in the same clothes as those he wore at the rehearsal — Norfolk jacket and knickerbockers, and a flaming red cravat. He would perch himself gnome-fashion upon a high stool (a coloured toadstool would not have appeared as being out of place) from which he would direct the performance.

It did not require a particularly discerning musician to single out his son Rudolph as being the most talented of the group. When Rudolph lost his life on active service in World War II, England became deprived of a man and musician she could ill afford to lose; for Rudolph was also a delightful person.

Those army church parades

For the many thousands of civilian onlookers who up to the outbreak of World War II thronged Aldershot's Wellington Avenue, particularly during the spring months when its chestnut trees were out in their full beauty, the Sunday morning military church parade provided a spectacle magnificent in its display of martial ceremonial and pride of regiment; for the various branches, the cavalry, the artillery and the infantry appeared to enter into a tacit agreement to vie each with the other in matters pertaining to pride of person and of regiment.

However smart their parade turn-out may have been, the PBI ('Poor Bloody Infantry') must ever have considered themselves as starting at a decided disadvantage when coming up against the stiff opposition from across the other side of the avenue; for the cavalry officer resplendent in his Savile Row-tailored uniform, his mirror-surfaced Sam Browne belt, sword-scabbard, riding boots and spurs, cut an imposing figure. So too the cavalry trooper with his highly polished steel sword-scabbard and spurs, the canary-coloured 'grips' of his riding breeches and his aiguillette.

Each regiment headed by its band marched to church at its prescribed regulation pace. Thus the cavalry marched at the slowest pace of all, which was 112 paces to the minute. Next came the Royal Artillery whose regulation pace was 116 steps to the minute; next the infantry at the standard pace of 120 steps per minute, and finally the Light Infantry and the Rifle Regiments (the 'Black Button Wallahs') whose prescribed pace of 152 steps to the minute suggested a pressing urgency on their parts to enter into commune with their maker.

Towering over all this in the near-distance was the massive equestrian statue of the Duke of Wellington.

All this outward show and glitter was one thing, but for those taking part in the parades it could quite often be another, for the rigid parade-ground discipline and divine service were not ready mixers. There was, for example, the true case of the soldier who was reprimanded by his NCO for not removing his headgear smartly enough when about to enter the church — "Take yer bleedin' 'at orf yer dopey bastard — aint yer woke up to it yet that yer abaht to enter the 'ouse of Gawd?"

Each individual soldier was permitted to attend the church of his own denomination; but this did not circumvent the army regulation which ordained that church parades were compulsory. It was a known fact that at enlistment the more resourceful recruit would state the name of some way-out religion 'that never was' in his attempt to dodge permanently these parades.

There was the case of the soldier who, feeling aggrieved at the compulsory side of it, wrote to G.B. Shaw, asking his advice. Shaw advised him not to attempt to fight the regulation but to regard the church simply as just another pile of bricks and mortar. The post-war fashion of the soldier writing to his MP had yet to come.

Little wonder then that this system inspired most, if not all, of our boys (myself not excluded) to make a token offering by giving the collection bag a resounding rattle before passing it on.

The church parade 'duty band' was responsible for playing the voluntaries and accompanying the hymn-singing. Most army chaplains' favourite hymn appears to have been the *Church's One Foundation* which invariably was sung to S.S. Wesley's tune *Aurelia*. It was a favourite also with the soldier congregations; and as much as I personally disliked the tune, it was none the less a moving experience to hear this untutored soldiers' choir of several hundred voices unite in so powerful and full-throated a rendering of it.

As with every other profession, the Army Chaplains' Department was made up of good chaplains and bad ones, or perhaps I should say, successful chaplains and unsuccessful ones. As I remarked earlier, the most outstanding preacher during my 10 years in Aldershot was the Reverend Yelverton, who commanded both the attention and the respect of his soldier congregations.

At the other end of the scale was the sort of preacher who found it necessary to get through to his soldier congregation by resorting to some cheap puerile tactic, such as a jocular reference to the army rissole — the eternal refuge of the destitute-of-ideas type of army padre.

I recall one army padre of the early 1920s, whose subject for one of his sermons was selfishness. He chose for his text the words of the current song-hit, *I love me*!

I love me,
I love me,
I'm wild about myself.
I love me,
I love me,
My picture's on the shelf.
I look myself right in the eyes
And say that you're just fine, etc.

The trouble with this particular preacher was that he lacked the personality to capture the troops' attention (which admittedly must have been no easy matter). His mumbling manner failed even to raise a snigger, for the troops could have gone to Aldershot's notorious 'Blood-Tub' theatre where they would have heard the same song put across by a chorus of semi-nude happy-looking girls, and have been spared the moral platitudes into the bargain.

The most pathetic example of this inept manner of approach was that of a very young and obviously inexperienced army padre. The text for his sermon was hope.

There is a well-known picture in the Tate Gallery painted by George Frederick Watts which he named Hope. Watts himself tells us 'All the strings of her instrument [a harp] are broken but one, and she is trying to get all possible music out of her poor tinkle.' Hope!

hoping she can play her tune even though her harp has all its strings broken but one. Hope! So do not despair, soldiers, Hope!

At the time (it was during my year in Bordon Camp) I could not help but feel that the preacher might have had some success had he tried putting that sort of stuff across a Mothers' Union meeting, but hardly across a brigade of seasoned soldiers. Perhaps more than any other single factor, I would say that it was pathetic showings such as these, which was responsible for calling into question the whole concept of the compulsory military church parade.

We knew the Reverend Anderson as 'The Scrounger', for virtually every one of his sermons included a begging appeal to the pockets of his soldier congregations. When eventually he retired he was given a living in the delightful village of Boldre in the New Forest. Although officially retired from the army, he remained on the active list insofar as his self-assumed prerogative over the Royal Artillery (Mounted) Band was concerned. "You simply must come down and play for my Church Fete" he would implore us. Go down we did, played (without a fee naturally) and entered wholeheartedly into the spirit of wild abandon which characterises the average church fete; for there were hoop-la stalls, weight-guessing competitions, and a fortune teller, whose astonishing accuracy surprised everybody until it was discovered that he was the local bank manager in disguise.

But the event which sent both Vicar Anderson and his flock into chaste raptures of delight was the novelty raffle. I purchased the winning ticket. The prize was a nanny goat, which I straightway named 'Kitson' after the author of that learned textbook *The Evolution of Harmony* which I happened to be reading between the playing of pieces. But when it came to my claiming Kitson (who already I had decided to tether in the field that backed on to my 'digs' in Aldershot's Brighton Road), I was requested to defer matters for a while. "Surely you do not really mean to take her?" pleaded a typical church-fete-type woman of me. "You realise, don't you, that she has a very young kid, and that it would be sheer cruelty to separate them?"

Although they promised faithfully to forward Kitson on to me once her offspring had been weaned, she never arrived. Furthermore, I subsequently had good reason for suspecting that either the Rev. 'Scrounger' Anderson, or one of his church fete committee was charged with the responsibility of seeing to it that the current year's raffle-goat was well and truly pregnant at the time of the village's annual fete. I later discovered that so far as Boldre was concerned, goats never had been one of its export commodities.

From the musician's point of view, the finest army padre I had the privilege of working with was the Reverend F.N. Robathan. I found his ideas on church music to be so sound and stimulating as to invite him to address the Kneller Hall student body on the subject. (This was during 1943 when I was Acting-Director of Music.) Between us, we hatched a plot to oust the old 1891 *Cathedral Prayer Book* settings of *Versicles and Responses* (which by tradition were used throughout the British army) and in their place substitute Tallis's settings. We further decided to dispense with all instrumental accompaniment to both these and the *Canticles*, and to train the choir (comprised mainly of Kneller Hall students) to sing everything *a cappella* (unaccompanied).

All went well until we were paid an unexpected visit by the Chaplain General to the Forces who was senior to Mr Robathan (senior in rank, that is, but not necessarily senior in the degree of his holiness). 'The Bull' (as we knew the CGF) had stampeded his way down from Reigate, the wartime HQ of the South-Eastern Command.

"How dare you," roared the Bull, addressing the two of us separately and yet at the same time; "how dare you change my form of church service without my authority. You will change it back again by next Sunday." We meekly obeyed.

The Reverend Robathan was no less zealous a reformer in his own civilian parish than he was in his army one. He related to me how he came to lose the whole of his church choir in one fell swoop. By way of a change, he decided to supplant the choir's annual performance of *Messiah* by Bach's *Christmas Oratorio*. The choir objected, Mr Robathan insisted, and so the choir resigned en bloc. But once they learnt that their vicar, nothing daunted, was raising a new choir which stated its willingness to sing the *Christmas Oratorio*, the old choir relented and returned to the fold — to sing Bach's *Christmas Oratorio*.

The Kneller Hall Band was involved in some further encounters with the Bull. In 1943 I had to take the Kneller Hall Band to Reigate on one Sunday of each month to play for the South-Eastern Command church service which was held in Reigate Parish Church.

I was taken to task by the Bull, who objected to my choice of music for the voluntaries. "Why can't you play us something that we know," grumbled the Bull during the course of the final processional hymn. (He actually stopped singing for a while in order to convey to me his deep displeasure.)

The next time we played there, I appeased him with *Demande et Reponse* from the one-time popular *Petite Suite de Concert* by Coleridge-Taylor. "That's much better — much better," purred the Bull.

On another occasion he administered a public admonition to some of my men who were whispering to each other during one of his prayer sessions:

> (mf) Most heartily we beseech thee with thy favour to behold our most gra...
>
> (ff) There's a prayer on you men! There's a prayer on!
>
> (mf) ..cious Sovereign Lord, King George ....

I discovered his roar to be worse than his toss; for when it came to my relinquishing the acting Directorship of Kneller Hall, he visited War Office personally to ask that I be given a 'deserving appointment' as he put it.

And then there was my own commanding officer, Lieut.-Colonel Robert Lowe Sherbrooke DSO of the Sherwood Foresters.

"Mishter Nalden! What wash that frightful piesh of mushic you played ush out of church to? Shome Bach fugue, I shpose?" (It was a sensitive arrangement for Military Band of Prelude IV from Book I of the '48.)

It was a time-honoured tradition in certain circumstances that one of the lessons be read by a regiment's commanding officer. Colonel Sherbrooke's predecessor in office was Lieut.-Colonel Dumbell (sic). This particular service happened to be held in some Middle East station before the outbreak of World War II and was for soldiers only, as all families had been sent home because of the Arab-Jew clashes.

The lectern in this particular garrison church conformed to the standard army pattern, a massive brass spread eagle. Colonel Dumbell began reading the Lesson, using his normal stentorian parade-ground voice, which, understandably, caused an outbreak of tittering from his all-soldier congregation —

> And the Lord lifted up his voice and said . . . if you men at the back of the church don't shut up, I'll hurl the Book and the bloody turkey at you.

The Aldershot News — February 2nd, 1930.
Royal Garrison Church:
'In spite of the inclement weather, a good congregation was present on Sunday evening. The Rev. H.F.S. Collier, SCF preached a sermon on the words "Was lost and is found". The soloist was Musician Nalden (harpist), R.A. Mounted Band, who played the Adagio from Beethoven's "Moonlight" Sonata, and gave a much appreciated rendering of "The Bells of Aberdovey".'

'The Red Church' (as the Royal Garrison Church* is affectionately known) could hardly be described as an imposing structure. Even so, nobody but an insensitive person who has worshipped there could fail to be moved by that spiritual 'something' which is ever present.

That 'something', which is timeless, may be related in some mysterious way to those battle-scarred, time-tattered regimental flags which reach out almost defiantly from the northern and southern walls near the choir stalls; or to Subaltern Horatio Herbert Kitchener's pride in his having helped increase the church's congregation of 30 officers and men 'to a congregation of nearly 1000'; or to the invisible but strongly-sensed presence of the spirits of those thousands of British soldiers whose battle-decimated remains lie buried in 'some corner of a foreign field'. Or it is related maybe to the silent echoes of past military services, whose very simplicity was such as to be understood by the most simple of soldiery; or to the Roll of Honour which is set appropriately on the walls of the sanctuary, recording the names of former Royal Garrison Church chaplains who fell on active service.

Its font is yet another possibility, at which generation after generation of soldiers' children have been baptised into the Anglican faith, including my own daughter, Rosemary. Or this spiritual 'something' may be related to the countless memorial tablets which record past episodes of glory and personal deeds of heroism. One such tablet is mounted high on the wall at the church's south-eastern corner, and tells its own story, which is as romantic as any passed down to us by the century that saw Corunna, Waterloo, the Crimea, the Indian Mutiny, Rorke's Drift, Khartoum, Tel-el-Kebir and South Africa:

> Wounded, Helpless, Sick, Dismounted, Charlie Fraser, well I knew,
> Came the worst I might have counted faithfully on you.
> (Memorial to Lieut.-General Sir Charles Crawford Fraser, KCB, VC, 1829-1895)

It was during this same year, 1925, that there occurred an event which was to shape the future course of my life.

Mr Hillier was now taking a greater interest in my musical development (he must have forgiven me my prize-winning effort) by giving me personal lessons during the 'Young Hands' practice period. He would sometimes have Horace Barker and myself in his office together, when we would be

---

* Built in 1863 and consecrated on 29 July of that year. Affectionately known as The Red Church after the colour of its brickwork.

put *Through the Sharps*, a book of cornet studies in duet form written by Manuel Bilton*.

One day (it would have been towards the end of the year) I was told to report to the bandmaster's office. 'What have I done now?' I wondered. All I could think of were the cello lessons I was now taking surreptitiously from another boy, my old friend Fred Goddard. Perhaps it was that; and indeed it may well have been, for Mr Hillier opened up with: "Oh, Nalden — I've decided to put you on the harp. Now, I don't consider that there's anybody around these parts who is qualified to teach the instrument, and so from next year, I'm going to send you to be taught at the Guildhall School of Music. The Band Fund will pay for your first term's lessons, but after that we will expect you yourself to carry on paying. This will mean also that you'll have to find your own weekly rail fare to London and purchase your own study books and other music."

He continued: "There was a famous Welsh harpist named John Thomas, who used to practise for eight hours a day and was so poor that he used to wrap a blanket around himself in order to keep warm. He finished up by becoming harpist to Queen Victoria and King Edward VII. I won't be expecting you to do quite that number of hours' practice, but I do want you to appreciate the opportunity the band is giving you."

"Thank you, sir," was all I could say; for with the prospect that had opened itself up so suddenly and so unexpectedly, I was too overwhelmed to say more.

Once I left Tim's office, I found myself making some rapid calculations. I was still classified as a boy, being paid still at the rate of seven shillings a week, less the two shillings which were deducted for 'credits'. But I knew I had to wait only until the March of the following year when I would enter upon my 'man's service', which would mean an increase in pay. In addition I was still earning a little extra money as trumpet player in Dick Thairs's Felix Dance Band. (I should have mentioned earlier that the band's theme song, naturally enough was 'Felix keeps on walking, keeps on walking still. With his hands behind him, you will always find him' — 'Felix' being the hero of a silent cinema strip cartoon.)

And it was around this same time (fortunately for me) that we band boys decided upon forming our own union, whose rules laid down the minimum rates we should charge a man for 'cleaning up' his equipment for church parade. These rates were — uniform alone, 1/6d; card pouch,

---

* Manuel Bilton (1862-?) commenced his military career as a musician in my own Band. He was appointed Director of Music to the Royal Horse Guards (The Blues) in 1903. He professed openly to being a great admirer of Napoleon, which inspired his *Napoleon* Overture.

an additional 6d; and instrument. This was an optional extra, the charge here being calculated according to the size of each individual instrument; for after all, the player of a double B flat brass bass could hardly have expected to be charged the same rate as that paid us for cleaning a silver-plated cornet.

"What a bloody hope," ruled our union boss (who would have been either Bill Walden-Mills or Jock Harris). (The union was formed in the first place as a counter-measure against some undercutting practices which were beginning to creep in; but mainly in order to defeat the mean tactics employed by one sergeant-musician in particular, who would attempt to 'pay' for our services with a slab of home-made coconut ice.)

A thorough polishing of one of the bigger brass instruments could take several hours; so that some musicians got round the difficulty by purchasing their own silver-plated instruments. I chose a different way out, for some musicians hold that silver plating an instrument adversely affects its tone. So I purchased a brass french horn, which I used for all duties except church parades. My official 'issue' instrument would thus remain in its case from one church parade to the next, and thus require the minimum amount of polishing.

A few days before we were due to go on Christmas leave, Bill Soars entered the boys' room accompanied by the band's commanding officer, Captain (Quartermaster) 'Bill' Baillie, a dour, but thoroughly likeable Scot.

"This is the boy who is going to learn the harp, sir," said one Bill, addressing the other Bill.

Captain Baillie asked to see my hands (although I never quite discovered why). I held both my hands in front of me as though for a Saturday morning inspection. (Bill Soars regularly inspected both our hands and the insteps of our boots at the Saturday morning room inspection parade.) Whereupon Bill Baillie emitted a low-keyed "Wheeee!" which through the centuries we have come to associate with the Highland Fling and the Scottish Separatist Movement; for my hands were literally coal-black from my making up the fire.

Bill Soars came to my rescue by assuring Bill Baillie good-humouredly that my hands and fingernails were always clean for his Saturday morning inspection — which they were, out of my now built-in respect for Bill Soars.

At last I knew exactly where I was going; or at least I thought I knew.

And so came to a close my happiest year as yet of my life as a soldier — or rather as a musician of His Majesty's Royal Artillery (Mounted) Band.

Man's service

In the March of 1926 I entered upon my 'man's service', and also upon the first of my nine years' colour service, i.e. service with the Regular Army; for the three-and-a-half years boy's service I had just completed counted for nothing.

I was now permitted to wear civilian clothes when off duty, and issued with a PP (Permanent Pass) which authorised me to be away from barracks from 'after duty daily until 11.59 pm'. (Under very special circumstances only were boys permitted to remain out of barracks after 9.30 pm.)

Although the band at this time numbered some 50 to 60 musicians, only 25 of these were on its substantive strength. The remainder (with the exception of the boys) were classified as being 'attached' to the band. In effect this meant that should there have been an outbreak of hostilities, all 'attached' musicians automatically would have been 'posted' to combatant gunner units.

Although remaining on in the band, once I had turned 18 I was 'posted' (on paper) to the 1st Pack Brigade, which at the time was stationed at Ewshott, some four miles from Aldershot.

All pack brigades were equipped with mules. These animals were used in rugged or mountainous country (such as in Italy in World War I) for transporting smaller pieces of artillery and other equipment which was strapped on to their backs. Their drivers walked at their sides.

Had hostilities broken out between the March and November of that same year, I thus would have found myself literally saddled with two mules, for whose mental happiness and physical well-being I would have been held responsible. Fortunately (for the mules' sakes) this eventuality did not materialise. Even so, I do not mind freely admitting that forever ringing uneasily in my ears during these months was the phrase 'with a kick like the hind leg of a mule'; and that deep down within my subconscious there lurked the fear that this, the grooming of a couple of mules, could well be my ultimate and final fate.

Reasoning to myself that it was infinitely more desirable at my time of life to be playing a harp temporal rather than a harp spiritual, I had already decided should the dread day ever eventuate, that I would limit my grooming to the mules' respective fores-to-midships, leaving their midships-to-afts to take care of themselves.

Then on 24 November of that same year I was transferred from the 1st Pack Brigade to the 5th Light Brigade. I cannot tell you anything regarding the functions of a Light Brigade of Artillery, for although for a time on the strength of one (again on paper only) I never attempted to discover what it was all about.

"I was now permitted to wear civilian clothes."   From a band photograph, 1927

Finally, on 22 October 1927, I was placed on the substantive strength of the Royal Artillery Band. At long last I felt safe.

Once I had turned 18, my pay shot up meteorically from seven shillings to 19s 3d per week. This, together with my regular earnings from the Felix Dance Band, saw me comfortably off and able to pay for my harp lessons.

I attended the Guildhall School of Music for my first harp lesson in the January of 1926. My teacher was Galatea Thorpe. She had been a pupil of John Thomas, the same John Thomas whose career had been held out to me by Mr Hillier as a shining example of what could be achieved by a person of humble origins.

John Thomas (1826-1913) was known in his native Wales as 'Pencerrd Gwalia', i.e. 'Chief of all Welsh Minstrels'. This title was conferred on him at the Aberdare Eisteddfod in 1861. It was peculiarly befitting therefore that he should have been born on 1 March, which is St. David's Day. When he was 14, Thomas was taken under the wing of Ada, Countess of Lovelace (Byron's daughter) who sent him to the Royal Academy of Music, London. In 1872 he was appointed harpist to Queen Victoria, and on her death, to King Edward VII. Meanwhile he had been appointed Professor of the Harp at both the Royal Academy and Royal College of Music.

Galatea Thorpe always claimed for herself the distinction (or womanly satisfaction?) of having been Thomas's favourite pupil. And I could readily believe this; for she was no less richly endowed in personal attributes than she was in musical ones.

When I commenced lessons with her she would have been a little over 70 years old, which meant that the greater part of her professional life belonged to the closing decades of the 19th century. This was reflected in her professed tastes in music, style of playing, and style of living. During the early years of her professional career she had been harpist in the Hallé Orchestra.

When I enrolled at the Guildhall, there were two harp pupils besides myself — a Miss Shillington Scales, who travelled up from Cambridge each week, and a Mrs Atkinson. Ultimately I became Galatea Thorpe's sole pupil, and at her request, took my lessons at her home in Brook Green, Hammersmith. Thus, and without knowing it, I came each week to within a mile of the district in which my mother had lived out her own personal tragedy. The hour's lesson I had been receiving at the Guildhall now became extended to two, and sometimes to three hours, for such was my teacher's generous nature.

Her first decision was that I should have an Erard Gothic model harp in place of the band's Grecian model. (The Grecian model harp is the smaller of the two, and quite unsuitable for orchestral work. It was this model which found its way into the drawing-rooms of the Victorian upper- and middle-classes; for the ability to be able to play upon the harp or piano, or to sing, was a necessary accomplishment for the young Victorian lady.)

One of our men told me of a harp he had seen for sale in Guildford, whereupon Musician 'Bowler' Reilly promptly whizzed me over there on the back of his motor cycle. It was a Gothic model, whose owner was asking £70 for it. I was told that should it not sell, it would be auctioned by Messrs Puttick and Simpson. Mr Hillier decided to take a chance on its being auctioned — which it was. He gave me powers to bid up to the Guildford price of £70.

Galatea Thorpe joined me at Puttick and Simpson, whose catalogue listed another, and more handsome looking, instrument. This one was knocked down to us for £60, which I straightway borrowed from Mr Reginald Nichols, the then Secretary of the Foundling Hospital. Exactly half a century later I received a letter from his secretary, the late Dorothy Brooks, in which she recalled the day when I walked into the Brunswick Square office and coolly asked for the loan of £60 to pay for a harp I had just bought at an auction sale.

As Tim Hillier became my guiding force, so Galatea Thorpe became my inspirational force. Her gentleness of manner, together with her very real interest in me both as a developing musician and as a developing personality, left their mark on me; for I found myself consciously modelling myself on her.

She was quite amazed at my gift of being able to memorise. For example, I memorised without any apparent effort Bochsa's *Forty Progressive Studies*, and the same composer's more advanced *Twenty Studies*. I took to memorising all my music, including orchestral parts, simply because of the inherent difficulty of reading harp music at sight. As a result of my doing this, I neglected, and badly, the all-important aspect of sight-reading. It was a mistake on my part which I continue to regret, for as I myself have since discovered, the memory weakens, whereas the facility for reading at sight stays on.

During the same year, Mr Hillier changed me over from the trumpet to the french horn. Although by then I had bought a trumpet of my own (for the band issued cornets, not trumpets), it soon became clear that I could not continue playing both the trumpet and the french horn. I therefore decided, not without regret, to pull out of the Felix Dance Band (Dick Thairs magnanimously allowing me to keep my Felix the Cat emblem). At the same time I also handed in my resignation to the manager of Aldershot's Garrison Cinema, where I had been deputising for the regular trumpet player, Musician Harry Harrison. In doing this, I was simply anticipating (albeit unknowingly) that fateful day in 1929 when every cinema pit-musician in the United Kingdom lost his job; for the 'Talkies' had arrived, heralded in Aldershot by Al Jolson in *The Singing Fool*. The leader of the Garrison Cinema orchestra, a capable violinist, was compelled, and grateful even, to accept a position in our local branch of Woolworth's as storeman and packer. London's Archer Street, the traditional meeting place for musicians who either were seeking work, or seeking a deputy, became a pathetic sight.

I soon came to realise that musically, the french horn was a far more satisfying instrument to play than the trumpet. To take but one example, the late classical symphony; whereas the horn is kept going for most of the time and frequently has something interesting to play, the trumpet (if allotted a part at all) more often than not is restricted to the same two tonic and dominant notes as the timpani; and like that instrument the trumpet has to content itself all too frequently with joining in the general melee — when it comes round. This means that the conscientious trumpet-player is forever counting an interminable number of bars' rest. The not so conscientious trumpet-player is either doing crossword puzzles or filling in his 'pools' coupon.

Perhaps the greatest advantage I gained from this change of instrument was the ability to transpose music at sight, and at any given interval. It is a faculty that the would-be orchestrator and conductor simply must develop. Indeed, I have heard of more than one orchestral horn player 'taking it out' on the 'difficult' and the 'dictatorial' type of conductor: "Maestro, I have an F double sharp for the E flat horn — is that correct?" is the sort of awkward and manufactured question that the unpopular conductor may find himself being asked.

During these years I undertook voluntarily to learn something about instruments other than my own. I took private violin lessons from 'Winkle' Goddard, whose name has already come into my story; Mr Hillier permitted me to borrow a band viola and sometimes to sit on the back desk of the viola section, which among other advantages, gave me facility in reading the alto clef. From other players I learnt the basic techniques of the wood-wind family.

Army bands in 'home' stations were inspected periodically by the Commandant and Director of Music, Kneller Hall. Whether it was because of Mr Hillier's fear of Adko (for the very thought of these inspections struck terror into the hearts of many a bandmaster) or whether it was a genuine move on his part to further our musical education, Tim called a group of some of the younger band members together, and announced his intention of running a class in harmony. Some members of the class resented what they felt to be an unjustifiable intrusion upon their leisure time; for the weekly work assignment plus the lecture hour itself certainly made inroads into this. So Tim whittled the class down to the few of us who were showing a genuine interest.

My harmony lessons with Mr Hillier took place in his office, with himself seated at his table and myself standing stiffly to attention by his side. I am sure that Tim did not really require this of me, but this attitude towards one's seniors was so ingrained as to become second nature in every one of us.

"Here you have consecutive fifths, Nalden — you must learn to avoid them."

"Yes, sir."

"And here you have doubled the leading note."

"Yes, sir."

"And here . . . " etc. etc.

Although I could not see it at the time, Tim clearly had taken me under his wing (as far as military discipline would allow) and was quietly going about the business of helping me lay my musical foundations. He would frequently call me into his office and give me long and highly instructive french horn lessons; for in his day he himself had been a fine french horn player, and I believe, a pupil of the great Borsdorf*.

Looking back on all this, I feel bound to ask, what other institution in the whole of England could have offered concurrently, individual tuition plus orchestral experience on various wind and stringed instruments and the harp, together with coaching in harmony, and aural training? Very few, I would imagine. Even so, in common with most other army-trained musicians, I regarded the university-conservatory trained musician with a mixture of awe and envy; they in turn were all too often prone to look down upon the military musician with an amused contempt.

I recall Bandmaster Hibbert telling me of Sir Edward Bairstow's** remark: "We can smell your military bandmaster's stuff a mile off." Little wonder therefore that the degree of Bachelor in Music was referred to in army musical circles as 'The Bandmaster's Waterloo'.

Added to the individual training I enjoyed, there were of course the works we rehearsed; and I stress the word 'rehearsed' for there was little likelihood of our ever performing publicly the great majority of them. As I have already said, Mr Hillier was an orchestral man, who had little, if indeed any, patience with the military band, and made no effort to conceal this.

During the whole of my 10 years in the band we performed in public only two symphonies — Dvorak's *New World*, and Schubert's *Unfinished*. Yet we practised assiduously, as though in preparation for public performance, Mozart's great trilogy, Symphonies 39, 40 and 41, Haydn's

---

* Friedrich Adolph Borsdorf (1854-1923). Professor of the french horn at the Royal Academy and Royal College of Music. Member of the old Queen's Hall Orchestra, and the London Symphony Orchestra. His reputation as a performer derived mainly from his artistry as a chamber music player.

** Sir Edward Cuthbert Bairstow (1874-1946), Organist, York Minster, 1913-46; Professor of Music, Durham University, 1929-46.

Oxford, *London* and 88th symphonies, together with his cello concerto; eight of the nine Beethoven symphonies (the exception curiously enough being the *Eroica*); Mendelssohn's *Italian* and *Scotch* Symphonies; the Cesar Franck Symphony, Tschaikovsky's 4th, 5th and 6th Symphonies, Dvorak's 4th, and Sibelius's 1st and 2nd. Other works which we rehearsed but never performed included Bach's *Concerto in D minor for Two Violins* and his *Third Orchestral Suite*, most of the standard overtures, and Elgar's *Enigma Variations*.

I well recall our being dealt a severe box on our musical ears when Tim introduced us for the first time to Holst's *Planets*. This by the way was in 1923, just four years after the work's first performance, which in itself is an indication of Tim's enterprise.

None of us pretended to understand what this strange 'music' was all about. The main difficulty I think must have been the relative absence of one particular factor that we had come to expect in music, namely, a singable tune. Thus *Mars* appeared to us as nothing more than a noisy cacophonous jumble of sound, and *Neptune*, which is described by one writer as 'perhaps the most remarkable piece of pure orchestral impressionism ever written', simply failed to add up. However, we took far more readily to this same composer's charming but little-played *Japanese Suite*.

Tim's greatest moment perhaps came when one of our officers asked that the orchestra play Wagner's *Siegfried Idyll* during an officers' guest night dinner. It was one of the rare occasions I can recall of Tim betraying openly signs of genuine excitement and enthusiasm — to think that a gunner officer should actually request us to play *Siegfried Idyll*. We rehearsed the piece no less thoroughly than had we been preparing it for public performance. Yet inwardly all of us knew (as Tim himself must have known) that the music would be drowned out even in its louder passages by the clatter of crockery and the usual officers' guest night crescendo.

Tim was so earnest a musician as to carry his principles even into the Aldershot Tattoo. For example, the music he adapted as an 'accompaniment' to the Royal Artillery Musical Drive (a hair-raising display given by horse and gun teams*) was the *Vivace* from the first movement of Beethoven's *Seventh Symphony*.

Deeply introspective person that he was, Tim failed to realise that the sort of music the average tattoo audience enjoyed the most was not

---

* All manoeuvres were executed at the gallop. At one tattoo there was a tragic pile-up caused by a piece of mis-timing, in which a horse suffered a broken leg. It was shot on the spot and the drive called off.

Beethoven but the community-singing which preceded the tattoo proper. The vast audience was led in this by the white-ducked, white-sweatered megaphone-happy man who was loaned out to the tattoo by courtesy of the London *Daily Express*.

And our band placed the blame fairly and squarely on Tim's shoulders for the loss of a regular and lucrative private engagement, the annual Grand National Steeplechase. "What punter wants to hear the *Unfinished Symphony*," grumbled the men between themselves, justifiably, "when he has just lost a packet on an 'also ran'."

It was just this sort of thing, his failure to understand that an army bandmaster's job, whether he liked it or not, was to provide musical entertainment in the popular meaning of the term, that in part probably cost Tim his promotion; for although he was one of the army's outstanding musicians (not bandmasters), Tim was never promoted to commissioned rank.

It was my singularly good fortune therefore that I should have landed fortuitously in a service band with a musician of Mr Hillier's calibre at the helm.

Once he saw that I was in earnest with my harp studies, he released me from the hour's 'Young Hands' practices. As the morning rehearsal finished at 12 noon, this meant that I was now able to practise the harp certainly for no less than five hours daily, seven days a week. My french horn and other instrumental practice was in addition to this. Once I had finished practising, I would get down to working on harmony and aural training. I was given virtually the exclusive use of the pay office, and should this not be available, the use of Mr Hillier's own private office. It was then that I was able to browse through his collection of learned tomes which were housed in the glass case.

Once I had worked through Part I of Kitson's *Elementary Harmony*, Tim did not allow me to continue with Part II, but switched me over to the same writer's *The Evolution of Harmony*, and *The Art of Counterpoint*. Both these textbooks were largely beyond my comprehension, as for example, the *Art of Counterpoint's* chapter on *The English School of the Sixteenth Century*. It was then that I found it necessary to continue working after the trumpeter had sounded 'Lights Out', which I was able to do by blanketing the pay office's window.

In the meantime my harp lessons with Galatea Thorpe were a sheer joy, so that each week reached its climax at 11.36 am, my train's departure time for London. On fine days I would walk along the Thames Embankment to the Guildhall, and still arrive there in time to fit in an hour's practice before my lesson.

I was once in the middle of doing this when a professor from the room on the opposite side of the corridor burst unceremoniously through the double-glazed doors of the harp room, and without a word, took me by the shoulder and steered me into his own room. Here I became an unwilling member of an 'audience' whose other members no doubt had been pirated in like fashion. From this I could only presume that the professor's idea was to give his pupils (there were several present) experience in performing before an audience. Each time I moved to go, he would lead me back to my seat, making a series of imbecillic-sounding 'n 'n 'n 'n 'n 'n 'n's. In the end it was Galatea Thorpe herself who saved me, by interrupting his pupil's recital with "If you don't mind, he is my pupil." It was my first meeting with an eccentric.

On another occasion I ran into Dr Davan Wetton, who taught class-harmony at the Guildhall. "You simply must join my harmony class deah boy! I'm sure you'll enjoy it immensely!" Maybe I would have, but the still fixed bland smile turned me off the idea.

I once had an interesting encounter with a person who appeared to be one of London's more colourful and romantic street buskers. Walking one day down one of London's West End streets, I came across a pathetic sight; it was that of an elderly woman, wrapped in a shawl, and playing on a much run-down harp. We chatted, and after listening to her pour out her life's sad tale, I promised to let her have my discarded harp strings.

I related my experience to Galatea Thorpe, who asked: "Was she playing on an old Grecian harp?"

"Yes."

"Was her 'charity bag' suspended from the pillar of the harp?"

"Yes."

"Was she playing *Men of Harlech*?"

"As a matter of fact she was!"

It transpired that she eked out a very lucrative living not only as a street busker but as a bookie's runner. She had accepted a bet from Galatea, and had made off with her winnings. Formerly a regular 'pitch' of hers, Brook Green henceforth became 'one of those streets up which I dare not walk'. "In the long run she became the real loser" Galatea explained to me, "for I used literally to keep her in harp strings." It transpired also that *Men of Harlech* was the sole extent of her repertoire.

The moral to all this? Never be so guileless as to equate a harpist's character with the seraphic appearance of the instrument he or she plays upon. (This caution does not apply to the author, naturally.) For was it not a harpist named Bochsa who cost Ann her courtesy title of Lady Bishop? (Ann was the second wife of Sir Henry Bishop, composer of *Home Sweet Home*. His knighthood, which was conferred on him by Queen Victoria in 1842, is the earliest instance of such a distinction being bestowed upon an English musician. Ann eloped with Bochsa to Australia in 1839.)

With the loss of my additional income from the Felix Dance Band and the Garrison Cinema, money was becoming rather tight; for there were some hidden expenses which I had not bargained for — the midday and tea meals on harp lesson day for example. But relief was not far off.

My musical horizons were soon to be extended in another, and very worthwhile, direction; for within a little over a year of my commencing studies at the Guildhall, I found myself being engaged as an orchestral harpist by various amateur music societies.

One conductor who frequently engaged me was a young Royal College of Music student of Malcolm Sargent's. He was in the process of learning the rudiments of his intended profession through the only avenue then open to most of Britain's aspiring conductors, the amateur orchestra. This young man was George Weldon, who later became well-known as conductor of the City of Birmingham Symphony Orchestra. In this way I came to know a number of works by French composers such as Debussy, Ravel and Honegger.

Another fine musician I met in this same way was Susan Lushington. She was sufficiently wealthy apparently to be able to engage at her own expense certain of London's leading orchestral players, such as the oboist Leon Goossens and Claude Hobday, who played the string bass in the BBC Symphony Orchestra. One charming production of hers (which she herself conducted) was Bach's *Peasant Cantata* in costume.

And then there was a Mr Steele, who was conductor of the Camberley (Surrey) amateur Choral Society. He frequently engaged a number of our players. At one of his rehearsals there arose a dispute which concerned the moving of the piano. "Please stand back, ladies and gentlemen; these soldiers will move it" was Mr Steele's smooth solution.

"I'm sorry, Mr Steele," rejoined 'Sonny' Soars our oboe player, "but 'these soldiers' will not move it. In the first place we cease being soldiers when we are engaged professionally, and in the second place we are paid to do the job of a professional musician and not that of a stage hand." A shocked silence followed, but the rebuke was fully deserved; for all too frequently did we find ourselves exposed to this sort of arrogance.

Whether or not it was an old wives' tale I cannot say; but we in the band held the belief that players of double-reed instruments (the oboe and bassoon) were more prone than other wind players to contract tuberculosis. Our bassoonist, for example, would gargle daily with salt water as a precaution against this. 'Sonny' Soars died of this complaint at the early age of 34.

Mr Steele once gave me a special rehearsal session on my own in order to try me out on a particularly difficult passage in Elgar's *The Music Makers*. The difficulty arose from the frequent pedal changes, for every accidental in harp music involves the shifting of a pedal. I had already taken the part to Galatea Thorpe, who related to me how once she chided Elgar with "You just don't know how to write a harp part, Sir Edward."

A further orchestral engagement took some of us to Cranleigh School in Surrey. The concert was conducted by the school's music master, Maurice Allen, and included a bracing performance of Borodin's *Prince Igor Dances*, the boys providing the chorus.

I envied everything about Maurice Allen, for in him I saw reflected all that I myself would liked to have had — his public school background, his university training, his type of job, and his *savoir vivre*. And yet, some 30 years later, when he visited New Zealand as examiner for the Associated Board and we had him round to our home, I found that all the old envy had left me. I was still too sensitive of my own background history, regretfully, to remind him of the time I played under his baton.

At this same time I was becoming engaged frequently as a soloist, playing harp solos at such diverse functions as a Young Liberals' Rally at Guildford, a vicar's silver wedding party (where I discovered for the first time the never-to-be-forgotten taste of a chocolate eclair), an All-Troops' concert at Bordon in Hampshire (where I was 'raspberried' off the stage) and a Masonic dinner.

Having concealed myself from the meeting which took place after dinner, I found myself enjoying as good a feast as any I had hitherto enjoyed save one — the annual hunt dinner, with which the artillery officers at Bordon Camp softened up the local farmers over whose land they hoped to hunt during the coming year. I was discovered by a Masonic brother, who hustled me out of the room with a complete lack of ceremony and an almost indecent haste.

I gained quite a lot of experience in solo work by playing without fee at the Percy Illingsworth Institute of paraffin-cleaned bath fame*. The

* See p.226

warden (a clergyman) who lived in style in a house perched near the top of beautiful and secluded Crooksbury Hill, described my offer to play gratis as 'awfully jolly', and insisted upon my accepting a fee in kind. So we struck a mutual bargain whereby I was to be given a free supper following each recital, plus a free bath at any time I felt like having one. (I might add that he got the better of this particular part of our bargain.)

Mr Hillier used me in the capacity of harp soloist to the full. I experienced the thrill which comes to every young performer when for the first time he reads his name in the press (adverse criticism excepted, naturally). One press report read 'Specially admired were the harp solos of Musician C. Nalden, a quite youthful performer, and one with an inborn faculty for playing the harp. He has the makings of a fine performer.'

Some few days after one of our annual Royal Artillery Association charity concerts, we were due for our routine general's inspection. When the General reached me, Mr Hillier turned to him and said: "This is the musician who played the harp at last Sunday's concert, sir." At this, the General's aide-de-camp took over and addressing himself to me said: "I expect you've heard of my father; he was harpist to Queen Victoria and King Edward VII." He was Major George Ivor Thomas, who unbeknown to me was quartered in the very same Waterloo Barracks as myself. There was a romantic sequel to this.

I walked one day into Gould and Bolttler's music shop in London's Poland Street to purchase some harp music. Sitting in the middle of the counter was a pile of handbills. On the front of the handbill was a picture of John Thomas playing the harp, and on the reverse side this notice of sale:

The ORIGINAL HARP of this world-famed Maestro is FOR SALE. This Harp was bought by Mr Thomas from Messrs Erard, and was played by him everywhere until his death in 1913. Since then it has remained with his family.

The instrument is in perfect condition and with it are the original IVORY HARP KEY, etc. as used by Mr Thomas himself, and also a practically complete set of BOUND VOLUMES of Mr Thomas's FAMOUS COMPOSITIONS for the harp, many of them fingered and autographed by the composer.

Immediately I made for Messrs Erard's, where the harp was on display. The owner, I was told, was Major Thomas!

It did not even occur to me that a soldier wishing to speak to an officer could do so only through a substantive-ranking intermediary; for I went along to Major Thomas's room, knocked on his door, and without further ado made known to him my reason for calling.

"Oh! No! Nalden," he said, "you could never afford the price I expect my father's harp to fetch. The advertisement has gone all over the world, and I expect somebody from America, for example, to be after it."

It was a crestfallen me who left his room. However, some short time later, summoning up courage, I decided to try my luck for a second time.

"You're beginning to make a nuisance of yourself, Nalden," was how he greeted me this time. "Come to see me again in a few weeks' time, and if by then it is not sold, you may have it."

Not only did the 60 pounds I paid for it include the ivory harp key, etc.; it included also Thomas's stool and music stand, together with two volumes of *Welsh Melodies* arranged for the Harp by John Thomas and inscribed *Joan Denny 1879* and *1888*; and two volumes of Beethoven's *Piano Sonatas*, also inscribed *Joan Denny 1870*. Joan Denny was Thomas's second wife. Before marrying him she had been his pupil.

One particular engagement was surrounded by an air of mystery. An octet was formed from within the band, and we were told that we were to play at the famous Ranelagh Club. It was further explained that the engagement was in the nature of an audition, which could lead to an extended and lucrative engagement 'somewhere in Scotland'.

Shortly after we began playing, in walked none other than Captain Adkins, who was accompanied by the Ranelagh Club's sort of gentleman-manager, Sir George Hastings. Adko's face looked at once more fierce, more cross, and more colourful than ever.

We must have satisfied our auditors, for some few months later the eight of us took off for a six-weeks' engagement in Strathpeffer Spa.

Our duties were straightforward and simple — to give three performances daily in the Pump Room Gardens, and to provide a dance band for their Saturday night 'hop'.

They were six weeks of unalloyed bliss; idyllic in fact. The weather was mostly perfect, so that I was able to slip out for solitary walks over the purple-heather covered hills, and over the stone-strewn moors to the beautiful Falls of Rogie. We were taken by car to as far west as Gairloch, skirting the banks of lovely Loch Maree for a goodly part of the run.

In the spa's Pump Room Gardens we were permitted to play bowls, which is why I now play golf.

When this dream engagement ended, I vowed I would one day re-visit 'The Strath'. To my lasting regret I never did; for one or another set of circumstances prevented me from doing so. The nearest I came to it was in 1942, when I accompanied Lt-Colonel Adkins on an inspection tour of army bands within the Scottish Command. Our tour took us as far north as Inverness, a tantalising 24 miles short of Strathpeffer.

It was following the Strathpeffer engagement that I came to take a course in harmony in a roundabout way. Taking the spa waters was a Reverend Nelson DD and his daughter, Mrs Margaret Hake. Margaret was studying singing at the Royal Academy of Music, but confessed to being 'bored to death' with the harmony course, which was compulsory. So I worked her harmony assignments for her (which she passed off as her own) and had them marked by her teacher, who was Montague Phillips, the composer of the once-popular light opera *The Rebel Maid*. It was a sort of an eternal-harmonic-triangle, the cuckold of course being Montague Phillips.

It was with a heavy heart that I left 'The Strath' at the end of these idyllic six weeks with orders to rejoin my band which was playing in Sheerness, Kent. After one performance during which I had played a harp solo, a blind girl was led up to me. She introduced herself as a foundling of my own generation. And then there was that homesick Irish actor belonging to the repertory company which was playing for the season in Sheerness. He begged of me to play him every day *Believe me if all those Endearing Young Charms*, even though each time I played it tears would roll unashamedly down his cheeks.

It was one of life's more romantic assignments, and one which afforded a deep satisfaction. When some few years ago I recorded this piece, I vow I could still see the tears welling up in that lovable Irishman's eyes.

At about this same time I took on my first harp pupil, who was a Bandsman Lewis of the Royal Ulster Rifles Regiment, whose barracks were close to our own. Rather more vital a personality was Bandsman Lewis's brother Ted 'Kid' Lewis, who in 1915 gained the world's welterweight boxing title. The boys' mother ran a maternity home in Aldershot, which, so my harp pupil in all seriousness informed me, was 'somehow always full up at Christmas'. The moral? 'Beware the Ides of March', I would say.

Towards the close of the Guildhall's autumn term of 1928, my teacher suggested that I take a complete rest from the harp over the coming Christmas leave. Up to them I had been practising not only for a seven-day week, but during holidays as well. So I took her advice, leaving the harp back in Aldershot for the first time.

I spent a thoroughly relaxed leave in Chertsey, taking part in every snow fight that was going, for it snowed heavily during the January of 1929. It was this I believe which was responsible for the damage; for I had yet to learn that a musician must take care of his hands.

Once back from leave, I resumed my studies, plunging straight into my normal routine of some five to six hours' practice daily. And then something

294 Half and Half

went horribly wrong with my fingers. Ugly, purplish swellings appeared around their joints, rendering practice painfully impossible. I reported the trouble to Mr Hillier, who was most sympathetic, sending me with a special note to the Army Medical Officer.

The MO simply passed me on to his orderly with instructions that he massage my fingers. As this treatment failed to improve matters, I set out on my own account to do a round of local civilian doctors. Ultimately I appealed for help to my old school, which arranged for me to see their honorary orthopaedic surgeon, a Mr Emslie. He had my hands x-rayed but did not explain to me the nature of the damage. I was now able to resume practice, but for greatly reduced periods. And then one of my little fingers began gradually to stiffen until it became completely rigid in both its joints. (The little finger is too short to be used in playing the harp.)

At this point Bill Soars stepped in, and advised me to arrange an appointment with a bone-setter (as they were then called), who had successfully 'fixed' a dislocated knee of one of the Aldershot Traction Company's football team. He was a W.E. Blake of Charterhouse Square.

He certainly 'fixed' my little finger for me. I could have yelled with pain as he broke down the adhesions. He then warned "unless you obey implicitly my instructions, you will land up with both your hands in that" (pointing to the plaster wall). One of his instructions was that I must follow a strict diet. He brushed aside my protest that being in the army would render this treatment quite impossible.

When I left his rooms I felt as though I had struck rock bottom; three years' hard study, and now, it seemed, a blank wall once again.

Mr Hillier made the decision for me. "You must live out of barracks; and if you take my advice, you will look for a place which is far enough away to give you a good walk into barracks each day."

It was then that Mr and Mrs Barnes entered into my life.

I had first to explain to them my financial position; that my army pay, plus the ration allowance to which I now had become entitled, amounted to 35 shillings a week. Mrs Barnes scaled her charge accordingly. And when in the September of 1931 the Government announced drastic reductions of pay in the three armed services*, she reduced her charge, which enabled me to go on living with them.

---

* It was the inequitability of these pay cuts (which hit the lowest ranks the hardest) that sparked off the so-called Invergordon Mutiny. Whereas admirals' pay was cut by seven per cent, and lieutenant-commanders' by 3.7 per cent, a married with children able-bodied seaman's pay was cut by 10.5 per cent, and an unmarried ABS's by up to 25 per cent. The news of the mutiny caused panic withdrawals by nervous foreigners on the Bank of England's gold reserves, and so led to Britain's abandoning the gold standard.

Not only did this fine couple see to it that I was properly fed, but insisted also that I take time off on at least one day of the week and accompany them on their walks; for the two of them were great walkers. They introduced me to the many places whose names were already familiar through my acquaintance with Conan Doyle's *Sir Nigel*. We walked to Crooksbury Hill, through Moor Park (where they related to me the history of Stella's Cottage*), to Waverley Abbey, Sheephatch, Tilford (whose bridge was held by Sir Nigel), and to Somerset Farm where one could (and did) eat unlimited amounts of scones, jam and cream for one shilling. We walked to Farnham Park, and to the lovely once-secluded villages which are dotted in no set pattern on either side of the Hog's Back — Runfold, Normandy, Seale, Puttenham; and at Compton, we visited Watts Gallery.

They first awakened, and then stimulated, my interest in these several villages' charming old churches. In Compton Church for example, they explained to me the various architectural styles, beginning with its Anglo-Saxon tower, then on to its Norman chancel and its unique upper chamber of sanctuary, its Gothic windows and its various pieces of post-Reformation work such as its carved pulpit and canopy and carved altar rails. And it was from Compton Church that I came to learn exactly what an anchorite or hermit cell was like.

They took me nutting and blackberrying, and taught me the names of the various wild flowers. They explained to me the nesting habits of birds, such as the sand martin, which abounded in beautiful Moor Park.

The Barnes had one child, a daughter named Mona. When I first went to live with them, Mona was living with her uncle and aunt in Wimbledon, but once she returned to live in Aldershot, she too would accompany us on our walks. These walks generally took place at the weekends and on Wednesday afternoons. Mona had a healthy appetite, and just as every one of England's rural footpaths once led to a church (so Mr Barnes explained to me) so did every one of Mona's routes lead ultimately to The Brown Owl, Farnham's most exclusive (and most expensive) tea shop. This meant that my already precariously-balanced budget (for I was still paying my Guildhall fees) became dangerously close to toppling over the edge of the precipice. I decided therefore to put my problem to my fellow bandsman, the irrepressible and irresponsible Eddie Roberts, who had had a great deal more experience in such matters than I.

---

* Named after Dean Jonathan Swift's friend, Esther Johnson. The *Journal to Stella* contains the letters Swift wrote to Esther Johnson.

"Always go armed with a sixpenny bar of milk chocolate," advised Eddie, "and see that Mona eats the greater part of it" (which proved not at all difficult to effect). Yet once again was insolvency successfully staved off.

The actual cooling off of my burgeoning friendship with Mona came about as a result of my growing passion for dogs. I would borrow other people's dogs and take them with me on my country walks. Mona once came home from her London office job, tired probably and hungry, to find one of my borrowed dogs secured to the gate which led to the house's back entrance. When Mr and Mrs Barnes and I returned some hour or so later from wherever we had been, it was to find an almost hysterical Mona, shedding tears of white-hot rage. "It's come to a pretty pass, mother," she screamed, "when a girl can't enter her own home." The dog had kept her at bay for a full hour.

Even so, life for me had taken on a very different meaning. I quickly regained my normally good health, and the strength continued to return to my fingers. Above all, I had discovered that there was far more to life than shutting oneself up in a room all day and practising the harp. Farnham Park was only some few minutes' cycle ride from the Barnes's house, so I would run over there on many a summer's evening (entering it via Folly Lane) to read my books within its lovely and peaceful surroundings.

But the whole episode of my fingers had given a severe jolt to any ambitions I may have cherished of becoming a professional harpist, which was the career Mr Hillier had in mind for me. I had to face up to it that from now on I was liable at any time to have a recurrence of the trouble, which was some form of arthritis; and the appearance of some mysterious pains in the joints of my elbows and knees came as a further warning — for once out in 'civvy street', should there be a recurrence of the trouble, I would find myself with no other career to fall back on.

But there was a deeper reason which decided me upon remaining in the army. I was then 21 years old, and had known nothing other than a safe guaranteed sort of existence; for however rough and uncouth army life may have been, I could hardly be given the sack. This is precisely what service life can do to one — sap one's initiative.

It was this apparent inability to face up to life and strike out for themselves that led so many staff bandsmen to remain in the army until such time as they were literally pensioned off. In the background there always lurked this very real danger of one's willpower becoming atrophied; and at that stage of my army career, I was no less exposed than were others to this danger: for although by then I had completed but three of my nine years' colour service, inwardly I already knew that when my nine years were up, I would lack the courage to make a break and strike out for myself in 'civvy street'.

In order to have qualified for a full pension, a soldier must have served for a minimum of 21 years in the Regular Army, excluding whatever boy's service he may have done. And I would say that the greater proportion of the men who were in the band during the same period as myself chose to stay on for pension rather than risk going out into 'civvy street' — for those were the years of the great depression.

So I came to the conclusion that the only safe course open to me was military bandmastership. I therefore asked Mr Hillier to register my name at Kneller Hall for the students' entrance examination, which he did; but not before registering his personal disappointment that I should elect to make this, and not the harp, my career. That was in 1931.

Towards the end of the previous year Galatea Thorpe had broken to me the sad news of her impending retirement from the Guildhall. I was saddened by the fact that I was to lose not only a fine teacher but also one of my God-sent direction posts; for she had given me guidance in many matters other than musical ones. It is understandable that I should have heard many fine harpists in my time. Unhesitatingly do I place Galatea Thorpe's name at the top of my list of 'greats'; she was possessed of a superb technique, but for sheer artistry and musicianship, I have yet to hear her equal. I continued to go on seeing her, our last meeting being when she came to my wedding in 1935.

My new teacher was Gwen Melhuish, a young and attractive brunette. Although not conscious of it at the time, I came later to see that Galatea Thorpe's tastes in harp music were rooted firmly in the 19th century, which after all, was understandable. Gwen Melhuish made some radical changes. John Thomas's *Studies* were replaced by an arrangement for harp of the *Preludes* from Bach's '48', and works by 19th century composers in general by works of 20th century composers.

At one of my lessons Miss Melhuish asked whether I would consider accepting a three-years' harp scholarship at the Royal Academy of Music. I had the feeling that the offer was made not so much because of the standard of my harp playing, but rather because the academy was without a harpist for its student orchestra. It was with more than a little regret that I knew I must decline the offer; for I realised only too well that the army would never consider releasing me unconditionally for three full years; moreover I could not have afforded to live in London — but it hurt all the same.

For one short period in my life in the artillery band I was accorded the equivalent of being 'sent to Coventry'. Although officially as members of the Royal Artillery Band we were in the army, none of us in all truth could claim that we were soldiers in the true warrior sense of the term. Our horses were groomed and saddled for us, and all we were ever required to do was to loosen their girths and surcingles after a 'ride' before handing them over to our drivers (grooms), who referred to us sneeringly as 'gentlemen of the RA Band'. Moreover, none of us had so much as handled a rifle, and neither had we done any gun drill. Imagine our sense of indignation therefore when it was announced that for the future all Royal Artillery Band musicians would be required to undergo a course in gun drill before being eligible to qualify for their proficiency pay. Not a few of our musicians threatened (but only threatened) to 'put in their papers' (meaning, to retire).

Our instructor, oddly enough, was sympathetic to our cause, and promised to have us ready for our passing out parade in the minimum amount of time. In order to live up to his promise, we were trained in one, and only one, of a gun team's duties. These in the main were the breech server who loaded the gun, a second breech-server whose job it was to open and close the breech, and the gun layer who was responsible for the gun's correct elevation, range, and direction. I happened to be crash-course trained for the office of loader, and was ever fearful lest my opposite number rammed the breech home just that split second too soon to reduce my hand to a bloody pulp.

Our passing out parade was going off swimmingly, until the inspecting officer came over to our team. "Now," he said, "I am going to take away your gun-layer who has been killed." I was given the double office of loader and gun-layer. A target was set me by the inspecting officer.

"Are you satisfied that you have found the correct elevation and direction?" he asked me.

"Yes, sir."

"Quite sure?"

"Yes, sir."

"Then let me tell you" (making his own check on my laying) "that if that were a live shell in the breech you would blow our officers' mess to kingdom come." And then addressing the whole parade, "I can see that you have been efficiently trained, and that you have learnt in a matter of weeks as much as the average recruit would learn in a year. Even so, I hardly think that you yourselves would expect on this morning's showing to be classified as gunners of the Royal Regiment of Artillery. I'll inspect you again in a month's time."

I was made the innocent scapegoat for this. However, we were not re-inspected, and neither was our proficiency pay stopped. In short, we reverted once again into becoming 'gentlemen of the R.A. Band'.

The day arrived when I was to sit the entrance examination for Kneller Hall. My supervisor was a Lieutenant Hobbs who was liked by us all. He, and another gunner officer, Lieutenant E.W.F. de Vere Hunt, were, I believe, army 'rugger' representatives. The time allowed for the examination (a written one) was three hours, but well before half that time had elapsed, Lieutenant Hobbs explained to me that he must be in Twickenham in time for a rugby match. "Would you mind very much if I left you to get on with it on your own? You may take as much time as you like, you know."

Mr Hillier looked over my scripts before posting them to Kneller Hall. He did not appear altogether happy with some of my work, and went so far as to point out some of the errors in my harmony paper. Even so, both of us knew that for me, the entrance examination was a mere formality, and its result a foregone conclusion; for Adko had already asked of Mr Hillier: "When are you going to send me that harp player of yours?" In short, Adko knew a good commercial proposition when he saw one.

Kneller Hall confirmed that I had 'passed in', and that I was to report there on 1 April — a date no less portentous than 15 March or 5 November.

One of the qualifications required of a potential Kneller Hall student was that he must have held non-commissioned rank for not less than a year before being admitted to the bandmastership course. Some time before I sat the entrance examination, Mr Hillier had had me promoted to Acting Unpaid Lance Bombardier. Once in this rank, I would volunteer to take other NCO's 2-3 pm 'young hands' practice. This arrangement suited both parties; for it gave me some experience, however elementary, in conducting, and the person I relieved a clear run of afternoons off.

I was now an NCO, and as such, inherited certain indubitable rights. Henceforth I was entitled to be addressed by all ranks from field marshal down to private, as 'Bombardier' or 'Bomb' for short. I was now eligible to use the NCO's wet canteen. I could place any soldier in a rank below my own 'on the peg' or 'on the fizzer' (that is, on a charge). Although I could be 'bust' (i.e. reduced to the rank of gunner-musician) for conduct unbecoming of a Non-commissioned Officer of His Majesty's Armed Forces, I could not, as an NCO, be awarded a 'dose' of CB. In short, I was now a person to be feared and respected by all soldiers below me in rank, i.e. by boys and privates. But in the event none of these eventualities ever came to pass; for I did not take advantage of wet canteen facilities;

never was I addressed by any field marshal as 'Bomb'; I did not put anybody on the 'fizzer'; I was not 'bust', and I was neither feared nor respected any more or any less than I had been before the sewing on by Mrs Barnes of my 'milk stripe'.

A few days before leaving for Kneller Hall, I decided to celebrate by joining up with a party of our musicians who had arranged to see a mid-week FA Cup competition re-play between the two London giants, Arsenal and Chelsea. This was to be the first and last professional soccer match that I was to patronise. The ground was packed tight and we became separated from each other in the crush. I found myself standing next to a fierce-looking bowler-hatted gentleman replete with nicotine-stained moustache and discoloured teeth.

The two teams sprinted on to the ground accompanied by a deafening roar from the crowd; and finding myself becoming caught up in the general FA Cup contagion, I enquired of my neighbour: "What colours are Chelsea?"

"Er you pullin' me bleedin' leg, cock?" he replied, "cause if yer are, I'll tell yer what colours Arsenal are as well, an' in a way yer won't like neiver."

Clearly, it was quite beyond his comprehension that a soccer fan could be so crass ignorant as not to know the respective colours of Arsenal and Chelsea. It was as well perhaps that we were tightly packed.

On the day before my impending departure, Mr Hillier called me into his office. It was then that he advised me to take my university degree, adding pathetically, "and don't make the same mistake that I made in thinking you cannot do it." He then gave me this curious and unexpected piece of advice: "And when you decide to marry, I would look around if I were you for a woman who has a bit of money of her own." At that time the only woman I knew having money of her own, or rather potentially of her own, was Gladys, the daughter of a widow who owned an off-licence in Leamington Spa. This good widow had made it known to some of our musicians who regularly 'digged' with her, that the lucky man who married her Gladys would come into £1000 hard cash; moreover her Gladys would simultaneously inherit a like sum.

The only snag here was that the lucky man would inherit also Gladys's pair of frightfully bowed legs — hence the inducement. Naturally I did not mention this potential gold mine to Mr Hillier, for fear he might egg me on. (In the event, I married into a family which, like myself, was flat broke. My marriage was able to take place owing to the magnanimity of Messrs Samuel Brothers [St. Paul's] Ltd., [Founded originally in 1830], who came over handsomely by letting me have the whole lot of my bandmaster's uniform 'on tick'.)

On the morning of my departure I knocked once again on the door of Mr Hillier's office — this time to say goodbye to Perce Rudd, who had succeeded Bill Soars as Band Sergeant-Major.

Bill Soars had maintained a strict discipline, never relaxing for a moment his tight rein of office. Although we feared him, nevertheless we respected him for this; for let it be admitted that the staff-bandsman, frequently finding himself as he did with surplus time on his hands, was ever liable to fall a willing victim to indolence, with the resulting loss of self-respect. Although Bill was not in a position to dictate what we did during our off-duty hours, he dictated, and in unmistakable terms, exactly what he expected of us in our on-duty hours.

Perce Rudd was the precise opposite. His was a lovable nature, and he was far too kind a person to have been placed in control of a body of men. Human nature being what it is, and being no different from other mortals, we took full advantage of his kindness. Discipline soon slipped, and he himself would occasionally arrive late for a parade. He was renowned for his absent-mindedness and forgetfulness. When first I lived out of barracks, my 'digs' were some hundred or so yards up the hill from Perce's home. On one Sunday morning I happened to be free-wheeling down the hill which ran past his house on my way to join the church parade. Perce hailed me with "Hi! Charlie! Let me borrow your bike — I'm running late. It won't matter so much if you're late." When I arrived in barracks, the band was formed up and about to march over to the Royal Horse Artillery lines. "Come on, Nalden! Double up! You're holding up the entire parade," shouted Perce, who clearly had forgotten that only some 10 or so minutes earlier he had hijacked my bike.

Perce's end was a tragic one. He ultimately lost his hearing completely. Stepping off the kerb one night in the war's 'black-out', he failed to hear an oncoming car and was killed instantly.

When it came to my saying goodbye to Perce therefore, I was saying goodbye also to the person who had befriended me (inviting me frequently to his home, for example) and who had continued to give me words of kindly encouragement ever since the day he had congratulated me upon gaining my 'First'.

I was saying goodbye also to many other old friends and personalities whom I knew I was going to miss sorely.

Although I myself had never indulged in a 'harmless flutter' (except in the heart of course), I found it none too easy when it came to saying goodbye to 'the old firm', Musicians George Kemble and 'Bassooney' Hay, who operated within the band their own unofficial bookies' business. It was no less difficult saying goodbye to that inveterate punter Lionel Tebby, who had enlisted in the band at about the same time as myself, coming to us from the Nautical School Training Ship *Mercury*, whose honorary director was the redoubtable seaman and England and Hampshire cricketer, Commander C.B. Fry. It was from the Commander that Lionel learnt to use a straight bat (for he was a good cricketer); but I would wager any amount with 'the old firm' that it was not from the Commander that Lionel learnt to back gee-gees.

Lionel, ever bent on beating 'the old firm' (in which he seldom succeeded I'm afraid) enlisted the aid of a professional tipster who went under the pseudonym 'Arbejay' (J.B. Rennie). Should a succession of his none-too-cheap tips fail to yield a winner, Arbejay (who lived 250 miles away in the far north of England) would send Lionel the pressing invitation: "You simply must come up here and have lunch with me one day." And should an 'also ran' (which Arbejay had tipped to win) happen to be a mare, his stock excuse for its failure would be: "She happened to be in heat." How Arbejay came by this bit of inside information, whether through his field-glasses or straight from the horses' mouths themselves, Lionel was never able to discover.

And then there was Walter D — , an ex-foundling boy, whose official way of ekeing out a living (playing the oboe in the band) came a very poor second to his unofficial way, which was playing the drums in the Felix Dance Band and racing his two whippets. With his whippets' tails tucked permanently between their legs and Walter's figuratively so (he was seldom seen to raise so much as a smile, let alone a laugh), he came ultimately to be distinguishable from his two dogs only by virtue of their not wearing the King's uniform.

And I was going to miss, not 'Plum' Warner so much as his wife, who was to be seen hanging around the barracks on each successive pay day and asking: "'as anybody seen my 'ub?"

And I was going to miss my french horn 'stand chum', 'Nobby' Allsworth. Could I ever forget the day when we were practising Manuel Bilton's *Ceremonial March*. It differed in one important aspect from every other march we played, for it bore neither a duple, nor a quadruple, but a triple time-signature. Ducking his head low behind our music stand and pointing his finger at the ¾ time signature, Nobby whispered hoarsely: "Charlie, this march must have been written for them bishops, mayors and other blokes what can't keep in step."

And I was bidding farewell to 'Fatty' Davis, whom I had re-christened in the names of Dumpert Schimmelpenninck. Regularly each Saturday evening (Saturday being the day after the army's traditional pay-day) 'Fatty' betook himself to the Royal Antediluvian Order of Buffaloes in Aldershot's

Victoria Road, there to re-sign the pledge, following which ceremony he would proceed to delight the assembled herd of fellow Buffaloes by a soulful rendering of *Variations on Lucy Long* on his bassoon.

I could not say goodbye to gentle Stan Reddish, for already he had left the band. It was Stan, who, 10 years earlier, had put me at my ease. I met him for the first time in the band practice room, and addressed him as 'sir'. "You don't 'sir' we ordinary musicians; you call me either 'Reddish', or if you wish, 'Stan'."

And although it was long since I had earned an honest quid or two in Dick Thairs's Felix Dance Band, I was going to miss my earliest army pastor and mentor.

And finally, I was going to find it desperately hard when it came time for my saying goodbye to those lovable characters, Tom Stroud (who did so much to help all band boys) and Norman ('Sandy') Lane. Tom's deafness led to his premature discharge from the army on a miserable pittance of a pension. When no longer able to play his instrument, Tom was employed as band copyist, which earned him an extra threepence a day. It was Tom who was given the colossal task of copying out an entire set of orchestral parts from the score of Elgar's *Enigma Variations*. It was Tom who taught me the basic principles of music copying, insisting that, like Sir Arthur Sullivan, I use a 'J' nib for the purpose. Seldom do I play my recording of the *Enigma* without recalling Tom's mammoth feat.

And finally Norman. Norman was a real 'man's man'. At the outbreak of World War II, he surrendered his dead-safe position as an artillery band musician by requesting a posting to duty, which meant active service. He rose to the rank of major, and served with the Eighth Army through the North African and Italian campaigns. Apart from being twice blown up by land mines and torpedoed during the Sicily invasion, he came through the war unscathed.

King's Rules and Regulations ordained that I add two more (unpaid) stripes to the one I already had. The wheel had taken one whole decade to turn full circle; for once again I was a f...ing sergeant. And during that decade I had learnt all about surcharging a rail ticket.

My final lesson at the Guildhall was a sad affair. I had managed to stay on there as a student for a full six years. It is understandable that I should continue to hold the school in deep affection.

Although I was not then to know, it so proved that when I was bidding a goodbye to all these things — to the Guildhall, to the Royal Artillery Band, to the Barnes family and to beautiful Moor Park, Waverley Abbey,

Sheephatch, The Spotted Cow, Crooksbury, Seale, Compton, Puttenham, Tilford and the rest, I was bidding a goodbye also to the happiest of my 25 years' army service.

FOOTNOTES TO CHAPTER 20

1. G.M. Young, *Early Victorian England* (London, 1934), Vol.I, p.351.

21: The Royal Military School of Music (Kneller Hall)

Until the year 1857, British Army bands were supported by their respective regiments. Their bandmasters and bandsmen were civilian musicians over whom the War Office exercised no control; so that when hostilities broke out, not a few of these musicians adroitly opted out by applying for their discharge. This was indeed the case at the outbreak of the Crimean War, when many regimental bands ceased overnight to exist as it were.

Moreover, there was not the same co-ordination between bands as exists today. When, for example, the British troops held a grand review at Scutari in 1854 in honour of Queen Victoria's 35th birthday, the massed bands' rendering of *God Save the Queen* was hardly recognisable as such, for not only did they play it from different arrangements, but in different keys. This fiasco was one of the deciding factors which led ultimately to the establishment of the Royal Military School of Music.

There were in those days two bandmasters, James Smythe (1818-1885) and Henry Schallehn (184?-?). Schallehn was Bandmaster of the 17th Lancers, and also conductor of the Crystal Palace Band. These two men petitioned the Secretary of State for War on the state of military bands and the need for their reorganisation. It was fortunate that Schallehn had served under the Duke of Cambridge when he (the Duke) was commanding the 17th Lancers. The petition reached the Duke shortly after he had been appointed as the army's new Commander-in-Chief; and on 26 September 1856, he issued a circular letter which was addressed to commanding officers of regiments. The letter's preamble informed them —

>H.R.H. The Commander-in-Chief, with a view to relieve regiments from the great expense now consequent upon the necessity of employing professional musicians, civilians as masters of bands, has it in contemplation to recommend the establishment of a large musical class as part of the education of boys sent to the Royal Military Asylum, and for the instruction of persons sent from regiments to qualify for bugle-majors, trumpet-majors and bandmasters, whose training would require special time and attention.

The scheme took shape, and a Military Music Class was established at Kneller Hall*, a building provided by the Government in the village of Whitton, about 12 miles from London.

The Royal Military School of Music (as it is now styled) started on 3 March 1857, with Henry Schallehn as its first director of music. As I have already said, one of its foundation professors was Sir Arthur Sullivan's father.

On 13 August of that same year we see the Duke recording in his diary his journey by train 'to see the New Musical School I have formed. It seems admirably established and is working most satisfactorily. A charming locality and they play and sing wonderfully well'. **

And an entry for 28 May 1886, records a further visit when he was accompanied by Sir Arthur Sullivan — 'Heard the band in the chapel first, and then a fine and powerful band on the Parade Ground. Was very much satisfied with the whole condition of things, as was Sullivan, who said he had no sort of suggestion to offer for improvements.'

The memory of the school's principal founder, the Duke of Cambridge, is kept alive today by the public house of that name which stands almost

---

* Kneller Hall was built in 1709 by Sir Christopher Wren. It was burned down to first floor level and rebuilt in 1848. It is named after Sir Godfrey Kneller (1646-1723), the celebrated portrait painter whose residence once stood on this same site. Christopher Neve sheds an interesting light on Kneller's purchase of the Whitton property, and the effect it had for a time on the quality of his workmanship:
'He was knighted by William III in 1692, granted a baronetcy in 1715, and in the process made enough money to keep a coach and six and to live in style both in London and in the country, building himself a country house at Whitton, possibly designed by Wren, in 1709.
'Perhaps because he was trying to pay for Whitton, he had his worst decade from 1710 during which his work deteriorated badly.'
(From a review of the exhibition of his work at the National Portrait Gallery, London, in 1971.)

**The Duke himself was no mean performer on the piano and organ, but the temper of the times, when the English public schoolboy learnt to suppress his emotions, when the pursuit of art in whatever sphere was equated with effeminacy, led him upon his entering the army to give it up. In like manner, Major Thomas (who sold me his father's harp) told me the reason for his giving up playing the piano. It was because of the very real risk he ran of having his instrument smashed up by his brother officers.

opposite the back entrance to Kneller Hall, on the Twickenham-Hounslow road. It was more than a little ironic that in my student days the Duke of Cambridge pub for some reason or another should be declared out-of-bounds to all ranks. And the hapless student Freddy Burnett who married the landlord's daughter, put himself rather badly offside with the Kneller Hall authorities; so badly in fact as to decide him to accept the bandmastership of a regiment which was due for a 21-year tour of foreign service.

In direct contrast was the bandmaster who married one of the daughters of the proprietor of Kiddles Korner Kafe which was not placed out-of-bounds. He went on to become Lieutenant-Colonel, director of music of one of our crack guards' bands. And although not a beer drinker myself, I would wager that the Duke's mulled ale was by no means inferior to Kiddle's 'Kuppa', which invariably would arrive slopped in one's saucer. So why this unfair discrimination against the 'Duke'?

Having already read in *King's Rules and Regulations* the formidable syllabus laid down for the course in military bandmastership, it was not without some misgivings that I set out for Kneller Hall.

The subjects of the three-year course included harmony, aural and instrumentation, in which a student was examined at the end of his second year.* The syllabus also provided for training in orchestral and military band conducting, for a two-month course on each of the military band's instruments, and a nine-month course on each of the violin, cello and string bass. In addition, a student was required to conduct a number of church services (for which he composed the voluntaries) and to write a number of original compositions.

The intensive nature of the course itself was paralleled by the number of hours devoted daily to its several requirements. Excluding the early morning fatigue and drill parades which commenced at 7 am, a working day would start at 9 am and go on until 8.30 pm. Between the hours of 9 am and 1 pm students would be either in the classroom or on the bandstand. From 2 pm to 4 pm was given over to compulsory sport. More band practice followed between 5 pm and 7pm. The last hour of the day, from 7.30 pm to 8.30 pm was devoted either to more classroom work, or to instructing the pupils in music theory. The lateness of the day's final

---

* This was known as The War Office Examination.

lecture hour was designed to prevent students and pupils alike from going up to London, which was only some few minutes run on the electric train.

On paper, all this appeared most impressive and had it been put into full effect, would have resulted in our receiving a sound musical training; more sound even and certainly more comprehensive than the courses currently being offered by the Royal Academy and Royal College of Music. But I was soon to discover to my dismay that the Kneller Hall I had now entered was a very different Kneller Hall from the one I had left eight years earlier.

My first move was to approach Mr Robert Stannard, the professor of harmony and aural training, and discuss with him Mr Hillier's suggestion that I aim to take my degree. He agreed to mark any additional work I should put in, and made some valuable suggestions. With so full a day, this meant my rising just that hour or so before the 6 am Reveille call.

A double bombshell very quickly put paid to my enthusiasm. The first one came when student Les Statham and myself were advanced to War Office Class I (WOCI), which meant our sitting the all-important War Office Examination at the end of our first instead of our second year. The second bombshell missed hitting Les, but knocked me out with a direct hit — my name appeared on the list of the Ranelagh Orchestra, and the No.1 (playing out) band.

During the time I was a pupil (1923-24) apart from the opening week of the British Empire Exhibition, no paid engagements were allowed. This meant that the time of students and pupils alike was devoted entirely to study. When I re-entered Kneller Hall as a student, the hours allotted on paper for study were no different from those when I was there as a pupil; but what now took place during those hours was something very different. In the intervening years the school had undergone a fundamental transformation, from being an institution devoted solely to learning into one whose overburden of extra-curricular activities constantly got in the way of one's studies.

It was not as though these activities operated against the student body as a whole, for only those of us with the greatest commercial potential suffered, leaving the others free to pursue their studies. And I was one of the unfortunates who came in for it all. I rarely saw the inside of a classroom for the first six months of my all-important 'WOCI' year.

My first engagement, which was to last throughout the 'London Season' was with the Ranelagh Orchestra. My name was down to double on the harp and the violin. A protest (or perhaps I should say an explanation) on my part that I did not consider myself a competent violinist was smartly swept aside. And I simply was not a competent violinist, for as I have already said, I studied it for a limited period only in order that I might obtain a working knowledge of the instrument.

Apart from the hour between 7.30 pm and 8.30 pm the whole of each working day was spent in rehearsing the music we were to play in that impregnable bastion of England's most privileged society, The Ranelagh Club. We played in the club grounds on the Wednesday, Saturday and Sunday of each week of the season, which lasted from May to early August. Apart from a 30-minute break for afternoon tea and a rather more substantial break for dinner, we played continuously from 2.30 pm to 10.30 pm on each of these days.

We were allowed no concessions of any sort. For example, our morning orchestral practices went on until 1 pm, leaving us 90 minutes in which to push down a meal, change our uniforms, load the lorry, and arrive at Ranelagh in time to commence playing at 2.30 pm. Even though we seldom saw the inside of a classroom, our bi-weekly assignments in harmony and instrumentation had still to be in on time. Finding the time to do these assignments was our concern. None of us dared complain, for then we would run the very real risk of being returned to our respective regiments on the grounds of our being 'unsuitable material'.

Although we were being well paid for this engagement, we envied those students who were left free to get on with the job which allegedly we were all at Kneller Hall to get on with — that of learning army bandmastering. Never could it be claimed that the countless hours those few of us were made to spend in the Ranelagh Orchestra added one whit to our musical development or, more important still, to our training as potential bandmasters. The type of music we played was of the light 'popular' variety; and Sir George Hastings (who appeared to be the club's 'gentleman manager') would have remained perfectly content had we played no other piece than *The Doge's March* from Rossi's *Merchant of Venice* suite.

Even though the pay was good, we were never certain of receiving the full amounts due to us; for Director Adkins had instituted a system of fines whose purpose allegedly was that of keeping us alert. A wrong note (real or imagined, for Adko had the reputation among us of possessing a 'lousy ear'), a split note, a missed or an untidy entry inevitably would result in a fine. And alleged inattention to marks of expression would lead to a mass fine for the whole orchestra.

When this system of fining was leaked to the press in 1942, one popular Sunday newspaper commented: 'We understand that the students of the Royal Military School of Music are fined for playing wrong notes — except when playing music by Alban Berg, when it doesn't matter a great deal what notes they play'. (This wry, but uninformed comment serves simply to underline the fact that today's discord is tomorrow's concord.)

Playing as I was a group of harp solos at virtually every performance, I became a sitting target and at no small cost, I might add, both to my pocket and to my self-confidence. I found it no easy matter to hold my concentration against a background of "Nalden has played a wrong note — put him down for five bob; another wrong note, increase it to 10 bob", and so on. As the sole double-handed member of the Ranelagh Orchestra, I found myself smarting under the double injustice of being the only one of its members who was open to collecting a fine on two counts — the harp and the violin; for I sat immediately on Conductor Adko's right.

So early on I devised a method which stood me in excellent stead throughout the remainder of the 1932 season and right through the following season. And then I was found out in something like a thousand-to-one-against chance. My unmasking took place during a Winter Orchestral Concert Series practice. The violins were not making too good a job of one particular passage, the cajoling, sarcasm, and dire threats of extra practice which were being hurled at us by Band Sergeant 'Bill' Bailey notwithstanding. Bill (who I seem to remember fancied himself somewhat as a violinist) grabbed hold of my fiddle with "Now listen carefully, all of you, and I will demonstrate how I want it played." His 'demonstration' provoked an outburst of uninhibited laughter from the full orchestra — an ff tutti in fact; for not a sound came out of my violin — not even the sound of the bow scraping across the strings. As far back as the commencement of the 1932 Ranelagh season I had taken the fine-proof precaution of soaping my bow.

Another member of the Ranelagh Orchestra was fined on a highly debatable technicality. It so happened that the first violins with the exception of this one person were playing in their third position. Whipping round to this odd-man-out, Adko demanded angrily, "Why aren't you playing half-way up the buddy fiddle like the other buggers are doing? You're fined five bob" (which was the standard fine).

But Adko never fined himself for his own mistakes, as for example when he brought down both his arms in a mighty Thor-like sledge-hammer blow for the opening chord of *The Mastersingers Overture*, to be responded to by the gentle horn opening of Weber's *Oberon Overture*.

The money which accrued to the 'fine fund' was blown each year on a dinner at the Savoy Hotel which was attended by all those who had 'contributed' to this fund. The self-invited, non-fine-paying guests at these dinners would include the commandant, the adjutant, and of course, Adko himself. Matters did not end there; for it was Adko the self-invited guest who dictated to the Savoy what the menu should be; and it was Adko who kept a tally at the dinner itself of the number of champagne bottle corks that were popped: "For," as he explained to us, "I know these buddy Savoy wine waiters' wangles only too well." For our 'guests', these dinners were dirt cheap, but for us 'contributors' they proved themselves mighty expensive affairs. Student Ted Eames was commissioned to design by hand the front cover of each individual menu card — an enormous and time-consuming undertaking. One cover design consisted of an unusual barometer; unusual in that there were no weather variables — just Fine.

Those of us who had hoped for a break after the conclusion of the Ranelagh season were to be disappointed; for hard on its heels broke the news that the entire Kneller Hall Band, reinforced by an imported corps of army drummers (some 180 of us in all) was to participate in a tattoo to be held in Manchester's Belle Vue grounds. The rehearsals started up all over again, with the emphasis this time on marching. And as the tattoo was to take place after sunset, it meant our memorising the whole of the music we were to play when on the march.

Our accommodation (as I had now come to expect of engagements of this nature) was primitive in the extreme, the whole 180 of us being herded together in one enormous barn of a room. These were the conditions under which those of us who ostensibly were studying for the approaching War Office Examination were expected to work; for by then we had been reduced to what virtually was a glorified correspondence course. And yet we all continued to take it; we simply had to, for there was no alternative.

It was in the Manchester Zoo that I came to witness a practice so vile and so cruel as to turn me against the whole concept of zoos for the remainder of my life.

The reptile-house, unlike other of the zoo's houses, closed its doors to visitors during feeding times; and for good reason. The keeper invited a party of us to stay on and see his reptiles being fed. None of us knew what was coming. He explained that a snake refused all forms of food unless it were alive. We witnessed first the hideous spectacle of a chicken being fed alive to a massive python. It would have been revolting enough had the reptile made its kill immediately. Instead, it kept the poor bird, its head buried within its breast and literally trembling with fear, in agonised suspense for a full 10 minutes before seizing it and crushing it finally to death. And to a small but even more deadly snake, he fed a live rat, which was suspended by its tail from the trap in which it had been caught.

In God's name, does any zoo justify its existence if this sort of bestiality must be practised?

The tattoo took us in point of time to the beginning of October; that is, to within six months of our sitting the vital War Office Examination. And still we were being denied a consistent run in the classroom. Furthermore, between-times found us fulfilling engagements of a sundry nature, such as preparing marches for a commercial recording company, running up to Leicester to give a single concert in its de Montfort Hall, and broadcasting a programme over the BBC.

It was the nature of this, the BBC programme, which led to a first-class row between Adkins and the BBC. It resulted in a rupture which was to remain unhealed during Adkins's remaining 10 years as director of music.

The BBC objected to the style of our programme. The corporation complained, very rightly I felt, that this was not the sort of offering they would have expected from the 'crack' Kneller Hall No.1 Band, which after all comprised some of the most talented musicians of the British Army.

One of its items in which I featured was an arrangement for harp and two saxophones of the *Barcarolle* from Offenbach's *Tales of Hoffmann*. I clearly remember Adko's show of impatience at the studio pre-broadcast rehearsal when I made a plea for quiet in order that I might tune the harp. Another piece, which probably sparked off the row, was a sketch entitled *A Visit to the Dentist*. Here is the sketch's opening:

Narrator: Ladies and gentlemen — It was a typical English summer's morning.

Band: Opening of *Morning* from Grieg's *Peer Gynt Suite*.

N: The rain was beating against the windows!

B: The 'Storm' episode from *William Tell Overture*.

N: I awoke — my tooth was throbbing.

B: Slow semitone trill on xylophone.

N: So, I jumped out of bed!

B: Loud thump on bass drum.

N: But it was cold.

B: Brrr . . .

N: So I jumped back in again.

B: Louder thump on bass drum.

N: But the tooth throbbed more violently than ever, etc.

Here was a military band, with a potential greater probably than any other band in all the three services, being reduced to putting across this sort of drivel. Indeed, one version of the school song which acted as a prologue to each of our performances was in the nature of a synthesis as it were of the style of entertainment which was to follow:

We venture to present you
A show we hope will please
Of light and classical numbers
We'll do our best and so will prove
The Kneller Hall Band is here!

This sort of entertainment did of course appeal to a certain type of audience, but what it had to do with making bandmasters of us I was never able to find out.

One engagement in the September of my first year at Kneller Hall took us to Worthing. We presented a typically Adkins-all-stops-out-programme, which included Humperdinck's *Hansel and Gretel Overture*, some xylophone duets, *Rhapsody in Blue*, a group of sea shanties, *The Kneller Hall Symphonic Rhythmic Combination*, some harp solos and, of course, *A Visit to the Dentist*.

I was told by the 'Cat' (Adko's personal factotum) of his master's extreme annoyance when shown the concert's press notice. This was headed —
'Gifted Young Harpist'
and went on to report, 'Perhaps the most popular item in Sunday evening's programme was the harp solo "At the Spring" by Student C. Nalden, for which he was accorded prolonged applause. He gave "Annie Laurie" as an encore. Student Nalden is certainly a very gifted exponent of his instrument.'

"It'll give that little sod a buddy swollen head, that's what it'll do," Adko told his Cat, who in turn jocularly related the conversation to me. But that did not prevent Adko from admitting me some week or two later to studentship proper, for my six months' probationary period was now up.

Shortly after I had 'passed in' Adko ordered me to grow a moustache. "We're not going to buddy well run the risk of being accused of kidnapping the Lindbergh baby," he told me. The name stuck, especially with Commandant Jervis's daughter Monica, who referred to me as 'The Lindbergh Baby' during the remainder of her father's command.

For these engagements we carried around with us an enormous mass of heavy equipment which had to be loaded on to the roof of the 'No.1 Band bus'. In addition to the normal complement of military band instruments, we lugged around king-sized xylophones and vibraphones (which were fitted with electrically operated tremulants, naturally), bells, fanfare trumpets, banners, sousaphones, timpani, a plethora of percussion instruments and effects, the harp, and of course a number of extra saxophones for use in The Kneller Hall Symphonic Rhythmic Combination.

The weight was such as to require the bus to be equipped with a specially reinforced steel roof. (At least my generation of students was spared the perpetual loading and unloading of the Hammond electric organ, which subsequently was added to the existing welter.)

Just one session of loading and unloading was quite sufficient to convince me that I must find some other person to do it for me; for it became quite impossible for me to undertake this stevedore-type task, and, with hands all of a tremble, to follow it up with playing a group of harp solos.

The front seat of the 'No.1 Band bus' had been permanently removed in order to make a space for the percussionist's 'effects' box, a great six-foot coffin-like affair. This box served a dual purpose, for it became Adko's bed for the return journey to Kneller Hall. In connection with this, I should mention that in keeping with the style of the concerts themselves was our own stage backdrop. This was what must have been surely the world's largest Union Jack. Following a concert, it would be folded to the shape and size of the drum box, thus serving as a mattress for Adko's 'bed'.

It was following the Worthing programme that a somewhat inebriated Adko climbed unsteadily into the bus and straightway flopped down on his 'bed'. "Just one moment, sir," put in Student McKenna. "You haven't yet got the Union Jack underneath you. Mind you, sir, I would far rather be draping it over you; but if you wouldn't mind raising yourself just a little, sir . . .".

Such sallies had to be carefully timed, and it so happened that 'Mac' had timed this one perfectly, for it was taken in good spirit.

Already I had become sadly disillusioned with Kneller Hall. Even so, there was little I could do about it, for by then I had more or less burned my boats. The only way out was for me to apply to be returned to my regiment; but such a course was unthinkable.

It was about this time that I poured out my heart to Charlie Leggett, the cornet professor of my pupil days. It was then that he remarked more in sorrow than in anger: "This once great institution is now run for the benefit of one man, laddie — one man, laddie."

With winter now drawing in, apart from the odd engagement or two, those of us whose study periods had been played havoc with were allowed at last to settle down to serious work for the approaching April War Office Examination.

It was my good fortune that I should have been blessed with a 'good ear', for I knew that I need do a minimum amount of work only in order to pass the aural examination. In view of the amount of time I knew I was capable of saving in this subject, I decided upon clearing away one of the obstacles which was standing in the path of my ultimate aim, a university degree. This obstacle was the ARCM* Diploma examination which was made compulsory for all Kneller Hall students. ("Makes for an impressive show in the bandmasters' section of the Army List", was how Adko justified the compulsory aspect.)

I decided therefore to enter for this examination which was due to be held some short time before the all-important War Office Examination. Being in my first year, I knew myself to be running the risk of falling between two stools; but with Christmas leave just ahead, when I would be able to work without fear of interruption for a full month, I calculated the risk to be a worthwhile one.

Student 'Jock' McKenna (of Union Jack fame) who already had gained his ARCM Diploma, decided to cash in on the examination's Marks for General Impression clause. He pinned an 'ad' on the students' notice board which was worded something thus:

S T U D E N T S ! ! !

Why risk throwing away those vital marks awarded for GENERAL IMPRESSION when for a reasonable rental you may hire my suit
THE PURPLE EMPEROR

Then, satirising the advertisements which appeared in *The Musical Times* offering coaching by correspondence, the 'ad' continued:

The PURPLE EMPEROR'S most recent successes include THREE A.R.C.M.'s, ONE L.R.A.M., and one First Mus.Bac.(failed).

In the event, the risk was worthwhile, for I passed both the War Office, and ARCM examinations.

Immediately after these two examinations, the Ranelagh season started up all over again, interfering, as in the previous year, with my course work; for this year was to have been devoted to the writing of a group of original compositions, whose marks counted towards one's final placing. Yet again, it meant those of us in the Ranelagh Orchestra having to wage our usual battle against time in order that we have our 'competitions' in on time.

No sooner was the Ranelagh season concluded, than I received urgent orders to travel with my harp on the overnight train to join up with the No.1 Band which, under Adko, was doing a tour of major Scottish towns.

The Glasgow engagement proved itself a particularly taxing affair, for true to the Scots' reputation for canniness, the city corporation's contract required us to play not only in a different park on each successive day,

---

* Associate of the Royal College of Music.

but on occasions in a different park for successive programmes. But the engagement had its compensations, for I was able to meet once again one of my Strathpeffer friends, the Spa's secretary, Nance Emslie. And one elderly lady enquired of Captain Adkins whether his harpist would be so kind as to go along to her home and instruct her niece in the proper method of tuning a harp. I was more than happy to carry out this pleasant duty, for each tuning session was rewarded with a lavish afternoon tea and a handsome box of chocolates. I am sure by now that I have been forgiven from Above for the once or twice before my leave-taking when I deliberately put the charming young lassie's harp just that wee bit out o'toon.

The Dumfermline engagement stands out in my memory because of the swarms of mosquitoes which persisted in tormenting us, programme after programme, day after day, during the whole of our stay in that town. Even though Andrew Carnegie had endowed his hometown most handsomely, Dumfermline residents themselves still attributed the cause of their recurring pestilence to the curse of his millions. But I became threatened by a pestilence far more dangerous, in the form of a young Dumfermline widow. She was finally eradicated only when I revealed to her the amount of my army pay, which still stood at 28 shillings a week. Never again was I to experience as I did then so rapid a transformation of requited into unrequited love, or such fervent protestations of undying affection refrigerating into 'let's be good friends'.

With the Scottish tour behind us, the remainder of the year was broken up with the usual round of concerts.

Perhaps the most worthwhile of these was the annual performance we put on at the Richmond Star and Garter Homes, which still nursed a large number of permanently bedridden servicemen from the 1914-18 war. Some had lain on their backs for close on 20 years.

A great favourite with our audiences, more so even than *A Visit to the Dentist*, was the scena, *Round the World*.

A short time before I entered Kneller Hall as a student, Adko thought up the idea of students themselves writing original sketches for performance by his No.1 Band. For this purpose, students were divided into groups, and told bluntly to get on with it. Each group was allowed a substantial period in which to complete its assignment. *Round the World* was written by the most enterprising of these groups, which utilised some authentic national melodies by writing for them direct to the countries concerned.

One team was headed by a Student Jordan, whom I myself christened 'The Rake', by reason of his Simpson's of Regent Street tailor-dummy-type handsomeness and his pleasure-loving nature. The Rake was a tall, athletic figure with a slightly Roman nose, the result probably of his passion for diving in the swimming bath. His upper lip, as the romantic novel of the 1920's would describe it, was 'adorned with a slight moustache'.

The Jordan team's period of grace having expired, it was called upon by Band Sergeant 'Bruno' Brunsden, a well-intentioned but Adko-scared personality, to put its sketch, which it has named *The Fireman's Scena*, into rehearsal.

"Now," instructed The Rake (the team's leader), "when I raise my arm, the whole band will shout 'Cheer! Boys! Cheer!'" He requested an 'A' from the oboe, and proceeded to intone, "We fight the flames!"

Band: "Cheer! Boys! Cheer!" . . . Dead silence followed.

"Well, why stop?" asked Bruno.

"Well, as a matter of fact," apologised The Rake, "that is about as far as we've so far got."

It was just unfortunate that at the very time when he should have been devoting the major portion of his spare time into composing his *Fireman's Scena*, The Rake should have been paying ardent court to the reigning beauty queen of Twickenham, for whom he had developed a deep (but not lasting) infatuation.

The Rake was later to figure in another incident, which, had it not been for its deeper significance, would have been funnier even than it was.

The occasion was a winter orchestral concert. For these concerts, a student was required to give the audience a spoken synopsis of the work he was to conduct. On the morning of the concert itself, 'speeches' would be vetted by the commandant, who would either pass them, or suggest certain modifications.

The Rake faced his audience to deliver his synopsis. With the front row taken up by the commandant, the adjutant and Adko, speech making could be a nervy business, particularly so when Adko, armed with pencil and paper, would commence making notes from the moment a student started addressing the audience. The Rake's synopsis went something like this:

Ladies and gentlemen,

The next piece on the programme is a song by Henry Purcell, who is acknowledged by musicians the world over as one of the greatest if not the greatest of English composers. Purcell was born in 1659 and died in 1695 at the all-too-young age of 36. Who knows what heights this genius would have reached had he lived to complete man's allotted span of three-score years and 10?

The song you are about to hear is but one all-too-short example of his genius.

Choir: (whose music directs that they move their right hands as though strumming a banjo) —

Imitate the strumming of a Banjo during these bars

zum zum zum   zum zum zum   zum zum zum   zum zum zum   It was in the broad At-lan-tic,   Mid the

E-qui-nox-ial gales,   That a young fel-low fell o-ver-board   A-mid the sharks and whales.   He

dis-ap-peared like a flash of light   So quick-ly down went he,   Now he's mar-ri-ed to a Mer-mai-ed at the

bot-tom of the deep blue sea.   Sing-ing   Rule, Bri-tan-nia   Bri-tan-nia, rule the waves,

Bri-tons ne———ver   shall be   mar-ri-ed to a Mer-mai-ed   At the

bot-tom of the deep blue sea.

This all-too-short example of Purcell's genius turned out to be a rip-roaring sea shanty. Puzzled and amused glances were exchanged between the members of the orchestra. After the concert, following usual procedure, we crowded round the notice board to read Adko's comments. He had let it pass, confining what criticisms he had to make to the choir's singing. The Rake had it pointed out to him that the song was composed not by Henry Purcell, but arranged by Paddy ('Fatty') Purcell, who had been a Kneller Hall student some few years previously.*

The story spread rapidly through the school, the only person kept in the dark being Adko, for had it leaked to that quarter, The Rake's final placing might well have been in jeopardy. For some of us the incident was a thought-provoking affair, as it provided a silent, but not altogether happy, commentary on the standard of our training.

The outbreak of war found The Rake with his regiment in Hong Kong. He was killed, so I was told, by a bullet from the rifle of one of his own regiment's sentries. His love of diving and underwater swimming had rendered him partially deaf. On the night he was shot dead, he had failed to hear the sentry's challenge to halt and identify himself. The Rake, who was liked by all of us, did not deserve to die so young and in so tragic a manner.

There remained one more hurdle to clear before I could get down to degree work. This was the LRAM Diploma examination in conducting.

It was not compulsory for students to take this examination, and only a minority entered for it. This was due mainly to one of the examination's requirements which expected candidates to present performances on two instruments, with one of these being on an orchestral instrument.

Before making an entry I sought the advice of Robert Stannard, who felt that I should gain as much experience as I could before embarking on the degree course. Once my 'competitions' (original compositions) were completed, I enrolled with him as a private pupil in harmony. The lessons I had strengthened the opinion I already held for his being a fine musician and a first-rate teacher, for the combination cannot be presumed.

Another teacher whose help I sought was the lovable, unworldly 'Syd' Forrest, who was our cello professor. I was already taking lessons from

---

* Paddy was something of a wit and a natural comic. In the aftermath of what should have been a lucrative engagement for the Kneller Hall Band (which instead incurred a disastrous loss) it was Paddy who suggested a re-styling of the name to 'Captain Adkins and his Bugger Hall Band'.

him as part of my course. For a person with a smallish hand such as my own, a cello lesson with Syd was little different I would imagine from the mediaeval form of torture known as the Rack. He would take a firm grip on two adjacent fingers, cruelly forcing them apart with "Sharper — sharper — sharper — sharper still" until such time as my intonation was satisfactory. It was generally agreed that Syd was a professor one should avoid.

During one of my lessons with him, I asked a question concerning some fingering, explaining, naively, that it was in connection with my coming LRAM examination. "Now, Nalden," replied Syd in his always frank manner, "do you ask me this out of genuine love of the cello, or do you ask it (shrugging his shoulders) merely because of this examination of yours?"

"Oh! Out of a genuine love of the cello," I lied.

"Very good! Very good! Very good! Nalden. I'm so pleased to hear that, because it so happens that Student McKenna is unable to complete his course with me. I'm sure you would like to come in his place, now wouldn't you? Very good! Very good! Very good!

"Now coming to answer your question. Some players would finger the passage this way . . . whereas others may choose to finger it that way . . . On the other hand there is this way . . . and of course that way of fingering it. But, the world's greatest players, they would finger it thus. Why? Because we consider it the more musicianly way of doing it."

I sat the LRAM examination early in the new year, 1934. One of my examiners was none other than the hero of my Kneller Hall pupil days, Walton O'Donnell.

A minor confusion ensued when it was discovered that the music for my harp sight-reading test had not been provided. Never before, apparently, had an LRAM candidate in conducting been known to offer this instrument. A test-piece ultimately arrived. It was Debussy's *Ist Arabesque* which I read through quite fluently; too fluently in fact, for it prompted O'Donnell to comment on my marvellous eyesight. I had made the elementary error of leaving the music stand adjusted to the same height as it had been for my performance on the french horn, for which I had to stand. Luck was on my side, for had I not known the *Arabesque* from memory, never could I have sight-read the groupings of 'twos' against 'threes'.

That same evening I sat patiently on a seat in Waterloo Station waiting for Peggy to arrive from her home in Fleet; for pass or fail, I had promised to take her out to dinner (a Lyons Corner House affair, I'm afraid) and afterwards to the theatre.

In the post on the very next morning was my result; I had passed. The way was now fully cleared (so I thought) for degree study.

The first difficulty I had to face up to was that I had not matriculated. Having left school at 14 this was hardly to be wondered at.

There were (and I believe there still are) two universities, and two only, which open their doors to external students. These were the universities of Durham and London. London University included a foreign language requirement in its entrance examination syllabus, but not so Durham, provided a candidate took an additional subject in lieu of this. I discussed the pros and cons of this with Dr Charles Hoby, a Doctor in Music of Oxford University, whose chequered career had commenced with a musical education at the Royal College of Music, to be followed in turn by a period of service as Chief Bandmaster of the Punjab Frontier Force, Bandmaster of the Natal Rifles, Bandmaster under the London School Board, Organist St.Luke's Church South Kensington, and finally Bandmaster of the Royal Marines, Chatham Division. When I came to know him, he had retired from the Marines, and was ekeing out a living by examining for the Royal College of Music, and coaching for degree and diploma work — mainly, I believe, by correspondence. He invited me along to see him in his South Kensington flat.

"Although I admire your ambition and enterprise in thinking in terms of a university degree," he opened up, "you must understand, of course, that it takes a very clever person to pass the Bachelor of Music examinations . . . a very clever person indeed."

"What about Doctor of Music?" I enquired timidly.

"Well, of course, for Doctor of Music it takes pure genius . . . pure genius . . . pure genius. Now when I took my doctorate at Oxford in ought eight . . ."

We then came round to discussing the relative pros and cons of the two universities. "Durham," he explained, "is known as the poor man's university, for it is relatively easier to get into, but harder to get out of, than London. London on the other hand is quite the reverse, being more difficult to get into, but relatively easier to get out of, than Durham."

I listened to all he had to say, finally making up my own mind on the matter, which was to enrol as an external student of Durham. This was not a case of my thinking that I knew better than Dr Hoby; it went rather more deeply than that, for the reason accounting for my decision was an urgent one.

In those days, should a bandmaster unluckily 'click' a regiment's abroad battalion, he might well find himself serving for the greater part of his military career in one of Britain's then far-flung outposts of Empire. My own father-in-law's history provided a case in point. His 'tip' was the Band of the North Staffordshire Regiment, which either was about to leave, or had just left, England for a 21-year tour of foreign stations. He spent the majority of these years in India, the remainder being divided between Egypt and the Sudan. It cost him his health, for he died shortly following his discharge from the army, even though still in his 40s. To my lasting regret I was never to meet him.

The reason behind my decision to opt for Durham therefore was the time factor; for with hard study and my usual good luck, I estimated that I might pass the Durham entrance examination within six months. London's language requirement on the other hand could have kept me fully extended for years.

The next question was how and where to obtain coaching for the entrance examination? The only source I could think of was Bennett's Correspondence College of Sheffield. But I was put off this possibility by virtue of its paternalistic style of advertising. 'Let me be your Father' invited the picture of a benign looking bespectacled gentleman. I reasoned within myself that as, so far, I had managed rather more than tolerably well without a father, why should I now at this stage of my life take on an adoptive parent merely in order to pass an examination? Furthermore, I had always been under the impression, rightly or wrongly, that it was the father's place to pay for his son's education and not the other way round. So in the end I decided against accepting Papa Bennett's warmly proffered paternalism.

It was Dr Hoby who suggested that I take a correspondence course with Wolsey Hall, Oxford. The entrance examination for Durham was held twice yearly, and I wrote to Wolsey Hall saying that I wished to sit the mid-year examination.

In doing this, I had not reckoned with the current year's engagement list, which to my dismay was to prove heavier than ever; for in addition to playing at the Ranelagh Club, we were asked by the Hurlingham Club to provide an orchestra, also for the full London season.

Although it was not possible for me to be in two places at the same time, it was not beyond the realms of possibility for me to commute from one club to the other and play a group of harp solos in each. To make this possible, I was prevailed upon by Adko to send to Aldershot for my John Thomas harp. The one 'perk' that I enjoyed as a result of this double duty was that by timing things to a nicety, I could dine both at Ranelagh and at Hurlingham, which invariably I did.

On one occasion I had finished playing a group of solos at Hurlingham when a woman club member taxed me with "Are you foreign?" When I assured her that I was not, she said, "I would not have thought that an Englishman would have had the enterprise." I have often wondered since whether the enterprise and ingenuity which the British people were to display during the coming war years caused this patronisingly good woman to revise her opinion of her fellow countrymen.

On another occasion my bicycle chain snapped in two when I was midway between the two clubs. I had to abandon my bicycle and board a bus. As I made to sit down, one loud-mouthed male passenger enquired of me, "And wot would that uniform of yors be, mate?" I relieved my pent-up feelings of frustration (for it was a particularly hot afternoon) with "The Tottenham Court Road branch of the Salvation Army, mate." "I thought so, mate." (Our Kneller Hall uniform was frequently mistaken for that of the Salvation Army.)

We once got a close-up view of the then young and lovely Barbara Hutton as she left the Hurlingham Club dining room. I remember thinking enviously, "Here is a woman who has everything." I had yet to learn that material possessions and wealth are not conducive to happiness necessarily, but frequently conspire seemingly to operate against it. But on that occasion, Barbara Hutton, who was to know great unhappiness, looked radiantly happy, as did her male escort.

The number of hours we spent in rehearsing the music for, and playing at, these two clubs made it quite impossible for me to commence study for my entrance examination before 9 pm each night at the earliest. Even so, I made it a rule from the outset never to go on working beyond midnight — a rule I was more or less able to keep. But I found it quite impossible to keep abreast of Wolsey Hall's assignments, and was forever sending them half-crowns, which was their fee for rearranging a student's course work.

In addition to my already generous work-load, I was appointed 'Blue-Stick', that is, assistant teacher in harmony and aural training. The actual teaching side of it was not nearly so time-consuming as the marking of students' bi-weekly harmony and aural assignments, for these made deep inroads into a Blue-Stick's time.

It was at this time that I had a lucky escape, probably from certain death. I had left the classroom by a matter of minutes only, when some great chunks of the heavy plaster ceiling gave way, splitting clean in two the chair I had been sitting on. It was the same room in which Student Jones had delivered his 'Ancient and Obsolete Instruments' lecture a decade earlier.

In the meantime, a whole new world had opened itself up to me. One subject I chose to read for the entrance examination was Biblical history which, so I was told by one who already had taken it, I would find the softest of soft options. It turned out to be quite the reverse, and neither did my foundling years of reading from the scriptures prove so very helpful.

English embraced a number of set books, including *Julius Caesar*, Hardy's *The Return of the Native* and essays by Cowley, Steele, Addison, Hazlitt, Lamb, Leigh Hunt and others. I became an ardent admirer of Thomas Hardy and continued reading his novels until I was well into middle age. And whenever opportunity arose, I would run up to London for any performance that might be offering of Shakespearean plays.

I managed to keep myself physically fit by playing squash, tennis and golf, although never becoming really proficient at any of these. A former commandant, Colonel Dalyrimple, had designed a nine-hole golf course. It was a potentially murderous affair because of the criss-cross pattern of certain of its holes. Even so, during the whole of my three years at Kneller Hall, only one man was hurt by a ball, this, ironically, being the school's regimental sergeant-major. He was popularly known as 'Beefer' on account of his oft-pronounced sentence, "You'll be fer office in the morning," which meant appearing before the adjutant on a 'charge'.

In golf, as in all other matters, Adko was a law unto himself. For example, when things were not going too well for him in the Boosey and Hawkes Challenge Cup (or was it the Dunn* Cup?) he argued that nowhere in the rules of golf did it state that the putter could not be used after the manner of a billiards cue. And as one cynic put it, when you play Adko at golf, you take on not only him, but his caddie, his Alsatian dog George, and the commandant's daughter Monica at the same time. Unsporting though it may have been, student Geoff Hensby and I had no compunction in giving Adko's opponent's ball a gentle nudge — just sufficient to ensure that Commandant Jervis was able to hole a birdie two at the psychologically-hazardous over-the-sports-pavilion No.3.

I realised that sitting Durham's mid-year entrance examination was quite out of the question when it became known that the Kneller Hall Band was to sail for Canada on 11 August for the Toronto Centenary Exhibition. Ranelagh and Hurlingham orchestral practices were superseded by marching drill parades, which commenced at 7 am daily. I asked Durham University, therefore, for a postponement of my examination until the following January.

---

* Named after its donor, Captain 'Paddy' Dunn of the Royal Horse Guards (The Blues) and father of Lieutenant-Colonel Sir Vivian Dunn, former Director of Music, Royal Marines.

THOSE BAND PHOTOGRAPHS.

'Those Band Photographs' by George Smith.

Senior Student West was charged with the business of arranging the band for an official photograph. His carefully studied arrangement was straightway scrapped by Adko on the grounds that the conception related to the Boer War period's style of group photography. Pride of place therefore was allotted to a garish display of xylophones, vibraphones, bells, timpani, harps and the rest; the focal point of course being Adko's plumed cocked-hat — the self-same headgear in which he had dogged Sir Edward Elgar's every step at the British Empire Exhibition, and in which he had presented himself at Durham for the University's Doctor in Music Examination.* The two Bandmaster George Smith satirical cartoons which summed up perfectly the changing face of the army band was inspired by a photograph he actually had seen being taken. The bandmaster concerned was one of Adko's 'live-wire' directors of music, who followed closely in his master's footsteps.

The outward journey on the *Ausonia* was no luxury cruise, for on our very first day out it was announced that band practices would be held during the day, and compulsory smoking concerts during the evenings.

It fell to my lot to entertain third-class passengers with nightly harp recitals. Playing the harp in mid-Atlantic, especially should the boat be riding on either a roll or a swell, is not a pastime I can wholeheartedly recommend. It is not my idea of a relaxed ocean cruise, and playing the harp in a submarine would, I'm sure, prove a far pleasanter way of passing one's time at sea.

Travelling on the same boat was a party of British public schoolboys. One of the masters in charge of the party, a Mr Chilton (that was his name, I think), gave me a series of valuable tutorials in English history. They were to help me immensely in the January matriculation examination.

The engagement itself, which should have been a pleasant affair, turned out to be nightmarish, with Adko, ever jealous of his personal reputation, in his most choleric mood. Expressed in a different way, well before the engagement ended, the Savoy Dinner Fund for that year was over-subscribed. His mood was calmed somewhat by the series of excellent press reviews.

On the return journey, Students Charlie West, Les Statham and myself were detailed by Adko to join him after dinner each evening for a round of whist. On one occasion, the game went on literally until breakfast-time of the following morning. As my own pile of winnings mounted, Adko

* See p.339.

took to baiting me with "Shades of buddy Hillier — keeping a cool head by not drinking, and fleecing the buddy lot of us." At this, Les Statham gave my shin a vicious kick, at the same time motioning me to go outside with him. "Have you no bloody common sense, Charlie? For Christ's sake let the old bastard win, otherwise we'll be at it all bloody night." We conspired together to let the old bastard win, but it made no difference, for we went on playing just the same until it was time for us to breakfast.

On that same morning many of us were detailed to get our hair cut. I made a dash for the barber's shop to be well up in the queue. It was sound foresight on my part, for his shop was soon packed out. I was awakened by the barber a few hours later to find myself his last customer for the day. That same night I reported as usual for the round of whist.

Once back at Kneller Hall I resumed my course with Wolsey Hall. In the meantime, new English texts had been prescribed which, as I now see it, was all to the good; for they opened up further new horizons. I had now to read *Macbeth* and the Ellershaw edition of *Keats Poetry and Prose*, and *Milton Poetry and Prose* — all hitherto unexplored worlds.

My tutor for Biblical history was the Reverend Jauncey. From him I learned simply nothing, the reason being that his writing was quite illegible. I once had the temerity to add a note to an assignment he had marked asking for some clarification. Realising the uselessness of asking for a clarification of his clarification, I gave up, resigning myself to studying the subject (a difficult one) unaided.

And then out of the blue there broke the exciting news that Adko had accepted an invitation from the Australian Broadcasting Commission to form the ABC Military Band. And as he was to travel by boat, we calculated gleefully that we would be seeing the last of him for several months. From my own personal angle his absence gave me the longest uninterrupted period of study I had known since entering Kneller Hall 30 months earlier. It gave me time also to attend concerts.

During the London concert season, students were allowed complimentary tickets for orchestral concerts, generally for those given in the old Queen's Hall.* Surprising though it may appear, it sometimes proved well-nigh impossible to find takers for these tickets, so overburdened were all too many of us with worthless activities. But with Adko now on the high seas, we were able not only to attend these concerts but to enjoy them as well.

* The Queen's Hall, Langham Place, which accommodated some three thousand people, was opened in 1893. It was destroyed by firebombs in the great raid of 10 May 1941.

Adko arrived back in England shortly before Christmas. It was then that I was allotted a number of curious assignments.

The first of these was in connection with Adko's recently completed tour. Together with the Brown twins, Lewis and Harry (both of whom were fine clarinettists) I was told to report to the director's office. The three of us lined up outside his door, one of us finally plucking up courage to knock.

"Come in," rasped the familiar voice. "Now," opened up Adko, "I expect yor've all heard that I had an extensive and busy tour of Australia?"

Indeed we had.

"And I made a great number of new friends."

"Yes, sir."

"Now, what I want you three to do is to get pencils and paper and think up some appropriate wording to accompany the Christmas cards I'm sending them. There'll be hundreds of 'em; far too many for me to write, so yor'll have to write them yourselves; but as though they're coming from me. Understand?"

"Yes, sir." (The Christmas cards were aerial views of Kneller Hall.)

"You'll compose four different forms of message. Let's call them messages A, B, C and D. Message A goes to such people as high church dignitaries, cabinet ministers and so on. Message B will go to lesser officials, such as mayors and city councillors. Message C is for the many friends I've made, such as bandsmen, and so on. You are to refer to the bandsmen as 'the Boys'. Message D is for the girl friends I made. You will end this message with 'a little love and a kiss'. Nothing like a bit of fun at Christmas."

"Do you think *'Un peu d'amour'* might be better, sir?" I put in.

"Very good, Nalden, but the type of flapper I have in mind wouldn't know wot the buddy 'ell* I was getting at. No — leave it at what I said — 'a little love and a kiss'."

Adko cheerfully accepted my suggestion for Message C, which ran 'The Major will be with his Boys once again this Christmas — in thought'.

"That's buddy good, Nalden," (although the three of us had already voted it corny).

That same evening we were travelling to an engagement in the No.1 Band bus.

"Well, Nalden," questioned Adko, "how many cards did you manage to get off?"

---

* A characteristic expression of his.

"Quite a lot, sir."

"Everything going alright?"

"Well, I did make one small mistake, sir."

"What was that?" questioned Adko sharply.

"Well, sir, I . . . I . . ."

"Come on, man, out with it — what did you do wrong?"

"Well sir, I . . ., I . . ."

"Buddy well out with it, Nalden."

"Well, sir, by mistake, I posted a card containing Message D to the Bishop of Melbourne."

"You buddy-well what?"

Sensing that the joke had gone far enough, I had to admit that it was a leg pull.

"My Gawd, Nalden . . . for the moment you had me scared . . . If you had buddy-well had done it . . ."

I played in the orchestra for the end-of-year annual dinner of the Kneller Hall Club, which normally was held at the Criterion Restaurant. One of the specially invited guests was Albert Ketelbey, whose *In a Monastery Garden* netted him more money probably than the total amounts received by Bach, Mozart, Haydn and Beethoven during the whole of their respective lifetimes. Following dinner, Ketelbey came up to me and said, "I'd like to write a harp solo especially for you. If you'll first explain some of the instrument's technicalities I'll start working on it." Although nothing came of it, I have always cherished the compliment.

In the January of 1935, I sat and passed the Durham entrance examination, the Reverend Jauncey notwithstanding. Wolsey Hall promptly added me to the list of their 'recent successes' no doubt, and no less promptly sent me their price list for Wolsey Hall blazers and Wolsey Hall ties.

Running through a large stratum of our English society is that fine vein, 'that almost divine snobbery of very strong motive power, that keeps the Englishman from being content ever to be classed a workman or labourer, a priest or soldier or scholar, as men of other civilisations are, and makes him always desires to be a gentleman*, a word without equivalent in any other language'.[1]

Little snob that I myself once was (as for example when I instructed the Guernsey shop-assistant to wrap my purchase so that the wrapper's lettering 'Burton Tailors' faced inwards — ("Our firm is as good as any other firm, sir"), even I shrank from the temptation of peacocking around in a crested blazer and tie of a correspondence college. Oh! No! (On second thoughts perhaps it was a piece of divine snobbery on my part — a haunting fear of my being exposed via the Wolsey Hall crest as a graduate of a correspondence course college.)

It was now time for me to decide upon a coach who would guide me through the three examinations of the Bachelor in Music degree course. I was given a recommendation to study under a Dr Frederick H. Wood, himself a graduate of Durham University, and by repute a sound teacher. As he lived and worked in Blackpool, it meant yet another correspondence course.

Although I was to meet Dr Wood but three times, he became nevertheless another of my God-sent direction posts. In his long and frequent letters to me, he would discuss a whole range of topics, from the progress I was making, to politics, religion ("No doubt Jesus Christ was a Good Man, but to claim that He is the Son of God is blasphemy"), the progress of the war and psychic research** (as he himself preferred to call 'spiritualism'). Even when the war was in its 'phoney stage', with the German-Russian treaty still holding good, Dr Wood predicted the intervention of a powerful force on the side of the Allies — "it could well be Russia". He was a firm believer in the doctrine of reincarnation, and spoke to me in a rational manner of his existence on earth during the era of the Egyptian pharaohs. It was not until well after I had completed my degree that I was to meet him for the first time — at a public swimming pool in Guildford. He approached me with "You are Nalden!"

Once I received Dr Wood's nod of approval, I wrote to the Registrar of Durham University, making an entry for the approaching September examination.

---

* The author of *A Letter on Army Reform* published in 1855, defines a 'gentleman' as one 'whose parents shall never have been engaged in any retail trade, or in any mechanical or agricultural calling, by which they have earned their bread'.

** Dr Wood published widely in this field. His works include *Mediumship and War, The Egyptian Miracle*, and *Through the Psychic Door*, which is 'A fascinating glimpse into the next life.' It was the untimely death of his brother which started Dr Wood on his psychic research. "My brother is walking with me now," he once said to me, "right by my side."

I had by now become resigned to the fact that any private study I might undertake must be snatched at odd times, but mainly between the hours of 9 pm and midnight. As far as I was able to assess, the only major interruptions that were likely to occur during this, my final year at Kneller Hall (1935), would be those caused by the hated Ranelagh and Hurlingham seasons. In this, I had failed to reckon first, with an engagement which took us to Bentall's (Kingston-on-Thames) Cafe, where I had to play my harp within tipping* distance of the tea-sipping patrons' tables; and secondly, with the filming of *In Town Tonight* which forever afterwards found me viewing rather more sympathetically our actors' and actresses' marriage breakdown rates.

And I had failed also to reckon with one particular aspect of Adko's Australian tour, which in retrospect was to involve four of us in a lengthy exercise in music writing.

Adko thought he saw in Australia a market which was guaranteed to bring him in a regular and luctrative supplementary income. His idea was to flood the Australian market with arrangements from popular overtures and the like for orchestra and military and brass bands. He enlisted first the services of Les Statham, whose assignment was to string together in 'piano score' certain excerpts from the well-known overtures of Suppé, such as *Light Cavalry* and *Poet and Peasant*.

The next stage involved one of the Brown twins, George Savage and myself. Our contribution was to arrange Les Statham's potpourri for brass band, military band and orchestra. So eager was Adko to test out the Australian market, that he relaxed his own strict order and excused us the compulsory afternoons' sport session. In short, our noses were kept to the grindstone all day and every day until our respective tasks were completed. Adko's sole contribution was to name the work. He called it *Suppé Supreme* which, as one of our droll wits put it, "sounds like one of the courses we had at last year's Savoy Dinner".

Even so, the conductor's scores credited not the three of us, but Adko with being the arranger, and the fees found their way naturally into the 'Arranger's' and not the arrangers' pocket.

Far from receiving a fee, poor George Savage's military band arrangement threatened to involve him in a crippling breach of copyright court action. George must have taken a set of parts of his particular arrangement when he left Kneller Hall to take up his appointment as Bandmaster of the Royal Warwickshire Regiment. A year or so later, Adko decided to dispense with

* But I received none.

his formal inspections of bands, but instead to visit various seaside resorts, and (unbeknown to the bandmasters involved), make reports on their respective bands' entertainment value, turn-out and deportment.

It was by the greatest stroke of ill-luck not only that he should visit the seaside town in which George Savage's band was playing, but also that he should be present at the very performance which opened with "my *Suppé Supreme*", as Adko put it when relating to me the full story. The first George Savage heard of it was by way of a letter he received from Adko giving him the option either of paying him (Adko) as the work's arranger a 20 guinea performing rights fee, or of being sued 'in the High Courts of Justice' for some incredibly great amount. George settled on the first option.

Some few years later, I asked George why he had capitulated. "Because I was a young married man with family responsibilities" he told me. Although the technical details of arranging are too complicated to enter into here, I pointed out to him that as his so-called arrangement was simply a verbatim copy of the relevant passages in existing printed arrangements of Suppé overtures, he would have won his case hands down had he decided to accept the challenge of a court hearing; for George had taken the easy (or perhaps I should say the 'easier') way out. I met him one day leaving the music library with an enormous pile of music wedged underneath his chin. "What are you going to do with that lot, George?"

"If that bastard thinks I'm going to waste hours of my time in putting money into his pocket, he's got another bloody think coming to him."

Should any Kneller Hall Student of that era have found himself faced with the same dilemma, he would, I am certain, have acted no differently from George, and opted to pay the 20 guineas.

It was fortunate for me that the Australian market was interested only in the brass band arrangement; for the strain on my eyes, caused by the hours of unrelieved music writing in doing my one orchestral arrangement proved so severe that for years afterwards I was to suffer periodic attacks of pain which obliged me to sit in a darkened room.

Neither had I reckoned upon the arrival at Kneller Hall of the young and handsome Iraqi student, Albert Chaffoo, whose admission as a student gave me my second curious assignment. Albert, who was then aged about 17, had come to Kneller Hall under the official sponsorship of the Iraqi Government to undergo a course in bandmastership. Once he had completed this, he was to return to Iraq to become Director of Music of the Iraq Army.

I was instructed to report to the director's office. Adko spoke to me on matters concerning our new arrival and appointed me Albert's personal mentor, guide and friend. "You are not to let him out of your sight for one buddy minute," he instructed me. "We simply cannot afford to have complaints laid at our door by the boy's legation."

This was all very well, but there were times when this private-eye key-hole diplomacy could become somewhat embarrassing; for Albert was possessed of rather more than his fair share of good looks and personal charm; and like the majority of us he was of an age when two constitutes company and three a crowd.

Albert's first shock was administered by Adko. He bowled in one day to an orchestral rehearsal and noticing that Albert was dressed differently from the rest of us rasped: "Nalden, you will see that Chaffoo is issued right away with a proper student's uniform. I just won't have him walking around the place dressed like half officer, half scripture reader." A dejected Albert complained to me afterwards: "I no like that man's speech — I shall report him to my legation." Adko had thus created the very situation which he himself had declared must be avoided at all costs. On this occasion I managed to talk Albert out of going to his legation.

The next shock was administered by Albert himself. He came to my 'bunk' (room) one day, and asked where he might obtain some risque French photographs. These were not for himself, he explained, but for a friend in Iraq. It was now my turn to threaten to go to my legation; for as I explained, British customs officers were not over-accommodating on this sort of importation, and that should any such thing be discovered it would be me, his appointed guardian, who would have to stand the rap.

Albert adjusted remarkably well to our Western customs except in one important aspect; he could not take our food. His complaint was fully justified, for few of us could take our Western food, which at times was fit only for the pig-swill bin. I reported the matter to Adjutant 'Bobby' Jones, who told me to invite Albert to write out his own menus. Adopting as solemn an expression as I was able, I handed the adjutant this list:

	Breakfast	Dinner	Tea
Sun.	Fried sheep & cocoa	Fried sheep & cocoa	Sardine
Mon.	Fried sheep & cocoa	Fried sheep & cocoa	Sardine
Tues.	Fried sheep & cocoa	Fried sheep & cocoa	Sardine
Wed.	Fried sheep & cocoa	Fried sheep & cocoa	Sardine
Thurs.	Fried sheep & cocoa	Fried sheep & cocoa	Sardine
Fri.	Fried sheep & cocoa	Fried sheep & cocoa	Sardine
Sat.	Fried sheep & cocoa	Fried sheep & cocoa	Sardine

"If the boy wants fried bloody sheep and cocoa, then go and tell the cook-sergeant that he is to have fried bloody sheep and cocoa," was 'Bobby' Jones's ruling.

I do believe that Albert came to appreciate my guardianship, for he showed me many kindnesses of which some were quite touching. He once came to my 'bunk' and produced a box containing some smallish lumps of a white substance which I confessed to never having seen before. He had asked his parents to send the stuff over from Iraq especially for me.

"Try this," he invited. The piece I tried was deceptively heavy, and but for the fact of my good fortune in being possessed of a set of strong teeth, I might easily have broken some of them in my effort to bite through it. It had the texture of stick-jaw which either had been pre-stressed or finished off with a concrete filling.

"What is it?" I asked Albert.

"Manna" replied Albert solemnly, "the food that God sent down from heaven for the Israelites when they were wandering in the wilderness."

"Oh! No!" I replied involuntarily, "Had God rained this stuff down, He would have concussed the whole of the Twelve Tribes, which is hardly the sort of treatment He would have meted out to His Chosen People." But Albert remained obdurate: "I tell you it is manna."

My next somewhat unusual assignment, although given me as a form of punishment, proved an interesting one. In the 'bunk' next to mine lived the Brown twins and the 'Whitton Playboy', Bill Allen. Bill had one failing; he found it difficult to get down to study. It was said of him that when he came to conduct from memory *The Ride of the Valkyries*, he did so with a baton in his right hand and a stop-watch in his left.

I once decided to enliven the wall over Bill's bed. Unbeknown to him, and some minutes before the regimental sergeant major was due to make his round of Saturday morning rooms' inspection, I hung a framed nude over Bill's bed on which I had inscribed, 'To my own darling Willie, with all my love, Phyllis XX.'

I was duly hauled up, and given the task of cleaning and cataloguing the school's collection of ancient and obsolete instruments which was housed in the commandant's office. One of these instruments was a Serpent, so named because of its resemblance in shape to a snake in the process of crawling. This particular instrument was not in need of a clean, for it had been restored and polished by the studios which had borrowed it from Kneller Hall for its filming of *Lorna Doone*.

Another instrument was a German bugle, a relic of the 1914-18 War. Then there was a very ancient set of bagpipes, whose bellows had long since become atrophied and wizened with age, so that they resembled some withered-up out-sized prune. The temptation proved itself too strong. I singled out Albert from a group of students with "It is the Director's orders that you prepare a bagpipes solo for performance at the next grand concert.''

"I will not do this thing," choked Albert, "I shall go to my bloody legation.'' Albert, who was liked by us all, settled down well and truly to our Western ways of life — our food, our Adko, our oaths and all.

In the meantime, I was making steady progress with my studies under the sure guidance of Dr Wood.

The reigning Professor of Music at Durham University was Sir Edward Bairstow. He had succeeded Sir Joseph ('Chester') Bridge* some few years earlier, and had restructured the Mus.B. and Mus.D. syllabusses completely. Figured basses and Strict Counterpoint in the Five Species types of question which had served successive examiners for the greater part of the 19th and the early decades of the 20th centuries were swept roughly aside. Their places were taken by a type of question which required candidates to write in the Italian and English styles of composition of the 16th century.

These reforms meant that in future, examination questions were to be related to live music rather than to a system whose ends over the years had come to be mistaken for the means. Although at the time these reforms must have administered a nasty jolt to some of their systems, Durham music graduates in general should have every reason for being grateful to Bairstow. I certainly have. His demanding standards must have remained a controversial issue right up to his death in office in 1946; for candidates who were interviewed for the Durham professorship were, I understand, invited to give their opinions of the 'Bairstow regime'.

Bairstow had all the alleged characteristics of the north countryman — a dourness and an abruptness of manner to the point of his appearing downright rude. He showed little mercy to candidates, and as his successor, Arthur Hutchings, once remarked to me: "Anybody who completed their degree during the Bairstow regime was worthy of it.'' Even so, underneath all this seemingly gruff exterior there reposed a kindlier Bairstow, which on occasions would gently surface, as for example, when my Dr Wood made a personal appeal to him on behalf of a blind student of his. "Should I fail her do you think she will write another exercise?" asked Bairstow. "No,'' replied Dr Wood. Bairstow passed her.

---

* Sir Joseph Bridge was organist of Chester Cathedral, his brother Sir Frederick Bridge holding a similar position at Westminster Abbey — hence 'Chester' and 'Westminster' Bridge.

Dr Wood soon had me working on past Durham examination papers. I rather lost courage when for the first time I came face to face with questions which required a fundamental understanding of the music of 16th century English and Italian schools; for apart from Gordon Jacob's arrangement for military band of *A William Byrd Suite**, this idiom to me was akin to a foreign language.

To help overcome this lack, I made several excursions to Foyle's of Charing Cross Road where I found quite a collection of second-hand music of this period including, among other works, a copy of the Vincent Novello edition of *The Works of Palestrina, The Prince of Music* (which will give some idea of the date of this edition). This period's music, distinguished as it was by its almost total absence from current commercial gramophone companies' catalogues, and with myself being a non-pianist, compelled me to study it without resort to mechanical aids of any sort. It was a self-imposed discipline I have persisted with throughout my professional life, and one which I have never regretted. One could describe it as 'hearing music through the eye'. Long before I was to hear them in live performance I had, for example, come to know quite a few of Brahms's chamber works in this way.

This practice taught me also to read and write fluently in the now, alas, almost obsolete 'C' clefs, whose mastery by the music student should, I feel, be obligatory.

Armed with my purchases from Foyle's and further aided by R.O. Morris's *Contrapuntal Technique of the Sixteenth Century* and the Reverend E.H. Fellowes's *The English Madrigal Composers*, I came to discover not one, but two, new worlds; for hand in hand with the music of the 16th century English madrigal composers goes the charming lyric poetry of the same period — the poetry of Thomas Campion, of Robert Herrick, of John Donne and of John Fletcher:

> Come, Sleep, and with thy sweet deceiving
> Lock me in delight awhile;
> Let some pleasing dreams beguile
> All my fancies; that from thence
> I may feel an influence
> All my powers of care bereaving!
>
> Though but a shadow, but a sliding,
> Let me know some little joy!

> We that suffer long annoy
> Are contented with a thought
> Through an idle fancy wrought:
> O let my joys have some abiding!

I continue still to derive a deep spiritual satisfaction from both the music and the poetry of this period.

In the April of that year I was offered, and accepted, the appointment of Bandmaster of the 2nd Battalion, The Sherwood Foresters (The Nottinghamshire and Derbyshire Regiment).

At the time of my appointment, the 2nd Battalion was stationed in the Middle East, and having completed its 21 years' tour of foreign stations, was due to return to 'Home Service'. The Commanding Officer, Lieutenant-Colonel Robert Lowe Sherbrooke DSO, advised Kneller Hall that he would not be requiring me to join the battalion until its return to England. And so I stayed on at Kneller Hall for a further half-year. This proved itself the most unhappy period of my army life so far. I found myself literally ticking off the days to the time when I would be freed from the hated Kneller Hall atmosphere for ever.

The cause of my unhappiness was Adko. I rather suspect he was undergoing a personal crisis of some kind, for throughout the Ranelagh-Hurlingham season of that year, his mood became more fiery, and his temper more choleric than ever. It was the Ranelagh Orchestra which bore the full brunt of his irascibility. An atmosphere of unrelieved gloom and apprehension settled over the whole orchestra, which was hardly lightened by the raucous, prophet-of-doom-like screams of Ranelagh's peacocks.

My own personal bout of misery was sparked off by an incident which earned me the sympathy of the whole orchestra. It fell to me to tune the orchestra before each performance. The opening piece for one performance happened to be Suppé's *Light Cavalry* overture. As is well known, this piece opens with a trumpet call, which by the way is scored for two trumpets in unison. One of the two trumpet players had failed to take the elementary precaution of checking whether his part was marked 'Trumpets in A', or 'Trumpets in B flat'. In non-technical language, the opening trumpet call instead of sounding in unison, came out thus —

Far from chastising the trumpet player whose fault it was, Adko whipped round to me and screamed: "You sod! Are you supposed to have tuned the orchestra? You're a mere buddy bricklayer at the job and you're fined a pound." It apparently did not occur to Adko that the tuning of my harp, whose 40-odd strings were forever exposed to the mercy of the unpredictable English climate, was a far more exacting affair than the tuning of a couple of trumpets. The trumpet player who was at fault could hardly own up to the precise nature of his error — for that would have been tantamount to his telling Adko that he (Adko) was unable to distinguish between a minor discrepancy in intonation and a full semitone.

My 'punishment' did not end there. Before this incident took place, Adko had been taking his nephew Student Basil Brown (a future Director of Music, Kneller Hall) and myself to and from Ranelagh in his car. That privilege went also. Basil related to me that when returning that same evening to Kneller Hall, Adko remarked: "I suppose I ought to be ashamed of myself." Obviously he was not as my fine was not remitted.

The sole person in the Ranelagh Orchestra to escape all this was the pianist, Albert Gregory. Although Albert dressed in our student uniform, he was, in fact, a civilian. He was a graduate of London University, but because of the current depression was only too grateful apparently to earn money in this way. Albert was a public spirited person, for in addition to his being the Music Representative of the Senate of London University he was a member (and an active one at that) of the Kingston-on-Thames Town Council.

For a long time following that incident it appeared (to me at any rate) that no longer could I do anything right in Adko's eyes. It may quite possibly have been an expression of pique on his part that I (as one of his good commercial propositions) would shortly be leaving Kneller Hall; for when it came my turn to go, he said to me: "I made a big mistake in accepting you as a student. I should have started you off on a band sergeant's course" (which in effect would have added a further 18 months to my statutory three years' student's course).

A rewarding engagement during that same year was Kneller Hall's participation in the Empire Day Royal Command Concert given in the Albert Hall in the presence of their majesties, King George V and Queen Mary, whose silver jubilee year it was.

The Albert Hall presented a magnificent scene. The spectacle of the massed choirs which were representative of the four countries of the British Isles (and which occupied the whole of the ground floor), the BBC Symphony Orchestra under its conductors Sir Adrian Boult, Dr Malcolm

Sargent and Sir Landon Ronald, and the dignified splendour of the royal box itself, was for me a moving and unforgettable experience.

Dr Wood now considered me sufficiently well prepared to attempt the first examination of the Bachelor in Music degree.

I travelled up to Durham, putting up at the Three Tuns hotel, where a number of other candidates were staying. I became somewhat disheartened by their learned discourse, particularly that of one self-opinionated candidate who in smooth dulcet-toned accents recounted to the assembled company the number of mistakes he had detected in an organ recital of Sir Edward Bairstow's. The whole episode did little to preserve my already shaky confidence in myself. It would have been more sensible, I told myself, had I sought private board, not realising that this simply was life. My skin-deep feelings of inadequacy and inferiority had little difficulty in surfacing.

On the morning of the examination I chatted with the university janitor, whose company was somewhat more relaxing than was that of my companions of the previous evening. He remembered Adko a decade earlier sitting the Doctor in Music examination. It was not so much the person he remembered as the attire in which he presented himself for the examination — the bright scarlet tunic, the blue overalls and (I believe) the plumed cocked-hat.

For a 'small consideration' the janitor undertook to advise candidates by telegram of their individual results. My own wire read, "Sorry no luck this time. Janitor." Six months had been all too short a time apparently in which to prepare myself for an examination of this nature. "Bad luck, Nalden," consoled Adkins, "but you did tell me before you went to Durham that you didn't fancy your chances overmuch, didn't you?" Which I had.

However, my result sheet was sufficiently encouraging for me to decide upon sitting again.

My time at Kneller Hall was now up. The misgivings I harboured before entering were as nothing beside those which beset me now that I was leaving the place; for at 27 years of age, I became suddenly aware of the fact that I was about to take up my first-ever position of responsibility, a position for which (as inwardly I knew) I was inadequately prepared.

Up to now I had received, but seldom given, orders; and even when I had been compelled to give them, I intensely disliked the idea of doing so. From now on I would be responsible not only for the musical training of an army band, but also for its general discipline and for the recruitment to its ranks of new personnel (which in the event proved itself the most worrying and onerous task of all). And although as yet some few years away, I would be required to become versed in the London System of Accounting; for one of my band presidents (an old Etonian) was to protest to me his inability to cope with the balancing of the band accounts.

Skipping every intermediate rank, I had been promoted from gunner-musician (i.e. private soldier) to warrant officer class I, the rank next below that of commissioned officer, and a rank which was held by one other person only — the regimental sergeant-major. In its degree of rapidity, there was no other form of promotion comparable to it in any of the three armed services. As may well be imagined, this could be a potential source of dissatisfaction in some quarters; for the 19th century army reforms notwithstanding, promotion by seniority was still obstinately clung to by the diehard, reactionary, type of soldier (as later I myself was to learn). It would have taken a very liberally-minded RSM, for example, to accept without murmur a situation in which he himself had risen to his rank of WO Class I by the painfully slow process of step-by-step promotion (ultimately to arrive there in his late 30s or thereabouts), and in which his bandmaster, from being a private soldier, had been catapulted into the same rank at a comparatively early age, and paid an additional and substantial emolument in the bargain.

Already I was finding it strange, and not a little embarrassing, at being addressed by soldiers in ranks lower than my own as 'sir'; for hitherto, the only people to 'sir' me had been the likes of millionaire Selfridge of Oxford Street W.1. ('I remain, sir, your humble and obedient servant'), the royal tournament barber, and the tip-hungry railway porter or taximan. And although I was now allowed a batman, I never really became used to the idea of having my boots and buttons cleaned for me. But the aspect which frightened me most was the fact that never during my 13 years' army service had I done so much as one single day's real soldiering. Cossetted as I had been for 10 of these years in the Royal Artillery Band, I had never handled, let alone fired, a rifle.

I became more apprehensive still when those of my fellow Kneller Hall students who had 'roughed it' in line regimental bands warned me of the type of shock I must expect now that I was no longer a 'gentleman of the Royal Artillery Band'.

It meant that at this late hour I found myself questioning my own wisdom in leaving the artillery band; whether after all I should not have stayed on, and taken my chance in 'civvy street' as a professional harpist. And running frequently through my mind was Dick Thairs's parting quip when

I came to leave the artillery band: "So you have decided after all that you would like to be in charge of a band of unruly men."

And finally there was that disturbing paragraph in the letter I had received from Bandmaster 'Johnny' Hitch of the Cheshire Regiment: "Remember that an Officer is always an Officer, and a Bandmaster never one."

Arising out of all these misgivings there emerged one point upon which my mind was firmly made up; that I must regard my appointment to the Band of the Sherwood Foresters as a first step, as a temporary affair only. As to what the next step might be I had no idea. I knew myself to be destined ultimately for something quite different, but what that 'something different' was, I could not as yet foretell. I did not attempt to prognosticate what the future might hold for me. For the moment I knew that I was about to embark upon a career for which I was fundamentally unsuited and that I must persist with my degree study.

When in 1932 I left the Royal Artillery Band for Kneller Hall, I knew I had a great deal to thank it for; for everything in fact. But now, when it came to my leaving Kneller Hall, ungrateful and even arrogant though it may appear, I felt I had but little to thank it for. Neither has time caused me to alter my view; for I have tended to look back on my student days at Kneller Hall as one of life's disillusionments. I had experienced for the first time just what it meant to have one's ideals rudely shattered.

The greater part of my three years there had been taken up with playing at engagements which taught me nothing about the new and exacting career for which, supposedly, I was being trained.

Looking back on it all, I now see that the most worthwhile aspects of the course were Robert Stannard's excellent harmony, aural and form lectures, and the study we made of the several woodwind, brass and stringed instruments ('secondaries' we called them). I have ever had cause to be thankful that I took this part of the course seriously and had not, as one student boasted doing, taken advantage of Adko's alleged 'duff' ear, and bluffed my way through them by playing three scales and three scales only — those of C major and its relative minors. I do happen to know that there was more than a small element of truth in this student's boast.

The study of these instruments has stood me in excellent stead throughout the course of my professional life. It came to my rescue, for example, when I found myself faced with the business of having to teach band boys virtually from scratch. It helped me during my 23 years as honorary conductor of the Auckland Junior Symphony Orchestra; and it helped me on a number of occasions when I guest-conducted the New Zealand Radio Symphony Orchestra; for I would say that the conductor who has experienced at first hand the 'feel' of each of the orchestra's individual instruments starts out at a far greater advantage than the one who has not. Such experience is of inestimable value to the conductor of a youth, or an amateur, orchestra.

Insofar as the course in conducting was concerned, never were we allowed to come to grips with the sort of conditions we would meet in our respective regimental bands. It never occurred to the director, apparently, that this massive Kneller Hall band of 160 performers might on occasions have been broken down into say, four bands of 40 performers; for this would have brought us face-to-face in far more realistic a manner with the sort of conditions we would be meeting after leaving Kneller Hall. Never would any of us inherit a band of the size and quality of the Kneller Hall Band.

Because of the Ranelagh-Hurlingham seasons, the Scottish tour, the trip to Canada and the rest (most of which coincided with the summer concert season) I suppose I could not have conducted the Kneller Hall Band on more than some half dozen occasions — and this in three years.

I received instructions to report to Whittington Barracks, Lichfield, where the 1st Battalion of the Sherwood Foresters was stationed. It was to be this battalion's last home station before commencing its long tour of foreign service.

I went in to take my leave of Adko, who, happily, was in one of his all-too-rare expansive moods. "Well, Nalden," he opened up, "Yor've been a perfect little sod since yor've been here, haven't you? All the same, I've grown fond of you, and I shall miss you and your 'arp wot once'."

He then came round to the subject of marriage. "Tell me, Nalden, are you thinking of getting married?" to which I replied, "Yes, sir." Knowing rather too well his views on marriage I dreaded what might be coming next; for no paternal counselling on his part would have caused me to change my mind, or my wedding plans, which unbeknown to him were already settled.

Whether his overtly opposing the institution of marriage as such was the outcome of his own marriage's breakdown I could never quite make out. But whatever the cause, he could at times deal with our 'marrieds' and our 'about-to-get-marrieds' with great severity. He was forever preaching to us on the folly of getting married.

"You can take it from me," he would say, "that once you're married, you'll be kicking yourselves around the barrack square for the remainder of your miserable lives." And following one of our Savoy dinners he put it to us: "The choice is yours; dinners like last night's affair if you remain single, or fish and chip suppers for the remainder of your buddy lives if you marry. But you can't have it both ways.''

I recall the case of one student who requested leave to get married. His request was granted; he was allowed time off from after the morning's band practice up to the starting time of that same afternoon's public concert — that is, from 1 pm to 3 pm.

On another occasion Adko had returned somewhat sooner than expected from a personal visit to the USA. It was a Saturday afternoon, which was observed as a half-day's holiday (except, naturally, for the Ranelagh-Hurlingham orchestras). Disregarding this, he called a snap rehearsal for No.1 Band, riding rough-shod over any arrangements its individual members may have made. One student was already in the train bound for Yorkshire in response to an urgent message because of his wife's unduly long period of child-labour. He had got as far as Peterborough when he received a telephone message ordering his immediate return to Kneller Hall. And this student happened to be particularly 'well-in' with Adko.

The officially recognised minimum age at that time for a soldier wishing to get married was 26, when he would become entitled to various allowances. But riding rough-shod over the army regulation on the matter, Adko made his own regulation. As Student Lester once poetically expressed it: "He doth bestride the narrow world like a Colossus.'' Adko ruled that whether or not he had reached the official marrying age, a student must not wed before his third and final year. He reasoned that it was unfair on the husband's part to expect his wife to forego dances and the rest while he buried himself in his work; and "How can a man possibly give of his best when he is rogering his wife every hour of the buddy day and night'' — which nauseated not a few of us.

Some years after I had left Kneller Hall there was the case of Adko's actually ordering a married student to live in barracks, apart from his wife, on the pretext that

Peggy.

married life was working to the detriment of his oboe playing. The student objected and was promptly told that he would be returned to his regiment. In desperation (having nothing further to lose), the student made a personal appeal over Adko's head to higher authority, which his rank entitled him to do. Adko's counter-move was to call in the army medical officer and attempt to persuade him to testify that the student's marriage had caused his work to deteriorate — which the MO refused to do. This was the first time during the whole of his 20 years as Director of Music Kneller Hall that Adko had been successfully challenged. To give him his just due, never did he attempt to 'take it out' on the student concerned.

And so there I stood, waiting to go, but wondering what he was going to say next.

"Tell me," he continued, "you're not thinking of marrying the girl you were dancing with all night at the last Kneller Hall Ball, are you?"

"Why not, sir?" I asked.

"Because she's too thin. You should get a hold of a jolly plump type like Student ——'s wife; the fatter ones are easier to live with."

Maybe they are; but having had no experience personally of living with 'a jolly plump type' I was in no position to debate on this. At the same time, whereas Student ——'s marriage to the jolly-plump-type person broke up, my own lasted a full 40 years.

Adko wound up, surprisingly, with: "In your case, Nalden, I think marriage would be a good thing; it will give you an excuse for not using the Sergeants' Mess."

I duly arrived at Whittington Barracks and reported to the adjutant. "We've nothing for you to do here," he explained half apologetically, "so we'd better send you on a spot of leave, don't you think?" When I told him of my marriage plans he replied, "In that case you may take all the leave you want; but be sure to advise your new commanding officer once you intend joining your unit."

I recall that same night hearing over the BBC the news of Italy's invasion of Abyssinia.

Next morning, the adjutant broke to me the news as to where my battalion was to be stationed. It was to be the most absurdly improbable of improbable military stations — the Channel Island of Guernsey. And my regiment was to be stationed there for three years.

Before leaving Lichfield for Fleet, the home of my future wife, I was invited by my 'opposite half' who was Bandmaster George Smith of the 1st Battalion the Sherwood Foresters, to join him on a specially-conducted tour of a nearby coal-mine. I am not normally given to feelings of claustrophobia, but on this occasion, particularly when we were obliged literally to crawl through a tunnel on our bellies, I most certainly was. And it overcame me again when our guide shaded his Davy lamp for us to experience a state of pitch blackness. It is from that time that my sympathy has gone out to miners, and of course to the 'wretched blind pit ponies', which even then were being used in certain British collieries.

George Smith was a serious minded, deeply introspective person. He had no time for class privilege, nepotism and the rest, and was not afraid publicly to air his views on such matters. For example, he made an embittered reference to the unbridgeable gulf which then divided 'Gentlemen' Officers from 'Other Ranks' when he wrote, 'The tendency in modern armies is towards mechanisation, and, much as we must deplore the necessity of giving "other ranks" free automobile rides, the "full marching order begad, while I ride a horse" attitude will disappear one day.' And this in a military magazine!

In a letter he wrote me during the war from North Africa when things out there were not going too well for us, he said, 'The desert is full of flies and "Old Boys", hence our present unhappy situation.' And, 'Don't you believe a word you read in the magazines and novels about the "Mysterious perfumes of the East"; for the women out here stink like polecats.'

I am quite sure when Colonel Somerville reminded us of the field marshal's baton which allegedly reposed in each of our knapsacks, that George Smith's silent reaction (for he was present at this particular prize-giving ceremony) was 'What utter balls!'

It was by sheer coincidence that the Smiths were to name their first-born Jonathan, and the Naldens to name theirs, David.

The Staffordshire town of Stone is only a score or so miles from Lichfield, so before returning south, I made time to visit my old Foundling Hospital chaplain, the Reverend Stork and his wife Alice in their charming old-world vicarage. It was the last time I was to see them. Mrs Stork predeceased her husband, who was to live on to the ripe old age of about 93.

We were married in the October of 1935 at All Saints Church, Fleet (Hampshire). (It was at Fleet incidentally that Sullivan wrote part of *Yeomen of the Guard*.)

Peggy's arrival at the church was announced by a fanfare of trumpets sounded by members of my old Royal Artillery Band. The string orchestra accompanied the service and at my request played a number of pieces which recalled nostalgically memories of services in Aldershot's 'Red Church'.

We spent our honeymoon in the Isle of Wight. Staying in the same house as ourselves as a 'permanent', was a clergyman who harboured the odd notion that honeymooners were intensely interested in the skin-burrowing habits of the African tick and other arachnida. We read in the English newspapers a short time later that this same clergyman has been summonsed and fined for ill-treating his dogs, by towing them behind his motorcycle literally at breakneck speeds through the streets of Ryde.

FOOTNOTES TO CHAPTER 21

1.   R.H. Mottram, *Early Victorian England*, I, p.185.

St Peter-Port, Guernsey, From The Pool by Henry Wimbolt.

22: *The Sherwood Foresters*
(The Nottinghamshire and Derbyshire Regiment)

GUERNSEY

To the Rock of Hospitality and Liberty;
To this Corner of old Norman land
Where dwells the noble little People of the Sea:
To the Island of Guernsey, austere but sweet.

Victor Hugo, *Toilers of the Sea*.

Nestling between the Cotentin Peninsula and the Bay of Mont St. Michel in the north of France are the Channel Islands of Jersey, Guernsey, Sark, Herm and Jethou. Just to the west of the tip of the peninsula is the Island of Alderney.

From their geographical position it would appear more consistent were these islands part of France, as indeed they were up to the time of the Duke of Normandy's successful invasion of England in 1066. Ever since then, they have remained loyal to the British Crown, even though to this day some Islanders continue to acknowledge the reigning monarch not as King of England, but as Duke of Normandy.

Ease of access, immigration, and the ravages wrought by the Germans during their wartime occupation of the Islands have combined to rob certain of them of some of their former charm and beauty. When, for example, we lived in Guernsey, a tiny island of a little over 24 square miles, the population was about 42,000. By 1971 it had increased to almost 54,000, giving a population density of 2250 to the square mile, against a population of 840 to the square mile for the same year in England and Wales. To these figures must be added the thousands of holiday-makers who flock to the Island each year.

Some of the Channel Islands' permanent residents were attracted there by reason of the sheer beauty of the islands themselves, and others by the relatively low taxes on incomes and luxury goods such as perfumes, wines, spirits and tobacco.

Perhaps the most lovely and least spoilt in the archipelago is the tiny island of Sark, which to the poet Swinburne became the Garden of Cymodoce. It was this island which was the setting for Jerrard Tickell's charming but tragic *Appointment with Venus*. Sark boasted having the smallest harbour in the world; so small in fact that the Guernsey-Sark inter-island ferry found it necessary at times to transfer its passengers to a smaller craft in order to land them. With one exception (a tractor), motor-driven vehicles are banned by Sarkese law. When we lived in the islands, a current story had it that in order to circumvent their own law the Sarkese imported their tractor, took themselves to their own court, found themselves guilty, fined themselves, but still retained the tractor.

Making the journey to Guernsey by air is infinitely more convenient than journeying there by sea. But the sea-going passenger has one distinct advantage over the air traveller. It is the unique view he gets of Guernsey Harbour, Castle Cornet and the little town of St. Peter Port beyond — an unforgettable experience to those with an eye for God- and man-made beauty.

Although we arrived there in November, the conditions which greeted us were akin to those of a lovely summer's morning. There was scarcely a ripple on the harbour pool, and the slight haze created the effect of bringing the looming silhouettes of the town's buildings gradually into reality.

I duly reported to the adjutant, who informed me that the battalion would not be arriving on the island until April of the following year. Meantime, my duties simply were to teach the dozen or so band boys. I volunteered to act as schoolmaster pending the battalion's arrival — an offer which was accepted.

The adjutant read me part of a letter he had received from Colonel Sherbrooke, the battalion's commanding officer. It spoke of his intention to despatch the regimental dance band in advance of the main body, and of his expecting to find it 100 per cent improved by the time he himself arrived in Guernsey. Fortunately (for me) the plan did not eventuate; I say 'fortunately', for although I had had experience in playing in dance bands, I had never trained one.

The undemanding conditions of my new life presented me with an unparalleled opportunity to resume work on my degree studies. Peggy was perfectly content to sit day after day, week after week and month after month, either reading or knitting — an occupation she had just taken up. Her first effort in this art was to knit me a sweater into which she worked the maroon and green colours of the Sherwood Foresters. Unfortunately she used too heavy a ply, so that each successive wearing of the finished article saw me becoming more and more a reflection of the then Surrey cricket captain, P.G.H. Fender, whose near-knee length sweaters consistently attracted the attention of the *Daily Mail's* sports cartoonist, Tom Webster.

Not profiting by her mistake, and using an even heavier ply, she went on to knit herself a magnificent full-length dressing-gown, which she had to abandon when it became evident that its ever-increasing length required the services of a team of train-bearers.

I was now beginning to feel the reaction from the intense pressures of my Kneller Hall years, and in particular from the concentrated work on *Suppé Supreme*. As I mentioned in the previous chapter, I was compelled to sit for hours at a time in a darkened room; also my headaches were now occurring with greater frequency and severity. So I decided to 'report sick'. I was admitted to Netley Military Hospital for observation. The army specialist attributed my chronic headache condition to the fact that I had made the rank of warrant officer Class I at the tender age of 27. I was too respectful of rank to attempt to prove him wrong by explaining that I had been a sufferer from early childhood. So he shrunk my turbinates by cauterisation, prescribed the newest-on-the-market painkiller, and sent me off on 'a spot of sick leave'. His treatment, although well-intentioned, proved quite ineffectual.

When ultimately I returned to Guernsey, the battalion had arrived from the Middle East.

The main body of the battalion was quartered in Fort George (since demolished) which dated from 1782 — and looked it. Both the fort itself, and the Martello Towers which stood as guardians of Guernsey's southern coast, were built because of the growing threat of an invasion by France, who four years earlier had declared war on Great Britain.

The band was quartered in Castle Cornet, which stands a half-mile out to sea. In earlier times it was accessible from the mainland only at the very lowest tides, but is now linked to the town of St.Peter Port by a mole.

Castle Cornet has a turbulent and bloody history of its own. It dates back to at least the 14th century, and for centuries after was constantly changing hands between its local defenders and the French. During the English Civil War, when the Parliamentarian Party enjoyed the support of the majority of Guernseymen, the Royalist Governor entrenched himself in the castle, which was his official residence. The castle withstood an eight year seige, during which time the defenders were reduced to feeding off limpets.

Even so, I doubt very much whether the castle's long and romantic history consoled my bandsmen for their primitive quarters. Even less did the band boys appreciate the castle, when during the 1938 war scare they were allotted one of its dungeons as their practice air raid shelter. No harm would have accrued had they heard the all clear signal. Unfortunately it was not for several hours after the initial air raid warning that they were missed.

Some two centuries earlier, a group of islanders who were appointed Parliamentary Commissioners for Guernsey were incarcerated by Sir Peter Osborne, the Lieutenant-Governor, in 'one of the deepest dungeons under the lower ditch — a place so subterranean and humid that our hair became wet, and from thence we were unable to see light but through the keyhole'. So you now know what sort of privations my poor band boys suffered. A soldier's life indeed is 'terrible 'ard'.

I was told on the day after I arrived back from sick leave to report to Colonel Sherbrooke. It was a summons I had long dreaded; for already I had been briefed on what to expect from that quarter. Three incidents involving the colonel had already been related to me, of which two implicated the band.

The first incident occurred during a battalion parade, when he rode over to the band to find out for himself why the three trombonists were not playing.

"Why aren't you men playing your instruments?" he demanded.

"Because we have 32 bars' rest, sir," came the confident reply.

"Thirty-two bars rest be damned! Bandmaster, it's time you taught your men that there's no bloody rest in my battalion. Start playing at once."

The setting for the second of the three incidents was the battalion's parade ground in Khartoum. The battalion was drawn up, the band with its back to the River Nile. I do not recall exactly what it was that sparked off the incident, but Colonel Sherbrooke bellowed: "Drum Major, give your band and drums the order 'About turn'!"

Drum-Major: "Band and Drums, er-bout . . . turn!"

Colonel Sherbrooke: "Now give them the order, 'Quick march'!"

Drum-Major: "Band and Drums, quick . . . march!"

Colonel Sherbrooke: "And don't you dare give them the order 'Halt'!"

Drum-Major: "Sir!"

I can only presume that the good Lord engineered a second Red Sea-type miracle, when the waters of the Nile became 'a wall unto them on their right hand, and on their left'; for both band and drums arrived in Guernsey at full strength, which included Derby XV, the regimental mascot ram.

The third incident was hardly calculated to foster good race relations.

The colonel was having a long-distance telephone call from one end of India to the other, but was getting nowhere apparently in making himself understood. "Put a white man on the phone" he roared. His reply to the protestations of the person at the other end of the phone that he was a white man was: "You're not a white man! I can see you from here. Your arse is as black as the ace of spades!"

It becomes a little difficult to reconcile this choleric (and characteristic) outburst of the colonel's with the fact that one of his illustrious forebears, Robert Lowe (who later was raised to the House of Lords as Viscount Sherbrooke), is said to have vied with Mr Gladstone 'in aptness of classical quotation'.

Can it be wondered at therefore that I viewed the prospect of meeting him with not a few misgivings? I was not to be disappointed; for he soon revealed himself as 'a soldier full of strange oaths . . . sudden and quick in quarrel'. With formal pleasantries quickly over, he charged into the attack for my not having arranged a comprehensive tour for the band of English seaside resorts. My mouth instantaneously dried up, and my temples tapped out their own version of the morse code. Temporarily *hors de combat*, I found myself unable to blurt out that I had in fact carried out, and at my own expense, an exploratory tour of south coast resorts from Hastings to Bournemouth; neither could I pluck up courage to explain that no seaside entertainments' manager would dream of employing a band that was completely unknown, unless, of course, its bandsmen wore kilts.

He next grilled me as to what arrangements I had made for the band to have regular feet and arms inspection. I cottoned on to the feet part of it, for I was after all now a member of a foot-slogging regiment. But arms inspection? I suppose I must involuntarily have made a passing glance either at his or my own arms, for he shouted, "Not those arms, you bloody fool! I mean guns! weapons! rifles!"

Fortunately for me Adjutant Ingall gallantly waded in to my rescue . . .

"Being an artilleryman, I expect Mr Nalden dealt only with the big fellahs, sir."

"Of course! Of course!"

Mercifully the colonel knew nothing of my dealings with the 'big fellahs' nor (even more mercifully) with the 'little fellahs'; for section XIII of my

Army Book 64 Soldier's Service and Pay Book which gives a record of a soldier's Annual Range Practices (Table RL or T or Machine Gun Courses) is completely blank.

The warnings given me by my fellow Kneller Hall students of the shocks I was to experience as bandmaster of a 'line' regiment were proving themselves, unhappily, to be all too true.

To add to my mood of dejection, I received news from Durham that I had failed the First Examination for a second time. Worse still, my marks if anything, were less satisfactory than those of the previous September examination. I drew little comfort from the news that Bairstow had passed only four of the two dozen or so candidates who had sat the examination.

In the meantime Peggy and I were discovering the beauties of the Guernsey countryside, and more particularly those of the flower-strewn cliff walks from Jerbourg Point to Pleinmont Point. We would take in a different bay on each of our tri-weekly walks. Never had we seen anything so beautiful as these cliff walks in the early spring; for then the cliffs and the gentle intersecting valleys are strewn with carpets of wild bluebells, daffodils, primroses and golden gorse, 'as if God's finger touched but did not press'.

Our favourite bay was Moulin Huet, in the Parish of St. Martin's. It is more rocky than every other of Guernsey's bays. One of its rocks was named Andrecot by the Guernsey people, and up to the early years at least of the present century, 'every boat's ensign dipped in his honour and a small oblation [was] flung to him "for luck" by the fishermen of St.Martin's parish as they sail[ed] past'.

In our second year there, we spent our entire savings on a secondhand car. This we used as a means of reaching the more distant parts of the island to explore on foot the various inland parishes and their beautiful old churches. And in the late summer and early autumn we would motor out to the west coast, evening after evening, for the sole purpose of beholding the sheer beauty of the setting sun and its warm after-glow. To stand gazing upon a Guernsey sunset is akin to inflicting upon oneself a form of exquisite torture. Its nearest parallel in music is the closing section of Elgar's Second Symphony. It has no like parallel in words.

In the winter evenings we played badminton and squash together; but I resisted firmly Lieutenant Astle's suggestion that I join the regimental rugger team; for I had been badly concussed at Kneller Hall when brought down by The Rake in a 'friendly' soccer game.

I must have become somewhat discouraged after failing the Durham examination a second time for I did no degree work at all during the summer of 1936. Instead I surrendered myself to the delights of sea bathing in one or another of Guernsey's heavenly bays. Indeed, I might well have gone drifting along in this manner had I not received an almost sharply worded letter from the Registrar of Durham University, asking whether or not I intended sitting the coming September examination.

September came round. I sat, and passed.

And then there occurred one of those strange incidents which from time to time and for no apparent reason, flit across the pages of one's life.

On the same day as the notification of my examination result arrived, there appeared on our doorstep my old Foundling Hospital friend, Maria Kenny. I recall her as being beautifully dressed, but carrying no luggage of any kind beyond her stylish handbag. She had travelled from England to Jersey (mistakenly thinking us there) but arriving penniless had been obliged to sleep the night in St.Helier's police station. She talked to us a great deal of her unhappy experiences in the mental hospital from which she had recently been discharged. She stayed with us for a week or so before returning to England.

Neither Peggy nor I ever really understood exactly what had prompted her to throw herself upon us unheralded, virtually penniless, and without a single item of overnight luggage. Clearly, she was an unhappy victim of circumstance. We never saw her again. I learnt some years later that she had died, aged about 48, after a long illness and much suffering.

The second examination for the degree of Bachelor in Music was held in the September of each year. This gave me a full year in which to prepare for it. In scope it was a great deal more demanding and far reaching than the first examination, but encouraged by Dr Wood, I decided to make an entry.

It was when I began reading for this examination that I came to realise the musical backwater this otherwise idyllic island really was. When at Kneller Hall, at least I had Robert Stannard to whom I could go for help. But here in Guernsey there was just nobody; nobody at least who could help me with my academic work. But in the end I discovered this to have its advantages; for being thrown virtually upon his own resources, the external student finds that he must delve more deeply, read more widely and question more closely than the internal student, who of course is given positive guidance as to the ground he must cover.

I would sometimes go to St. Stephen's Church, where the organist, dear old Mr Matthews (who by then must have been well past his 80th year) would play to me from his voluminous collection of Bach's organ works. He had studied in Germany, and in his prime must have been a fine organist. His German training left its mark, for he was ever critical of certain English organists who, he declared, played Bach's fugues at 'far too fast a tempo'.

Another remarkable musician I met was a Mrs Gardner, who owned Guernsey's exclusive and staid Old Government House Hotel. Our common meeting ground was the harp for she had been trained as a harpist and as a pianist. I never heard her play the harp, but as a pianist, particularly for one of so advanced an age, she was quite remarkable.

She might well have been adopted by the film actress Margaret Rutherford as her prototype. One of the hotel's guests had been Reginald Foort, the well-known cinema organist of the 20s and 30s. "I believe," she once said to Foort, "that your cinema organ is a remarkable instrument. I understand you can actually imitate anything on it, from a cat-fight to a dog running around with a tin can tied to its tail." Reginald's half-stumbling, half-apologetic reply (so she told me) was that once away from his cinema organ, invariably he went to the one great love in his life, Bach.

Mrs Gardner loved to relate the story of how she defied Guernsey's chief constable throughout the entire 1914-18 war by refusing to hand over for internment her German-born gardener. Guernsey law at that time did not give the police the right to enter private premises where no actual crime had been committed. And so Charles the gardener remained an internee of the Old Government House Hotel throughout the war, never daring so much as to put one foot over its threshold.

Mrs Gardner introduced me to her close friend, Frederick Dawson (1868-1940). In his day, Dawson had been one of England's foremost pianists. 'Grove' records: 'He was 10 years old when his ability to play the whole of *Das Wohltemperirte Klavier* [the "48"] from memory brought him to the notice of Halle . . . His reputation stood high in continental cities, especially Vienna and Berlin.' It was all the more remarkable therefore, that Mrs Gardner was well able to hold her own when she joined him in playing the two-piano version of Brahms's *Variations on a Theme* by Haydn (St.Antoni Chorale).

It was Frederick Dawson who befriended the English composer, William Baines (1899-1922) who is remembered today, not through his compositions (which were greatly admired by Dawson), but by the memorial raised to him in the Primitive Methodist Church at his native Horbury in Yorkshire. One of Baines's compositions is an eight-bar *Prelude** which he dedicated to his mother. Dawson told me that he played this piece over to himself

---

* This *Prelude* is engraved on the William Baines Memorial Plaque, which may be seen in the gallery of the Horbury (Yorkshire) Methodist Church.

every night before retiring to bed. Like William Baines, I owe Dawson a great deal, in that he helped me considerably to extend my knowledge of piano music and to appreciate good playing.

Another frequent visitor to Guernsey (whose spiritual home it was) was John Ireland; but although I knew his Guernsey friend, Andrew White (who was the most vague and unbusinesslike businessman I have ever met)* I was never privileged to meet him.

As I have said, on the academic side I had to fend for myself the best I could. Among my mechanical aids were a piano (which I bought for 30 shillings and later sold for exactly half that price), a wind-up portable gramophone, a number of records, and of course, a radio.

It so happened that the year 1937 afforded me the most favourable conditions for study I had so far experienced, thanks in an oblique sort of way to Colonel Sherbrooke.

Good soldier that he was, the colonel in many respects was an exacting person. One of his first tidying-up processes after his arrival in Guernsey was to have the rear wall of the regimental squash court knocked out and rebuilt some few inches further back, so that it conformed to regulation dimensions. The many regiments in the past who had used it had either not noticed the defect or had been content to accept it as it stood; but not so 'Fizzer'.

He next transferred all his energies into a quite different project. The PRI's** clerk, Sergeant Chapman, was a thin, emaciated looking person, who bore all the outward signs of one who suffered from pernicious anaemia. He walked one day into Stonelake the chemist on official regimental business. Giving Mr Stonelake a knowing wink, Sergeant Chapman proceeded to startle him with: "I think a couple of dozen gross should tide me over the next week or two."

Perhaps the worst disgrace that could befall a regiment was for it to run a high incidence of VD; and whether or not one agreed with the colonel's enlightened plan (enlightened for those days, that is) of free condoms for all ranks, it meant the battalion leaving the island with a clean slate, and the saving of more than one soldier from falling an unwilling victim to that loathsome scourge; for penicillin had yet to be discovered.

---

* I happened to be in his music shop when a customer asked whether he had a certain gramophone record in stock. "I'm very sorry, but I haven't," he answered her. After she had left the shop, he admitted to me: "I just might have it, but I couldn't be bothered to look for it."

** President Regimental Institutes.

The colonel next turned his attention to an area of land just outside the walls of the fort itself; it was a good piece of ground going to waste. In no time he had this converted into the regimental piggery. Officers were invited to buy shares in it (although I do not recall seeing its listing on the London Stock Exchange). Considerations of hygiene were of paramount importance, and in order to bring this home, he had a directive published in Regimental Part I Orders which laid down that 'The Officer of the Day will report immediately any smell he detects within 20 yards of the Regimental Piggery.' This order set me musing to myself as to whether our officers' public school-Sandhurst education had been really necessary.

At the end of the piggery's first financial year, a proud colonel brought to the notice of the entire battalion through the medium of Part I Orders that it had returned somewhere in the region of a 100 per cent dividend to its shareholders. Thus was his undying faith in his own business acumen fully justified; and thus were his critics and the faint-hearted who had reacted overcautiously to his initial floatation, effectively silenced.

Bandmaster, The Sherwood Foresters.

The colonel had every reason for being proud of his undoubted business ability, for after all, had not the Battalion Pioneer Squad constructed the sty at no cost to anybody?; had not the battalion 'Janker Wallahs' (defaulters) provided him with a free labour force, and had not the pigs' wash come free of charge from the regimental swill bins?

Next, it was the turn of Belvedere Field, which we sometimes used as a parade ground. The criss-cross pattern of its roads was, in the colonel's eyes, all wrong. And so he called me in to his office one day to explain regretfully that he must use my bandsmen as part of a battalion road-construction labour force. This went on for most of the spring and early summer months, leaving me virtually free to get down to study. (During the Occupation, the Germans managed to out-Sherbrooke Sherbrooke, by constructing a vast underground hospital beneath Belvedere Field.)

The road building proved itself to be not the end of things, but only the beginning; for hard upon its completion came our annual six weeks' camp in Jersey, when the bandsmen reverted to their traditional wartime role of soldiers first and musicians second. This gave me yet another long and virtually uninterrupted period for study. It also gave me time for exploring Jersey itself.

Although I never considered either Jersey's harbour or its town of St.Helier as attractive as their respective Guernsey counterparts (St.Helier having lost much of its original character in its 'modernising' process), I did find inland Jersey even more beautiful than inland Guernsey. Its churches are every bit as interesting and beautiful as those in Guernsey. The most charming of these perhaps is the grey-granite, stone-roofed church which nestles beneath the cliffs at the far end of St. Brelade's Bay. Standing in the same grounds is the Chapelle des Pecheurs, which, tradition has it, was built by St.Marcouf for Jersey fishermen, and is the oldest church in the Channel Islands. (I seem to remember seeing the graves of German prisoners-of-war who died on the Island during World War I.)

It is hardly to be wondered at that such beauty should have become the inspirational force for John Ireland's Orchestral Prelude *The Forgotten Rite*. In Ireland's own words: 'It is a work I felt much about. I wrote it after being alone for six weeks in Jersey, and one felt so intensely, so painfully, in fact, the indescribable beauty of the light, the sea, and the distant other islands. At that time, one felt that the very thinnest of veils separated one from the actual reality behind all this smiling beauty.' I know just what Ireland meant.

Neither is it to be wondered at that 'all this smiling beauty' should have given birth to a Peter Monamy and a Sir John Millais.

One of Jersey's interesting personalities I was frequently to meet was Lady Trent, widow of Lord Trent (formerly Sir Jesse Boot, founder of Boots Cash Chemists Ltd). My band played in her spacious grounds (which she threw open to the public) two or three times during each of the six weeks we were in camp.

It was in camp that I came to know some of the Sherwood Foresters' officers rather more intimately. I became particularly fond of my band president, Major H.L.B. Mills who although losing an arm in World War I, was able to drive a car as expertly as most other men: of Major 'Mouse' Wright (who was so nicknamed on account of his having slept through a heavy World War I German bombardment), and of Captain Bobby Stott.

Early one morning Bobby called me over to his tent, and assuming a tone of mock severity, questioned me: "Are you the man responsible for this?" 'This' was a noticeboard which had been 'lifted' the night before by some of our young subalterns from a nearby farmhouse, and hammered into the ground immediately outside Bobby's tent. It read —

I had to tell him that I was not the architect of this schoolboyish prank, even though I envied secretly the subaltern whose idea it had been.

Although inwardly overjoyed at the thought of returning to my beloved Guernsey, it was not without a great deal of regret when it came for us to leave Jersey. The band was to return there later to participate in the island's famous annual Battle of Flowers. The winning entry was a charming 18th century period piece, *Swing as we go*, matching in beauty the delicate pastel shades of the flowers which adorned the float.

Durham University had allowed me to sit its first examination in Elizabeth College, Guernsey, but for the second examination, which included a viva voce, I was required to travel to Durham, a full two-days' journey. Never before had I felt so well prepared.

My viva voce examination was conducted by Dr Gordon Slater, the then organist of Lincoln Minster. We came to the prepared score, which was Vaughan-Williams's *London Symphony*. "Now," he shot at me, "I would like you to find for me one particularly remarkable piece of scoring" (a somewhat ill-judged question, I thought, on a symphony which played for the best part of an hour).

Although I had studied the work in depth, and was able to answer his other questions, this particular one found me guessing rather wildly. "Here it is," he said, pointing to the passage at the end of the *Scherzo* where clarinets and harp (harmonics) double each other. "Nothing quite like it has ever been done before, has it?" Weakly I agreed with him; for I lacked both the confidence and the courage to contradict him by pointing out that Berlioz had done something closely similar in his *Danse des Sylphes*. I did tell him, however, that I was a harpist, at which point the examination became conducted in reverse as it were, with Dr Slater questioning me on the instrument's technicalities for his own enlightenment. (I met Dr Slater in 1940, following an organ recital he had given in Derby Cathedral. I related to him my reluctance to 'correct' him at our viva voce session of three years earlier. "So you thought I was one of those?" he quipped jocularly.)

This time I decided not to take advantage of the janitor's telegraphic service; I regretted not doing so when my result, a pass, reached me a few days later. Another of the successful candidates was a Frederick Coley, who a few years later was to teach my son the piano when he entered Portsmouth Grammar School.

The third and final part of the Durham degree required candidates to write a musical 'exercise', the academic term for an original composition. Acting upon Dr Wood's advice, I chose to write a work which included the harp.

At the end of the year, I attended the annual dinner of the Kneller Hall Club in London. One of the specially invited guests was Sir Percy Buck*, who had been one of my Durham examiners. When I mentioned to him that I was writing my exercise he advised: "Don't be afraid to write a tune, and if you use a key signature, then let it be meaningful. We get so many exercises these days which state solemnly 'String Quartet in F major'; yet one may go through several of its pages before coming across the note F, let alone the chord of F."

We spent our Christmas leave at my mother-in-law's home in Fleet. Even though it meant seeing her family, Peggy disliked the idea of leaving 'our' Guernsey even for a few weeks as much as I did myself. On our return journeys we would make for the upper deck of the cross-Channel steamer in time to catch an early morning glimpse of our beloved Guernsey.

It was on one of these leaves that we came to meet Major Tom Whaley, late of the Royal Warwickshire Regiment, which was formerly Field-Marshal Montgomery's Regiment.

It appeared that Peggy's mother had succumbed to the major's pitiful pleas and had taken him in as a boarder. (Perhaps out of deference to his standing in society, I should say, as a paying guest.)

We had already been regaled by Peggy's sister Joan with stories relating to Tom Whaley. He apparently enjoyed his whisky, so we presented him with our duty-free allowance of that spirit, which immediately established between us the most cordial of relations.

Joan had written to tell us of the major's reaction to an illuminated copy she had done as a schoolgirl of Kipling's *If*.

"Bai Jove, Joan," he said, screwing his (plain glass) monocle into his right eye, "Did you realleh do all this by yourself?"

"Yes, Major Whaley."

"Jolleh, jolleh good show, Joan. But you don't say you made up those wonderful words as well?" (The major was educated at Harrow.)

When making his plea to be taken in as a PG, Major Whaley assured my mother-in-law insofar as the breakfast meal was concerned, that he would cause her no work at all; for he intended carrying on with having the same breakfast that had stood him in excellent stead ever since his subaltern days — a plate of cold pickled pork, washed down with a pint of beer.

---

* Following Sir Percy's death in the October of 1947, a current story told against him was related by the *London Daily Telegraph and Morning Post* columnist, Peterborough: His fellow professor [at the Royal College of Music] Sir Frederick Bridge, was taking a class of girl students in the Tonic Sol-fa with a movable 'doh' when Sir Percy Buck knocked at the door. "Who's there?" called out Sir Frederick. "Buck," was the reply. "Well, you can't come in here now, Buck. The room is full of does," Sir Frederick cried.

This once led him into an highly embarrassing situation. As a senior regimental officer, he once found himself sitting at the mess dining table directly opposite the colonel of the regiment who was paying the battalion a courtesy visit. Major Whaley called over one of the mess waiters and in a low undertone gave his order for breakfast. Some short time later the mess sergeant came to where he was sitting, clicked his heels, and in full hearing of the colonel of the regiment, asked: "Is it correct, sir, that you wish to have your beer brought to you in a coffee pot?"

I was once on the point of going out when Major Whaley pulled me up with: "Good God, Nalden! You're not going out dressed like that, sureleh?"

"Like what, sir?" I asked.

"Without wearing a hat. It's only cads, you know, who don't wear hats." Which accounts in part as to why to this day I seldom go out attired like a cad.

He sometimes played host to his former commanding officer and his wife, Colonel and Mrs Marriott. Mrs Marriott was opposed to her husband's drinking spirits of any kind. Tom circumvented that one by inviting his old CO to try some of his 'white sherry'. The stratagem paid off until the colonel's lady herself once decided to try some of Tom's special 'white sherry'.

When boarding with my mother-in-law, he developed three hobbies — gardening (at which he became a fair hand), making dove cotes, and collecting second-hand boot-scrapers which (being perpetually insolvent) he invariably gave away as wedding presents. He insisted that we take one of his dove cotes back to Guernsey. Peggy was not at all sorry (quite relieved in fact) when finally it collapsed, for our cocker spaniel Rob misunderstood consistently the purpose of its being there.

Major Whaley was 53 when he married for a second time, and promptly expired on his wedding night — 'done in' no doubt by a surfeit of conjugal affection and white sherry.

My degree result reached me at a time when the battalion was rehearsing interminably, day in and day out, for its forthcoming ceremony of Trooping the Colour. We trooped the colour twice in each year. One of these ceremonies was held in honour of the King's birthday, and the other on 20 September (known as Alma Day) to mark the gallant part played by the Sherwood Foresters (then the 95th Regiment of Foot) in the Battle of the Alma, which was fought and won by the Allies in 1854.

For the Alma Day parade, Colonel Sherbrooke conceived the romantic idea of dressing the colour party in authentic period uniforms; and as a final touch of authenticity, that its members grow side-whiskers.

I must admit that the colour party made an impressive sight, particularly our Corporal Stevens, whose great natural height (his Shako adding an extra dozen or so inches) and massive physique had him towering not only above the remainder of the colour party, but over the entire parade.

This authentic touch was all very fine from the spectators' viewpoint, but hardly so from that of the colour party; for during the growing period of the side-whiskers its members were confined to barracks, lest their Crimean-period appearance brought the good name of the battalion into disrepute with the local townspeople.

It was for one of these trooping of the colour parades that I took it upon myself to ring a change of tune for the inspection part of the ceremony. The inspection tune played not only by us, but by every other band in the British Army apparently, was _May Blossom_:

The band had no sooner commenced playing my substitute tune when my attention was drawn to Colonel Sherbrooke, who from the majesty of his mount was making frantic gesticulations with his stick, which I correctly interpreted as a signal for us to stop playing.

"Mr Nalden," he roared from his end of the parade ground, "Bachelor of Music or no Bachelor of Music, I won't have you tampering with my inspection tunes. I don't know what it is you're playing, but I don't want to hear it again. In future you will play the tune we all know, and you will not change it without my express permission."

"Which tune do you want, sir?" I bellowed back.

"You know as well as I do — 'He peed on the old Colonel's doorstep'," he roared back in reply.

On another occasion the parade was being taken by the second-in-command, Major 'Mouse' Wright, on Fort Field. The battalion was drawn up at one end of the field, with the band at the other.

On the order 'Battalion . . . Quick march!', we struck up with the march beloved by circus bands the world over, *Blaze Away*.

We were promptly stopped by a succession of waves from Major Wright's stick.

"Get that together, Mr Nalden," he shouted.

We went through a second, a third, and finally a fourth attempt at 'getting it together' before it dawned upon me exactly what Major Wright was getting at. As I was anxious not to prove the major wrong, I decided upon a diplomatic solution, by instructing all the lower instruments to move one bar to their left, and all the upper instruments one bar to their right. It came out like this:

My diplomacy had paid off. "That's better, Mr Nalden," bawled the Mouse.

There was a good deal of this sort of philistinism in the army (both genuine and affected), even more among the officer class than among the 'other ranks'. It behoved one to learn to accept this sort of thing with good grace and with humour; for to 'correct' one's superior could have disastrous results. Rarely in the army did one encounter an Archibald Wavell.

Shortly before leaving Guernsey for our annual camp in Jersey, I received advice from Durham that conferment of degrees was to take place on 28 June. I was unable to attend, and so was 'capped' in absentia. It was not my regimental duties which prevented me from travelling to Durham, but a telegram despatched from Guernsey just three days before the graduation ceremony — 'Son arrived 5.30 am. Both well.'

Colonel Sherbrooke granted me extended leave, followed by weekend leave for the remainder of camp. "You are the only man in the battalion I could possibly do it for," he revealed to me in a corner-of-the-mouth 'strictly between you and me' sort of aside. I could not be altogether certain whether this was intended as a compliment or otherwise.

Mrs Gardner, who had a big say apparently in the management of the Lady Ozanne Nursing Home, arranged for Peggy to have 'her' room. David was baptised by the Dean of Guernsey in the Town Church, whose oldest parts are believed to date from the reign of King John.

A little later, the dean, accompanied by his curate, called on me, not in his official capacity as dean, but as a sufferer from sciatica. He had been told that a gut string worn next to his skin would relieve his sciatica. I thus enjoyed the unique experience of measuring up a real live dean round his middle, and fitting him up with one of my gut harp strings, which happened to be a fifth octave G, the longest string but one. Out of respect for the cloth, I decided against fitting him with the longest string of all, known as 'fifth octave F', for its purple dye (denoting in New Zealand, second-grade meat) tends to run in hot or humid conditions.

I cannot recall whether it was Dr Wood or myself who first raised the idea of my going on to read for the doctorate. I do however recall Dr Wood's advice that I should get down to work with the least possible delay; for, he reasoned, all too many of his students' early ambitions had cooled because of their tardiness in making a start. I would have taken his advice and made an immediate start had it not been for an obstacle which was lurking constantly and uncomfortably in the background.

Some years earlier Kneller Hall had instituted its own 'Advanced Certificate' examination with the idea presumably of gaining complete control over promotions to guards and other commissioned-rank staff bands. It meant that however strongly backed and however highly qualified a bandmaster might be, he could not look forward to promotion until such time he had gained this new qualification.

Modelling itself on the army's famous psc (Passed Staff College) qualification, it was given official recognition by War Office, and holders of the certificate were entitled to append the letters psm (Passed School of Music) after their names. ('Pepper, Salt and Mustard' as one disgruntled bandmaster dubbed it.)

There were several good reasons for causing disquiet among potential psm candidates. One of these was the regulation which restricted candidates to a limited number of attempts. Another was Adko himself — that he should be a member of the examining body; for some bandmasters who had fallen foul of him (no difficult accomplishment) felt, rightly or wrongly, that the die was already loaded heavily against them.

Shortly after our return from camping in Jersey I was advised of an impending band inspection by Kneller Hall — which had me worried, for I had seen very little of the band since the spring. I was questioned, or put more accurately, I was probed in a diplomatically-phrased manner, as to Adko's social status; whether he was a 'gentleman' or a 'ranker' officer. It was the matter of suitable accommodation in the Officers' Mess and of hospitality generally. Adko himself solved the difficulty by staying at the Old Government House Hotel*.

It was Adko himself who suggested that I call on him in his hotel, "and bring a bottle of whisky with you, Nalden. It's buddy silly having to pay the hotel price of 12/6d for it when you can get it from one of the town's stores for eight bob."

It gave me the greatest pleasure that same evening to rub in as hard as our difference in rank would allow, that contrary to what he himself preached, a man could be married and yet study at the same time.

"Yours is an exceptional case, Nalden, and if you're sensible you'll take her out for the evening sometimes and really do her proud." This was the only concession he would make.

He then broached the subject of the coming psm examination, asking why I had not made an entry, and at the same time making it clear that a Bachelor in Music degree was not sufficient a qualification in itself for ultimate promotion.

I reminded him of the regulation which required a bandmaster to have been with his band for a minimum period of five years before making an examination entry. He waived this aside, which left me with no alternative other than to put my name down for the coming November examination.

Our dream years in Guernsey were rapidly coming to an end.

We were advised of our next station, which was to be Bordon Camp in Hampshire. This item of news was broken to us, not by War Office,

---

* A class barrier was erected around this hotel, which was officially reserved for officers' use only. 'Other ranks' were forbidden to use it. The fashion for disgruntled soldiers to air their grievances to their local MP's had yet to arrive.

but by an English brewery firm which, by recourse to some secret source of inside information, had managed to get in just that one step ahead of War Office's official notification.

One of the brewery's representatives quickly ingratiated himself with our Sergeants' Mess members by the proven technique of "What'll you have?"; and by his answering "Oh! definitely!" to any and every question or opinion which might be put to him regardless of whether or not inwardly he was in agreement with them. Poor unwilling sycophant! How I pitied him his mode of employment; but with the jobless figures still running all too high, what else was there for a man belonging to his particular social stratum to do?

'Definitely' happened to be the 'in' word of the 30s. Its over-use once so exasperated one British judge as to move him to instruct witnesses to stop using it. I recall Colonel Sherbrooke inspecting a new intake of recruits, and the reply made by one of its number to a question which had been put to him — "Definitely, sir!"

"Did you hear that?" put in the colonel in an aside to his adjutant, "Earmark him straightaway as a company clerk."

A short time before we left Guernsey, a major row blew up which I seem to recall led to the resignation of one of the island's senior police. It appeared that a prison official who was doing his early morning rounds noticed one of the cell doors slightly ajar, and the cell itself empty. He waited around, and some little time later, in walked the cell's inmate. It transpired that the prisoner simply walked out of his cell after dark each evening, slept the night at home, making prison again in time for the early morning roll call. An 'inside job' if ever there were one.

Because of the smallness of the island, drunkenness could be effectively controlled. An offender would be photographed holding a board in his hands (and generally with a broad grin spread over his face) on which was recorded the period of his disqualification from entering any of the island's pubs. Copies of the photograph were circulated to all pubs and displayed in some prominent position.

And taking a leaf out of the same book, one of the town's businessmen, a gents' outfitter, regularly displayed in his shop window a list of bad debtors.

The end of the battalion's stay in Guernsey coincided with the end of Colonel Sherbrooke's military career, for he had now reached retirement age. He farewelled the battalion during the course of a special parade, which was held on a bitterly cold November morning.

Surveying the parade from the heights of his horse, he opened with:

"Novembah appears to have been my fateful month. I was born in Novembah, gazetted in Novembah, married in Novembah . . . "

Voice from band: "And for —'s sake peg out in Novembah."

For all his irascibility, his autocratic manner and his apparent contempt for the world's civilian population in general, I came to admire the man as being the real professional soldier through and through. If not the ideal battalion commander (his choleric outbursts tended to rule him out of that category) he was a man, I felt sure, who would spontaneously undertake any act demanding bravery without thought for his own personal safety. In that way, he must have made an ideal leader of men in the 1914-18 trench-type warfare.

DNB has this to say about another of his forebears, Sir John Coape Sherbrooke (1764-1830):

> At the storming of Seringapatam he commanded the right column of assault. He was knocked down by a spent ball as he mounted the breach, but quickly recovered, and Baird said in his report: 'If where all behaved nobly it is proper to mention individual merit, I know no man so justly entitled to praise as Colonel Sherbrooke' . . . He was second in command to Wellesley in the campaign of 1809 . . . Wellington long afterwards told Lord Stanhope, 'Sherbrooke was a very good officer, but the most passionate man, I think, I ever knew'; and he mentioned as an instance, that in his (Wellesley's) own presence at Oporto his interpreter so irritated Sherbrooke that he could hardly keep his hands off him . . . Wellesley wrote to Sherbrooke to impress upon him that he must not abuse commissariat officers, however much he might think they deserve it.

This also is the Colonel Sherbrooke I knew — exactly, in fact; for I recall our Lieutenant-Quartermaster 'Napi' Barber confiding in me his disgust that Colonel Sherbrooke should refer to him openly as a 'fornicating imbecile'. Napi was so outraged as to consider seriously making a personal appeal to the King, which his commissioned officer rank allowed him to do.

Even so, I personally was most sorry to see Colonel Sherbrooke go.

And then I had to thank his wife Eileen for her gift to me of her fine collection of piano music.

None of us could then foresee that within a year the Channel Islands would be under German rule:

that the inevitability of invasion would split island opinion right down the middle, sowing the seeds of a harrowing and long-lasting bitterness between those who decided to leave and those who decided to stay on;

that for no given reason all males and their families who were not of direct Channel Islands' descent would be sent to internment camps in Germany;

that one Channel Islander (a Jerseyman) would be incarcerated in the Belsen hell for his harbouring an escaped Russian prisoner;

that Guernsey's beautiful coastal scenery would be scarred by a mass of hideous concrete fortifications;

that the charming old Gouffre Hotel which was once owned by the parents of my son's godmother would be wantonly sacked;

that pigs would be kept in the basement of Guernsey's exclusive Old Government House Hotel;

that Jews would be registered on a special register and that 'every Jewish-owned business would be indicated by a special notice as a Jewish undertaking';

that those who remained on in the island would discover, as their besieged 17th century forebears had discovered, new tastes in foods such as limpets, treated seaweed, and 'tea' made from pea-pods, desiccated carrots and cured bramble leaves;

that in the war's final phase the near-starving population would be reduced to killing off their dogs to provide themselves with food, and to rummaging in near-empty garbage bins;

that the day would come when elderly lady cat lovers 'might be seen painfully scrambling over the rocks at low tide with unsuitable tools in unpracticed hands to detach limpets that they might take home, boil and mince for their fastidious pets';

that the famous Guernseys' and Jerseys' hitherto abundant milk yield would gravely decrease through the islands' acute shortage of cattlefood;

and that 'the association of empty-headed Guernsey women with German soldiers' would become a contributory cause of the more than five-fold increase in the island's illegitimacy rate.

Neither did any of us foresee that Colonel Sherbrooke's wife, Eileen (who had been most kind to me on a number of occasions), would become the central figure in an incident which threatened to develop into an ugly situation. Here is the story as told by Ralph Durand in his *Guernsey under German Rule*:

> A silly practical joke led to the detention of Mrs Sherbrooke, the wife of an officer on service in England, on a charge of having made signals from the roof of her house to British agents concealed in the bushes in her garden. She was not imprisoned but was strictly confined to her house in the charge of a series of German officers, one by day and one by night, who took up their quarters in her drawing-room. As she was not allowed to use her telephone and a sentry was posted at her front door to forbid entrance to her house, her friends did not know of her plight till one of them chanced to

enter her house by the back door over which no guard had been set. The Germans naturally questioned Mrs Sherbrooke's two maid-servants as to her alleged hostile activities. They broke down under cross-examination and admitted that the charge brought against her arose from an anonymous letter which they themselves had concocted as a joke. Mrs Sherbrooke was therefore released from arrest, but the maid-servants were sentenced to imprisonment, one for nine months in Jersey and the other for six months in Guernsey. It should be added that the German officers appointed to be Mrs Sherbrooke's temporary gaolers carried out their duties with tact and consideration. The practical joke had given the German authorities a great deal of trouble. Every night for some considerable time before Mrs Sherbrooke's detention they attempted to catch her and the non-existent British agents in the very act of communicating with each other. During these nights it was not British agents but German police who hid in the bushes in her garden. It was natural that they should resent being put in a ridiculous position by others.

A great lump rose in my throat as we steamed out of that most unlikely of unlikely military garrisons. Part of that lump remains and is ever likely to remain.

We arrived in Bordon Camp on one of the most bitterly cold nights I can recall, the iced-up roads making our march from the station to our new barracks literally a foot-slogging exercise.

BORDON CAMP

The few memories I retain of Bordon Camp are unhappy ones.

I recall the year 1924 when a particularly callous murder was committed. The Bordon branch of Lloyds Bank was a wooden red-tiled hut, set back a few yards from the London-Portsmouth road and partially surrounded by pine trees. The manager, a Mr W.E. Hall, was found shot through the head, his murderer getting away with a little over a thousand pounds. Within days of the murder, a Lance-Corporal Abraham Goldenberg, whose regiment was stationed in Bordon, was arrested and charged with the crime.

The murder was a premeditated affair in that Goldenberg, in his ultimate confession, admitted to 'politely borrowing' a revolver from a Major Lewis when he was out of his quarters and 'borrowing five rounds' from the machine-gun store. His motive, so he said, was to obtain money so that he could marry. One of the more unsavoury aspects of the case was Goldenberg's attempt to implicate another man named Meredith, who, Goldenberg alleged, had fired the shots whilst he (Goldenberg) was keeping watch outside the bank. Goldenberg was found guilty and following his counsel's unsuccessful plea of insanity, was hanged at Winchester Gaol.

A few years after this, while I was still in the artillery band, I was invited to play some harp solos in a concert which was to be staged in the Bordon Garrison Theatre. The stipulated dress for male performers was dinner jacket, which in itself was something of an incongruity for an all-soldier audience. One section of the audience clearly did not appreciate the beauties of *Believe me if all those endearing young charms* (all ill-advised choice on my part) and let me know in true barrack-room fashion just what they thought of my harp and me to the point that I was compelled to discontinue playing.

Samuel Butler, who came to this country (New Zealand) in 1859 and settled in Canterbury, once complained: 'It does not do to speak about John Sebastian Bach's fugues to "rowdy-hatted" sheepmen of Canterbury.' The theory I hold is that these same rowdy-hats repatriated themselves and were the progenitors to a man of my Bordon Camp audience.

And shortly before my regiment was due to move to Bordon, the wife of a bandmaster friend of mine who was stationed there had a most unpleasant and frightening experience. She received through the post a letter from an anonymous writer who alleged he had seen her in the embraces of another man. The writer invited her to meet him after dark in a lonely nearby wood. She drove to the spot, accompanied by her husband, who was crouched in the rear of the car and armed with a heavy spanner. It was as well for all concerned that the would-be blackmailer failed to turn up, for clearly there could have been yet another Bordon Camp murder.

It is hardly surprising therefore that I should have developed a dislike of the place even before we moved there.

Had War Office tried its worst, it could hardly have chosen a station which was further removed aesthetically from the one we had just left. Although some permanent barracks in brick were beginning to be put up, our own lines named Martinique Barracks consisted of row upon row of comfortless wooden huts. Not far removed from the soldiers' quarters were the 'other ranks' married quarters which had been named by some person with a misguided sense of humour after famous English hunts, such as Quorn, Belvoir and so on.

From the common soldier's point of view, the place was dead, for apart from the garrison theatre and a newly-opened garrison cinema, there was nothing — not even a soldiers' home.

One of the finest addresses for the defence at any army court martial was given, I was told, in Bordon itself, when the young defending officer, in making his plea for mitigation, brought home to the court in vivid fashion what a hell-hole of a station Bordon Camp really was. He pointed out that unlike his fellow officers who could run up to 'town' in their cars, the soldier who was stationed in Bordon had every provocation for committing so-called crime; and while admitting that such behaviour could not be condoned, he made the plea that the court take into consideration the frustrating conditions under which the Bordon-stationed soldier lived.

Even so, being stationed in Bordon had its compensations. One of these was that we were living in the very heart of some of the most charming country in southern England, with Gilbert White's Selbourne a mere five or so miles away. And with tennis and squash no longer readily available, I joined Blackmoor Golf Club, one of the most picturesque courses, surely, in the county. (How I came to be admitted to membership still has me baffled, for it was stuffed with army officers and other formidable-looking gentlemen.)

Another compensation lay in the fact that stationed directly opposite us was the Duke of Wellington's Regiment, whose bandmaster, Frank Ashton-Jones ('Jonah') had been in the same War Office class at Kneller Hall as myself, and who was, without doubt, the finest musician of the lot of us. Why he ever took to joining the army remained a mystery. All he would tell us was that one day found him singing as a choral scholar in Winchester Cathedral, and the next scrubbing tables and forms in the barracks of some wild Scottish regiment.

Because of the amazing range of his voice (which even the great castrato Farinelli might have envied), his services had been in constant demand for our Kneller Hall smoking concerts.

He was the only honest 'con' man I have ever met. We named him 'La Gazza ladra' (The Thieving Magpie) for no student's pens, pencils, rubbers, manuscript paper, hair-cream, soap, girl friends, batons, or anything or everything, were considered sacrosanct in his eyes. But we all loved him for his vagaries.

Jonah was forever in deep financial difficulties. While at Kneller Hall he solved his problem by taking rather more than full advantage of one of Messrs Samuel Brothers's (of St.Paul's Churchyard E.C.) special 'sprat to catch a whale' customer services, which encouraged students to obtain their goods 'on tick'. And so periodically Jonah would emerge from Samuel Bros. with yet another tailor-made suit — which he would promptly pawn.

Once he had left Kneller Hall, his increased rate of pay notwithstanding, he found to his personal discomfiture, that the deadly combination of being stationed in Malta, running a flash car and a none-too-cheap new wife, and with no benevolent Samuel Bros. in the background, did rather less than nothing to help him straighten out his by now dire financial position.

And so he devised a seemingly fool-proof system of paying his debts, into whose mysteries I myself became not altogether unwillingly initiated; for so basically honest were Jonah's principles.

"Oh! Boyo," he opened up to me, at the same time pressing into my hand a post-dated cheque for £10. "Could you let me have a cheque straightway for £10?"

It so turned out that I was merely one of an extensive clientele, whose members ranged from the firm of Boosey and Hawkes, all bachelor and widower bandmasters within a 30-mile radius, his mother-in-law's grocer at Eastleigh, to the local garage proprietor. When one of his post-dated cheques became due for payment, he would honour it simply by borrowing (and straightway banking) a like amount from another of his clients, who would be handed a post-dated cheque in exchange. Thus was the wolf kept at bay.

And then one day the inevitable happened: the Bordon bubble burst when a cheque (a sizeable one apparently) bounced. Jonah received a rip-snorter of a letter from his bank manager informing him that the thousands of pounds which had passed through his account notwithstanding, he might consider taking his worthless business elsewhere.

At the time my regiment was under canvas near the charming village of Thursley. Peggy had motored over from Bordon with a picnic tea which the three of us settled down to enjoy under one of Tilford Green's shady trees. What should have been a delightful episode turned out a miserable flop. Jonah spent the whole afternoon deeply engrossed in his most recent bank statement, attempting to discover just what had gone wrong with the 'system'. He finally blurted out the one and only comment that was to pass his lips — "Boosey and Hawkes might at least have had the bloody decency to warn a bloke that they were going to bank a day earlier than usual."

Some few weeks after our arrival in Bordon, I sat the psm examination. For some months past I had been stuffing my head with a lot of useless information (with not enough of it as it turned out) in preparation for the dreaded instrumentation paper.

We were seven candidates in all, of whom three had been students when I was a pupil at Kneller Hall. One could sense the tense atmosphere as each of the papers was handed out; for the future direction of our respective careers in the army rested upon the outcome of this examination. A pass would mean almost certain advancement, either to a 'minor' staff band, or a 'major' staff band, whose director of music held commissioned rank. Either way, it would mean a permanent 'home' station, with the odds of eight to two on in the cases of commissioned directors of music*, of its being in the London district. With a directorship of music would go also a substantial increase in pay allowances and pension, and should one's band be stationed within 10 miles of Charing Cross Station, a substantial 'London allowance' in the bargain. A fail would mean soldiering on in the same warrant officer rank, moving stations every three years, and (in view of a new regulation) the virtual certainty of 'clicking' a tour of duty abroad, with its attendant problem of educating one's children.

As for my own reaction, I can only say that I felt doubly tense, for having recently completed my university degree, a fail either in harmony or aural would have been humiliating in the extreme.

It did not help matters when Adkins strode angrily into the room while the aural examination was in progress and rebuked the student who was dictating the tests from the piano for his allegedly making things too easy for us. The reason for this inexcusable behaviour soon became apparent. On that same morning he had received news that judgment in a court case in which he was suing a well-known gramophone company for alleged breach of copyright had gone against him. I believe the costs set him back by some thousands of pounds.

There was one aspect of the examination at least which inspired confidence in candidates — that the examining board included Sir Adrian Boult, Sir George Dyson (who was then Principal of the Royal College of Music), and the Director of Music of the Grenadier Guards, Lieut.-Colonel George Miller. The two other examiners were Adkins himself and the commandant, Colonel R.H.R. Parminter DSO, MC.

During my viva voce examination, Sir George Dyson sketched out these four notes on his blotting pad —

and proceeded to ask:

---

* There were then 10 Directors of Music — the Brigade of Foot Guards (5), the Household Cavalry (2), the D. of M. Kneller Hall, the Band of the Royal Engineers, and from the musician's viewpoint the most desirable of all, the Royal Artillery (Woolwich) Band, which in those days boasted an orchestra and a military band of over 100 members. As a boy I attended the annual concerts given by the orchestra in the old Queen's Hall.

"Of what famous movement is this the first subject?"

A: "Mozart, Symphony No.41 in C ('Jupiter')."

Q: "Who wrote four symphonies in the keys of which the above notes are the tonics and in the same order?"

A: "Brahms, 1 in C minor, 2 in D, 3 in F, and 4 in E minor."

Q: "Who wrote four symphonies in the four keys a tone lower than the above?"

A: "Schumann, No.1 (the 'Spring') in B flat, 2 in C, 3 in E flat (the 'Rhenish') and 4 in D minor."

."Very good." commented Sir George. "How did you come to know all that?"

Somewhat naively I suppose I admitted coming across the same question when working through a Durham Doctor in Music examination paper.

"Did you now?" chuckled Sir George. And then, rather proudly, "I was the examiner who set that question."* (A curious question to set, I thought, in a D.Mus.paper.)

The commandant next had a go at me. One of his questions was: "Let us suppose you were playing at some seaside town and one of your bandsmen fell off the platform and broke his leg. What would you do about it?"

I suggested first making the man as comfortable as possible, asking whether there were a doctor in the audience, and calling an ambulance. None of these was the answer the commandant was looking for.

"You would first find out where was the nearest military hospital, to save putting the Government to unnecessary expense."

And next I came to facing Adko across the examination table. From the very outset it resembled far more closely a cat-and-mouse act rather than a music examination.

Cat: "I want you to state what in your opinion is the ideal instrumentation for an eight-piece dance band."

Mouse: "One alto saxophone, one tenor saxophone . . . "

Cat: "Yes?"

Mouse: "er . . . one trumpet, one violin, one string bass, piano and drums."

Cat: "And?"

Mouse: (quizzically): "And, sir?"

Cat: "Yor've only named seven — I asked for eight."

* Oh! had I but then known that the final movement of Symphony No.13 in D by Haydn opens with precisely this same four-note pattern.

Mouse: (panicking) "And another alto saxophone . . . no, . . . no, sir . . .
        make it a trombone."
Cat: "Make up your buddy mind; what is it to be — another buddy
        saxophone or a trombone?"
Mouse: (I forget which of the two I opted for; but at the time I could
        not but help thinking to myself what an unfair question it was,
        and how loaded it was in the examiner's favour; for it had neither
        a 'right' nor a 'wrong' answer. No different in fact from examining
        a chess player and asking him to state the ideal opening moves
        in a game of chess.)
Cat: (who in the meantime tosses mouse up in the air with his right
        paw and catches him as he comes down in his left, but not before
        making a feint as though to drop him altogether.) "Now, I want
        you to tell me everything you know about the cornett — not the
        military band cornet, but the one spelt C-O-R-N-E-T-T."
Mouse: Gives correct technical description, fills in some historical details,
        and goes on to enlarge: "There were three sizes in use, the small
        treble cornett, the ordinary cornett and the great cornett."
Cat: "Very good! Nice to know that some bugger has been doing his
        homework."
Mouse: (emboldened by his success and knowing Adko for the bluffer that
        he was), enlarges by giving the respective compasses of the said
        small treble cornett, the ordinary cornett and the great cornett.
Cat: (making further notes behind his cupped paw) "Quite right." My
        bluffing (for I had made up the compasses as I went along) had
        paid off handsomely.

But the greatest farce of all, which would have been hilariously funny
had not men's careers been involved, was the instrumentation paper, which
Adko himself had set.

In the allotted space of three hours candidates were expected to:

(i)   transcribe an extract from a military band arrangement of Bach's
       Organ *Fantasy and Fugue* for the 'Grand Organ as a solo in the true
       Bach style'.

(ii)   make a conductor's score of a goodly portion of Variation VII, *The
       Adventure of the magic horse* from Strauss's *Don Quixote*, and 'score
       same for a military band of 25 performers' (the music copying involved
       in itself being out of all proportion to the time allotted for the complete
       three-hour examination).

(iii) score the *Largo* from Beethoven's *Piano Sonata Op.106* for a military
       band of 25 performers, and

(iv) answer a group of 'side-questions' which among others required candidates to state what they knew of the 'seven cylinder' trombone, to explain its use and to state the reason why it was not used in the military band; and to 'Give the pitch of the ancient cymbals, and explain what is meant by their "classical" use.'

These questions would have been fair enough had they been put to an aspirant for the presidency of the Galpin Society, or to the tv quiz candidate who was coming perilously close to winning a commercial soap firm's prize of an XJS model Jaguar car plus a round-the-world all-expenses-paid trip; but to include them in a supposedly serious music examination?

Immediately after sitting this paper, one candidate had the temerity to ask Adko (in a pupil-master sort of approach) how he thought the harp glissando in *Don Quixote* should have been scored. "A roll on the buddy cymbal, boy — a roll on the buddy cymbal."

In tossing off this solution it did not occur to Adko that the military band's one allowable percussionist would already have had rather more than enough on his two hands in his rolling on the tympani and in his being required at the same time to keep the indispensable wind machine going at full blast.

Equally absurd questions continued to be put to psm candidates after Adko had been more or less compulsorily retired from the army. I recall for example seeing Bandmaster Basil Brown emerge from his psm viva voce examination wearing a face blacker even than the proverbial thunder. He had been asked by the military examiner, Captain Dave Jones of the Royal Engineers, to state what he knew about the Tromba Marina.

The follow-up to this question was quite amusing. News of it reached the ears of co-examiner, Sir George Dyson. During the psm examiners' meeting which took place at the Royal College of Music, Sir George took Dave Jones gently by the arm (so it was related to me by the then Kneller Hall commandant, Major A.T.B. Bignold-de Cologan) and led him up to one of the college's show-cases of ancient instruments. "And this, Captain Jones," he said sweetly, "is a Tromba Marina."

I recall a similar case some few years ago when invited to sit on a panel which was to examine a member of the New Zealand Royal Marines Band, who was seeking promotion to commissioned rank.

"Now, what is a Chest of Viols?" asked the Marines' examiner of the candidate.

"Sorry, sir, I don't know."

"You don't know?" came the shocked reply. "I consider it most frightfully important that you should know what a Chest of Viols is."

The setting of this 'clever' type of question is of course nothing more than a pathetic attempt on the part of the military examiner to impress his civilian counterpart. It all stems from the sense of inferiority which dogs (often quite needlessly) the services' musician — myself at one time not excluded.

My result was read out to me by our new commanding officer, Lieut.-Colonel Gamble — passes in all subjects except instrumentation.

I could sense (rightly or wrongly) that my fail in instrumentation did not entirely please the colonel; for although I had not exactly tarnished it, neither had I enhanced the illustrious name of the Sherwood Foresters.

Postscript on the Ancient Cymbals:

Cecil Forsyth in his *Orchestration* tells us,

> These were in common use by the ancient Egyptians, Greeks and Romans. Specimens of Egyptian cymbals are still in existence. They were made either of brass or of mixed brass and silver, and varied in diameter from 5½ to 7 inches. There are several sets of Greek cymbals in the British Museum. One sweet little pair, 3½ inches in diameter, is complete with its tiny chains and rings. It gives out a clear F# in alt.
>
> Berlioz reintroduced these small ancient cymbals in *Les Troyens*. In doing so he showed his sound antiquarian taste by having them tuned to a definite pitch . . . their effect is charming, but they are better when used in the classical manner, that is to say, played in rhythm by a large number of dancers, than when employed singly in the orchestra.

My readers will now see for themselves why it is so frightfully important for a military bandmaster to know the pitch of the ancient cymbals and to know what is meant by their 'classical use'.

With the psm examination mostly behind me, I settled down to the rather more satisfying work of studying for the Doctorate in Music.

As I have already explained, each infantry regiment consisted of two battalions, a 'home' and an 'abroad' battalion, so that rarely, if ever, the 'twain did meet'.

The meeting of the two Sherwood Foresters battalions was thus an historic occasion.

It so happened that our 1st Battalion had completed its three-year tour of duty in Jamaica and Bermuda, and was on its way to the Middle East. It was accorded the almost unprecedented privilege of being permitted to break its journey at Southampton in order to join its sister battalion in a regimental reunion. Naturally enough, we were to act as host battalion.

One of the festivities was a reunion of members of the regiment's *Old Comrades Association* — ex-servicemen who had maintained their links with the regiment. One of these old comrades, a real 'old sweat' if ever there was one, persisted in claiming that I had served with him in the famous Bantam Division* of World War I. I tried but without success to convince him that at the time of the Bantam Division's existence, I could scarcely have been hatched, let alone have become one of its member cocks.

"But surely you remember old Topper Brown," he persisted, "'e must have been even shorter than you is."

"Topper Brown?"

"Yeah, Topper Brown. 'e was the bloke wot reckoned all us Bantams suffered from Duck's Disease."

"Duck's Disease?"

"Yeah, Duck's Disease — 'e called the Bantams the Duck's Disease Brigade, cos 'e reckoned that all our arses were too near the ground. Now d'yer remember 'im?"

Throughout the remainder of the day he continued to embarrass me with, "Wotcher, me ol' bantam cock, ow's yer fight? Comin' over to the mess?"

Clearly, he had no respect either for rank, or for a university graduate — none whatever; the most outrageous case of applied irreverence in fact that I have ever experienced.

The reunion also brought George Smith and myself together again. Although he had made a number of gloomy, but uncannily accurate, predictions as to England's ultimate fate, not even he could foresee the day when the Bermuda which he had just left (and loved) would be traded in for 50 obsolete World War I destroyers of the United States Navy.

The climax to our Sergeants' Mess festivities was to be a dinner, at which we were to play host to our sister battalion's Sergeants' Mess members.

"Nothing by way of expense will be spared," explained our regimental sergeant-major, "in going towards making this a memorable occasion." This prompted my suggestion that an orchestra to provide music during dinner was a must. It put a lucrative engagement in the way of my old Band of the Royal Artillery.

---

* The formation of the Bantam Division during the 1914-18 War was the idea of Lord Kitchener who had been impressed by the number of men who were below the standard of military height. 'They were all wee chaps, standing no more than 5 feet 1 inch above their boots, and, for the most part, less than that.' (Quoted from *The Great World War*, ed.Frank A. Mumby, London, 1917, Vol.VI, p.46.)

Next, where to dine? This clearly had to be Farnham's exclusive old stage coach inn, The Bush Hotel, which at the time was managed by a gentleman-hotelier type. At our invitation he came to Bordon bringing with him some one or another club's menu, which he thought might be of some help to us in planning our own dinner. Apart from the club's motto (which was in Latin) the specimen menu was in French, which neither my warrant officer colleague nor myself pretended to understand. (At the same time I did wish that he would spare me the embarrassment of his phonetic cracks at certain of the courses' more unpronounceable names.)

With this part of it settled, the hotelier returned to discuss the format of the menu card itself. Pointing to the club's motto he asked: "Any ideas on this sort of thing?" My regimental sergeant-major colleague immediately came across with: "I don't know how you feel, Bandmaster, but my feeling is that we would have done ourselves well enough already; no, I don't think we'll have a further course, thanks all the same."

One of the year's events I dreaded most was the Aldershot Tattoo. I recall once having to search out my band president, Captain Hugo Meynell (incidentally one of the most charming men I have ever met) from among the vast concourse of the tattoo's performers. Although I was successful ultimately in tracking him down, recognition was made no easier on account of his being attired in 17th century period costume, which was set off by an enormous plumed hat.

I found it all very thought-provoking, even at this late hour, June 1939, with Austria annexed and Czechoslovakia totally subjugated, and with an outbreak of war with Hitler's Germany seemingly inevitable, that here was the British Army playing its annual summer's game of 'once-upon-a-time'. And as though cocking a snook at Hitler's tirades and bloodcurdling threats, the massed bands of the Aldershot Tattoo changed the final exit march from whatever it was to *Who's Afraid of the Big Bad Wolf.*

With the signing in the August of that year of the Russo-German pact of mutual non-aggression (which was to have run for 10 years) we all sensed that war was close at hand — imminent in fact. Even so, apart from the odd lecture from one of our officers on what action we should take in the event of an air-raid warning, and apart from our own particular married quarter being declared a command post (which was evidenced by the addition of a couple of red fire buckets filled with sand), life went along in the same unruffled, complacent manner. Late though the hour was, it was still not considered too late, apparently, by one commercial advertiser, who in all seriousness asked, "Why not have your dog dyed to match the colour of your favourite dress?"

In common with millions of others we listened to Neville Chamberlain's broadcast to the people of Britain which told that as from 11 am on that morning of Sunday, 3 September, a state of war existed between Britain and Germany.

As in World War I, all army bandsmen automatically assumed the role of battalion stretcher-bearers, and bandmasters together with band-boys were posted to their respective regimental depots.

Peggy and I packed what few sticks of furniture we had, and sent them down to Winchester, where Peggy's mother was now living.

Discounting our initial removal from Guernsey, this next move was to prove itself as being the first of a score or so changes of residence we were to make before settling finally in a permanent home of our own — in New Zealand.

I drove Peggy and David down to Winchester, and a day or so later left Bordon for our regimental depot in Derby.

NORMANTON BARRACKS, DERBY

With my bandsmen now serving in France, there was all too little for me to do at the regimental depot, my only official duty being one of instructing a mere handful of band-boys. I was not sorry, therefore, to fall in with the suggestion that I assume the role of the Depot's PAD (Passive Air Defence) Officer. I took over this duty from Lieutenant 'Staggers' Stephens, whose father, by an odd coincidence, happened to be chaplain to the Foundling Hospital*. I talked to Lieutenant Stephens about my doctoral studies; whether, with a war now on, I should continue or abandon them 'for the duration'. His reply was unequivocal and encouraging. "What difference either way will it make to the conduct of the war whether or not you continue studying? Of course you must go on." And so go on I did.

As PAD Officer I was responsible (among other duties) for taking what action I deemed necessary to minimise the effects of incendiary-bomb attacks. I was given a free hand to enter all barrack buildings' lofts and have the local Royal Engineers knock holes into dividing walls in order to create freedom of access.

In my zeal for my new job, I reprimanded the manager of the local tannery for his fobbing off on to us a whole consignment of leaky wooden

* The Reverend E.C. Stephens, Chaplain 1935-1946.

casks, which were to form part of our primitive fire-fighting equipment. I was put right on this by a faintly-amused factory foreman, who explained that I must develop patience; for in all good time the wood would swell.

A further responsibility was to provide slit trenches in sufficient number to accommodate the whole of the depot's personnel. Once again I met with frustration, for the heavy rains and snowfalls which attended the 1939-40 winter led to the trenches becoming first flooded, and finally frozen over. This in turn led to a written complaint laid against me by my own band-boys — 'that when we were suffering from coughs, colds and sore throats, Bandmaster Nalden did make us remove ice and snow from the slit trenches'. Zealous though I was, it seemed that whatever course of action I took, I simply could not assist the war effort.

Early on, the commanding officer, Lieutenant-Colonel Fenn, decided to inspect the depot's PAD arrangements, and accompanied by 'Staggers' Stephens, Lieutenant Walton (the gas officer) and myself, he decided first to inspect the wooden hut which had been converted into a first-aid centre. A small porch, hung with a heavy anti-gas curtain, had been built on to the existing building, with its entrance set at right-angles to the door of the hut itself.

"Are you all quite satisfied that a stretcher could negotiate this angle?" enquired Colonel Fenn of us.

"Quite sure, sir," came our confident reply.

"Then we'll try it out," suggested the Colonel.

A stretcher was produced, and sure enough we were able to negotiate the angle, always provided that the stretcher was tilted sideways at an angle of something like 180° and the casualty made to walk. One of our number muttered something about the possibility of strapping casualties on to the stretcher — a suggestion which was received by the colonel with a somewhat lesser degree of enthusiasm than that in which, in all good faith, it had been proffered.

Such was the state of Britain's preparedness at the outbreak of war.

Towards the end of the inspection tour, Colonel Fenn summarised: "We have seen the gas de-contamination centre, which I understand is for both men and women?"

"Right, sir."

"And we have seen both the men's and women's first aid posts."

"Yes, sir."

"What I now want to know is, what arrangements have been made for casualties who are both gassed and wounded?"

We guided him to a room which had been especially equipped for that purpose.

"Now," he asked, "who is to use this, men or women?"

"Both men and women, sir."

"Both men and women? We simply cannot have men and women using the same room — surely not?"

We respected our commanding officer for the highly-principled man we knew him to be; but was this not taking matters rather too far? A man who is both gassed and wounded finding himself lying next to a woman who also is both gassed and wounded and . . . ? Oh! No! Surely not that? But the colonel was adamant. He ordered the equipping of a second gassed-and-wounded centre, thus satisfying himself as to the decorousness of the two gassed-wounded sexes.

Colonel Fenn must then have been somewhere in his 50s. "Dickens," he once confided in me, "should not be read until one is reasonably well on in life; that is the time really to appreciate him."

He was a regular soldier of the old school, and one who held on grimly in the old Duke of Cambridge manner to service traditions in general and regimental traditions in particular. I happened one day to be in his office when he was discussing with adjutant Captain Nevitt the army dentist's application to be quartered in the officers' mess. "We extend this as a courtesy to the medical officer, but never to a dentist!" Such was the Regular Army's rigid caste system.

On the eve of the ATS* being quartered in Normanton Barracks, Colonel Fenn called a special parade. Adopting a Churchillian 'Singapore has fallen' tone of voice, he informed the parade that women were to share our barracks, adding, "And remember this: I look to all of you, every one of you, to conduct yourselves like gentlemen."

Now, throughout the course of my story, never wittingly have I taken what is conveniently termed 'author's licence'.

Consider the following story from Malcolm Tillis's *Chords and Discords* (1960):

> My last nine months in the Army . . . were spent as a member of the R.A. Portsmouth Band . . . I knew that all the members of Service bands were regulars, but this did not stop me from asking the Band Master . . . if he was short of a string player. He said he was always short of string players, ordered me to bring my instrument at the double, and, without any further preliminaries, commanded me to play on the spot . . . I was only required for the string pieces: these included Ivor Novello selections and, the piece de resistance, the Ballet Music from *Faust*.

* Auxiliary Territorial Service — The women's branch of the army.

Now this is an example of what I would term 'author's thumping good licence'. And I should know; for I happened to be Tillis's allegedly Ballet Music *Faust* loving, 'execute everything at the double', commanding him to 'play on the spot' bandmaster.

So when I tell you that within a week of the ATS contingent's arrival in our barracks a complaint was lodged, not by the women, but by the men, concerning the females' loud and persistent use of language that would shock the sensibilities of the proverbial trooper (whose most ribald volley of oaths by comparison would fall upon the ear like some polished phrase from Jane Austen) — when I tell you this, you will accept it as 'gospel' and not shrug it off with a faintly incredulous smile as an example of 'author's licence'.

Shortly after this incident, I myself managed to run mildly foul of the senior ATS officer, a Mrs Heath-Gracie, who was the wife of the local cathedral organist. It happened like this:

Memo. for PAD Officer
    This girl complains that her gas mask does not fit her, although we
    both agree that there is nothing wrong with the mask itself.
    I request that you take urgent and appropriate action please.
                              (Signed) Lieut. H. Heath-Gracie

Memo. for Lieut. Heath-Gracie
    Ref. to your memo. concerning the gas-mask.
    If, as you say, there is nothing wrong with the mask itself, the only
    course of action I can take is to recommend that the girl's face be
    re-modelled to fit the mask. This would be a pity, for she is a real
    stunner.
                              (Signed) C. Nalden, PAD Officer.

Lieutenant Walton baled me out of this one by assuring Lieutenant Heath-Gracie that this was not intended as a piece of insolence on my part.

One effect of the introduction of military conscription (which in the September of 1939 was extended to all men between the ages of 18 and 41), was the lowering from 26 to 21 the age at which a married man became entitled to draw marriage and child allowances. It was a measure which was the cause of no small degree of dissatisfaction among the 'regulars', who for generations past, had they elected to marry before reaching 26, had drawn nothing beyond their basic pay. It became a common daily occurrence to read this sort of thing in our Depot Part II Orders:
Marriage

Pte Smith to Anne Jones, 20.10.1939.
> Marriage allowance is granted to Pte. Smith w.e. from this date.
Child Allowance
> Pte. Smith is granted children's allowance in respect of the following:

George Smith	born	19.1.1927
Joseph Smith	born	16.6.1928
Alice Smith	born	20.10.1930
Frederick Smith	born	1.12.1936
Maud Smith	born	14.2.1939

The hapless Private Smith had perforce to run this gauntlet of undesirable publicity in order that he qualify for these allowances. 'Intimidated, Governor, intimidated', as Alf Doolittle would say.

Rationing was introduced early. The only member of the depot personnel to escape this was the regimental mascot Derby XV who by the way had travelled up to Derby in our convoy. At a time when men were being limited to one soap coupon per week (or was it one per month?) and when women became obliged to forgo their Friday night shampoo ('Friday night is Amami night', ran the well-known shampoo advertisement), Derby XV, so the ram orderly confided in me, was accounting for a goodly-sized packet of Lux for each of his weekly baths. Derby was later packed off 'for the duration' to Chatsworth, the ancient seat of the Dukes of Devonshire, where, to his delight (the ram's, not the Duke's) he was treated no differently from any other ram, in that his regimentally-imposed state of celibacy became abruptly terminated.

Britain's state of ill-preparedness for war was brought home to us in a minor way in our own depot. When in May 1940 Germany invaded the Low Countries, we were obliged to 'stand to' for one hour after sundown and for one hour before dawn. We had so pitifully few rifles and light automatic weapons that it was found necessary to ferry backwards and forwards each day the weapons that were being used by recruits at the practice rifle range, which was a score or so miles away. This meant that during the daytime the depot was virtually defenceless.

I myself was issued with a revolver, an obsolete model which would take a special type of bullet only. Never before having fired a revolver, I sought some instruction in its use. It was refused on the grounds of a shortage of that particular type of ammunition. "And don't let the Germans take you prisoner armed with that weapon," cautioned Major 'Mouse' Wright cheerfully, "or they'll shoot you out of hand."

"Why's that, sir?" I asked.

"Because it fires dumdum bullets*."

And when I took the band to a Foresters' unit in Buxton Spa, I saw something which would have lowered to minus zero the morale of even the most stout-hearted and optimistic of Englishmen. It was a squad of men being instructed in rifle drill, their 'rifles' consisting either of broom handles or of weaponry on loan from the local museum. (This was shortly after Dunkirk.) "They will at least have mastered their basic rifle drill by the time they come to be issued with the real thing," explained their commanding officer to me.

It was immediately following Dunkirk that a War Office directive called for the reformation of regimental bands, which, as I have already said, were automatically disbanded at the outbreak of war. There can be no doubt as to the wisdom of this move, which was designed as a morale-raiser. For example, I had found rooms for my wife and son in a doctor's house in Rosehill Street. In the February of 1941 the Luftwaffe made an unsuccessful attempt to knock out the important Rolls Royce works. Instead, it dropped a stick of bombs in our own locality, damaging without exception every one of its houses, and completely knocking out No.13.

The civilian population's morale was hardly raised by the steady and persistent fall of snow which followed the raid. Even so, when a company of Sherwood Foresters, headed by its band, made a march through the bomb-stricken areas, the people turned out in full force, their cheering at times beating the band at its own noise-making game.

One bomb which failed to explode buried itself in the grounds of the Arboretum, which was immediately facing the house in which my family was rooming. Everybody in the area was evacuated pending the bomb's defusing. The bomb disposal officer, a cheery captain probably in his mid-30s, took me over to see the brute, but not, I might add, until after it had been defused.

I met this same officer some few months later, and scarcely recognised him as being the same man. In the intervening months he had had one of his young officer assistants blown to bits, and he himself now resembled a man grown pathetically old long before his time. Even so, not a word of complaint about his potentially suicidal job ever escaped his lips. It was shortly after this meeting that I left Derby for good, and I never learnt what became of him. Never since have I ceased to admire both his, and all other bomb disposal personnel's, indomitable bravery.

---

* A kind of soft-nosed bullet that expands on impact and inflicts laceration. Use of the dumdum has been classified as a war crime by a number of international conventions, including the Hague Declaration of 1907. (O.D.)

One good reason why the Germans failed to hit the Rolls Royce works was the effectiveness of the smoke screens which were laid down each month as the moon was about to take on its full circle. This was accomplished by means of thousands of closely-spaced galvanised-iron oil-burning stoves. They burned a mixture of paraffin and crude oil, belching out a constant stream of thick black smoke, whose foul fumes managed to penetrate even the most efficiently sealed-up houses. It must have been sheer hell for sufferers from chest ailments.

To be admitted as a candidate for Durham University's degree of Doctor in Music, a graduate had to be of at least 13 terms' standing from the completion of his bachelor's degree. I fell far short of this requirement, but harbouring that feeling of uncertainty which was the lot of all servicemen, my request to sit the March 1941 examination was granted. I was far from being prepared, and I was failed. That was on the debit side. But on the credit side I had gained some valuable examination-room experience in being required to sit five three-hour papers on consecutive mornings and afternoons. And again on the credit side, when preparing for the examination I came across this:

> Tossing his mane of snows in wildest eddies and tangles,
> Lion-like March cometh in, hoarse, with tempestuous breath,
> Through all the moaning chimneys, and 'thwart all the hollows and
>   angles
> Round the shuddering house, threating of winter and death.
>
> But in my heart I feel the life of the wood and the meadow
> Thrilling the pulses that own kindred with fibres that lift
> Bud and blade to the sunward, within the inscrutable shadow,
> Deep in the oak's chill core, under the gathering drift.
>
> Nay, to earth's life in mine some prescience, or dream, or desire
> (How shall I name it aright?) comes for a moment and goes —
> Rapture of life ineffable, perfect — as if in the brier,
> Leafless there by my door, trembled a sense of a rose.
>
> (William Dean Howells)

I chanced one day to pass Colonel Fenn and find him engaged in an earnest, low-toned conversation with a high-ranking officer whom I had not seen before. It was quite apparent that whatever it was they were discussing was of a most serious nature. It all came out a day or so later when we received into our barracks an ill-assorted body of troops, representing so it seemed every regiment of the British Army. They had come to us direct from Dunkirk.

As a serviceman myself, then of some 18 years' standing, I well remember how deeply moved I was by the pathetic spectacle provided by these men (many of whom clearly were still bewildered) as they formed up in two extended ranks to be issued with the barest necessities of a soldier's kit, such as socks, underclothing, towels and shaving gear. Many of them were without caps and battle-dress blouses, for in common with the 335,000 other troops who managed to reach England, they had either lost or jettisoned their all, barring the clothes they stood up in. There they stood, the dejected remnants of a defeated army.

The depot quartermaster, Major Warmer, made history by dispensing with the customary red-tape which required the soldier to 'sign on the dotted line' for each article of kit issued him. Instead, he simply listened to each individual man's needs, and with a 'that's good enough for me' attitude, saw to it that they were met. Knowing just what these men had so recently been through, it was sound psychology on his part. "We'll answer all those awkward questions later," was his remark to me.

One man who was a music graduate of London University had acquired a painful stammer, which told its own harrowing story. Another, a Sherwood Foresters' sergeant, related to me how he literally bit the dust in his agony of fear as the German Stukas persisted in their relentless dive-bombing attacks. "Under conditions such as those," he blurted out, "we are all the same. Once we began flinging ourselves flat on our guts, there was no longer any such thing as officers, sergeants and privates. We suddenly all became equal; all the same — just plain men — scared men."

Late in the July of 1940, we took in a further contingent of troops which had been evacuated from St.Nazaire. It included some of the survivors from the ill-fated evacuation ship *Lancastria* which was sunk by a stick of four heavy bombs that scored as many direct hits. Colonel F.E. Grigg who acted as ship's adjutant estimated that the total number aboard well exceeded 9000. Of this number no more than 4000 survived what has been described as 'by far the worst disaster ever to befall a British ship'.[1]

One of the survivors was Bandsman Haynes of the Sherwood Foresters, who at the time could have been little more than 18 years old. According to Haynes one of the bombs by a lucky, or unlucky, fluke (depending, naturally, upon whose side you were on) whistled clean down the ship's funnel. But this was not destined to be the end of the survivors' troubles; for as Haynes went on to tell me, they then found themselves floating targets for enemy machine gunners. Being a strong swimmer, Haynes managed to keep afloat until picked up by another of our boats. Our Bandsman Johnson, a non-swimmer, failed to make it.

It was a joy for me to meet once again my Bordon-days' band president, Captain Meynell, who had fared rather better than most by his managing to hang on to his 'British Warm' (overcoat).

We spent our Christmas 1941 leave in Winchester. Shortly before I was due to return to Derby, I received a telephone call from Churchill House, North Camp, Aldershot, which was the wartime home of the Royal Military School of Music (Kneller Hall itself having been requisitioned by War Office 'for the duration').

My caller was Student Charlie Adams, who was Lt. Colonel-Commandant Adkins's 'cat'. Adko was now commandant and director of music rolled into one. Adams explained that Adko wished me to relinquish my band and return to the school as harmony and aural teacher. He further explained that there would be a small drop in my extra-duty pay, which Adko suggested I should regard simply as a casting of my bread upon the waters. The biggest bait, however, was the concern expressed by Adko about my doctoral studies. "Tell him," he instructed Adams, "that he will have ample time for study."

The 'mighty colossus' then proceeded to reveal his hand. Charlie Adams continued: "When you return to Derby you will be telephoned by a Major Inglis-Jones of War Office. He will offer you the Royal Artillery (Salisbury Plain) band. The commandant says you are to turn it down, no matter how heavy the pressure."

Although I was to be given time to 'think about it', I gave Adams my answer straightway — that I would relinquish my band and return forthwith to the school; for much as I disliked and feared even the thought of re-entering that atmosphere all over again, to have refused would have been tantamount to committing promotional suicide. I would have been stuck on Salisbury Plain for the remainder of my days — such was Adko's power and hold over the British Army bandmaster. And I recalled his words to me on the subject of 'his' psm Diploma: "I do not regard a university degree in itself as a sufficient qualification for promotion — you must also have 'my' psm."

Sure enough, immediately upon my return to Derby, I received a call from Major Inglis-Jones offering me the Royal Artillery Band. As instructed, I turned the offer down.

"I know that Colonel Adkins would like to have you with him at Churchill House," the Major persisted, "but this is an opportunity which I don't think you can afford to let pass."

I felt bound to refuse a second time.

"You realise, don't you, Nalden, that in turning this down you might eventually find yourself falling between two stools" — which is precisely what I was to do.

But in the circumstances I could hardly expect to convince a War Office official that I was acting under duress; that I was being morally blackmailed. Neither could I tell him that the option to my re-entering an atmosphere which I had come to dislike and distrust, was for me to live out the rest of my soldiering days in a place which had the reputation of being one of the most desolate and God-forsaken of all army camps; for by that time the band had been moved from Salisbury Plain to Larkhill Camp, which literally is off the (AA) map. With Larkhill being so close to Stonehenge I would of course have had opportunity to attend its annual Druidic Midsummer Day ritual, but I could not bring myself to regard that exciting prospect even as sufficient compensation against spending a lifetime in Larkhill Camp.

I recall a story involving a Mr Simpson, a one-time Bandmaster of the Royal Artillery (Salisbury Plain) Band, who at the time of this incident was close to retiring age. It appears that he was reprimanded by a young and raw artillery subaltern for saluting in a lethargic manner. "All I can say, sir," Simpson replied, "is that my saluting has satisfied generals and even field marshals."

And so it came time for me to say farewell to Normanton Barracks. I was sorry in some respects to be leaving, but not in others. It was only a few weeks before all this happened that I had managed to re-settle my family in capacious St.Barnabas Vicarage, whose incumbent, the Reverend Thornton, we knew from our Guernsey years. I recall Mr Thornton, a bachelor, proudly showing us a handsome set of aluminium kitchenware which he had recently purchased. Shortly afterwards he sacrificed the whole lot (but not before bashing it out of any recognisable shape) in response to an urgent appeal for aluminium by our aircraft industry. It was with more than a tinge of regret that we left the peace of the vicarage.

On the other hand, sadly, we had lost Colonel Fenn. His successor was an entirely different kettle of fish. His opening snarl to me was: "I'll give you until tomorrow morning to get your car out of my barracks." It was no easy snarl to comply with, for apart from a small ration to accommodate the elderly and infirm churchgoer, petrol supplies for the private motorist by then had ceased; and rightly so.

And then there was this further and quite unexpected reason for my eagerly anticipating a speedy departure. The barracks's NAAFI grocery store had been burgled by a group of my bandsmen. My Band Sergeant Dobson inadvertently stumbled across the stolen goods and dutifully had informed me of it. I found myself giving evidence therefore against the bandsmen culprits. Shortly after this had happened, Dobson tipped me off in his habitual mournful tone of voice about a conversation he had overheard. "I heard one of the men say that should there be an invasion you'll be the first one to go, sir."

"What makes them think that?" I asked.

"Because you're to be shot in the back, sir."

As the Merry Men of Sherwood Forest ever were renowned for their deadly marksmanship, my departure for southern and safer climes came as a not altogether unwelcomed event.

FOOTNOTES TO CHAPTER 22

1. This and the following quotations are taken from Ralph Durand's *Guernsey under German Rule* (London, 1946).
2. Quoted by N. Bonsor, *The North Atlantic Seaway*, Vol.I, p.118.

23: The Royal Military School Of Music
(Churchill House)

"Well, Nalden," opened up Commandant Adkins quoting (as was his wont) from the Scriptures, "he was lost and is found" — a singularly inappropriate observation I thought; but I could hardly tell him so.

"And so you managed to put it across Jingles?" (Major Inglis-Jones.)

"Yes, sir."

"Yes, he got on to me about it. Said he had never before heard the like of it — a buddy bandmaster having the nerve to turn down a staff band appointment. But what I said to him was: 'Far better be a curate at Lambeth Palace than a vicar of some buddy remote country parish.' I was not slow to grasp the point of his analogy, which like many another of his quips was witty up to a point, but singularly inapt; for not even the most abject of sycophants would openly have flattered Adko by likening him in any way to the Primate of Canterbury. Neither was I slow to grasp its ominous inference.

He then went on to discuss my extra-duty pay, which turned out to be a tenner less than the figure quoted me over the telephone by Charlie Adams.

There then emerged the real reason for his pulling me back to Churchill House. "It isn't so much to teach the students" he explained, "as to help me in here. In other words, you may consider yourself from now on as general factotum to the great Pooh-Bah himself."

"Now," he went on, "your first job is to learn to forge my signature — and don't forget to use green ink."* This was the most outlandish order

---

* Another of my somewhat more unusual duties was to open and read Adko's mail to him while he lay, full-length, Roman fashion, in his bath. From my own personal viewpoint I can only lament that the bubble bath had yet to be invented.

by far, surely, that I or any other soldier, past or present, had ever been given. The idea behind the order was that I sign the odd letter or two in his absence. I sometimes found myself actually composing personal letters on his behalf, such as the one to the adoring female who was sending him regular and generously-filled food parcels from Canada.

"Now go down to the library, Nalden, and when you have given it the once over, come back and tell me what you think of it." I thought I detected a hint of smug satisfaction in his voice.

The library was given pride of place located as it was in an imposing room on the left of the entrance hall, and clearly designed to catch the eye of the Churchill House visitor. I could make neither head nor tail of the shelving system, which appeared to have nothing consistent about it whatever. A harmony book might have as its next-door neighbours a history of music and *Proceedings of the Musical Association*, which in turn might have as their respective next-door neighbours a copy of Adkins's *Treatise on the Military Band* and Percy Buck's *Acoustics for Musicians*.

It was in desperation that I sought out the librarian who was a student. The explanation was an exceedingly simple one, and one which I should have rumbled straightway. Adko had instructed the librarian to arrange the books in their respective size order, but in reverse of the normal army parade ground system, so that the tallest books were on the left and the shortest on the right.

After mastering Adko's signature, my next task was to amend the school's copy of *King's Rules and Regulations*, a job which normally would be given to the least intelligent of a regimental orderly room's clerical staff. A sudden and unexpected visit by Adko to the room in which I was working found me not pasting in amendments but reading some book or other on music. I had been caught red-handed.

I felt bound to state my case and remind him of his promise to allow me ample time for study. As matters then stood I was in far worse plight than I had been back in Derby, which was bad enough; for with one minor modification, the hours of work at Churchill House were exactly as they had been at Kneller Hall. The sole modification was that afternoons were no longer given over to compulsory sport. In my own case I was expected to go on working during the afternoons at this sort of thing. I went on to tell him that I had entered my name for the March Doctor in Music examination.

I received but scant sympathy.

"What do you do after evening classes?" he asked (these still being held nightly from 7.30-8.30).

"I study, sir."

"Yes, I realise that — but until what hour?"

"About 11 o'clock, sir."

"And what do you do after that?"

"I go to bed, sir."

"What's wrong with your working until two or three in the morning as I used to do? And let me tell you this, Nalden, my batman had instructions to wake me up with a cup of tea at 7 o'clock, no matter what time I may have gone to bed."

There was just no arguing against this sort of clap-trap.

I left his office a most unhappy man, for I knew there was nothing I could do about it. There was no returning to Derby, for in the meantime my vacancy had been filled by another man. I realised that I had become virtually stateless; that I had fallen between those two stools Inglis-Jones had warned me about.

I should have pulled out of the coming March examination, for even back in Derby my band duties which included a fair amount of touring had left me with relatively little time for concentrated study. And now this.

But I sat the examination and fared little better than in the examination of a year earlier.

Also, I was fast coming to the point of sensing the need for some personal tuition; for I had now been working by the correspondence method and in total isolation, musically speaking, for almost a decade.

So I wrote Dr Wood asking him his advice as to whether I should make a break with Durham and transfer to London. This would mean my having to sit part of the Bachelor of Music degree all over again, but being stationed, as I was, so near London, I was now in a position to avail myself of the opportunity for personal tuition. Dr Wood's reply decided me upon making the change.

The move to Churchill House and the resulting reduced establishment, saw Adkins becoming Commandant and Director of Music rolled into one. For a man of his, shall we say, unorthodox methods, his newly-acquired status created at the same time a potential source of danger — to himself.

His first big mistake was to give lavish dinner parties. At a time when the food served up by a graduate of the Aldershot School of Cookery's famous six-weeks' crash course was considered good enough for the likes of General Montgomery and his Middle East staff, Adko had managed to acquire the services of none other than Private Bertorelli, of London's famed Charlotte Street restaurant of that name. The excellently cooked food for these dinner parties would be served by white-mess-jacketed soldier waiters, with background music provided by a student orchestra.

One honoured guest was the local brigadier, who clearly was not impressed either by the lavishness of the meal or by the display of ostentation which went with it. This sort of thing may have been all very well in times of peace, but hardly appropriate at the very time that Britain had lost Singapore. Adko was decidedly uneasy throughout this particular party and with good reason; for unwittingly he had driven the first nail in his own coffin.

To Adko's credit, however, was the fact that he had every available square inch of Churchill House ground under cultivation, and saw to it personally that the ground was 'double dug', which hardly endeared him to the soldier-gardeners. I would say that the entire mess of about 50 men was kept in vegetables of various sorts for several months of the year — so productive was the kitchen garden.

In 1942 the band was invited to play in Canterbury Cathedral for the enthronement of Dr Temple as the new archbishop. I was given the interesting assignment of selecting and arranging the music and rehearsing our particular part in the ceremony. I took it for granted that I would be included in the Canterbury party. It was to become one of my life's greater disappointments when Adko, pointing to the telephone on his desk, told me that I was the only person he could spare to deal with incoming calls!

Although in the past he had shown me certain kindnesses, it was in cases such as this that nobody, not even his own blood relations (of whom three were army musicians) escaped this hard and selfish side of his nature. He knew only too well what this once-in-a-lifetime experience would have meant to me, but it was this total lack of consideration for the feelings of others that alienated the sympathies of so many people. In this particular instance there were others on the staff, his own personal batman, for example, who were quite capable of answering a telephone, and to whom the cathedral service incidentally would have meant very little, if indeed anything, at all.

The subsequent broadcasting of some of 'his' (Adkins's) fanfares threatened to lead to a further breach of copyright action on his part, which was called off only when the BBC agreed to settle with him out of court. His private view of the BBC was that it resembled a giant octopus. The BBC's private view of him was . . . (let mortal flesh keep silence).

I was given unlimited access to the Churchill House files, which enclosed between their buff covers many of Adkins's personal letters and documents. That olive-green cabinet housed between its four steel walls some of the most pathetic tales of human misery I had yet encountered.

With the coming of spring, Adko decided upon carrying out a series of band inspections, which in peace time were dreaded by most British army bandmasters; for although at one end of the scale an 'outstanding' inspection report could lead to a staff appointment, at its other end it could, and frequently did, lead to a 'bowler hat'.

It fell to my lot to map out the itinerary, which proved itself an exacting and exasperating exercise; for I was totally unversed in the intricacies of the railways' ABC timetable; and with Adko to contend with I was quite fearful of putting a foot wrong. I was also to accompany him on these tours, and participate in the band inspections themselves by questioning bandsmen on musical matters generally.

It was not difficult for me to sense on occasions not only that my presence was not welcomed, but actually resented, particularly so by the odd bandmaster or two who had been students at Kneller Hall when I myself was there as a pupil.

Some bandmasters, taking the short-term view, accepted into their bands civilian musicians who had been called up for war service*. This led to some prickly situations — the civilian musician for example who considered himself a cut above his military counterpart. A case in point was the lovable Bandmaster Joe Needham's Berkshire Regimental Band. I was about to question his flautist, when placing a restraining hand on my shoulder and assuming an accent faintly redolent of that of his deceased French-born wife, Joe cautioned me with, "Non! Non! Non! Nalden. You mustn't question 'im, 'e 'is a BBC arteeste.''

This particular inspection tour took us to such far-removed camps as Reading, Cardiff, Wrexham, Chester, Hounslow, Manchester and so forth. The grossly overcrowded trains (one became accustomed to standing in their corridors throughout long journeys), coupled with the unpredictability of the railways' wartime services, combined to make these tours no picnic. And added to the inspection reports which I was expected to write at the end of each day, I found myself for the first time since my boy's service saddled with the chore of cleaning two sets of uniform — my own and Adko's; for Adko having to clean his own uniform was unthinkable.

In the late summer of that same year Adko decided to inspect bands in the Northern and Scottish Commands. He became uneasily curious when out of the blue Major Inglis-Jones announced his intention of joining us for part of the tour. Ever afraid as he was of top brass and anybody and

---

* A case in point being the Griller Quartet, which joined the Royal Air Force Central Band as a string quartet.

everybody connected with War Office, Adko attempted to comfort himself with the self-propounded theory that 'Jingles', bored with the prospect of sitting at his desk in Whitehall all day, was attaching himself to us by way of a pleasant diversion. I preferred to reason coldly how it would affect me personally — that Inglis-Jones's joining us would mean my now being saddled with three sets of uniform. How very right I was, and how dismayed I became when meeting for the first time this six-foot plus, brass-buttoned, outsize Sam-Browned, size-12-booted guardsman. And as a warrant officer class I, I could hardly hand him a copy of the union rates which operated during my band boy days.

Because of our invariably tight schedule, fitting in the midday meal was sometimes a problem. This was solved by Adko, who instructed me to write in advance and 'invite' bandmasters to pack lunches for our train journeys. As the tour progressed, Inglis-Jones became more and more amused (rather than impressed) with the day-to-day spectacle of bandmasters vying with each other seemingly as to which of their number could outdo the other in the excellence of the fare, and of their accepting wartime rationing not as an obstacle, but as a challenge.

The climax came when one bandmaster, attaching rather more importance to his inspection report than to the physical well-being of his own children apparently, topped off his lunch hamper with a bag of oranges. "But Adko," quipped I-J, "I thought oranges were only for children under five."

Drink on the other hand was something different, for its acquisition presented no problem at all. By pretending that Churchill House was an officers' mess (when in point of fact Adko was the only resident officer there), Adko had been obtaining from the NAAFI monthly supplies of wines and spirits equivalent to about four dozen officers' rations. When preparing for these tours my instructions were to allow for half a bottle of whisky per day, plus an additional bottle for each week we were away, plus a bottle of port per week, plus a syphon or two of soda.

This miniature off-licence, together with a half-dozen *Military Band Journals* (which were taken as sight-reading tests) went into my own personal bag. This was a capacious portmanteau of solid pigskin which was just (but only just) capable of standing up to this grossly unfair demand. By basing a calculation on the fact that a full bottle of whisky weighs a trifle under three pounds, a little simple arithmetic will give the reader a fair idea of my bag's weight at the commencement of a three-weeks' tour.

On one journey, Inglis-Jones made to move my bag from the train to the platform. "Good God, Nalden! Whatever have you got in here?" he asked. "John Brown's body?"

"No, sir. John Haig's body," I replied with some 87 per cent truth.

We duly arrived at our northernmost point. This was Fort George which is some little way beyond Inverness and the then regimental depot of the Seaforth Highlanders. As we approached the forbidding-looking barracks, we were greeted with strains coming from the fort of *Will ye nae come back again.*

"I wonder who that's in aid of," asked Adko quizzically.

"We may be certain of one thing, sir," I replied.

"What's that, Nalden?"

"That it's not in aid of you, sir."

Neither was it. It was the Highlanders farewelling King George VI who had been visiting the near-by scene of an air crash in which his brother, the Duke of Kent, had been killed.

I was required periodically to telephone Churchill House and report any happenings to Adko. Towards the end of the tour, Charlie Adams who was at the Churchill House end of the telephone, sounded decidedly uneasy. It appeared he was being asked some awkward questions relating to paid engagements by a mysterious 'somebody' at War Office. Neither he nor I liked the sound of it one little bit; but knowing Adko's inherent fear of War Office, we decided for the moment that I should not tell him.

The reason behind this mysterious questioning and also for Inglis-Jones's attaching himself to us became evident, painfully so, on the day following our return to Churchill House. Adko was told to report to the local brigadier, the same brigadier who had dined with him some few months earlier. He read out to Adkins a number of charges and peremptorily placed him under close arrest. This was in the September of 1942. The denouement was swift. Less than three months later, Adkins was tried by general court martial on 21 different charges, which in the main arose out of his allegedly improper distribution of engagement monies, his system of imposing fines, obtaining wines and spirits from the NAAFI by false pretences, and his misuse of official railway travel warrants.

For his defence counsel, Adko briefed Mr Henry Maddocks, one of the foremost barristers of the day. He was found 'not guilty' on 18 of the 21 charges, but 'guilty' on the remaining three, which related to his misuse of railway warrants, ordering a sergeant to pay a fine for an offence against discipline, and obtaining wines and spirits from the NAAFI by making a false statement. His sentence was that he be severely reprimanded. His position in the army became untenable when War Office appointed as commandant a man who was junior to himself (Adkins) in rank.

Even though he was not actually dismissed the service, it was a sad ending, nevertheless, to 'a grand career, unique in the history of English and military music' as his defending counsel put it. He had enlisted as a band boy at the age of 14 (this giving him 43 years' army service) and had risen to become the army's most influential musician. It was even more sad that his long and distinguished career should have been abruptly terminated when he was within three years of a normal and honourable retirement.

At one point in his trial, Adko made the point "there was a practice known from generals down to band boys called 'wangling'." Adko might well have flown one rank higher; for it was Field-Marshal Lord Kitchener (under whom Adko had served in the South African War) who instructed his director of military intelligence to "Loot [Khartoum] like blazes"; who let it be known to his director that he wanted "any quantity of marble stairs, marble pavings, iron railings, looking glasses and fittings; doors, windows, furniture of all sorts."[1] But there existed one fundamental difference between the two men — Kitchener was Kitchener and Adkins was Adkins — the one considered as being irreplaceable, the other apparently not.

By reason of his rule by fear, his seeming lack of sentiment and consideration for others and his active discouragement of marriage among students, Adkins (unwittingly maybe) had erected around himself an impenetrable barrier which appeared to shut out any true friendships, and which resulted instead in a great personal loneliness.

And after the court martial? Military musical circles continue to this day to be divided on one of the moral issues involved — should or should not Colonel Adkins have been informed against by a wearer of the same cloth (i.e. by an army bandmaster) which had been the case?

There occurred one minor episode, a consequence of the NAAFI wines and spirits wangle. On the day following Adko's arrest, a certain senior chaplain to the forces, whom I had long suspected as being something of a humbug, came specially to see me in Churchill House.

"Oh, Nalden! I was asked to interview an officer who is under arrest," was his opening gambit; "and when I saw who it was, I just wept. So very sad, Nalden."

"Yes, sir, very sad."

"Oh, by the way," he added, as though as an afterthought, "is it true that Colonel Adkins kept a book with the names of friends to whom he supplied liquor?"

"Yes, sir; as a matter of fact my own name is in it, as he let me have a bottle of brandy for my mother-in-law."

"You wouldn't know, would you, Nalden, whether my name is in it?"

"I'm afraid it is, sir," I answered untruthfully. Had he not been the humbug I knew him to be, I would have provided instant relief to his tormented soul, by telling him that the book had long since been consigned to the flames by the faithful Charlie Adams. But as it was, the malicious streak I have in me led me to add to, rather than detract from, this otherwise holy man's sense of discomfiture. He was, in fact, another of my dear old foster-mother's 'bleedin' ol' 'ippercrits'.

For the best part of the year following Adkins's arrest, I was acting director of music. One of my first moves was to re-establish relations with the BBC, which I think I am correct in saying had remained unrepaired since the Kneller Hall Band's unfortunate 'dentist' broadcast performance in 1932.

One of our broadcast performances served to demonstrate to us how anxious Britain was to maintain good relations with Argentina. It was stressed by the BBC that our performance must be 'live', which meant our broadcasting somewhere around 2 am. I questioned this, and the answer given me was that reception of BBC relays to the Argentine was so clear that they were able to distinguish between a 'live' and a pre-recorded performance.

So anxious was Britain to preserve good diplomatic relations (all connected I appear to remember with Argentina's exports of beef to Britain) that she (Britain) was not prepared to take the risk of offending her, not even in a seemingly unimportant way such as this. I was announced as 'Carlos Nalden', an attempt on the BBC's part no doubt to hoodwink Argentinians into believing that the conductor came of good bull-fighting stock.

My next move was to invite musicians prominent in their respective fields to deliver lectures to our students. One of these was Dr Boyd Neel, who had already established himself as a pioneer in the field of baroque and early classical orchestral music. Another lecturer was Hubert Foss, writer on music and editor of *The Heritage of Music* series. Following his first lecture, I invited him to have a drink.

"Beer, thanks, Nalden — make it a quart, please."

I was subsequently told by a friend of Hubert's that it was around this time that his third marriage had broken up, which might well have been the motivating factor behind his asking for a quart. But whether his quart-quaffing was by way of celebration or done in sheer desperation, I never discovered.

One interesting engagement in which the Kneller Hall musicians took part with myself conducting was a mammoth concert held in the Royal Albert Hall in aid of the Musicians' Benevolent Fund. Among those taking part were Dame Myra Hess, the BBC Orchestra under Sir Adrian Boult, and the actor Esmond Knight, who had lost his sight in the Hood-Bismarck action. The most moving moment of the evening came with Knight's reciting Laurence Binyon's *For the Fallen* and the Kneller Hall trumpeters' responding to it with Sir Arthur Bliss's *Fanfare for Heroes.*

We played also for the premiere screening in London of *The Life and Death of Colonel Blimp*, with Roger Livesey in the title role. I remember well the audience's good-humoured chuckle and its gradually gathering momentum when one of the film's characters cautioned another, "Never trust a politician." Sitting in this first-night audience was Winston Churchill.

I inherited the responsible but pleasant task of steering the current War Office class through its final examinations. The class in return paid me the gracious tribute of naming itself The Nalden Class. It was a signal honour, for never before in the history of the Royal Military School of Music had a bandmaster been accorded this distinction.

Perhaps my most revealing experiences at that time arose out of my appointment to the Music Committee of ENSA. Although as army representative I contributed very little to the general discussions, I did manage to take in a great deal. I had my eyes opened for the first time to the petty kind of back-biting that went on in the more exalted musical circles, which in my innocence I had imagined to be the sole prerogative of the lowly service musician. One target for attack was Sir Malcolm Sargent. The conversation went something like this:

A: "And I then said to him 'Sargent, you're a liar'!"

B: "And where may I ask would Doctor Malcolm Sargent of the Brains Trust be now?"

C: "In Spain, I believe."

A: "And let's hope he remains there."

It did not occur to these people apparently (or did it?) that England's music at that time was every bit as much in need of a 'Flash Harry' as was its army of a flash 'Monty'.

Several of my stories, I am sometimes reminded, sound decidedly tall. Even so, I do not shrink from vouching for their authenticity — yea, every one of them. It is simply that during my unusually varied lifestyle I have encountered people and situations that are not likely to be encountered by, say, the 9 to 5 office worker, the 5 to 9 (am) nightwatchman or the 9 am to 11 am London stockbroker. Could any person for example parallel my experience of being enrolled as a harp student at a London school of music, and at the same time have hanging over his head like some threatening Sword of Damocles the grim reality of finding himself at any

Above: The Nalden Class, Churchill House, 1943.
Author - front row, third from right.
Below: The Belle Vue Class, Kneller Hall, 1933.
Author - front row, third from left.

given moment being held responsible for the everyday well-being of a couple of mules? So I do not hesitate to vouch for the authenticity of this experience.

Following Adkins's arrest in the September of 1942, I was more able to devote myself to concentrated study for the approaching second Bachelor of Music examination at London University. It was during the course of sitting this examination that I ran into the most improbable of examination candidates. His object in sitting the examination (so he explained to me in conspiratorial tones) was not to pass, but to fail; that he had presented himself regularly for this examination, year after year, with the avowed intention of failing it. It appeared that part of his assignment as a contributor to a certain (unnamed) music journal was to record his impressions as an examination candidate on the quality of the University of London's Bachelor in Music degree papers.

Premissing that a pass could cost the fellow his job, I used frequently to find myself musing as to whether the poor chap's hitherto run of good luck came to an end by his being so beastly unfortunate as to fluke getting through.

During my time at Churchill House I had completed the London Bachelor in Music degree, and passed instrumentation to complete the psm diploma.

psm certificates are signed by the school's commandant and director of music. I must some day put forward my name for inclusion in the *Guiness Book of Records* on the grounds of being the only psm diploma holder ever to have signed his own certificate, which I did in the capacity of acting director of music.

On the very day after sitting the instrumentation paper I felt desperately ill. I reported sick to the nearest army medical centre, which happened to be located in the Army School of Physical Training in Aldershot's then famous Queen's Avenue. From the conversation that was going on between other soldiers who had reported sick (most of whom were wearing the traditional striped PT Instructor's jersey) it became apparent that the ASPT's medical officer harboured but little sympathy for his soldier patients. This was borne out by one instructor who emerged from the surgery, looking quite ghastly. "What did he give you?" came the stock question. "Two days excused swimming," came the dejected reply. I should add that we were then in the throes of a particularly severe English winter.

But to me the MO showed the utmost kindness, taking the step, unusual for an army medical officer, of visiting me during the period of my compulsory confinement to bed.

The MO was New Zealander, Jack Lovelock.

Although the findings of the general court martial had been promulgated early in the January of 1943, no move was made to appoint a successor to Colonel Adkins until the following July. Three of us were short-listed, the other two being a good deal senior to myself.

I do not conceal the fact of my being bitterly disappointed when the directorship did not come my way; for only some short time before his arrest, Colonel Adkins had confided that he was seriously considering recommending me as his successor.

At this distance of time, I now see that War Office's decision was a just one. As a serving soldier myself, I should have acknowledged gracefully (other things being equal) that a Mons Star was a more fitting qualification for promotion in the army than was a university degree. And the new director, Meredith Roberts, had a Mons Star.

Furthermore, I now see that the reforms which I intended to introduce (had I been given the position) would have had me dubbed a reactionary; for however much I disliked the about-turn which military band music had executed during the Adkins regime, there can be no disputing the fact that he instituted a form of entertainment which appealed to a vast section of the general public.

Having been involved (albeit as an innocent bystander) in the Adkins affair, it was clear that no longer could I go on working in Churchill House.

I was given the choice of two 'minor' (i.e. non-commissioned) staff bands — the Band of the Royal Military College, Sandhurst (which would have had me following in the footsteps of Sir Arthur Sullivan's father) or the Royal Artillery (Portsmouth) Band, which was then stationed in Chester. Although allegedly I was given a free choice in the matter, some mild pressure put on me by Major Inglis-Jones induced me to opt for the Royal Artillery.

At about this same time an appointment of a quite different kind was made — that of Bandmaster to the newly-created ATS (all-women's) Band. I like to think that in appointing as it did a serving male army bandmaster named Monk*, War Office had in mind to 'play it safe'. After all, with

* Bandmaster H.C.F. ('Charlie') Monk of the Essex Regiment.

'100 girls and a man' involved, could one really blame them their cautious approach?

FOOTNOTES TO CHAPTER 23

1. Philip Magnus, *Kitchener* (London, 1958), p.148.

24: His Majesty's Royal Artillery (Portsmouth) Band

The story of my remaining few years in the army is mainly one of missed appointments, frustration, and a growing sense of dissatisfaction with service life in general.

The first commissioned appointment to pass me by was the Band of the Royal Engineers, which, as Colonel Adkins had strongly hinted, was to be my stepping stone from the Sherwood Foresters to Director, Royal Military School of Music. It was a band I would very much liked to have had, mainly because of its fine orchestral tradition.

The Royal Engineers' retiring director of music, Captain 'Dave' Jones, knowing Colonel Adkins's intention of appointing me as his (Captain Jones's) successor, did his best to have me at least granted an interview. But to no avail. Understandably perhaps, the appointment went to the second senior of the three of us who had been interviewed some few months earlier for the Royal Military School of Music appointment.

The next commissioned appointment to occur (for which I was short-listed) was a no less desirable one. It was director of music of the Royal Marines Band, whose permanent station was Plymouth. The retiring director had been none too well apparently, and was leaving the service on medical advice. He was Major F.J. Ricketts*, better known as Kenneth

---

* Major Ricketts enlisted as a boy in the Band of the Royal Irish Fusiliers, his instruments being the cornet, piano and organ. He went through Kneller Hall and was appointed Bandmaster of the Argyll and Sutherland Highlanders in 1908, a position he held for close on 20 years. He served as Director of Music, Royal Marines (Plymouth) Band from 1930 to 1944.

J. Alford, composer of what is perhaps the most whistled, the most played, and certainly the most royalty-conscious of any military march ever written — *Colonel Bogey.*

I understand that *Colonel Bogey* had netted its composer a small fortune well before the royalties from the film *Bridge on the River Kwai* netted him (or rather his widow) a second small fortune. One obvious reason for its success was the addition of the bawdy words with which its opening is now universally identified. Even so, this in itself should not be counted a fortunate break for the composer, for *Colonel Bogey* stands firmly on its own two feet as a fine bracing march. And it is a well known fact that Ricketts himself regretted the addition of the words.

The story as to how the march came to be so named is a fascinating one. Ricketts composed it shortly before World War I, when he was bandmaster of the Argyll and Sutherland Highlanders. He was playing a round of golf when he received a warning signal from a fellow golfer who happened to be an army colonel. The colonel's style of warning was not the customary 'Fore!' but two shrilly-whistled notes —

from which the march *Colonel Bogey* ultimately evolved.

I was told at Plymouth that one applicant for the position was the proprietor of a spectacular rough-riding show from America's wild west, whose name was something like Don Pedro and his Cossacks (a curious blend of Spanish and Russian). The Marines' orderly room sergeant told me that Don Pedro's application (which he addressed personally to Major Ricketts) ended with, 'What with my big reputation and your little outfit, we should be able to make quite a go of it.' Don Pedro was not short-listed.

The audition consisted of our conducting the Royal Marines Orchestra and Military Band.

Following the second day's auditions, I chanced to meet Major Ricketts and the Marines' adjutant in Plymouth. Major Ricketts had some highly encouraging things to say to me. The adjutant was even more encouraging, leading me to expect that I was to be offered the appointment.

With one notable exception, these Marine band appointments almost invariably had gone to serving army (not Marines) bandmasters. (The notable exception was Lt-Colonel Sir Vivian Dunn, who I believe was appointed to the Portsmouth Royal Marines Band straight from the Royal College of Music, where he had been a student.)

The Plymouth appointment was epoch-making in that for the first time in living memory it went to a serving Royal Marine.

My disappointment was greatly offset by this charming letter:

Dear Mr Nalden,

Before I leave Plymouth today I feel that I must send you a line to say how much you impressed me by your really admirable performance at the two days' audition: I am sure it could hardly be improved upon.

Though the G.O.C. Royal Marines decided to appoint a candidate from the Royal Naval School of Music — a natural choice perhaps — this fact cannot detract from the excellent impression you made on the Board.

You have my deep sympathy in missing the appointment by so narrow a margin, and I trust you will not meet such misfortune in your next venture.

Should another vacancy occur, whether it be Navy or Army, I hope you will look to me for a testimonial which I will gladly give with full confidence in you.

Yours sincerely,
F.J. Ricketts.

In my view, Kenneth J. Alford's marches stand head and shoulders over all others, the famous Sousa's marches not excluded.

Rather like Sir Arthur Sullivan, who would have preferred his fame ultimately to rest upon his serious works (such as his one grand opera *Ivanhoe*), so Ricketts I suspect yearned secretly for more public recognition of his serious works. I gathered this impression from a conversation I had with him before leaving Plymouth. He told me of a woman who was introduced to him on her insistent request following a church service at which had been sung his own setting of the *Te Deum* and *Jubilate*. "All she wanted to talk about" Ricketts told me, "was *Colonel Bogey*. She had always wanted 'so very much' to meet the person who composed this nice tune. "But not a word," he complained almost bitterly, "about my *Te Deum* and *Jubilate*."

I have always regretted that I was not to know this unassuming man rather more intimately. He died in 1945 within a few months of his retirement.

I was particularly fortunate in being stationed so near to the city of Chester, even though, as it turned out, it was to be for so short a time: for in addition to the joy of exploring this city of ancient walls and old timbered houses, I came to know the cathedral organist, Malcolm Boyle, and his assistant, Dr Roland Middleton.

My new band was essentially a touring band, visiting gunner units in all areas of the Western Command. This meant our spending relatively few days of the year back at base. But during the few days we were back there, I made it my business to visit the cathedral as often as I could. Malcolm Boyle would invite me up to the organ loft during services and persuade me to hum a short phrase upon which he would straightway improvise in a masterly and musicianly fashion. In turn, Dr Middleton was no less a master of the art of improvisation. He had taken his degrees at Durham University, and like myself had studied under Dr Wood.

Leaving Churchill House meant that I was back once again to working for my Mus.D. by correspondence. I would like to have had some personal coaching from Dr Middleton, but my new band's extensive touring programme (something over 300 days in each year) and its subsequent move away from Chester, precluded any possibility of this.

Even so, Dr Middleton did undertake to supervise me in the writing of my musical 'exercise'; for here, my frequent periods of absence from Chester did not matter nearly so much.

I look back upon my association with this almost painfully shy, self-effacing person as one of my life's happiest musical experiences; and I continue to count myself fortunate that I should have come under the influence of so fine and accomplished a musician. For Roland Middleton was just that.

It was in the February of 1944 that I received the disturbing news from my wife who was now living in a flat in Farnborough (Hampshire) that the house had suffered bomb damage; and could I possibly get leave to go down to her. I was granted short leave on compassionate grounds.

Had I caught my train connection at Waterloo Station I would have arrived home in the early evening; but a visit by the Luftwaffe kept many thousands of us confined for most of the night in the depths of London's underground railways.

I duly arrived at Farnborough Station at about 4 am and was not sorry for the few miles' trek through the snow; for it was instrumental in restoring some feeling in my numbed extremities. I arrived home to see a light burning in our kitchenette. With most of the windows shattered, Peggy was making some porridge in a futile attempt to warm herself; for it was a bitterly cold winter's night. In company with the occupants of the bottom flat, she had spent the night of the raid with David (then aged five) huddled beneath an 'Anderson' air-raid shelter. The woman who was living in the downstairs flat told me privately that she (Peggy) was the most calm and relaxed of them all.

At approximately 2 am on the following night, Peggy woke me to ask that I take her to hospital. Rosemary was born some three hours later.

I quote this incident as being typical of the countless thousands of similar examples of stoicism that were displayed by the womenfolk of the several warring nations. I do believe it is at times like these that woman is given an added strength.

My own behaviour on this occasion was not upheld as being quite as heroic as Peggy's apparently. Having no telephone of our own, my next-door neighbour, who happened to be the local coal merchant, had offered us the use of his telephone when it came time for Peggy to enter the maternity home. I had not counted upon this happening in the early hours of the morning, and feeling a little diffident about waking at 2 am a person whom I hardly knew, I am alleged to have asked Peggy whether she might manage to delay matters for an hour or two.

It was a matter only of weeks after Rosemary's birth that I evacuated my family to Holmfirth in Yorkshire; for Hitler had unleashed the first of his frightful and indiscriminate weapons of destruction, the V1.

Being stationed at Chester was far too good a thing to last, so I was not at all surprised to learn that we were to move south to Park Hall Camp in Oswestry, which was a vast artillery training centre.

In common with most other military garrisons, Park Hall Camp boasted its own garrison theatre. But it went one better than most camps, by having its own resident cinema organist, who was Private Reginald Stone. (As I have already said, 'Reginald' was the 'in' name for cinema organists.)

The camp adjutant told me the story of how it all came about. A new recruit named Stone had asked permission to bring his instrument into camp so that he might provide a little light entertainment for the other chaps. "Most certainly," was the adjutant's ready response. Whereupon some few days later he was confronted with a request from Private Reginald Stone for the loan of a couple of the regiment's three-ton lorries plus a sizeable fatigue party; for his 'instrument' turned out to be an electronic cinema-organ, a full-scale affair replete with any number of loud speakers which were housed in enormous boxes such as might have been constructed for containing the remains of some ancient family of Norse giants — hence his request for the lorries and a fatigue party.

Thereafter each cinema session was graced with a 10-minute interlude featuring Private Reginald Stone at the console of his very own Mighty Wurlitzer.

As I have said, we were a touring band, literally a band of itinerant musicians. Our tours took us throughout the north-west of England as well as through Wales and Northern Ireland.

I found lovely Northern Ireland a land of curious contradictions. All honour, for example, to the architect who designed the army barracks at Lisburn which is some six miles south of Belfast. The site on which these barracks were built must formerly have been a stretch of wooded countryside. But instead of employing those indiscriminate bulldozing tactics which all too frequently are a prelude to building construction, the impression I gained was that the architect planned the barrack buildings around the trees, thus ensuring a minimum of felling and a maximum degree of conservation.

Added to this was the colour of the brickwork which harmonised perfectly with the park-like setting. In place of the hideous yellow-coloured bricks which characterised all too many of 19th century England's barracks, workhouses, lunatic asylums and public bath-houses, the barracks in Lisburn were built with a delicately mottled, soft-toned, brick.

In stark contrast to this were the houses of the poorer people, in which chickens strutted at will, pecking at what they could find on the brick-tiled or earthen kitchen floors.

And then there was the Salvation Army officer who tapped me on the shoulder when I happened to be standing on the edge of a pavement in Newry's main street. Having suffered from the British army's system of compulsory church parades for close on a quarter of a century, I was in no mood to receive the Word of God as preached by the Salvation Army. "Son," he said, "if you're looking for some clothes without coupons [i.e. black-market stuff] the shop is standing right behind you. It'll cost you a couple o' bob a coupon."

And when in Downpatrick I made time to visit the Anglican cathedral. Prominent in its grounds is a great boulder which marks St. Patrick's burial place — at least, that is what Northern Ireland's protestants will tell you. When I told the woman serving in the local bookshop that I had just been visiting St. Patrick's burial place, her face hardened into a tight-lipped expression, and her narrowed Irish eyes were no longer smilin'.

Whipping round, she drew a brand new book from off the shelf with, "Take that back to your barracks, and when you've finished reading it,

come back here and tell me where St. Patrick is buried. I'll tell you now,''
(jerking a thumb contemptuously in the direction of the cathedral) "it's
certainly not in that place.'' Some Catholics claim that St. Patrick's burial
place is at Croaghpatrick in the neighbouring county of Armagh, and
others that it is way up on some distant hill in County Down.

One quaint practice in Northern Ireland relates to its milestones.
Travelling say from Belfast to Londonderry, the first milestone might be
engraved "Londonderry 77 3/8 miles". From that point on, each successive
milestone will continue to have engraved on it those three-eighths of a mile
— 76 3/8, 75 3/8, 74 3/8, diminishing finally to "Londonderry 3/8 mile".
It had not occurred to engraver Patrick apparently that he could have spared
himself a great deal of unnecessary work had he placed his first milestone
just those three-eighths of a mile nearer Londonderry.

And it was in Northern Ireland that a gunner officer of rare
understanding took it on himself personally to provide me with some
reading material. It was set out before my arrival on a table by my bedside.
It became my initial introduction to C.S. Lewis through his *Screwtape
Letters*.

Northern and southern Ireland have some curious ways of scoring off
each other. Travellers on British Rail will be familiar with the notice 'Please
do not flush this lavatory while the train is standing at a station.' 'Except
at Portadown' I once read in a border-crossing Irish train.

I found the Welsh people different again. For example, whereas I never
heard a word of Gaelic spoken during my several tours of Northern Ireland,
I observed on more than one occasion how the Welsh people would switch
from English to speaking in their native tongue the moment one entered
a railway carriage. And many years later when being shown round a Welsh
university library, my guide, who was the professor of music, also broke
into Welsh when speaking to members of the library staff. At such moments
as these one becomes temporarily deaf and dumb. For all I knew the
professor may have been saying "He's one of those Kiwi —'s that humbled
our lads at Twickenham.''

Indeed, I found far more evidence of a resurgent nationalism in Wales
than I did either in Ireland or in Scotland.

A timely word or two about the legendary regimental sergeant-major
may not be amiss. Fire-breathing dragons on the parade ground though
many of them may appear, my own experience has been that once off duty
they can be the most gentle of men and endowed with an almost child-like
sense of fun (as opposed to a sense of humour). I remember one particularly
burly-looking type who was RSM of a gunner unit in South Wales. I
remember him chiefly by reason of his being the ugliest man by far that

I have ever come across. He happened to be particularly fond of my band and would personally see to it that we were well looked after when visiting his unit.

"Yer won't git much out o' yer solo cornit player ternight badgy," he once threatened me.

"What makes you think that?" I asked.

"Cos I'm gonna stand in front o' 'im an' suck a lemon."

I could not restrain myself from asking whether he thought the lemon was really necessary. Slow at first to see my point, once he had tumbled to it he shook with laughter, remarking, "I can't understand even now 'ow me wife came to marry an ugly bugger like me."

His wife, who had a chocolate-box type of prettiness and as an erstwhile children's nanny had managed to assimilate something of the 'U' class manner of speaking, played almost consciously the part of beauty to his beast. But Oh! My! wasn't the beast proud of showing off his beauty!

One of my more interesting experiences in an otherwise routinely-dull touring programme occurred during a visit to a gunner unit which was encamped on an earl's estate in the Midlands.

I received a personal invitation from the earl to see his collection of pictures, which I appear to remember included a number of fine Gainsboroughs. The earl then took me on a personally-conducted tour of his once-stately home. We went through room after room in various stages of bareness and disrepair. Some of the bedrooms, for example, had nothing in them — not even carpeting or beds. The earl may have sensed that I was taking all this in, for he paused in one particularly sparsely-furnished room, and placing his hand on my shoulder explained, "My family has been poor ever since it entertained Edward VII."

"How long did he stay?" I asked.

"About a week."

"But surely, sir," I replied, "just one week's stay shouldn't have reduced the family to being permanently poor?"

"You obviously don't know what a visit from King Edward involved."

Christopher Hibbert spells it out in rather more detailed fashion in his *Edward VII*:

'In the first place, his hosts were often required to accommodate an entourage of almost Elizabethan proportions. It was not unknown for the King to travel with two valets, a footman and a brusher; with a lord-in-waiting, a groom-in-waiting, a private secretary and two equerries, all of whom had their own servants; with two chauffeurs, two loaders for the King's guns and a loader each for the guns of the gentlemen attendants; with a gentleman-in-waiting and two ladies-in-waiting for the Queen, who also brought a hairdresser and two maids; with two detectives, two police sergeants and three constables; and with an Arab boy whose sole duty it was to prepare the royal coffee, which he served to his master on bended knee. The number of pieces of attendant luggage was likely to be equally prodigious. In the King's trunks alone there would be as many as forty suits and uniforms and twenty pairs of boots and shoes even for a visit which was to last for no more than a week.'

One place we visited regularly was Birmingham, mainly to entertain the city's factory workers. During our earlier visits I would sometimes do some quiet swot in the tranquil atmosphere of the city's war-scarred cathedral precincts. But as the war progressed, couples would desecrate the place by carrying out their love-making behind its tombs and headstones. An occasional visit by the military police would see the place come suddenly alive with soldiers and their girls of the moment.

In 1944, the Director of Music of the Coldstream Guards, a Major Windram, was nearing retiring age. I had cause to visit him during that year on some semi-official business. I must have cut a pretty unimpressive figure with him, for he confided in a mutual friend who lived in Shrewsbury that he (Windram) could not see in me his successor "however well qualified he may be".

"We have to remember," he explained to our mutual friend, "that we directors of music have sometimes to discuss certain matters with His Majesty."

I thus viewed my prospects of promotion in that particular quarter as virtually nil; for a word whispered in some lordly lug or earlish ear (and the Brigade of Guards was not exactly wanting in Peers of the Realm) would most certainly be listened to, especially should it concern the closing up of its exclusive ranks to a rank outsider.

In the event, Major Windram had no say in the matter, for fate was to intervene in a most tragic manner. On Sunday, 18 June 1944, a 'V1' scored a direct hit on the Guards' Chapel during morning service killing Major Windram, five members of his band and 120 of the congregation.

Once again I was short-listed and invited to attend War Office for interview. Candidates were interviewed in order of seniority. Duggie Pope (who was given the appointment) overshadowed me by some three years in seniority and approximately double that figure in inches.

Thus was I thwarted of the honour of meeting personally His Majesty King George VI, and of seeing my name appear among the list of credits at successive tv screenings of *Dad's Army*.

In general, most bandmasters promoted to commisioned rank managed to keep their sense of proportion, but it was the odd one who looked upon his elevation (quite mistakenly) as the equivalent of his progressing a good six rungs up the social ladder.

While I was a student at Kneller Hall we held social functions of varying kinds to which directors of music automatically would be invited. To guard against possible gate-crashers, guests were required to produce their invitation cards to the gate sentry. On one of these occasions, Captain Samuel S. Smith, director of music of the Life Guards, tall, debonair, in short the very model of a cavalry officer, arrived resplendent in full evening attire, but minus his invitation card.

"May I please see your invitation card, sir," asked the sentry, who was a stocky dour Scot.

"I'm awfully sorry, but I quite forgot to bring it," replied Sam Smith.

"Sorry, sir; my orders are that I must not admit anybody who hasn't an invitation card."

"But look here, I'm Smith of the Guards" replied Sam loftily.

"And I'm Jones of the KOSB's*" retorted the sentry, "but you still can't come in unless I see your invitation card."

Our touring duties were absurdly light, as most gunner units could employ us only in the evenings. Quite often the dance band only would be required. This meant that the majority of us could go for days at a time with virtually nothing to do. I was thus able to study for long periods, and simulate actual examination room conditions, by working previous years' degree papers without fear of interruption. But once back in Park Hall Camp conditions were not always quite so accommodating.

I arrived back from one tour to find the peace and quiet which hitherto had prevailed in my living quarters being rudely shattered by a seemingly non-stop musical performance. The artist concerned was a singer possessed of an uncommonly powerful (but lousy) voice and lots of stamina. He appeared to be accompanying himself on a badly out-of-tune ukelele, an instrument which had been made popular by the comedian George Formby.

With my examination now only a matter of weeks away, and finding myself quite unable to work under such conditions, I strode angrily along

* King's Own Scottish Borderers.

the passage, rapped on the offender's door and without waiting for the customary 'Come in', entered — to meet rather more than my physical match in one Sergeant Ronnie James, who only a few weeks earlier had wrested the British lightweight boxing title from Eric Boon by knocking him out in the 10th round.

After highly complimenting Ronnie on his developing musicianship, I explained to him my dilemma. He proved himself to be one of the nicest men I was privileged to meet during the whole of my army service. He must have been a devoted family man. Even then he was speaking of taking his wife on a sea cruise once the war had ended and told me of his plans to box in Australia. Having as I do a total abhorrence of the so-called 'noble art', my heart bled profusely for Ronnie when I read of his Australian defeat. But knowing the man, I would say that he would have taken it philosophically, looking upon it, I am sure, as the means of providing for his wife an extended holiday cruise.

In the December of that year (1944) I was given leave to sit the Mus.D. examination. Once I learned that I had passed, I settled down to concentrated work on the exercise, which I planned to complete in time for the 1946 examination. Dr Middleton, who was now organist of Chelmsford Cathedral, continued to supervise this and on the odd occasion I would make the journey from Oswestry to his home for a personal lesson.

In the July of the following year we were visiting a gunner unit in Milford Haven when I was asked to take an urgent call from Oswestry. My band president who was at the other end of the line had received advice from Kneller Hall of a newly-created commissioned appointment. Was I desirous, he asked, of being considered for the appointment of director of music to the Royal Indian Air Force Band? The position would involve a 'normal tour of duty in India' (four years).

The appointment did not appeal greatly to me, mainly on the grounds that it would mean a four years' separation from my family. I was anxious also to complete my exercise for the 1946 examination, which I could hardly expect to do should I be posted to India. On the other hand, I was getting simply nowhere by remaining in the army, for by then I had been stagnating in the same rank for over 10 years and still without any prospect of promotion. It was as though some powerful but hidden hand was consistently working against me. So I replied that I was desirous of being considered for the appointment.

Three of us were short-listed, my friends Vic Hayes and 'Edgar' Wallace being the other two. And this time I was the senior contender.

Another hidden hand (or was it the same one?) placed itself on my shoulder just as I was about to go in for my interview. The three of us had been discussing the pros and cons of the job when Vic Hayes, pulling a wry face, remarked, "The one aspect that puts me off is having to train a native band." I knew nothing of this. It transpired that whereas Hayes and Wallace had been sent copies of the conditions of appointment in full, the Kneller Hall authorities for reasons best known to themselves had sent me an extract only, which did not include the reference to a native band. I was furious at what I could see only as a deliberate deception on Kneller Hall's part.

I was called in to meet the interviewing board, a formidable array of Royal Air Force officers which included Wing Commander 'Rudy' O'Donnell, director of music of the RAF Central Band. The president paid me the graceful compliment of suggesting that the Royal Air Force would welcome me into its ranks. This made it less easy for me to turn down the appointment. But turn it down I did, giving as my reason the information I had just received from Vic Hayes.

"Don't you like native bands?" asked one of the board's members. I tried to explain as tactfully as I could that native bands were normally taken by Kneller Hall students who had failed to complete their bandmastership course, or by bandmasters who had reached the end of their respective army careers. (I should explain that this had nothing whatsoever to do with racism, a topic which in those days was seldom if ever discussed. It was simply unheard of for a bandmaster with his career still ahead of him voluntarily to quit the British army for a colonial band.)

The next one to be interviewed was Vic Hayes, who also turned it down. This must have pleased his father, for a short time after the interviews had taken place, he told me that his army service in India had undermined his health. And so the appointment went to 'Edgar' Wallace, who subsequently became director of music to the RAF Central Band. He was not to complete in full his tour of duty in India, for within less than three years of his taking up the appointment, royal assent had been given to the Indian Independence Act.

Towards the end of the year, my band, which had been augmented by the Royal Artillery (Salisbury Plain) Band, was detailed for a tour of gunner units in the British Army of Occupation on the Rhine. This meant our being stationed in Larkhill for a few weeks before our departure in order that the two bands might rehearse together. I was given an insight into what my permanent lot in life would have been had I accepted the Salisbury Plain Band those two years earlier. For officers, life on the Plain could be quite pleasant. They had a magnificent and comparatively new mess (which some thinking people felt should have been built only after the rank and file had been decently housed), their own golf course, and with the easing of petrol rationing, ready means of getting away at weekends.

But for the average soldier it must have been deadly. For the soldier's wife, even more deadly. Her drab married quarter (which looked out on to row upon row of even more drab army huts) stood in far too sharp contrast with the officers' mess. Her shopping facilities were virtually limited to the camp's NAAFI and the mobile fish-cart whose owner incidentally acted as the camp's unofficial bookie. Quoting a *bon mot*, he was forever reminding his clientele, "You can back with me for a win or a plaice." Never by the way did I hear any of the soldiers' wives complain of their suffering from our present-day malady, diagnosed as 'suburban neurosis'.

Our tour of Germany turned out to be the most stimulating and enjoyable experience of the whole of my service life. I fell in love with the German countryside; I fell in love with the mediaeval town of Hamelin, where I visited the Rattenfangerhaus, from which, as legend has it, the Pied Piper 'stept into the street' to abduct the town's children; and for Hahnenklee in its fairy-story picture-book setting high up in the Harz Mountains it was love at first sight.

It was here that I skated in the company of two German schoolgirls, of whom one clearly was more roundly educated than the other. As we skated she related to me in perfect English a story she had learnt at school which told of an English working-class family's way of spending a holiday. This particular family spent its holiday at Margate. Mornings commenced with the family eating jellied eels bought from a kerbside barrow. Following this, the family divided up, with mum and the kids repairing to the sands and dad to the boozer. Each day ended with the family re-uniting in the fish and chip shop. There was rather more than a little truth in this story which clearly was intended to implant in the German girls' minds the drab ritualistic way of life of their plebeian English counterparts.

In stark contrast to Hahnenklee were the German towns' and cities' rubble-blocked streets; the thin wisps of blue smoke which curled up from the seemingly uninhabitable ruins that once were houses; the German girls who were openly prostituting themselves in exchange for Allied soldiers' sweet and cigarette rations; the hastily improvised military burial grounds dotted around in various parts of the countryside which told of minor but bloody and decisive skirmishes; the evergreen-strewn grave of lately executed

Irma Grese*; and the Christmas Day spectacle of German men and women prisoners exercising themselves behind barbed-wire compounds which a few months earlier had held Allied prisoners.

In the report I submitted on the tour, I see that I recorded the one major disaster which befell us. This struck when the courtesy visit we paid to the 51st Highland Division happened to coincide with its New Year's Day celebrations — 'We made our exit on the following day in the regimental coal lorries unnoticed apparently and the Highland Division is still blissfully ignorant no doubt of our visit.'

I had managed to complete the presentation copy of my exercise by the end of the German tour and was able to submit it in time for the 1946 examination. It was accepted, the degree of Doctor in Music being conferred on me in the June of that year.

Shortly after our return from Germany the band was moved to its pre-war station, Portsmouth. I was allocated a married quarter which backed on to the house in which George Villiers, Duke of Buckingham (now named Buckingham House**) was assassinated by John Felton in 1628. It is grimly ironic that the house adjoining Buckingham House should be named after the Duke's assassin.

Portsmouth suffered some severe bomb damage which had taken its toll of many historic buildings including the Garrison Chapel. This was the old Domus Dei founded in 1214 by Peter des Roches (or, as some claim, by Peter de Rupibus, Bishop of Winchester) for Christ's poor and dedicated to St. Nicholas. One historical monument to escape damage was the Sally Port in Broad Street 'from whence heroes innumerable have embarked to fight for their country'; and from whence Nelson embarked to fight his last battle and to meet his last enemy.

One of our first duties when in Portsmouth was to meet the *Queen Mary* at Southampton, whose most distinguished passenger was Sir Winston Churchill. He had returned from the USA, fresh from delivering his famous Westminster College Fulton Address which had caused a furore by his reference to 'an iron curtain [that] has descended across the continent'.

---

* Irma Grese was found guilty on 16 November 1945, of mass murder and whippings at Belsen concentration camp, and sentenced to death by hanging. An appeal for clemency was rejected by the British Commander-in-Chief, Field Marshal Montgomery. She was hanged at Hamelin and buried a little way outside the town. Irma Grese was a mere 21 years of age.

** No.10 High Street. In the same street is The George hotel, in which Nelson frequently stayed. His bedroom is preserved intact.

Sir Winston was the first passenger to disembark, which he did to the accompaniment of some loud cheering and (although played down in the following day's papers) to some equally loud booing. I remarked to a nearby spectator on the base ingratitude of people. In reply she asked whether I had forgotten the fate of our boys whom Churchill had sent to the Dardanelles.

In the winter of 1946-47 Britain was experiencing a most severe period of cold weather with unabated frosts, snowstorms and blizzards. Fuel stocks were well-nigh exhausted, for coal output had failed to keep pace with consumption.

My band was instructed to take up position shortly after dawn on 1 February 1947 (a bitterly cold morning) on a desolate stretch of Portsmouth's foreshore, and told to 'blow like hell until the *Vanguard* is out of sight'. The *Vanguard* was sailing from Portsmouth for South Africa with the royal family on board.

It was by sheer bad luck that the royal tour of South Africa should have coincided with this 'never-to-be-forgotten winter'; for it touched off some ill-informed and quite hurtful criticism back in England. There was a certain degree of dissatisfaction also among the *Vanguard's* crew, the prospect of their wintering in South Africa notwithstanding. This piece of information reached my ears through the naval ratings' confidante, who was the manageress of Portsmouth's newly-opened NAAFI Club (a post-war experiment in the armed services' social welfare).

The ratings complained at their being allotted what remained of the ship's deck space after the two-thirds allocated to the royal party, and the other third to the officers and 'hangers on'. As a measure of retaliation the ship's laundry staff was resolved upon starching a certain article of the royal women's underclothing.

The *Vanguard* returned to Portsmouth to be welcomed by a lovely English spring. My band was detailed to form part of the guard of honour.

The King look bronzed but tired, I thought. The young princesses looked quite charming in their simple frocks which were of the same delicate shade of pink as those they had worn for their grandfather's silver jubilee thanksgiving service in 1935; it was the same shade of pink also that the then future Queen of England was to wear over three decades later for her own silver jubilee thanksgiving service.

The approach (but only the approach) to war-grimed Portsmouth Station positively gleamed under its new coat of paint.

In the meantime more psm examinations had been held and passed by bandmasters of whom some were senior to me in terms of army service. This meant that I was liable yet again to be pushed a further rung or two down the promotional ladder. I had already been warned by another army graduate in music that far from finding my doctorate an asset I would find it a liability. His prognostication was proving itself to be only too true.

I decided therefore to take the unusual and (for me) bold step of writing a letter to my band president for consideration and forwarding to higher authority. It was not a letter of complaint; in it I drew attention to Colonel Adkins's remark which he made to me when I was about to leave Kneller Hall to take up my bandmaster's appointment — that a university degree plus 'my' psm would add up to a stonewall case for promotion. I went on to point out that I had worked unremittingly for a number of years with this assurance in mind, only to discover that advancement was as far away as ever it had been.

At about this same time, Bandmaster 'Tin' Plater of the Royal Tank Regiment, wrote a letter on his own account in which he pointed out that with only 10 'major' staff band appointments allotted to the whole of the army, the vast majority of bandmasters, however well qualified and senior they might be, could never hope to attain commissioned rank. Plater would by then have served in the same rank of bandmaster for over 20 years; for he was about to leave Kneller Hall as a bandmaster when I arrived there in 1924 as a pupil.

Whether it was the result of either or both our letters, a few months later it was announced that a number of bandmasters of certain 'minor' staff bands were to be promoted to commissioned rank — and my band was one of them. Paradoxically Plater's Royal Tank Regiment was not included, although this anomaly was later rectified.

About this time there became directed against me a mysterious campaign of pinpricking and petty complaints. It culminated in my being instructed to report to the brigadier, Royal Artillery Southern Command, whose headquarters were in Salisbury. At the time I was enjoying a spot of leave which of course had to be interrupted. It was fortunate that I should have had a good friend in the HQ's chief clerk, who tipped me off beforehand as to the source of the complaints. The suspicions I already harboured as to whom it might be were now confirmed; and I knew the root cause of it all to be what Lord Vansittart once described as 'that most potent engine of evil in the human frame' — jealousy.

Throwing my normal reticence to the wind (for I knew it had to be either the one or the other of us), I told the brigadier that I was fully alive to the source of his information, and had reason for believing that the complaints were deliberately inspired. I went so far as to ask whether he would support my application for transfer to another regiment, for the person I named as being behind it all was himself a gunner. I asked the brigadier whether he did not think it strange that never before had anything of a like nature happened to me.

The brigadier proved unusually sympathetic, and although he said little, it was no mere coincidence I felt that the pinpricking abruptly ceased. All the same it had given a further severe jolt to my faith in human nature.

But well before all this happened I had become conscious within myself of a developing sense of disappointment and frustration with service life in general. Seniority was still God and Colonel Blimp still his prophet. I had come to loathe the very sight and smell of our routine mode of transport, the army three-ton lorry; then there was the habitual cursing and swearing which went on in the several sergeants' messes I had to visit.

I was beginning to feel a growing repugnance at having to order my fellow men about, especially certain of my bandsmen, for whom I had developed a strong liking and in some cases, an affection. Allied to this were the uncomfortable feelings of guilt I experienced when encouraging young boys of 14 and 15 to enlist into a way of life against which I myself had soured. Above all, there were those frequent and unhappy disruptions to my family life which were occasioned by our still heavy touring programme; for I was finding it more and more difficult to effect the adjustment from family life to barrack-room conditions and vice versa.

A further cause for dissatisfaction was the type of music we were compelled to play. During our time in Oswestry when we were able to augment our string orchestra and play with some fine pianists (the late Norman Greenwood being one of them) we were able to mount a series of worthwhile concerts in the camp's YMCA hut. But now in Portsmouth we were back once again to a monotonous diet of Ivor Novello selections and xylophone solos.

The news that at long last I was to be promoted left me cold; for this particular promotion was simply an automatic affair.

Looking back on it all, I see that little of this was the fault of the army, for the fault lay mostly within myself. It was simply the surfacing of a deep-rooted psychological condition which up to now, consciously or unconsciously, I had managed to suppress. I must have known all along, albeit within my subconscious, that I was not cut out for the career into which I had been pitchforked. With these and other misgivings now taking root, I came to think seriously of leaving the service.

I have been fortunate in that work, even when it has involved extended periods of intensive study, has always come easily to me. Never have I felt the need to goad myself into getting down to work. But I was now beginning to feel a little jaded; for I had been studying without any appreciable break for a full 20 years.

Even so, if I was to make this break, there still lay ahead one necessary undertaking. I must learn to play the piano in however elementary a fashion. In this I was fortunate in finding some excellent teaching locally. And to assist me in my new project, an uncle of my wife's offered to lend me his portable 'dumb' keyboard which would help me keep in practice when touring; for among other duties my band had been advised of an impending tour of the Middle East.

I let it be known to my musician friends that I was on the lookout for employment outside the army.

I first wrote to John Thorpe, a friend and fellow-student of my Kneller Hall days. John was bandmaster of the Bedfordshire and Hertfordshire Regiment, and being stationed in Bedford, a wartime home of the BBC, had managed to secure for himself a position with the corporation's permanent staff. I sounded him as to my own prospects for a similar appointment. "Doctors of Music around here" he wrote, "are as two-a-penny as unpaid lance-corporals. Your best bet is to hang out for one of the army's posh jobs."

I wrote to my old coach, Dr Frederick Wood, who replied to the effect, simply, that it was high time the army recognised my qualifications by promoting me.

I next arranged a meeting with a friend of my Kneller Hall days, Albert Gregory*. His advice (tempered, one suspected, by his pre-war near-poverty existence) was no different from that of Thorpe's and Dr Wood's — "Make your career the army. You'll find that unless you're a member of the establishment, your university qualifications will count for very little."

Undeterred, I continued to persevere by enrolling with the University of London's graduate employment bureau and by scanning *The Times Literary Supplement*. It was the latter medium which decided me upon enrolling with a London educational employment agency. I discarded the idea at the form-filling stage which asked for detailed information of one's education, from 'prep' school onwards.

I made half-hearted applications to the then newly-formed Yorkshire Symphony Orchestra which was currently advertising for a conductor, to Bromsgrove School in Worcestershire for the position of music master, and

* See para 3 of p.338 -

to Portsmouth City Council which was about to establish the post of music organiser, presumably for the County of Hampshire. (Was it a coincidental pointer to my ultimate destination and destiny I was later to wonder, that my daily route to our band practice room should have taken me via Southsea's Auckland Street West?).

I stress that my applications for these three positions were half-hearted affairs, for I was all too conscious within my own self of the fact that the greatest obstacle which stood in the way of my finding suitable employment in 'civvy street' was the constantly-nagging sense of inadequacy and lack of self-confidence. It was mainly this which turned my thoughts to the then-fashionable 'in' thing — emigration — emigration to one of the dominions where one's origins did not count.

With this in mind, I made personal visits to New Zealand House and its Australian counterpart, and sounded out an ex-foundling boy who held a prominent position in Australia's Broadcasting Commission.

The Channel Island of Guernsey is at its loveliest in the spring when its cliff walks become covered with an untamed profusion of wild bluebells, daffodils, primroses and bright yellow gorse. We spent a holiday there in the particularly lovely spring of 1947 which was to prove itself the harbinger of the most blameless and seemingly never-ending summer that England had known for many a year.

During our stay I received a letter from a Professor Hollinrake which enclosed particulars of a lectureship in music to be established by Auckland University College, New Zealand. A friend of mine had spoken to him of me, and he had sent me details of the appointment 'just in case you might be interested'.

We met in New Zealand House (which then was in the Strand), when 'Holly' encouraged me to submit an application. This I did, ultimately receiving a cable from the college offering me the appointment.

At the very same time, an official announcement gazetted by War Office listed the names of the staff bands whose bandmasters were to be promoted to commissioned rank. My band was among those listed.

I had to make a momentous decision; whether to play safe by remaining on in the army, or whether to sever the umbilical cord which throughout my life had attached me to institutionalised living of one kind or another, and step out into the unknown.

My accepting the college appointment would mean a substantial drop in salary, a less generous pension scheme, relinquishing a secure job, uprooting my family for an unknown country at the other end of the world, and embarking upon a career which was as far removed as it was possible to be from the one (and only one) lifestyle I had known since I was a boy of 14. Moreover, the College's conditions of appointment spoke of the arrangement as being 'terminable at any time after the three-year period by either party on three months' notice'.

This is how the pros and cons of the two jobs were put to me by the War Office representative of army bands to whom I had gone, not to seek advice but to enquire about my release from the army. I freely admit that his gloomy warnings made me go hot (literally) under the collar and caused my throat to dry up.

It was in this sorry state that I arrived home to be given the most severe and prolonged 'Lady Macbething' ever, for Peggy had far greater faith in me than had I in myself. She would not hear of my turning the whole thing in (which I myself was now wanting to do), but gently insisted that I see it through. It was her womanly insistence, together with a minor but annoying incident, which resolved me finally upon the signpost I should follow.

In the late summer of that same year, we were detailed as duty band for a tattoo to be staged in Southsea Castle. All profits were to go to Royal Artillery charities. (However well-intentioned the tattoo's promoters may have been, I failed to understand why ex-servicemen whose physical and mental illnesses were the direct result of the recently-fought war should be made to suffer the indignity of being treated as objects of charity.)

The tattoo was held after dusk, which meant that certain of the music we were to play had to be memorised. One of these pieces was the *Introduction to Act III* of *Lohengrin* — a military tattoo war-horse. Due to first-night 'nerves' possibly the *Introduction* may not have sounded so readily familiar shall we say to some ears (including my own) as it should have done. Next morning I found myself on the mat facing the same brigadier who had interviewed me at Salisbury.

"I have received a complaint from a high-ranking officer," he said, "who was present at last night's tattoo. He complains that your band played out of tune."

Had it not involved me in yet another petty but annoying situation I would have regarded this complaint with some amusement; for the brigadier's remark appeared to imply that the higher an officer rose in rank the more acute his sense of musical pitch became; that promotion and a finer aural perception automatically went hand-in-hand.

The impression I personally had gained — and this after a full quarter of a century's army service — was the very reverse of this; rather was it one of a second lieutenant setting out on his military career with acute 'perfect pitch', but after several campaigns spent in 'seeking the bubble reputation even in the cannon's mouth', of his finishing up completely tone-deaf by the time he reached field-marshal's rank.

And this impression gains strength from no less an authority than Lt-Colonel G.J. Miller, one time director of music of the Grenadier Guards and senior director of music of the Brigade of Guards. Writing in the summer 1956 issue of *Tempo* he relates the difficulties he met with when attempting to persuade his GOC to agree to the Band of the Grenadier Guards changing its pitch from 'high' to 'low' or 'continental' pitch:*

> At the beginning of this century the national schools of music and indeed the majority of the large permanent orchestras of the country had decided to come into line with the rest of Europe and adopt 'low' pitch. For years I had been sadly 'out of the picture' in the Grenadier Band's annual visits to France, where I had been unable to join with our colleagues of La Garde Republicaine in combined performances of the National Anthems of our two countries.
>
> This therefore was the burden of my argument with the GOC. He called a committee of officers together to parade with the bands of the Grenadier and Coldstream Guards for a demonstration of the two music-noises: the one band with instruments in high and the other (ours) in low pitch: we were to play alternately.
>
> The 'learned committee' listened profoundly but could come to no decision. No one could detect any difference and concluded it was a lot of fuss about nothing.

To resolve my own personal dilemma required some quick thinking on my part. I suggested to the brigadier that the high-ranking officer who made the complaint might possibly have mistaken for faulty intonation the passage of 'modern' harmonies towards the end of William Walton's *Crown Imperial March* (which also we had played).

"Perhaps you would like to hear the passage, sir?" I suggested. Yes, he would very much like to hear it.

Before getting the band to play it, I explained to the men what it was all about, at the same time affecting an appealing look of deep despair. The band took my SOS and reacted quite splendidly; for its response to my mute appeal resulted in the said passage's emerging more like pure post-romantic Schonberg than Walton.

---

* 'High pitch' (known as Old Philharmonic Pitch) is A = 452.5 vibrations per second. 'Low' (or New Philharmonic Pitch) is A = 439 v.p̣.s. It was not until 1929 that British military bands finally made the change from 'high' to 'low' pitch. The cost involved would have been astronomical, for it meant scrapping entirely all 'high pitch' wood-wind instruments, and modifying all brass instruments.

As I stood back regarding my band with feelings of relief mingled with pride and gratitude, a slightly dazed brigadier said "I see just what you mean, Mr Nalden. I'll report to the general what you have told me."

By this time my mind was thoroughly made up (thoroughly made up, that is, by Peggy) that I would accept the New Zealand appointment. I submitted therefore a formal application for my discharge.

According to my successor, Kneller Hall was angered at my turning down a commission, which, he told me, they likened to 'Teddy giving the English Throne a kick in the pants'; for mine was the one and only case in Kneller Hall's 90-year history of a bandmaster doing just that.

In my prevailing mood of uncertainty this news of Kneller Hall's attitude hardly helped matters; for although Kneller Hall was not to know it, I was far too apprehensive of what lay ahead to indulge in any smug feelings of having scored off them — or indeed off anyone else; for buzzing around in my mind was our local boot-repairer's chance remark, "You're not scared, are you?"

Not scared? In all truth I was scared stiff. Here was I about to step out some 12,000 miles into the unknown, and saddled to boot with the responsibilities of a wife and two very young children. As to my new job of university lecturer (so ran my thoughts), had I not been foolhardy, even impertinent, in accepting it? For far from having had lecturing experience at university level, I had never been afforded opportunity even of attending a single university lecture. But my greatest deficiency in this respect was, of course, that indefinable 'something' which one gains from the corporate life of a residential university.

Moreover, my fears and feelings of uncertainty were hardly lessened by a sombre article by New Zealand writer Anthony Alpers, which appeared at this same time in one of Britain's national newspapers. I recall the whole tenor of the article *The Return of the Immigrants* as being decidedly discouraging to the would-be emigrant.

Partially off-setting Alper's gloomy picture was the kindly encouragement given me by the late Dr Kenneth Stallworthy and his wife May. At the time Dr Stallworthy was on the staff of Portsmouth's St James's Psychiatric Hospital and completing the Diploma in Psychiatric Medicine pending his return to Auckland's Avondale Hospital.

The last I was to see of my band was on Portsmouth Station, where I went to farewell it as it left for its tour of the Middle East. It was a tour I would have liked to have shared with them, but fate had decreed otherwise.

And then came the breaking point. Something within me snapped once I had sold up and moved to my mother-in-law's house in Broadstairs, where we were to spend the intervening period between my discharge from the army and our setting out for New Zealand. New Zealand House had arranged passages for us on the *Rangitata* which was due to sail on 1 January 1948, the same day which saw the nationalisation of Britain's railways.

I was ordered to bed by the local doctor, and permitted to sail only on the understanding that I be cared for in the ship's hospital.

Here I counted myself fortunate, for conditions on board were hardly conducive to the relaxed atmosphere of a holiday cruise. The *Rangitata* had yet to be re-converted from its wartime role of troopship, which meant that it put to sea with something approaching three times its normal peace-time passenger complement. The cramped conditions on deck served to intensify to an almost unbearable degree the petty squabbles and the rest which are the commonplace of any extended boat journey.

My papers on discharge shewed me as having served in the army for a total of 25 years, 108 days.

My 'Leap over the Wall' brings to an end my personal version of '*A Soldier's Tale*'.

PART III

MILD OR RELATIVELY SO

25: Mild — or relatively so

When asked by an army friend what his ambition was, Basil Spence replied, "To build a cathedral." As it became Spence's ultimate vocation to build a cathedral in stone, so it was to become mine to build a cathedral in sound. To how many individual people's lots has it fallen to be architect of a cathedral in sound — meaning a conservatorium of music? One in several millions?

We landed in Wellington early in February, and travelled to Auckland that same night by the 'Limited'. A generous University College had arranged accommodation for us (at our own expense) at the old Waverley Hotel. I certainly did not receive my money's worth from my first night there, for I was prevented from sleeping until the early hours of the morning by the non-stop music recital which came from a juke box in the milk bar opposite. I awoke to find that my voice had deserted me completely. In the circumstances this was just as well perhaps, for no sooner had I returned to my room from breakfast than there came a confident knock on my bedroom door. It was a young and obviously enterprising reporter.

"Dr Nalden?" he enquired. I merely nodded. ('Another of those uncommunicative Poms', he must have thought.) "I'm from the *Auckland Star*, and would like to have your opinion of music in New Zealand," he went on.

I must by then have been in New Zealand certainly not more than 48 hours (of which a third had been spent in the train) and the only music indigenous to the country of my adoption I so far had heard had come from the aforementioned juke box. I beckoned him to come closer, indicating in mute fashion that I wished to whisper something in his ear. Sensing a highly confidential opinion and possibly a sensational scoop for his paper, he readily obliged. "Come and see me again in something like six weeks' time," I whispered in his ear — which he did. Although our paths never crossed again, I have often wondered how far up the journalistic ladder this enterprising person had climbed.

During our voyage out here, I recall remarking to my wife that although I was about to take up a purely academic post, I felt strangely convinced that the work which lay ahead of me was to be predominantly in the field of practical music. Once I had taken up my duties at the college, it was not difficult for me to see that there was ample scope in this field.

I was taken aback somewhat at the balance, or rather the total lack of it, between the facilities currently available to the academic music student and to his performing counterpart. The syllabusses of all four New Zealand university music departments were adapted exclusively to the needs of the academic student, to the total exclusion of instrumentalists. Indeed, one of the earliest criticisms I heard levelled against our own music department, and this more than once, was that a student could graduate as Bachelor in Music even though he be incapable of playing a note of music — which was true.

All four university colleges' prescriptions for the Bachelor in Music degree course read very much like those of Cambridge University; but we had no parallels to England's colleges and academies of music, so that music as a university discipline was a very lop-sided affair.

One of my duties was to train and conduct the college's Music Club Orchestra, whose players came from several different faculties. One cellist had the disturbing habit of getting ahead of the beat. I tried to get around this by giving him a handicap of the odd bar or so (the exact number of bars being determined by the tempo of the piece), in the hope that we might at least alight on the final chord together. Another cellist would be fingering away busily on one string, while bowing on another.

And the intermittent spasms of welkin-shattering, barbaric barking, welling forth from the french-hornist (my otherwise good friend, the late Professor Tom Rive) provided a peculiarly apt answer to the nostalgic sigh of Walter Scott's line, 'O for a blast of that dread horn'.

Tuning the orchestra posed a further problem; for example, clarinettists with 'high' and 'low' pitched instruments. In those days we had to take a liberal attitude to intonation.

In 1950 I was appointed honorary conductor of the Auckland Junior Symphony Orchestra. This orchestra, the result of the farsightedness of the late Gordon Cole, had been established in 1948 with a view to meeting the needs of young musicians once they had left school. My association with the orchestra was to last for 23 years, during which time I was supported by an active committee, headed by the perfect chairman-secretary partnership of the late Roy Kendon and Joye de Vere.

The most touching moment of my long and happy association with the orchestra came some 18 months after I had resigned as its conductor. I was driven by my family to a secret destination to find myself confronted with a grand assembly of well over 200 past and present players and committee members, of whom some had come from as far afield as Christchurch, Nelson, Wellington and Rotorua. Between them they had formed an ex-players' orchestra which, rather in the manner of the Siegfried Idyll orchestra, had been holding secret rehearsals over a goodly number of months. So well kept had the secret been that when it did come, the surprise, which was akin to that of the television series *This is Your Life*, was total. Indeed the party organisers might well have named it 'This is Your Life' — for my years with the orchestra spanned virtually the whole of my working life in New Zealand.

It was befitting that the person who for well over a year had worked unremittingly on the scheme should have been Pat Harrop; for I regarded it as being a form of penance on her part; her way of atoning for her attempt some few years earlier at putting one across me —

"So you wish to enrol in instrumentation?"

"That's right, Prof."

"You know that I teach the subject?"

"That's why I chose instrumentation."

"What other subjects are you enrolling in?"

"No others, Prof.; just instrumentation."

Fishing around for a personal compliment, I asked, "And so of all the university subjects you are eligible to enrol in, you are choosing to enrol in one that I teach?"

"That's right, Prof."

So taken off balance was I with this graceful form of flattery that for a moment (but only a moment) my heart threatened to rule my head.

"That's fine, but as much as I appreciate the compliment, I'm afraid there's one snag; you see, I expect students enrolling in instrumentation to have done at least stage II harmony, but preferably stage III — and you haven't done either?"

"No, Prof., but in my particular case I don't think that really matters."

"Oh?"

"Well, you see, Prof. I was going to ask you for a full exemption from lectures and assignments."

"?"

"Well, you see, Prof. it's like this: I've simply got to find somebody who's prepared to enrol me in some subject or other, otherwise I don't qualify to compete in the inter-varsity winter tournament."

One likes to believe that the phenomenon of the many New Zealand youth orchestras which in recent years have come into being is the result at least in part to the early lead given by the Auckland Junior Symphony Orchestra.

One of my earliest AJSO rehearsals was attended by Michael Bowles, who succeeded Anderson Tyrer as conductor of the New Zealand National Orchestra (as it was then known). Michael Bowles insisted in characteristically Irish fashion that I have breakfast with him, when between stewed fruit and cereals we discussed musical matters generally.

Shortly after this I received an invitation to conduct the National Orchestra — an invitation which was to be repeated on several occasions. It was a case of working again with old friends, as long before this, I had been associated with the orchestra as deputy harpist and french horn player.

I came to learn that however glamorous to the layman the conducting of a full symphony orchestra may appear, to be doing this intermittently can involve one in considerable mental strain — be he a university lecturer or a Conservative Prime Minister of England. For let it be faced that in many a professional orchestra there are players who are at least the equal of, and sometimes superior to, the person on the rostrum.

A sympathetic leader (or perhaps I should say 'concert master') will always endeavour to put the nervous guest conductor at his ease — which is just what that lovable person the late Vince Aspey (whom James Robertson once hailed as a genius) always did with me. The combination of his fine musicianship and his almost childlike ingenuousness produced as capable and as natural an orchestral leader as any conductor could wish for.

Vince could display a ferocious wit calculated to demolish utterly and completely any would-be opponent. I take the risk of relating just that once too often the most famous Vince Aspey anecdote.

It was during the early days of the National Orchestra, when the conductor, Anderson Tyrer, happened to be discussing with Vince some matter relating to bowing. Butting in (somewhat unethically it was thought), Francis Rosner who was sitting immediately behind Vince, volunteered "But

this [demonstrating] is the traditional way of bowing it, Mr Tyrer."
Whereupon Vince swung round to demolish him with "And I suppose that's
how old Nero bowed it?" And Vince asked of one of my university
colleagues in his characteristically quizzical manner, "I understand you
are one of those queer blokes that writes fugues?"

And mention of James Robertson (who as one-time resident conductor
of the National Orchestra accomplished a great deal more I feel than he
has been given credit for) reminds me of an incident which occurred during
his term as conductor of the New Zealand Broadcasting Corporation
Concert Orchestra. It fell to my lot to assist in finding players to fill in
the gaps in his orchestra, particularly in the wood-wind section. Even so,
James was not altogether happy. He complained bitterly to his leader during
the orchestra's first performance (an opera matinee), of his being fobbed
off with a hard-of-hearing clarinet player — until it was explained to him
that the player's deaf-aid was not in fact a deaf-aid at all, but an ear-plug
attachment for a pocket transistor receiving set; for the player concerned
had mastered the difficult art of playing his part and listening to the races
at the same time.

Another musician who was doing a great deal for New Zealand music
in general and for Auckland in particular was Georg Tintner. His finest
work, I would say, was with the old Auckland String Players, whose
performances were of professional standard. Tintner seldom used a score,
preferring instead to carry the music (which might be a complete opera)
in his head.

He had in one of our students a devotee named Leslie Thompson, himself
a no mean musician.

Permanently-puckered brow, temperamentally as taut and nervy as the
final movement of William Walton's 1st Symphony, school teacher by day
and office cleaner by night (this in order to finance his intended trip to
England), Leslie Thompson* symbolised the serious-minded university
music student of the early post-World War II years.

Now, Leslie was an ardent admirer of Austrian-born Georg Tintner, at
the time (c.1949) conductor of the Auckland Choral Society.

It was this admiration, coupled with a strong sense of moral duty towards
his family, which led Leslie along with two other enthusiasts to start an
all-night queue outside Begg's Queen Street music shop, whose entrance

---

* Leslie Thompson, one of our more outstanding students, graduated as Bachelor in Music in 1952. Mr Thompson is
permanently resident in Oxford, and although retired, continues to conduct the Oxford Studio Orchestra and act as music
critic for the *Oxford Times*.

was set back somewhat from the pavement; for Leslie was determined upon securing those three specific (but only those three specific) seats from which his family could observe Tintner conducting *The Messiah* from memory, and their own Leslie adding his personal weight to the work's vocal bass-line.

Leslie took up his position in the 'queue' at 1 am. At 3 am (so he himself later related) a torch was flashed in his face — by a police officer.

"And what might you three be doing here?"

"We're queuing."

"Queuing? Queuing for what?"

"The Messiah."

"The Messiah?"

"Yes — the Messiah."

"Who's he?"

"You know the Messiah, surely officer?"

"As a matter of fact I don't know the Messiah. What's he do — play the pianner or something?"

"Actually the Messiah's not a person."

"???????"

"It's an oratorio by Handel."

"So another joker called Handel comes into it?"

The situation was threatening to take on a sinister turn; for Auckland's co-leading music shop of those days stocked not only harmonicas (which in all truth are nothing more than mouth organs with a private school education), abundant copies of *The Rustle of Spring*, Associated Board and Trinity College Theory Papers and the *Harry Lime Theme*, but the leading brands also of washing machines, pop-up toasters and electrically-heated hair-curlers; in short, the professional burglar's dream haul.

But plausible spokesman that he was, Leslie succeeded in dispelling in part the officer's worst suspicions, that they were loitering with intent. So that, although not wholly satisfied (the proffered complimentary tickets notwithstanding), he allowed our dedicated trio to continue its business of queuing.

Thus it was, rather in the courtly tradition of Don Quixote of old, who, as a candidate for knighthood, kept a solemn night-long watch over his armour, that our three stalwarts pursued their lone vigil until Begg's opened its booking plan six hours later.

Now, this story is true in every detail. There still exists, however, a legendary sequel whose authenticity I, for one, regard with deep suspicion.

Our police officer, so the legend goes, in accepting the proffered complimentary tickets made his apologies in advance for unavoidable lateness.

It would so happen that his arrival coincided with the opening of the Hallelujah Chorus. In keeping with the tradition dating from the 23rd day of March 1753, the vast Town Hall audience to a man . . . (I do beg your pardon!) . . . the vast audience to a person rose to its feet.

Our hero, mistaking this for a spontaneous tribute to his magnanimity of the previous night, was heard to utter in a voice literally choking with emotion, "Please be seated . . . it was nothing . . . merely in the course of my duty."

At the 51st bar, when sopranos and altos unite in their triumphant shout, "King of kings, Lord of lords", our hero, now well-nigh prostrate with pent-up emotion (and being the modest man that he was) could take no more. He fled the hall in terror never to return.

And so it was that his acquaintance with *Messiah* became forever restricted to those 51 bars of the Hallelujah Chorus.

In the April of 1951 I found myself landed in hospital, the result of a severe burn which caused extensive damage to my left hand and arm. But for the skill of the plastic surgeon, Mr (now Sir) William Manchester, my harp-playing days would have been at an end. Due solely to his consummate skill (which gave me back full use of my arm and hand) I was able once again to pick up the threads and go on to give a number of harp recitals for Radio New Zealand, which in turn led to its according me the status of national artist.

It was my first insight into the New Zealand hospital system. I found the nursing service quite outstanding, the staff making it their duty seemingly to look after their patients' mental as well as their physical well-being.

And it was in Middlemore Hospital that I came to learn something at first hand about our Maori people. One of the finest men I have been privileged to meet was Mark Mete, a young Maori clergyman, who at the time was curate to the Vicar of Otahuhu, the late Reverend J. Pittman. Mark was intensely loyal to his vicar, and full of praise for the radio talks he gave when conducting *Morning Devotions*. Mark insisted that I listen to Mr Pittman's next talk, which happened to coincide with the morning of one of my operations. I had been given pre-op medication, and my ward blind lowered. Mr Pittman went straight into his subject, posing a rhetorical

"I can imagine no situation more terrifying."

question which somehow appeared to be directed at me personally: "Are YOU prepared for death?"

I switched off.

I came to love the Maori's own disarming brand of naïveté. A case in point is this authentic story which was related to me by that ardent Salvationist, the late Professor Tom Rive. It appears that there was a mass conversion to the Salvation Army faith among the King Country Maoris. They crossed over in their scores apparently.

"What was it that led you all to answer the Call?" they were asked by a specially despatched senior army officer.

"Well, to be quite truthful, Major," came the reply, "it was your free issue of the army's jerseys — we were able to equip quite a number of rugby XVs."

Was this a piece of artlessness? Or was it a shrewd tactical move on their part? For I can imagine no situation more terrifying than that of a six-foot, 16-stone Maori bearing down on one with the Army's motto 'Blood and Fire' emblazoned across the full width of his 44-inch chest.

During the July of 1955, the late Professor Galway, who then occupied the Otago University chair in music, wrote to Professor Hollinrake to tell him of his (Galway's) impending resignation on medical advice. I had met Victor Galway on the odd occasion only when he visited Auckland as our external assessor. It came as something of a pleasant surprise, and a boost to my morale therefore, when in this same letter he asked "Will Charles Nalden be an applicant for the chair? I sincerely hope so."

Professor Hollinrake appeared surprised when I told him that I did not intend applying. He had expressed similar surprise some few years earlier when I told him of my decision not to apply to be head of a newly-created music department in the University of Western Australia.

The truth of the matter was, I knew I had still a long way to go in learning my job. Although Hollinrake (and others possibly) may not have sensed it, I still was all too uncertain of myself; for my abrupt transition from army to university had not been accomplished without a great deal of inner conflict, which at times led me into deep depressions. Other factors which went to influence my decision were my work with the Auckland Junior Symphony Orchestra and family considerations; for I have never regarded either promotion or the attraction of a higher salary as being sufficient reasons in themselves for uprooting oneself and moving elsewhere.

Before that same month of July was out, Professor Hollinrake himself had died at the all-too-young age of 52.

'Holly' had held the chair of music for 20 years*, during which time he had accomplished much for the development of music both within the college and the community. It was owing to his initiative that the Master of Arts and Honours course in Music became established in all four of our university colleges; and just five weeks before his death our own college council had approved the institution of a diploma course for executant musicians — the fulfilment of an idea which had been occupying Holly's mind ever since his return in 1948 from a tour of universities in the United States.

In some ways 'Holly' was a strange, and I suspected lonely, person. So wedded was he to his work, and so seriously did he take it, that I have known him to accept at least part-blame for a student's failure. Thus when one of his stage I students wrote of 'the trance position of the second subject into the key of the tonic', he held himself to blame for not having expressed himself more clearly.

And when once paid a graceful compliment (albeit unwittingly) he twisted things round in such a manner as to cause hurt to me personally. The incident took place during a singing scholarship examination. One of his tests required the candidate to determine the time-signature of the piece he was playing, and then to begin conducting it. He began by playing the last movement of Beethoven's Violin Concerto. The candidate's attempt at conducting might have done credit to a racecourse tick-tack man, but hardly to Beethoven's Violin Concerto. Undeterred, Holly said, "I'll play the piece again and see whether you can state the period in which it was written." No — she could not make up her mind on that one either. In desperation Holly said, "I'll play it again: listen carefully this time and see whether you can name the composer."

Suddenly the candidate's face lit up, her frown of frustration translating itself into an expression of joyous recognition. Turning round to Holly, she blurted out, "Why! of course, Professor! It's one of yours!" (She was awarded the scholarship.)

Holly's reaction to my expression of uncontrolled mirth was to remark coldly, "It's as well that at least somebody thinks something of me" — not appreciating of course that a lot of us did think a great deal of him.

---

* Before Professor Hollinrake's appointment to the chair in 1935, professors of music were engaged on a part-time basis. In 1883 we see the college registrar reporting 'that he had communicated with the Vice-President of the Choral Society, Mr Fenton, the Resolutions adopted by this Council with reference to the institution of a professorship or Lectureship of Music; that he had also, as directed by the Committee on Lectures, inquired what guarantee would be given for payment of a portion of the salary from the Choral Society, and to what amount.' Auckland had to wait a further five years before the chair in music was established. It was filled by Herr Carl Schmitt, who was paid a yearly salary of 'one hundred pounds and the ordinary College fees payable by students', against the £700 paid to the other college professors.

In the November of the same year an unofficial approach was made to me regarding the Otago chair in music, their first advertisement not having succeeded in attracting a suitable candidate. I was assured of 'a 95 per cent chance of being appointed' should I apply. But again I said no, even though it meant running the risk of falling between two stools; for applications for the Auckland chair had yet to close.

I had by then been acting head of department for some five months, and was beginning to realise just what running a university department could mean. I soon discovered (as I put it in my farewell speech to members of our senior common room) the subtle difference between the party game of musical chairs, and the university game of chairs in music. In the former, one grabs a chair the moment the music stops; but in the latter the music stops the moment one grabs a chair. I was fast becoming a reasonably able, if reluctant, administrator.

It was the result of this experience of acting as departmental head, together with a good deal of urging from my friend and ever helpful colleague Tom Rive, which decided me upon applying for the Auckland chair.

Establishing a conservatorium of music

When appointed to the chair in the following year, the first question asked of me was — did I feel that Professor Hollinrake's conservatorium scheme should be proceeded with or scrapped? There was of course no alternative answer for me to give, even though the weaknesses in the proposed course structure were (to me at any rate) all too apparent.

An article I was invited to contribute in 1965 to the 60th Jubilee number of *Kiwi* (the literary magazine of the University of Auckland) presents a fair picture of the diploma course's development up to that year:

A Conservatorium of Music within the University

'The Greeks, Romans, have graced music, and made it one of the liberal sciences, though it now becomes mercenary. Your princes, emperors, and persons of any quality maintain it in their courts. All civil Commonwealths allow it.'

The Anatomy of Melancholy: Music a Remedy —
Robert Burton (1576-1639)

In short, dear student reader, they all had it — except New Zealand. The long delay in acknowledging the need for a conservatorium of music in this country may of course have been the early missionaries' endorsement of Plato's stern philosophy which forbade wine and music to all young men, 'because they are for the most part amorous "ne ignis addatur igni" lest one fire increase another'. Or of course it may have been these same early missionaries' no doubt sincere, but foredoomed attempt to counter the already threatening omnipotence of the oval-shaped god — for had not Roger North in his *Musicall Gramarian* of some two centuries earlier warned that 'the thought of some folks may run upon a dance, ye hurry of football play, all which Bizzarie ye masters of musick will undertake to represent'.

Whatever the reason for delay, on one point my mind is firmly made up; it is this: that had our sporting fraternity earlier been made aware of the latent powers of music — had our angler friends for example, known that 'The gentle strains of Arion's lyre made fishes follow him' (thus sparing themselves the expense of spinners), or our annual duck-shooters (if we believe Calcagninus) 'that birds are much pleased and attracted by musick' (thus eliminating unnecessary expenditure on decoy ducks), or our deer stalkers (if we believe Scaliger) that 'harts and hinds are exceedingly delighted with it' (thus opening up undreamed-of possibilities for mass extermination) — had they known all this, I remain unshakeably convinced that a full-scale conservatorium of music in this country would long ago have been a living reality.

Prior to the establishment in 1956 of this University's Executant Diploma Course, New Zealand offered virtually nothing in the way of conservatorium training for the practical musician. What practical training facilities there were existed solely in the hands of the private music teacher. This was good enough up to a point, but the supply of good music teachers varied from centre to centre, and in the early post-war years there already were signs that the younger generation of musicians was not content to embrace a profession that offered highly irregular hours of work, indifferent monetary rewards, but a guaranteed goodly lash of virulent mothers' tongues during Music Competitions Week. Moreover, the formation of the National Orchestra in 1946 greatly aggravated an already problematical situation (the dearth of good music teachers), by drawing extensively upon the country's finest instrumentalists, many of whom were not only orchestral players, but teachers as well. Indeed, it would not be going too far to claim that in gaining a national cultural asset, the manner in which the National Orchestra came into being disrupted the country's balance musically, from which even now, almost twenty years later, it has yet to recover. The vacuum that was created literally overnight still exists, and must continue to exist until practical training (conservatorium type) schemes such as our own are established at strategic centres throughout New Zealand.

It is true that in 1950 the then Heads of the four University Music Departments made a concerted and honest attempt to introduce a degree course in music that admitted practical performance as a subject. Their heretical proposal struck the Academic Committee of the old University of New Zealand apparently as a bolt of lightning in the heart of a virgin forest, for it was promptly thrown out on the grounds of its being 'non-academic'.

When informed of the Academic Committee's decision one certain Professor of Music was seen to cross himself and heard audibly to murmur (in an irreverent invocation to Music's legendary Patron Saint) "My sainted Aunt Cecilia!"

Not content with declaring it a heresy of the type which three centuries earlier would have ensured the four professors to suffer the same fate as that of Galileo, this same committee proceeded to rub a pinch of academic salt into the wound, by admitting a new Bachelor in Music and Honours degree course; so that, whereas the academic musician could now read at any one of the four university colleges for the Diploma in Music, or for

"Thus sparing themselves the expense of spinners" by Garth Tapper.

Above: "Harts and hinds are exceedingly delighted with it."
Below: "I will make YOU the envy of your friends."

the degrees of Bachelor in Music and Honours, Doctor of Philosophy and Doctor in Music, the aspiring violinist or pianist had to content himself at best with what teaching (if any at all) was available locally, and at worst, with enrolling with Professor H. ('Send no money in the first instance') Becker of London, who guaranteed to teach you (by correspondence) to play the Grieg and the Schumann piano concertos in six months' progressive lessons. ('His friends laughed at him — until he sat down to play. I will make YOU the envy of your friends' sort of thing.)

At this time New Zealand was thus unique, in that she was the only country in the world boasting a Western cultural tradition, yet having no conservatorium of music. It followed that many of the students who enrolled for academic music courses at this time did so neither from choice nor from conviction, but simply because there were no practical courses offering. By reason of outlook and natural endowment, many of our music students would have been far happier working and studying in the practical, rather than in the academic, field; and it was by no means uncommon for these 'conservatorium types' either to cross over to an Arts course, or to abandon the Mus.B. course altogether.

However, in 1954, our own University College (as it was then) approved a 'blue print' for a practical music course, the brainchild of the late Professor Hollinrake, and in the same year, the Music Advisory Committee of the Department of Internal Affairs recommended that:

> In the event of a three-year Executant Diploma Course for the practice of music being inaugurated at Auckland University College, this meeting is prepared to recommend the allocation of six three-year bursaries of £150 per annum . . . for selected students undertaking full time study for the Executant Diploma.

Because of Professor Hollinrake's untimely death, it fell to me to inaugurate the new course, which had its first intake of students in 1956.

It thus became the first officially sponsored Conservatorium of Music (though in miniature) in the country's history.

The magnificent gesture of the Department of Internal Affairs in allocating us the six bursaries (which it was understood were to be awarded annually for a trial period of five years) was dulled somewhat by the fact that 'at least one member of the Committee' [of the Internal Affairs Music Advisory Committee] 'is having second thoughts'. And this, mark you, after the course had been running exactly one year. More in anger than in sorrow I replied:

> To me, it seems incredible, that a Course set in operation, the result of a unanimous vote by the Music Advisory Committee, should be queried after exactly one year's duration.

My temper was not improved by another member's suggestion that the Course after all should be transferred to Wellington.

On the home front, things were made no easier by the resignation of two of our part-time teaching staff just prior to their giving their first lesson, and by a third uprooting for an overseas trip in the second of the three years' course.

These early setbacks at least had the great advantage of placing our course at the cross-roads; if it was to go on, it became increasingly obvious that it must be given official recognition by the Education Department for bursaries, and continuity ensured by staffing it with a core of salaried full-time teachers. We got both; a fully sympathetic University Council gave us all that we asked for, and so within six years of the Executant Diploma Course's inauguration, we were able to attract a full-time salaried teaching staff whose names (as one private music teacher put it) 'would grace the Calendar of any Conservatorium of Music'. And to safeguard the teachers' own standards, they were employed on a teacher-performer basis, with the condition that they give a limited number of public performances within the University. This has resulted in an unbroken series of highly enjoyable chamber music concerts, graced by the continued co-operation of the English Department, and disgraced by the almost total absence of staff and students from the concerts themselves.

So much for the Muse of Poetry. What of the erudite side of the Course? In my most recent Annual Report to Council I was able to write:

> It is gratifying to report that the Executant Diploma Course continues to make a positive contribution to the music profession.
>
> Since the course's inception, some twelve instrumentalists have swelled the ranks of the New Zealand Broadcasting Corporation's Symphony and Concert Orchestras*, one violinist is playing with the Scottish National Orchestra, and another player has been engaged by the Northern Sinfonia of England; a further three players joined various Australian Symphony Orchestras; four Diploma holders were subsequently awarded overseas scholarships for post-graduate study; a further three are on the staff of the N.Z.B.C. and some seven have entered the music teaching profession.
>
> Meanwhile, further 'Overtures to an Accommodating Council' are being secretly composed behind the Music Department's Red Corrugated Iron Curtain.**

---

* One of this number (Gordon Skinner) subsequently became principal bassoonist of the N.Z. Radio Symphony Orchestra, and another (Melbon Mackie) co-principal bassoonist of the Covent Garden Opera and Ballet Orchestra.

** This is a reference to the corrugated iron building which housed the Music Faculty for a full 20 years.

Thus became established New Zealand's first Conservatorium of Music, thanks mainly to the generous measure of support given me by Vice-Chancellor Kenneth Maidment.

It could, I suppose, be counted as one of the more paradoxical twists in the history of music that whereas Dr Charles Burney, through no lack of enthusiasm and enterprise on his part, should fail in his attempt to establish within the walls of the Foundling Hospital what promised to be England's first conservatorium of music, it should fall to the lot of an ex-foundling boy some two centuries later to become the person largely responsible for establishing New Zealand's first conservatorium of music.

Interlude — I become a Knight for a Day

I was once quite puzzled to find in my university mail-box a letter addressed to 'Sir Charles Nalden'. It was from a professor of music of an Australian university thanking me for my kind letter of introduction in favour of Mr — . 'Once he settles down,' the professor's letter went on, 'I am sure he will be able to contribute to the progress and general musical activity of the university.'

In my reply, I pointed out that there must be some misunderstanding, for I had not written on behalf of the young gentleman concerned. The professor of mathematics of this same Australian university had received a similar letter of introduction written supposedly by our own professor of mathematics, the late H.G. Forder.

I was then sent a copy of the letter allegedly written by myself:

Dear Professor,

Allow me to introduce one of my quite outstanding students to you. He will soon be starting studies in Mathematic's [sic] Honours at your University and I am taking this opportunity to write to you before I leave for England. His name is — and he has taken so far studies in Music under my direction and Philosophy and Maths. He has 3 degrees (B.Mus. B.A. B.Sc.) in the 3 subjects and is only 21. The reason I should like you to get in touch with him is because he has a large number of MS of New Zealand and young English composers . . . besides being himself a very skilled pianist and organist in the Contemporary and Ultra-Contemporary field. Taking 3 firsts in 3 consecutive years has led myself and members of other faculties to take a very special interest in him . . . I feel there is tremendous talent in this boy and I feel sure you would be very interested to meet him and hear his music and his views about music and its philosophy . . . I feel if I introduce him to you, you won't be surprised at some strange young man bursting in on you. I hope he will give you as much pleasure from his knowledge of music as I have had teaching him, but in many respects I seem to have learnt from him. He has a great gift for combination of diverse fields like Science, Maths, and Philosophy to use them as one in his own description of music and art.

My Best wishes to you and your staff and thanking you in anticipation,

Yours Most Sincerly [sic]

Sir Charles Nalden D.Mus. (Lond.Camb.)

K.C.M.G. F.R.H.

(P.S. I am sorry that I won't be able to receive any replies as I am leaving tomorrow for England.)

It subsequently transpired that the protege from whom I had learnt so much had been excluded from our own university because of his poor academic record.

As for Professor Forder's reaction, he was consumed with a burning envy, complaining bitterly to me of the unfairness of it all; that I had been created an FRH (whatever that might signify) and a Knight Commander of the Order of St. Michael and St. George, whereas he had remained a mere university professor.

Even so relatively small an incident as this can result in a big and unnecessary waste of a head of department's time. Some members of the non-university public do not appreciate fully the extent of the administrative load carried by a university head of department. As Denis Brown, one-time professor of physics, put it to me, "They demand the highest qualifications from applicants for a chair, and promptly turn the successful candidate into a full-time administrator." And Freddy Chong, one-time professor of mathematics, once told me that the ever-nagging presence of his departmental administrative duties well-nigh drove him to despair.

After administering an expanding department for close on 20 years, I can say that keeping abreast with one's subject — reading, listening to new recordings, and adequate lecture preparation — becomes less and less easy and finally quite impossible. Insofar as they relate to heads of university departments, the stories one so frequently hears concerning those long university 'holidays' should be disregarded: for they are in the nature of pure folk-lore.

Music — A joy for life?

As the one-time subject convenor for music, I fought (and lost) a 12-year battle with the Universities Entrance Board* to have musical performance included as a subject in the University entrance, bursaries and scholarships examinations.

· Our private music teachers will tell you that once their pupils reach the appropriate age, many of them feel compelled to confine their instruments to their cases for months at a time for fear of failing their school examinations. These virtually enforced breaks in their musical studies, coinciding as they do with the vital formative years, must operate to the permanent detriment of their executant technique.

It is time that we in New Zealand came to acknowledge the importance of including in our schools' examination syllabusses subjects that are relevant to students' lives; and that we rid ourselves once and for all of the mistaken notion that music is a luxury, a superficial pleasure, fit only for 'long haired aesthetes'.

My fight with the entrance board was not on behalf of the young and aspiring professional musician only. It was fought also on behalf of the elderly woman (who will never forgive me for calling her that) who makes the ferry crossing each week to the mainland, motors the 70-odd kilometres to Auckland, puts up for the night in a motel, repeating the whole process in reverse on the following day, so that she might enjoy her two-hours' orchestral practice. This was Margaret Richter (since deceased) who was a pupil at St Paul's Girls' School, London, when Gustav Holst was music master. (His *St Paul's Suite* was composed expressly for the school orchestra.) I was fighting for the likes of the elderly man who came to me in a distressed state brought about by his wife's threatened intervention between him and his weekly string quartet practice; for the busy doctor who 'took her grade VIII' on the violin at the age of 50 or thereabouts and who never willingly forgoes an orchestral practice or a weekend orchestral school.

Meanwhile, we must look forward hopefully to the day when an enlightened University Entrance Board will no longer stand in the way, as it does at present, of our young people's musical development. The board may be assured that unlike many another subject which is promptly dropped once the scholar has his examinations behind him, musical performance, should it be introduced, will enjoy a far greater survival rate simply because of its far greater promise of becoming one of life's lasting interests. The insuperable difficulties which are said to stand in the way of my proposed scheme's introduction, together with those members of the UEB who will

---

* One of the functions of the UEB is to make regulations and draw up prescriptions for the University entrance, bursaries and entrance scholarships examinations.

not (as their counterparts in other countries have done) make an honest attempt to find a solution, must be swept into limbo, with the imposition that the Limbo Library be limited to copies of Dr Agnes Savill's *Music, Health and Character*, Edward Heath's *Music — A Joy for Life*, and to the works of others who similarly have discovered the part that music can play in the course of their professionally crowded lives.

Reconciliation
In which Half-and-Half total up to make one Whole.

'As is so often the case,' one writer suggests, 'the legitimate offspring is much less interesting than the bastard.'[1] Although for obvious reasons it would be imprudent for me to comment one way or the other on this, what I will say is that my life has been infinitely more interesting than that of many a union's legitimate offspring; for I have had a charmed existence, owing everything to providence, with providence owing me nothing.

At one time I envied the English public schoolboy his inherited advantages; the class of society into which he was born and the apparent ease with which he moved around in whatever type of company he may find himself. Above all I envied him his unique style of education which provided him potentially with so great a start in life as to leave the English council school and institutionally-educated boy forever trailing in his wake. In short I envied him his fortunate accident of birth which foolishly I would compare all too favourably with my own 'accident' of birth.

My years in New Zealand have changed all that; for now in the autumn of my life I am able to see that the whole of my *Bitter* half was simply in the nature of a preparation for the work I was destined to do during my *Mild* half.

My ideas on the meaning of education in general and of university education in particular have likewise undergone a change; for I have come to see that the true scholar regards those tangible pieces of evidence in the form of certificates, diplomas, degrees and the rest simply for what they are — official acknowledgments of certain levels of scholastic attainment. I am able now to see that a university degree in itself can be of little value unless it be regarded as a passport to further and still further learning. This was the sermon that I preached to those of my senior students who were near to completing their initial degrees. For my text I took a passage from J.C. Masterman's *To Teach the Senators Wisdom*:

> I reaffirm my belief that men should come to the University for the love of learning. I should like, then, to see the University as a place of learning, where learning was honoured for its own sake, where

those came who loved it, and where the lovers of truth and knowledge pursued their studies without any thought of their ultimate objects or of positive results.[2]

I offer one final reason as to why I no longer envy those who are born into the establishment:

> 'I'm glad I was born poor. Poverty gives one so much more than riches — the priceless gift of real ambition.'

> — Sophia Loren.

Postlude

Surely Thy loving-kindness and mercy have followed me all the days of my life.

> Praise thou the Lord, O my soul.

FOOTNOTES TO CHAPTER 25

1. Gerald Abraham, *A Hundred Years of Music* (London, 1938), p.69.
2. J.C. Masterman, *To Teach the Senators Wisdom* (London, 1952), pp.177-8.

Charles Nalden was born in England in 1908 and raised in London's Foundling Hospital. At age 14 he began his long career with various British Army bands rising to bandmaster after study at the famous Kneller Hall and London Guildhall. He emigrated to New Zealand in 1948 to take up a lectureship in Auckland University College, now the University of Auckland.

He was appointed to the chair in music in 1956 and in this capacity played the central role in the establishment of New Zealand's first conservatorium of music.

He has conducted the New Zealand Symphony Orchestra on a number of occasions as well as appearing as a casual player on his principal instrument, the harp. He has also given frequent broadcast talks on music.

His book *Fugal Answer* was acclaimed by Watkins Shaw (Music and Musicians, October 1972) as 'the most penetrating and precise treatment of the subject available'. Another publication *A History of the Conservatorium of Music* was the author's personal contribution to his university's centenary celebrations.

His work with amateur orchestras spans the whole of his years in New Zealand.

On his retirement in 1974 the University of Auckland elected him Emeritus Professor of Music and in 1976 he was awarded the CBE for Services to Music.

Photo: Wendy Nalden, taken on the author's eightieth birthday.